# Country Inns and Back Roads

"Why should not the New Englander be in search of new adventures?"

THOREAU: *Walden*

# Country Inns and Back Roads

VOLUME XI

BY THE BERKSHIRE TRAVELLER
Norman T. Simpson

THE BERKSHIRE TRAVELLER PRESS
Stockbridge, Massachusetts 01262

THE BERKSHIRE TRAVELLER TRAVEL SHELF
Country Inns and Back Roads, North America
Country Inns and Back Roads, Europe
Country Vacations, USA
New Brunswick Inside Out
Canada's Capital Inside Out
Montreal Inside Out
The Inn Way . . . Switzerland


FORTHCOMING:
The Inn Way . . . Caribbean (September 15, 1977)

Library of Congress #77-77593
ISBN #0-912944-42-0
Copyright 1977 Berkshire Traveller Press
Printed in U.S.A.

COVER PAINTING BOOK DESIGN AND DRAWINGS: Janice Lindstrom


Printed in Dalton, Massachusetts by The Studley Press


Second Printing

# PREFACE

What is a country inn? Back in the 1968 edition I quoted a remark to the effect that "a country inn is an inn in the country." In some ways this is still rather descriptive. The word "country" implies an escape from urban pressures and demands and not only conjures up euphoric bucolia but a welcome innocence associated with the American past. An old definition of an inn is "a place where you can get board, lodgings and comfort for yourself, and feed and a stall for your horse." The horses and stalls have gone but the emphasis on simple values is still highly desirable.

Each inn is original and unique, a reflection of the personalities and tastes of the innkeeper-owners, who are more than likely on hand to make their guests feel at home. This presence generates a strong feeling of involvement. I refer to it as "personal hospitality."

In 1966, the first year that *Country Inns and Back Roads* was written, I invited a group of the innkeepers and their wives for dinner and discovered that they were delighted to have the opportunity to exchange ideas and help solve common problems. We had such a good time that first evening that we decided to meet again the following year and thereafter. From those early meetings has evolved something that I can see now was inevitable: The formation of an independent innkeepers' association which would provide a forum for innkeepers to continually exchange ideas and supply each other with mental and moral support. These meetings continue and the Association is thriving. Membership invitations are extended to inns selected for the book. Dues are nominal.

From the very beginning I looked for inns that I felt would continue to operate for many years to come. Consequently there are a number of inns that have been included each year since the late 1960's. The innkeepers' young families have grown up and some are even carrying on their parents' innkeeping tradition. When inns change hands it is our general practice to omit them from subsequent editions until the new innkeepers have the opportunity to become firmly established. A steady stream of letters has assured me that this sense of continuity is most important.

Incidentally, I receive many, many welcome letters each year. Through them I am richer for some deep and lasting friendships. Many letters recommend inns that I haven't visited, some contain praise for inn-going adventures, and a few have criticisms. In the case of the latter, the information is passed on to the individual inn. I am in continual contact with each inn and try to revisit as many inns as possible each year.

## RATES

I do not include lodging rates in *Country Inns and Back Roads* because the very nature of an inn means that there are various size lodgings, with and without private baths, in and out of season, and plain and fancy decoration. It is the unanimous opinion of the innkeepers that travelers should be encouraged to call ahead and inquire about the availability and rates of the many different types of rooms.

European Plan (E.P.) means that rates for rooms and meals are separate. The American Plan (A.P.) means that meals are included in the cost of the room. Modified American Plan (M.A.P.) means that breakfast and dinner are also part of the room rate. Some inns include a Continental breakfast with the lodging. Rates in inns are comparable to those in hotel, motel and resort accommodations in the same geographical area. To me this represents a travel bargain for there is so much more offered at a country inn. The italicized paragraph following the account of my visits to each inn provides factual information and travel directions.

## OBJECTIVES

In the 11 years of its publication, this book has never intended to be a total guide to country inns in the United States and Canada. It contains my continuing experiences visiting a carefully selected group of inns in each region. The purpose is to encourage travelers to visit country inns in or out of the book, wherever they may be located, and to experience this unique type of personal hospitality which has roots going back to biblical days. Because there are always changes taking place at country inns each year, some inns going out of business or changing hands, and new inns being discovered, I feel a new edition is neccessary every twelve months.

## THE FUTURE

What of the future? It looks wonderful. I will continue to write and publish *Country Inns and Back Roads, North America* as long as there is a need for information on personal hospitality. Other travel books published by The Berkshire Traveller Press include the growing *European Edition of Country Inns and Back Roads*, and also books written by Margaret Zellers, an extremely capable travel writer who shares every bit of my enthusiasm for country inns. Her books are titled, *The Inn Way . . . Switzerland* (to be published in June 1977) and *The Inn Way . . . The Caribbean* (to be published in September 1977). Margaret and I expect to share our explorations for personal hospitality everywhere in the world in many, many more books.

For new readers, welcome to the wide wonderful world of country inns as an interesting alternate style of travel. One reader refers to this as a "wish book." He says: "We may not be able to go to all the places you write about, but we wish we could." It is our wish for all of you to enjoy my happy experiences in country inns everywhere.

Norman T. Simpson
Stockbridge, Massachusetts
March 1977

# CONTENTS

Preface

Arizona
    LODGE ON THE DESSERT, Tucson 296
    RANCHO DE LOS CABALLEROS, Wickenburg 298
    TANQUE VERDE, Tucson 294

California
    BENBOW INN, Garberville 307
    HARBOR HOUSE, Elk 304
    HERITAGE HOUSE, Little River 306
    NORMANDY INN, Carmel 309
    OJAI VALLEY INN, Ojai 313
    SUTTER CREEK INN, Sutter Creek 302
    THE INN, Rancho Santa Fe 315
    VAGABOND HOUSE INN, Carmel 311
    WINE COUNTRY INN, St. Helena 300

Canada
  Quebec
    CUTTLE'S TREMBLANT CLUB, Mont Tremblant 330
    HOVEY MANOR, North Hatley 332
    WILLOW PLACE INN, Como 334

  New Brunswick
    ELM LODGE, St. Stephen 336
    MARATHON HOTEL, Grand Manan Island 340
    MARSHLANDS INN, Sackville 342
    ROSSMOUNT INN, St. Andrews 338

  Nova Scotia
    INVERARY INN, Baddeck 344
    KILMUIR PLACE, Northeast Margaree 346
    MILFORD HOUSE, South Milford 348

Ontario
GRANDVIEW FARM, Huntsville 328
OBAN INN, Niagara-on-the-Lake 326

Prince Edward Island
SHAW'S HOTEL, Brackley Beach 351

Connecticut
BOULDERS INN, New Preston 24
CURTIS HOUSE, Woodbury 18
GRISWOLD INN, Essex 20
MOUNTAIN VIEW INN, Norfolk 26
SILVERMINE TAVERN, Norwalk 22
WHITE HART INN, Salisbury 28

Florida
BAY HILL CLUB, Orlando 249
BAY SHORE YACHT CLUB, Ft. Lauderdale 255
BRAZILIAN COURT HOTEL, Palm Beach 253
CHALET SUZANNE, Lake Wales 251
LAKESIDE INN, Mount Dora 247

Georgia
KING AND PRINCE BEACH HOTEL, St. Simons Island 245

Indiana
Historic New Harmony
DURBIN HOTEL, Rushville 269
NEW HARMONY INN, New Harmony 266
PATCHWORK QUILT, Middlebury 271
RED GERANIUM AND SHADBLOW RESTAURANTS, New Harmony 268

Kentucky
BOONE TAVERN HOTEL, Berea 237
DOE RUN INN, Brandenburg 231
ELMWOOD INN, Perryville 235
INN AT PLEASANT HILL, Shakertown 233

Louisiana
    LAMOTHE HOUSE, New Orleans    257

Maine
    ASTICOU INN, Northeast Harbor    111
    BLACK POINT INN, Prouts Neck    115
    CAPTAIN LORD MANSION, Kennebunkport    117
    CLAREMONT, Southwest Harbor    113
    DOCKSIDE GUEST QUARTERS, York    119
    GREY ROCK INN, Northeast Harbor    114
    HOMEWOOD INN, Yarmouth    121
    ISLAND HOUSE, Ogunquit    123
    OLD FORT CLUB, Kennebunkport    125
    SQUIRE TARBOX HOUSE, Westport Island    128
    SUDBURY INN, Bethel    126
    WHISTLING OYSTER, Ogunquit    130
    WHITEHALL INN, Camden    132

Maryland
    MARYLAND INN, Annapolis    198
    ROBERT MORRIS INN, Oxford    196

Massachusetts
    ANDOVER INN, Andover    47
    BRADFORD GARDENS INN, Provincetown    30
    BRAMBLE INN, Brewster    35
    INN AT DUCK CREEKE, Wellfleet    33
    INN FOR ALL SEASONS, Scituate Harbor    43
    JARED COFFIN HOUSE, Nantucket Island    39
    LONGFELLOW'S WAYSIDE INN, South Sudbury    45
    NAUSET HOUSE INN, East Orleans    37
    RALPH WALDO EMERSON, Rockport    49
    RED INN, Provincetown    32
    RED LION INN, Stockbridge    53
    STAGECOACH HILL INN, Sheffield    55
    VICTORIAN, Whitinsville    41

VILLAGE INN, Lenox 57
YANKEE CLIPPER, Rockport 49
YANKEE PEDLAR INN, Holyoke 52

Michigan
    BOTSFORD INN, Farmington Hills 278
    STAFFORD'S BAY VIEW INN, Petoskey 280

Minnesota
    LOWELL INN, Stillwater 288

Missouri
    CHESHIRE INN, St. Louis 282
    ST. GEMME BEAUVAIS INN, Ste. Genevieve 284
    WILDERNESS LODGE, Lesterville 286

New Hampshire
    COLBY HILL INN, Henniker 87
    DANA PLACE, Jackson 108
    JOHN HANCOCK INN, Hancock 89
    LOVETT'S, Franconia 91
    LYME INN, Lyme 93
    NEW LONDON INN, New London 107
    ROCKHOUSE MOUNTAIN FARM, Eaton Center 95
    SPALDING INN CLUB, Whitefield 97
    SQUAM LAKES INN, Holderness 99
    STAFFORD'S-IN-THE-FIELD, Chocorua 101
    WELLS WOOD, Plainfield 103
    WOODBOUND INN, Jaffrey 105

New Jersey
    MAINSTAY INN, Cape May 192

New Mexico
    RANCHO ENCANTADO, Santa Fe 292

New York
ALGONQUIN HOTEL, New York                    138
ALMSHOUSE INN, Ghent                          136
ASA RANSOM HOUSE, Clarence                    140
BEEKMAN ARMS, Rhinebeck                       142
BIRD & BOTTLE INN, Garrison                   143
BULL'S HEAD INN, Cobleskill                   145
CLARKSON HOUSE, Lewiston                      147
GLENN IRIS INN, Castile                       148
GREENVILLE ARMS, Greenville                   150
HOLLOWAY HOUSE, East Bloomfield               152
LINCKLAEN HOUSE, Cazenovia                    154
OLD DROVERS INN, Dover Plains                 160
OLIVER HOUSE, Ancram                          156
REDCOAT'S RETURN, Tannersville                166
SPRINGSIDE INN, Auburn                        158
SWISS HUTTE, Hillsdale                        162
THREE VILLAGE INN, Stony Brook                164

North Carolina
HEMLOCK INN, Bryson City                      214
HOUND EARS LODGE, Blowing Rock                220
NU-WRAY INN, Burnsville                       212
PINE CREST INN, Tryon                         218
SNOWBIRD MOUNTAIN LODGE, Robbinsville         216

Ohio
BUXTON INN, Granville                         273
GOLDEN LAMB, Lebanon                          276
WELSHFIELD INN, Burton                        275

Pennsylvania
ACCOMAC INN, Wrightsville                     169
CANDLEWYCK INN, Green Lane                    171
CENTURY INN, Scenery Hill                     172

FAIRFIELD INN, Fairfield    174
INN AT STARLIGHT LAKE, Starlight    176
MOSELEM SPRINGS INN, Moselem Springs    177
OVERLOOK INN, Canadensis    179
PINE BARN INN, Danville    181
PUMP HOUSE INN, Canadensis    184
1740 HOUSE, Lumberville    186
STERLING INN, South Sterling    188
TAVERN, New Wilmington    190

Rhode Island
   INN AT CASTLE HILL, Newport    59
   LARCHWOOD INN, Wakefield    62
   1661 INN, Block Island    63

South Carolina
   ROBERT'S OF CHARLESTON, Charleston    244
   SWORDGATE INN, Charleston    242

Vermont
   BARROWS HOUSE, Dorset    68
   BLUEBERRY HILL, Goshen    70
   CHESTER INN, Chester    72
   GREEN MOUNTAIN INN, Stowe    74
   INN AT SAWMILL FARM, West Dover    76
   INN ON THE COMMON, Craftsbury Common    85
   KEDRON VALLEY INN, South Woodstock    77
   MIDDLEBURY INN, Middlebury    79
   NORTH HERO HOUSE, North Hero    81
   VILLAGE INN, Landgrove    83

Virginia
   ALEXANDER-WITHROW HOUSE, Lexington    209
   GRAVES MOUNTAIN LODGE, Syria    203
   GRISTMILL SQUARE, Warm Springs    201

HOLLYMEAD INN, Charlottesville                205
OLD CLUB RESTAURANT, Alexandria               210
WAYSIDE INN, Middletown                       207

Virgin Islands
  St. Thomas
    PELICAN BEACH CLUB                        356
    VILLA OLGA                                355
  St. John
    GALLOWS POINT                             358
  St. Croix
    KING CHRISTIAN HOTEL                      360
    KING'S ALLEY HOTEL                        361

Washington
  CAPTAIN WHIDBEY, Coupeville                 319
  FARMHOUSE, Port Townsend                    317
  LAKE QUINAULT LODGE, Quinault               321

West Virginia
  COUNTRY INN, Berkeley Springs               222
  DROVERS INN, Wellsburg                      228
  GENERAL LEWIS INN, Lewisburg                224
  RIVERSIDE INN, Pence Springs                226
  WELLS INN, Sistersville                     229

Index

# Southern New England

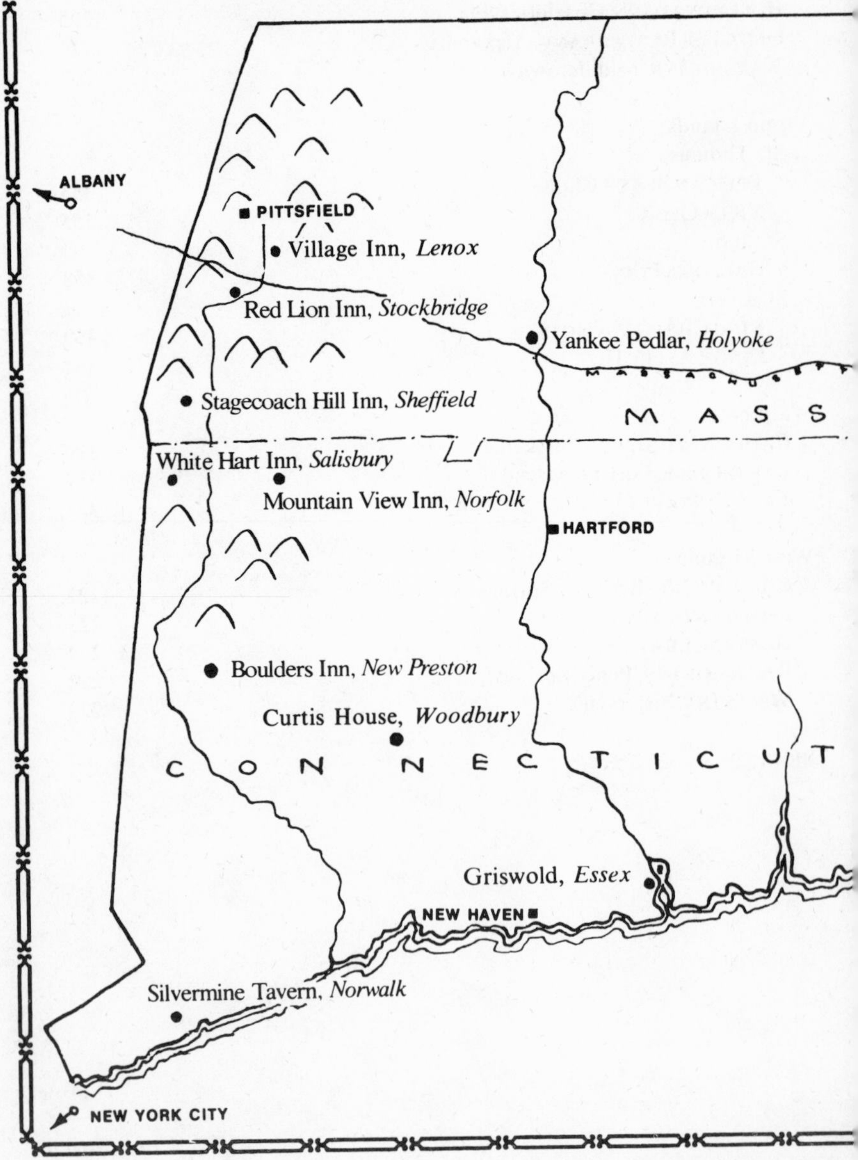

ALBANY

■ PITTSFIELD

● Village Inn, *Lenox*

● Red Lion Inn, *Stockbridge*

● Yankee Pedlar, *Holyoke*

MASSACHUSETTS

M A S S

● Stagecoach Hill Inn, *Sheffield*

White Hart Inn, *Salisbury* ●

Mountain View Inn, *Norfolk*

■ HARTFORD

● Boulders Inn, *New Preston*

Curtis House, *Woodbury* ●

C O N N E C T I C U T

Griswold, *Essex*

NEW HAVEN ■

Silvermine Tavern, *Norwalk* ●

NEW YORK CITY

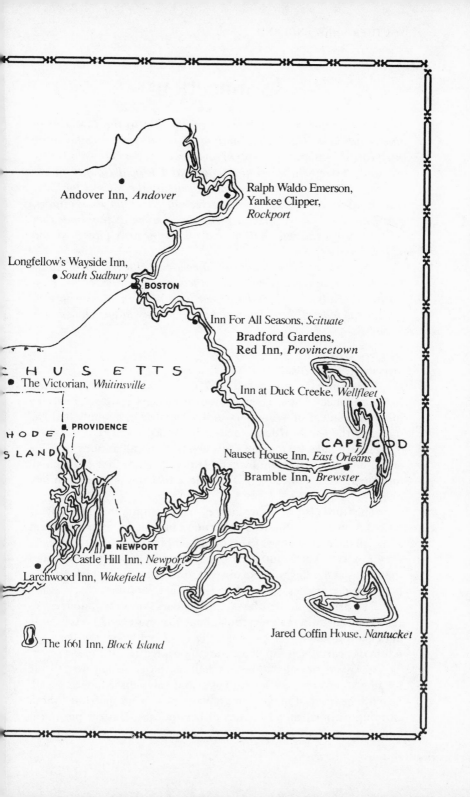

Andover Inn, *Andover*

Ralph Waldo Emerson,
Yankee Clipper,
*Rockport*

Longfellow's Wayside Inn,
*South Sudbury*

**BOSTON**

Inn For All Seasons, *Scituate*

**Bradford Gardens,
Red Inn, *Provincetown***

C H U S E T T S

• The Victorian, *Whitinsville*

Inn at Duck Creeke, *Wellfleet*

HODE
SLAND

■ **PROVIDENCE**

**CAPE COD**

Nauset House Inn, *East Orleans*

Bramble Inn, *Brewster*

■ **NEWPORT**

Castle Hill Inn, *Newport*

Larchwood Inn, *Wakefield*

The 1661 Inn, *Block Island*

Jared Coffin House, *Nantucket*

# Connecticut

*Most people want to get out of the city to the Connecticut hinterland in a big hurry, and as a result some of the more interesting roads are passed up in favor of the super highways. There are some extremely interesting roads in Fairfield County in the vicinity of Greenwich and Norwalk. Certainly the Merritt Parkway and the Connecticut Turnpike do very nicely as far as Westport, but from there on we suggest picking out some of the roads that lead north up through Wilton and on up through Litchfield and past Danbury.*

*One of the prettiest roads in Connecticut is the section of Route 7 which starts in Gaylordsville, goes through Cornwall Bridge, West Cornwall, Falls Village and Canaan into Western Massachusetts. For several miles, the road runs right next to the winding Housatonic River.*

### CURTIS HOUSE
### Woodbury, Connecticut

"Yes, since the inn opened in 1754, I believe we are the oldest inn in Connecticut." The speaker was redhaired Gary Hardisty, himself a life-long resident of Woodbury and a member of a family that has operated the Curtis House since early 1950.

"There have been quite a few changes and alterations over the years, and many different owners. However, since four of them, all unrelated, were named 'Curtis' I believe that this is an appropriate name."

The Curtis House by any name is a real country inn experience. I visited it on a chilly Saturday afternoon in January after a pleasant snowfall the night before. Everything combined to make it idyllically New England. The countryside was at its best in a white mantel, and the towns and villages in northwest Connecticut, with 18th century homes and churches, gleamed in the bright sunshine.

The drive from the Massachusetts Berkshires (Woodbury is in the Connecticut Berkshires) took about 90 minutes and I was eagerly anticipating lunch. As I opened the old front door, the heavenly odors of hearty New England cooking wafted toward me.

I walked through a narrow hallway past the stairway to the lodging rooms on two floors above, and entered the low-ceilinged, heavily beamed dining room. Waitresses were bustling about carrying trays laden with plates of beef pot pie, Yankee pot roast,

roast beef hash, scallops, and blueberry pancakes. The room was filled with happy people including quite a few families of students at the local prep school. I was given a quiet table in the corner, and my visit to the Curtis House began in earnest.

My luncheon included a delicious fresh fruit and sherbet cup, hot muffins, and a beef pie. From the desserts I chose an apple crisp which was served with vanilla ice cream. I noticed that the dinner menu offered these things and much more, including sweetbreads, roast beef, and quite a few fish dishes such as broiled bluefish.

I was delighted to discover that there were 18 lodging rooms in this old inn, many of them with canopied twin or double geds. Twelve of the rooms have private baths. There are four more modern rooms in the nearby Carriage House.

Later, I chatted with Gary Hardisty in the living room with the fireplace and wide floor boards. He explained that the large inn signs outside were the work of Wallace Nutting who included many of the Woodbury buildings in his book *Connecticut the Beautiful.* Gary explained that Woodbury was one of the antiquing centers of New England and there were many, many antique shops on Routes 6 and 47. The Glebe House which was the birthplace of the American Episcopal church is only a ten-minute walk from the inn.

Gary explained that as a rule dinner reservations are not accepted with the exception of New Year's Eve, Mother's Day, Easter and Thanksgiving.

I learned that almost everything on the extensive menu is prepared from scratch and the inn does all of its own baking. Those warm muffins at lunch really hit the spot.

19

After spending the remaining part of the afternoon browsing through the village, I left Woodbury and the Curtis House as the setting sun created great red and orange streaks over the snowy hills and the lights of the inn were already casting their warm beckoning glow. This was the way it's been for well over 200 years.

*CURTIS HOUSE, Route 6 (Main St.), Woodbury, Conn., 06798; 203-263-2101. An 18-room village inn, 12 mi. from Waterbury. Open year-round. European Plan. Lunch and dinner served daily except Christmas. No pets. Antiquing, skiing, tennis, platform tennis, horseback riding nearby. The Hardisty Family, Innkeepers.*

*Directions: From N.Y. take Sawmill River Pkwy. to I-84. Take Exit 15 from I-84 in Southbury. Follow Rte. 6 north to Woodbury. From Hartford take I-84 to Exit 17, follow Rte. 64 to Woodbury.*

## GRISWOLD INN
**Essex, Connecticut**

It was Christmastime in Essex. I had an appointment for lunch at the "Gris" with Margaret Zellers, the author of the forthcoming Berkshire Traveller Press book on the Caribbean inns. She was driving over from her home in nearby Connecticut while I drove down from Stockbridge.

I was glad for the chance to be here because I really wanted to see this beautiful village and inn during the holiday season.

I was delighted to encounter Vicki Winterer in front of the "Gris" and she was bubbling over with holiday enthusiasm.

"Bill and I feel very special about Christmas here," she said. "We had an honest-to-goodness old-fashioned Christmas tree lighting in Griswold Square." She indicated an interesting group of late colonial and early Federalist buildings, and restored barns just across the street from the inn. It is now a very attractive collection of shops.

"Through the church bulletins and posting a notice on the bulletin board in the post office, we invited all of the townspeople to come here for the official lighting. The Eastern Brass Quintet, whom we have invited here for other occasions, played some beautiful hymns and anthems, the minister said a prayer and then the First Selectman flipped the lights. It was just wonderful. Everyone applauded and we all felt so good and close together. There were a few guests at the inn that night and they, of course, were most welcome.

"Afterwards, we served some hot beverages and sang Christmas carols. It was the nicest feeling. That's why we love the town so much,

because everybody comes and enjoys these things."

Readers of previous editions of CIBR are undoubtedly familiar with the Griswold and Essex. In many ways the interior design of the inn reflects the many aspects of the history of the village. For example, the Steamboat Room is the dining room whose decor and furnishings simulate the dining salon of a riverboat of a hundred years ago. On one wall of the room is a mural depicting Essex as it appeared at the turn-of-the-century. The entire picture rocks slowly creating the impression for people in the room that they are on a moving ship.

Other dining rooms provide an opportunity to exhibit an impressive collection of firearms, marine oils, Currier & Ives steamboat prints and various steamboat artifacts including ships' clocks, masthead lights, and bells.

During the Christmas season there were all kinds of wonderful reminders of the season including a sleigh filled with gaily wrapped packages and several Christmas trees in other dining rooms.

The outside of the inn was decorated with festoons of evergreens, in which were nestled dozens of tiny white lights. This decorative theme was carried across the street to Griswold Square where the lampposts were trimmed with greens tied with red bows.

The food at the Griswold is basically American. There are all kinds of local fresh and salt-water fish, and also beef and lamb dishes that have been popular in this country since its beginning. A Hunt Breakfast is served every Sunday which includes great long tables of fried chicken, herring, lamb's kidneys, eggs, grits, creamed chipped beef and special sausage.

21

It was great fun to visit the "Gris" during the Christmas season, and I am telling the story of my experiences, because they do, indeed, reflect the excitement and good times which I've had in all other seasons.

For more than 200 years the "Gris" has continued to provide food, lodging, and entertainment for all who desire.

*GRISWOLD INN, Main St., Essex, Conn. 06426; 203-767-1812. A 16-room inn in a waterside town, steps away from the Connecticut River, and located near the Eugene O'Neill Theatre, Goodspeed Opera House, Ivoryton Playhouse, Gillette Castle, Mystic Village, Valley Railroad and Hammonasset State Beach. Some rooms with private baths. European plan. Complimentary Continental breakfast served daily to inn guests. Lunch and dinner served daily to travelers. Hunt breakfast served Sundays. Closed Christmas Eve and Christmas Day. Day sailing on inn's 44-foot ketch by appointment. Bicycles, tennis and boating nearby. Victoria and William G. Winterer and A.W. Lovell, Innkeepers.*

*Directions: From I-95 take Exit 69 and travel north on Rte. 9 to Exit 3, Essex. Turn right at stop light and follow West Ave. to center of town. Turn right onto Main St. and proceed down to water and inn.*


## SILVERMINE TAVERN
### Norwalk, Connecticut

The first thing I heard was the sound of happy people singing. It was approximately one o'clock in the afternoon and the voices were jubilant and ringing. I learned that this was a special luncheon at the Silvermine for the Newcomers Club and the voices were those of the "Blue Notes," a large chorus of women who sing in barbershop harmony. I always think of a country inn as being a very logical place for things like this to happen. Entertainment and a great deal of community activity have always been in abundance at inns.

I wandered over to the glassed-in terrace overlooking the outer deck and mill pond, which on this January day was covered with snow. The trees were now bare and the winter birds like chickadees, bluejays and cardinals were flitting from branch to branch. In the summer it is almost idyllic with the serene mill pond and the resident ducks and geese.

Turning back into the dining room my eye caught the pewter serving plates at each table setting, accompanied by white napkins and crystal goblets. The atmosphere on the inside on this chilly winter's day was considerably enhanced by a warm crackling fire in one corner.

A small poster announced the Thursday night buffet which included soup, roast beef, corned beef, fried chicken, salad, dessert and coffee. Besides the Thursday buffet there is an innkeepers dinner on Friday night, and on Wednesday during the summer there is a barbecue. One of the most popular events, especially with the people from Fairfield County and vicinity, is the Sunday Brunch buffet, which has as many as twenty-five different offerings on the big tables.

One section of the dining room has been sheltered from the rest by a group of large benches with high backs. There is a little lounge area with old-fashioned wooden arm chairs and candles on each of the tables. The artifacts, art work and decorations at the inn seem to span the years from the Colonial era through late Victorian.

The Silvermine is an inn with many different attractions. It consists of a rambling structure housing the restaurant and some of the tidy inviting guest rooms. The original part of the building is over 200 years old. The mill is located on the waterfall next to the inn and was one of the oldest operating mills in the area. There is also a country store which used to be the general store at this crossroads and is now used as a gift shop.

The inn is another family operation with Frank Whitman, Sr. and Jr. both very much involved. Things are done in a quiet, conservative New England manner and gentlemen are requested to wear jackets on Friday and Saturday evenings.

I hope the next time I visit it will happen to be one of the days that the "Blue Notes" are entertaining again. I can still hear their rendition of "Won't You Come Home, Bill Bailey?"

*SILVERMINE TAVERN, Perry Ave., Norwalk, Ct. 06850; 203-847-4558. A 10-room country inn in the residential section of Norwalk. Long Island Sound and beaches 6 mi. away. European plan includes Continental breakfast. Lunch and dinner served to travelers daily. Open year-round. Closed Christmas Day and Tuesdays during winter. Golf, tennis and fishing nearby. Francis C. Whitman, Innkeeper.*

*Directions: From New York or New Haven via I-95, take Exit 15. Pick up the new Rte. 7 going north. At the end of Rte. 7 (approx. 1 mi.) turn right, go to first stoplight, turn right. At next stoplight by firehouse turn right onto Silvermine Ave. Proceed down Silvermine Ave. about 2 mi. to Tavern. From I-84 and Danbury take old Rte. 7 south to Norwalk. Watch for Kelly Greens ½ mi. south of Merritt Pkwy. on the left, turn right on Perry Ave. opposite Kelly Greens. Follow Perry Ave. 2 mi. to Tavern. From Merritt Pkwy. take Exit 39 south on old Rte. 7 and follow directions above.*

## BOULDERS INN
### New Preston, Connecticut

During the past eleven years I have been guided by letters from readers who have been looking for inns that meet particular needs. Many such inquiries deal with "family inns"—places which have country inn hospitality and personal involvement but which are also ideal for families. This means a lot of outdoor recreational facilities plus rainy day diversions.

Among several inns in this category is the Boulders Inn which is located on the shores of Lake Waramaug in northwest Connecticut. The Boulders is a real family affair. Dick and Jane Lowe are in their 27th season and it is the 42nd year for the inn, which was started by Jane's parents as their family summer home. Dick and Jane's two sons, Russ and Tucker, are also very much involved in the operation of the inn as they have been for many years.

Actually the Boulders offers a great many things that appeal to people of all ages. Beautiful Lake Waramaug provides marvelous swimming, boating, sailing, rowboating, fishing and other water sports. The high hills behind the inn cover 250 acres and have miles of trails marked for hiking to Pulpit Rock and the Pinnacle. During the winter these same trails are perfect for cross-country skiing. The inn

also has its own lift for a little downhill skiing and sledding and when the lake freezes over there is skating.

Rainy days are well provided for in the huge oak-beamed barn which is also an inviting spot for an evening before the fire. There are dozens of indoor games and activities. There is also a barbecue one night a week.

Additional outdoor activities that have universal appeal are tennis on the inn courts, golf and riding nearby. There is also the American Indian Archeological Institute with their trails and guide to "Connecticut's Last 1200 Years." Located as it is in a picturesque corner of Connecticut, there are many interesting parks, nature preserves, museums, fairs, concerts, theatres, church suppers, back-roads, antique shops and beautiful drives in the area.

Accommodations at the Boulders vary to provide for both families and couples. Some rooms are in the main building which is above the lake in a beautiful park-like surrounding. Others are scattered around in small lodgings on the hillside and in the valley.

In the dining room, where the walls and pillars have been built out of huge local stone, there is a large collection of antique utensils, and a fieldstone terrace offers a fine view of the lake and hills.

However, the Boulders really spans the generation gap. The last time I visited there I enjoyed my dinner with some people who had been coming to the Boulders for thirty-five years. I asked them what they like the most and both of them replied in concert: "We like the peace and quiet."

*BOULDERS INN, Lake Waramaug, New Preston, Conn. 06777; 203-868-7918. A 30-room year-round resort-inn, 1½ mi. north of*

*New Preston, 20 mi. from Danbury. All plans available. Breakfast, lunch and dinner served daily to travelers from late May to mid- September and some weekends through the year. European plan and breakfast available rest of year. Monday dinner served to house guests only. Rooms and breakfast only on Thanksgiving. Closed Christmas. Tennis, swimming, boating, sailing, fishing, hiking, skiing, tobogganing. Golf and riding nearby. Dick and Jane Lowe, Innkeepers.*

*Directions: From I-84, take Exit 7 and follow Rte. 7 north to Rte. 202 (formerly 25) through New Milford. Proceed 8 mi. to New Preston then 1½ mi. to inn on Rte. 45.*

## MOUNTAIN VIEW INN
### Norfolk, Connecticut

I first visited the Mountain View Inn in the late sixties. Since that time, I have been there in mid-summer during the Yale Music School concert season and at the height of the foliage season which is so glorious in northwest Connecticut. I have also visited several times during the Christmas season when the inn is so beautifully decorated, and at Thanksgiving a few years ago when I enjoyed not just turkey, but goose, ham and duck.

I've talked about the food which is the result of Karl Jokinen's 25 years of experience as a chef. The menu includes frogs legs, Smithville ham, pork chops, loin of pork, stuffed shrimp, Boston scrod, steak Tartare, chicken Papillote, bay scallops, veal curry, Gaspé Bay salmon in an aspic mold, fresh squash with remarkable seasonings, an avocado salad with orange dressing, and duck l'orange.

The duck is crisp on the outside, delightfully warm and tender on the inside, and the sauce defies description. They frequently serve baked apples stuffed with mincemeat. The crowning touch comes when Joan Jokinen pours a little cointreau over everything and applies a match.

In the past I have also followed the progress of 10-year-old Jenifer Jokinen who does a great deal of the Christmas decorating in the inn and Karl's son Larry who is now 18, an experienced cook, and a great help to his father in the kitchen.

I have also referred to the fact that Karl is not only an excellent chef but loves to work with his hands and has made a great deal of the furniture that is used in the inn. He is also an expert with clocks. There is even one clock that runs backwards.

The last point illustrates the one thing that I never have mentioned—the sense of humor that I think is so wonderful to find in any innkeeper and is so abundant in Karl's makeup.

I don't believe in all these years I have ever seen Karl without a wonderful smile on his face and both he and Joan radiate cheerfulness and good humor to all of their guests. Karl usually comes out of the kitchen after all of the main dishes have been prepared and moves from table to table with his white chef's uniform and hat exchanging pleasantries with his guests. There is usually at least one hearty laugh at each table.

Karl and Joan are great visitors at other CIBR inns and one of their favorite places is the Rabbit Hill Inn in Lower Waterford, Vermont, which has another innkeeper with a great sense of humor, John Carroll. When the two of them get together I can always count on some kind of monkeyshines.

Once I asked Karl about his cheerful disposition. "Well, he said, "we love innkeeping and we love the people who come here and enjoy our inn. And there are still times when a sense of humor is as valuable to an innkeeper as a good recipe for duck l'orange."

*MOUNTAIN VIEW INN, Norfolk, Conn. 06058; 203-542-5595. A 7-room village inn, 40 mi. west of Hartford in the picturesque Litchfield Hills. European plan. Breakfast, lunch and dinner served daily to travelers except Mondays and Christmas Day. Open year-round. Golf, tennis, hiking, swimming, mountain climbing, bicycles, ice fishing, Alpine and xc skiing nearby. Karl and Joan Jokinen, Innkeepers.*

*Directions: Norfolk is on U.S. 44 which runs east-west. North-south roads which intersect 44 include U.S. 7, I-91, and U.S. 22. Inn is located off Rte. 44, ¼ mi. on 272 South.*

## WHITE HART INN
**Salisbury, Connecticut**

I was seated in one corner of the White Hart Inn with Innkeeper John Harney who was using some diversionary tactics, as usual, to take the third checker game.

The setting was perfect. We were surrounded by nostalgia as thick as creamery butter that might have come from an old-fashioned churn in the corner of the Country Store. John reached out and handed me a glass jar with wintergreen sticks. I kept my eye warily on the board and indicated my preference for molasses.

"Let me tell you about tea," said John. "If all the cups of the world's favorite beverage consumed annually were placed side by side it would stretch 11½ miles. We have been importing teas from East Africa, Ceylon, Indonesia and China, and, with the help of Mr. Stanley Mason who started the business a number of years ago, we are turning out what we think is the best tea obtainable.

"Of course, all of this is most appropriate considering what seems to be happening to the price of coffee. I think that we have made a real coup."

I was now convinced that John's desire to win at checkers at any cost had led him to distract my attention with conversation. There was enough at the White Hart to distract my attention anyway. For instance, in the Country Store there were the enticing aromas and scents of soap, candles, sachets, fresh breads, pastries and donuts. There were new items on the old shelves such as bright yellow ceramics with handpainted French and Belgian peasants, hurricane lamps, baskets, signs, a marvelous collection of spices, and even (oh, horrors) an old-fashioned coffee grinder.

The White Hart Inn has been here for 100 years and John insists that he has been here for 110! The past few years have seen some most interesting changes at the inn but there seems to be no change in John. "Oh, I'll be here for another hundred" he said.

The inn is in the Currier & Ives northwest corner of Connecticut where there are winding roads, picket fences, old colonials, high hedges and many lakes. It is the countryside for leathers and tweeds, for long walks, cross-country skiing and antique hunting.

The White Hart is a rambling old place with many fireplaces and chimney corners. The guest rooms in the main house are big and comfortable but those in an annex nearby are a bit more standardized.

The emphasis is on American cooking but occasionally some unusual things are added to the menu. "We're ready for just about anything," says John.

The Christmas Holiday season is also great fun here because of the gingerbread village that has been created by Olive Dubois for one of the rooms of the main lobby. There are houses, churches, mills, schools and little shops made from gingerbread, and all lit up with little lights.

"Let me take you downstairs and show you where we mix the tea," John said. I protested that we ought to finish the game. "Oh, the game," he said. "Well, I won that ten minutes ago."

*WHITE HART INN, Salisbury, Conn. 06068; 203-435-2511. A 25-room village inn, 55 mi. west of Hartford. European plan. Breakfast, lunch, dinner served to travelers daily. Alpine and xc skiing, ski-jumping, golf, swimming nearby. John Harney, Innkeeper.*

*Directions: Exit the Taconic Pkwy. at Millbrook, N.Y. Proceed east on U.S. 44 to Salisbury. Inn is located at Jct. of U.S. 44 and 41.*

# Massachusetts

*Long before the Massachusetts Turnpike became the principal route between Boston and the Berkshires, Route 20 was the way to go. It was quite an adventure then, sharing the road with the trucks. It is still possible to cross the state on Route 20 but I would suggest that the Turnpike is best used between Ludlow and Westfield, thus eliminating the traffic of Springfield and its environs. Route 20 between Westfield and West Stockbridge winds its way among some of the attractive hill towns such as Russell and Huntington. In Chester, I like to stop in at Mr. Pease's haberdashery store which is located about half a block from the main road just across the bridge over the Westfield River. The building dates back to around 1910 and has some fascinating decorations. The ceilings on the first floor are of molded tin. Route 20 continues its twisting way up across Jacob's Ladder and down into the Berkshires via Lee.*

## BRADFORD GARDENS INN
### Provincetown, Massachusetts

The light from the fireplace, so welcome at any time, flickered over the low ceiling of the bedroom and glanced off the polished headboard of the bed and bureau. I pulled the counterpane up under my chin and luxuriated in the delicious comfort of actually having a fire in my bedroom in the morning. Six of the rooms at Bradford Gardens have their own fireplaces, and one has a Franklin stove.

The front window of my room overlooked Provincetown Harbor and the shapes of the old houses, shops, and churches became more visible in the early morning light. The side window overlooked a beautiful rose garden with over 200 plants. It also includes several flowering fruit trees, and many chairs and chaise lounges are scattered about. This is also where an outdoor fireplace is located which is used by some of the guests to do their own cooking should the spirit move them. Breakfast is the only meal served at the Bradford Gardens, but Jim Logan, the innkeeper, is happy to explain the specialties of the various Provincetown restaurants.

I remained in bed until the very last minute and then hustled downstairs to meet Jim and the other guests at breakfast. On this particular morning we had eggs Franciscan. However, there are several different dishes offered on successive mornings. During the summer, lighter breakfasts are served in the Rose Garden.

It's very tempting to stay on and on at the Bradford Gardens Inn because there is so much to do in the immediate vicinity. The inn is located away from downtown Provincetown, but well within walking distance of all of the quaint shops and wharfs, the Pilgrim's Monument, the museums, and the dozens of other things to enjoy. The great Cape Cod National Seashore is only minutes away. It's fun to rent bicycles and use the many special bicycle paths that have been laid out among the sand dunes.

The Bradford Gardens Inn is rather small and quite informal. Guests become acquainted readily because Jim sees to it that everyone enjoys themselves.

Each one of the lodging rooms has its own character and a descriptive name such as the Alcove Room, the Honeymoon Suite, the Chimney Nook and the Jenny Lind Salon, which has a real Jenny Lind spool bed. A great deal of care has been taken in furnishing each room with 19th century American furniture. There are many original works of art in the parlor. The inn also has three deluxe units with kitchens and fireplaces for groups up to six.

I made my first visit to Bradford Gardens in the fall of 1973, and it has been great fun to watch its growth during the years. Letters from readers praise the breakfasts, the comfortable rooms, the growing art collection and the feeling that someone actually cares.

My good friend, John Venner, who was the co-owner of the inn, passed on during 1976. Jim Logan is doing a splendid job and the Bradford Gardens is continuing to grow.

*BRADFORD GARDENS INN, 178 Bradford St., Provincetown, Mass. 02657; 617-487-1616. A small 8-room village inn with working fireplaces overlooking Provincetown Bay. European plan includes complimentary breakfast. No other meals served. Open year-round. Within walking distance of Provincetown harbor and shops. Bicycles, swimming, riding, tennis, golf and dune buggies nearby. Jim Logan, Innkeeper.*

*Directions: Follow Rte. 6 to Provincetown.*

## RED INN
**Provincetown, Massachusetts**

Provincetown in September! The clean sea air has a pungent quality. The sun takes a few minutes longer to make its morning debut, but it is every bit as warming and as generous as in August, inviting noon and afternoon swimming at the numerous nearby Cape Cod beaches. The Provincetown shops may not open until 10 or 11 a.m. but it is much more fun browsing. The back streets with their twisting and turning lanes seem more private and personal when there are fewer people about.

When I shared some of these thoughts with Ted Barker during a leisurely luncheon at the Red Inn he responded with enthusiasm. "September is really ideal. Our staff takes a deep breath and begins to enjoy Provincetown too. There is elbow room and the village returns to its quiet, private status. Marci and I like to walk up Commercial Street to 'do' the shops and see some of our village friends."

Marci and Ted Barker and various members of their family have made the Red Inn a genuine Cape Cod institution. In a tourist-oriented locality where new restaurants arrive with the birds in spring each year and permanently close their doors in the fall, the Red Inn has thrived with each passing year.

"I believe the fact that we are a family-run restaurant makes a big difference in our service," said Marci, who joined us for a moment at our table overlooking the harbor. "Do you know I counted sixteen members of our family who were working at the inn at the same time during the summer. There were sons, daughters, in-laws, nephews and cousins—a real 'old time feeling' which made it lots of fun."

Marci and Ted already had been operating the inn for quite a number of years before I made my first visit in 1974. This sense of permanency is one of the features that I look for in deciding which of the many fine inns and restaurants that I visit each year should be included in this book.

During the past years I have written extensively about the menu which includes various cuts of western beef, a great variety of seafood dishes, and lobster (which seems harder to get with each passing year). I also raved about the super desserts including brandied peaches, strawberries Romanoff, strawberry shortcake which is made with an oven-baked biscuit and generous amounts of strawberries and honest-to-goodness freshly whipped cream. My favorite is a baked apple with a filling of brown sugar and cranberries and topped off with whipped cream or vanilla ice cream.

The waitresses are all dressed in very gay gingham costumes which harmonize beautifully with the pattern of the plates, a lighthearted floral design on a white background with blue edging.

Marci and Ted told me that an array of appetizers would be added to the menu for 1977 including oysters and clams on the half shell, baked stuffed clams, escargot, mushroom caps, baked onion soup, lobster and shrimp cocktail.

Well, luncheon was over and so was my yearly visit at the Red Inn. I took one long last look at the harbor and the flocks of seabirds looking for a meal on the wet banks as the tide receded.

"Come on, we'll walk up town with you," said Ted. "It feels good to take the afternoon off."

*THE RED INN, 15 Commercial St., Provincetown, Mass. 02657; 617-487-0050. A waterside country restaurant with a striking view of Provincetown harbor. No lodgings. Open for dinner every night of the year. Serving lunch April through December. Within walking distance of all Provincetown lodging accommodations and recreational activities and attractions. Ted and Marci Barker, Innkeepers.*

*Directions: Follow Rte. 6 to end of Cape Cod.*

## INN AT DUCK CREEKE
### Wellfleet, Massachusetts

"What a great evening." Larry Fox, long a good friend and fellow tennis-enthusiast, described our evening at the Duck Creeke Inn most succinctly. His wife, Billie, Karen Oleson and I all chimed in with similar sentiments. The four of us were out at

Wellfleet on Cape Cod to visit Larry and Gloria Casale and to wish them well with the restoration of this old inn.

The evening got off to a great start with little handwritten menus with reproductions of a red-feathered cardinal on them. Larry explained that the menus were done by Phyllis Howard, who also did the inn brochures. There were several interesting dishes and the four of us managed to sample everyone else's entrée. There were nods of approval all around.

Billie had the veal Marsala, Karen had the chicken roulade, I had the seafood roulade and Larry had the manicotti. All were excellent.

The atmosphere is equally impressive with a lot of individuality shown at different tables throughout the low-ceilinged dining room. Each table has its own set of chairs, and imported and domestic antiques are found everywhere. The walls have both engravings and prints of the 19th century, carefully collected by Larry and Gloria.

After dinner we all walked a few steps over to our lodging rooms in the Sea Captain's house, one of several buildings that comprise the inn. Built in the early 1800's it is an excellent example of the Federal period.

There are wide floor boards and skillfully carved mantelpieces which provide a journey into the past. The odd thing about this building is that the former owners created a most unusual feature in the rear of the building—they added a broad verandah with stately two-story pillars. The entire effect is that of a Louisiana mansion.

Gloria kept an inn for a number of years on the inner Cape, and

Larry has had a career in advertising, construction and real estate. Together they make an excellent team and get a great deal of help from Gloria's sons. John, for example, has a green thumb and is responsible for the plants that are scattered throughout the many houses of the inn. Mike is in charge of the Tavern next door, and the time I was there, another son, Steve was cooking. However, all of the cooking is either supervised or prepared by Gloria. In fact there is a funny little story connected with that: Larry said that a Boston newspaper called up and asked what kind of food they had—was it New England or haute cuisine? Larry said he thought a minute and said, "I don't know what to call it—it's Gloria's cooking."

Well, no matter what you call it, Gloria's cooking was superb that evening, and we are happy to tell the story of this inn.

Incidentally, Wellfleet is located on the inside upper forearm of the Cape, near the tip and has a picturesque harbor. It is just a few miles from Truro and Provincetown. I hope to have many more great evenings at the Inn at Duck Creeke.

*INN AT DUCK CREEKE, Box 715, Wellfleet, Mass. 02667; 617-349-9333. A 40-room inn near the tip of Cape Cod. European plan includes Continental breakfast. Lunch and dinner served to travelers daily. Open daily from May 15—Oct. 15 and on weekends and holidays in off-season. Reservations required in off-season. No pets. Ocean beaches, nature walks, golf, tennis, fresh water fishing nearby. Larry and Gloria Casale, Innkeepers.*

*Directions: From the Sagamore Bridge, take Rte. 6 to Wellfleet. Turn left at Wellfleet Center sign. Inn is located on the right about 500 yds. after making turn.*

## THE BRAMBLE INN GALLERY AND CAFE
### Brewster, Massachusetts

"Watch your head going up these stairs. This is a very low ceiling." Karen Etsell spoke just in the nick of time. I ducked my head and just missed the dormer which extends over the stairs of this 1861 house. Even with a green paper flag for a warning, only a midget could proceed without bending.

The Bramble Inn Gallery and Cafe (hereafter known as The Bramble Inn) is a dandy. In the first place it is a marvelous example of several features that I delight in finding in country inns. There is no question that it expresses the innkeepers' individual interests and personalities. If ever an inn had individuality without a single trace of the stereotype, it is The Bramble Inn.

The entire ambiance was an exciting experience for me. The basic colors are green and pink. For example there are green place mats and pink napkins held in place by very attractive flowered rosebud napkin rings. The walls and woodwork are sparkling white and the floorboards of differing widths have been refinished with a warm, brown patina. There are lots of plants hanging from the ceiling and lots of ivy to provide more accents of green.

However, the main decor of the inn is provided by a collection of watercolors, oil paintings, lithographs, pastels and wood lathe art. Wood lathe art is a combination of wood lathe blocks and barnsiding creatively arranged in a rough frame. Also scattered among all of these art pieces are photographs taken by one of the innkeepers.

The menu is very appropriate for brunch, a midday meal or late afternoon or early evening repast. I enjoyed immensely the Cape Cod clam chowder. Another homemade soup is also prepared daily and these are served with some positively scrumptious baked bread. There are two cheese plates, one called the Breakfast Cheese Plate which consists of small light cheeses for the morning meal. Most of these are the soft type cheeses accompanied by fruits and baked bread. The Luncheon Cheese Plate consists of fruits served with a choice of brie, Camembert, or Vermont cheddar cheese and the freshly baked bread. A delicious quiche and two crepe dishes (chicken and seafood) have recently been added to the menu. The dessert is something special and original called Bramble A La Mode an old-fashioned Cape Cod delicacy (according to the menu) of chopped raisins and cranberries gently sweetened and wrapped in a tender pastry. This is topped with vanilla ice cream. All of these simple offerings are served with an appropriate group of beverages.

There are but two lodging rooms at the top of the stairs. One with a double bed and one with two single beds. Both have flowered wallpaper and country furniture. There is a definite tilt to the doors and floors which adds to the fun. These rooms share a bath, and Continental breakfast is included with the room.

The Bramble Inn came into existence because Elaine Brennan and Karen Etsell decided that they would like to try their hand at innkeeping. Interestingly enough, both of them are professional social workers and Elaine (the partner who does photographs) is still working at her profession at the Barnstable High School.

Karen Etsell decided to resign her job as Director of the Cape Cod Retired Senior Volunteer Program when the Bramble Inn opened its doors. There is no doubt that each contributes something of herself to the Bramble Inn.

Now we are happy to welcome the Bramble Inn and its two talented and involved innkeepers, Elaine and Karen, to this group of inns.

*THE BRAMBLE INN GALLERY AND CAFE, Route 6A, Main St., Brewster, Cape Cod, Ma. 02631; 617-896-7644. A village inn with 2 lodging rooms and art gallery in the heart of one of Cape Cod's northshore villages. Lodgings include Continental breakfast. Brunch, lunch and an early light evening meal served daily except Mondays. Open May through mid-October. Small, intimate inn does not meet the needs of most children. No pets. Swimming, sailing, water sports, tennis, golf, recreational and natural attractions within a short drive. Elaine Brennan and Karen Etsell, Innkeepers.*

*Directions: Take Exit 10 from Rte. 6. Follow 124 to the intersection of Rte. 6A (4 mi.). Turn right, 1/10th mile to inn.*

## NAUSET HOUSE INN
### East Orleans, Massachusetts

A couple of years ago my good friend, tennis opponent, and attorney in Stockbridge, Fred Rutberg said that he would love to go to Cape Cod in the fall. He was looking for an intimate country inn preferably with antique furnishings in a quiet community on the south shore, and preferably not too far from the water.

"Fred," I said, "you have just described the Nauset House Inn. I think you will love it." To make a long story short, Fred went to the Nauset House that time and several additional times. Recently I had occasion to ask him what it is he likes most about the inn.

"It just seems nice," he replied. "I like the fact that it is well done and not at all plastic. On my first visit I was very much impressed with the way they organized the breakfast and the social hour at the

end of the day. It meant that you were able to get together but it wasn't like a community thing. You could attend to your own business, but if you wanted to find some people to talk to or to go to dinner with, you could meet them and spend the evening. They treat everyone so beautifully. I also liked the terrace out in the backyard orchard."

Since Fred had been to the Nauset House Inn recently, I asked him how things on the outer cape progressed during the Bicentennial celebration.

"Jack Schwarz said that the great Bicentennial Bathtub Race was a huge success and everybody came to the Nauset House Inn for breakfast afterward. On the 4th of July they had fireworks on the beach and Jack told me that everyone felt 100% American when it was over."

The Nauset House Inn is almost three-quarters of the way out to the end of Cape Cod within sight of Nauset Beach which has some of the best surf in New England. Breakfast is the only meal served and there is something different everyday, like the quiche Lorraine on Monday, cranberry muffins on Wednesday, sour cream coffee cake on Tuesday, french toast on Thursday. The maple syrup is right from the Schwarz's farm in Vermont. Since Jack and Lucy are also in the business of buying and selling antiques, all of the lodging rooms have been furnished with an extensive collection of handsome beds, chests, clocks, highboys, and other Early American antiques. They also have a tiny antique shop in the orchard behind the inn.

Fred's preference for the Cape in the fall is the choice of a wise traveler. "It's a great feeling" he said, "to be on Nauset Beach in the hot September midday sun and be able to look both right and left and see nary a soul. Bicycling on the by-ways is almost a private experience also.

"I like the Nauset House so much," said Fred, "that I have already made reservations for next fall. Why don't you come also and we'll challenge Jack to a game of tennis?"

*NAUSET HOUSE INN, P.O. Box 446, Nauset Beach Rd., East Orleans, Cape Cod, Mass. 02643; 617-255-2195. A 12-room country inn 90 mi. from Boston, 27 mi. from Hyannis. Breakfast served to inn guests only. No other meals served. Some rooms with shared bath. Open daily from April 1 to Nov. 15. No children under 10 yrs. No pets. Within walking distance of Nauset Beach. Riding and bicycles nearby. Jack and Lucy Schwarz, Innkeepers.*

*Directions: From the Mid-Cape Hwy. (Rte.6), take Exit 12. Follow signs for Nauset Beach. Inn is located ¼ mi. before beach on Nauset Beach Rd.*

*Nantucket had a very strange beginning. In 1659, Thomas Macy, a Puritan farmer who lived on the mainland, was heavily fined for giving shelter to four Quakers during a terrific storm. He was so outraged that he decided to "take up his abode among savages where religious zeal had not yet discovered a crime in hospitality." He bought Nantucket Island for 30 pounds and 2 beaver hats and established his first settlement. Today, Nantucket's attraction can be found in its cobblestone main streets and handsome old houses. Most of them date back prior to 1835.*

*Nantucket has several historic houses that are open to the public and the Nantucket Whaling Museum which houses ships' models and books of the era which made Nantucket the main whaling port. One of the most interesting features is a collection of portraits of captains of whaling ships. The South Sea Island Room features artifacts and art brought back by returning whalers and sailors. The oldest house on Nantucket was built in 1686 and contains period furniture and china. The Old Gaol was built in 1805 mainly for people unable to pay their debts.*

## JARED COFFIN HOUSE
### Nantucket Island, Massachusetts

It's difficult to believe that this sturdily built, Federal-style house is an inn. Only the discreet murmur of voices and muffled

39

*Nantucket waterfront*

clinking of silver from a tree-shaded patio gives its identity away. It seems just like the other handsome houses of Nantucket whaling captains.

It was good to see Phil Read again, and I was very pleased when I realized that I was going back to one of the Crewel Rooms, with those splendid four-posters and the beautiful antiques. Interestingly enough, I have met three other people in my travels about the country who have also been guests at the Jared Coffin House, and were also put into these Crewel Rooms.

Nantucket Island, "The Little Grey Lady Of The Sea," is located 30 miles at sea from Woods Hole, and natives do, indeed, live here year-round. During the summer and fall it is almost always necessary to make automobile reservations on the ferry. However, a car is not really necessary to enjoy the island to the utmost. A visit to the bicycle shop will not only provide wheels but also amusing diversion.

One of the most enjoyable seasons of the year is Christmas time. There are some quaint island customs for the holidays that have been carried over from the old whaling days. There have been many feature stories about Christmas on the island, and as a result it is almost always necessary to reserve many months in advance.

I enjoy just strolling along the winding streets, happily coping with the cobblestones, and bicycling out to look at the Scotch heather, wood lilies, and wild roses on the moors.

This kind of activity naturally makes for hearty appetites, and I particularly favor the Jared Coffin specialties such as quahaug chowder and bay scallops.

At a recent meeting of CIBR innkeepers and their wives, Phil Read received a standing ovation from all of us when he announced that he and Peggy, after years of being innkeepers of the Jared Coffin House are now the sole proprietors as well!

Visiting Nantucket is always a unique experience. Staying at the Jared Coffin House is probably the closest thing that I found to actually feeling like I am a native for a few days.

*JARED COFFIN HOUSE, Nantucket Island, Mass. 02554; 617-228-2400. A 41-room village inn 30 mi. at sea. European plan. Breakfast, lunch, dinner served daily. Strongly advise verifying accommodations before planning a trip to Nantucket in any season. Swimming, fishing, boating, golf, tennis, riding, and bicycles nearby. Philip and Margaret Read, Innkeepers.*

*Directions: Accessible by air from Boston and Hyannis, or by ferry from Woods Hole, Mass. Automobile reservations are usually needed in advance. (617-426-1855.) Inn is located 300 yards from ferry dock.*


## THE VICTORIAN
### Whitinsville, Massachusetts

Orin and Martha Flint are a part of the "new generation" of innkeepers. Like Tom and Sue Carroll at the Mainstay, Rick and Pat Sutfin at the Harbor House, Ken and Wendy Gibson at the Robert Morris, and Marty and Barbara Walzer at the Pine Barn, the Flints decided to go into the innkeeping business while they were young and grow with it.

Their inn turned out to be a beautiful old mansion in a "forest of Arden" setting with great collections of flowers, trees and birds, and a pond within walking distance.

The interior of this Victorian masterpiece is like a moment in time in 1885. They have furnished it with beautiful antiques, paintings, Oriental rugs and hundreds of books. Stepping inside the huge glass front doors, I was confronted with a sweeping staircase that led, as I learned later, to the bedrooms on the second floor. To the left was a sumptuous parlor done in blue and gold, and to the right was the main dining room, formerly the library.

Orin Flint, wearing a Victorian costume that could only have come from Angel Street, greeted me, and we sat for a few moments talking about the joys of innkeeping.

"Martha is the one that really provides the stability for us," he said. "She supervises all of the cooking and we make everything from the freshest ingredients. She loves dishes like French onion soup and mushroom soup, braised sweetbreads and oysters Florentine. We make our own bread, including homemade dill bread.

"Our typical dinners during the week are filet Madeira, boned chicken breasts in wine sauce, boeuf Bourguignon or prime ribs. We generally have one unusual entree each evening besides the normal menu. On Tuesday it could be blanquette de veau; Wednesday, sole Meuniere; Thursday, shrimps in beer; Friday, oysters Florentine; and Saturday, scallopini al citrone, which is something that makes a special night special. Our Sunday menu is a la carte. The Sunday brunch has a choice of quiche, eggs Benedict, onion soup, shrimp scampi or full dinners such as seafood Newburg.

At this point Martha came in and the three of us went on a short tour of the seven well-appointed lodging rooms.

Descending the stately stairway, Martha explained they make a great celebration of holidays. "We are open for all of them and we do special decorations for Christmas and Thanksgiving and the other holidays as well. We're not far from Foxboro where the New England Patriots play, and Boston is only forty-five minutes away. Providence and Worcester are only thirty minutes away."

I was delighted to find the Victorian. Martha and Orin are two sincere people with excellent taste. They are doing a lot of extra things that I always like to find at a country inn, be it a Victorian mansion or an Arizona guest ranch. They are personally concerned with making certain that each visitor carries away an understanding of their dedicated spirit of innkeeping.

I know I did.

*THE VICTORIAN, 583 Linwood Ave., Whitinsville, Mass. 01588; 617-234-2500. A Victorian mansion with seven lodging rooms available in a quiet town 15 mi. from Worcester, Ma. and 40 mi. from Narragansett Bay in R.I. European plan. Lunch and dinner served to travelers daily except Mondays. Overnight guests receive Continental breakfast. Very small pets only. Lawn games, ice skating, fishing on grounds. Golf and tennis nearby. Orin and Martha Flint, Innkeepers.*

*Directions: From Providence, follow Rte. 146 north and take the Uxbridge exit. From the traffic light in Uxbridge, proceed north on Rte. 122 approximately 1½ mi. to Linwood Ave. (there will be a sign on the corner saying "Whitinsville — Left"). Bear left here. The inn is a few hundred yards around the corner. From Worcester, follow Rte. 146 south to the Whitinsville-Purgatory Chasm exit. Proceed into Whitinsville and keep right at the set of traffic lights onto Linwood Ave. The inn is on the left at the other end of Linwood Ave. — about 1½ mi.*

## INN FOR ALL SEASONS
### Scituate Harbor, Massachusetts

"I knew that this was going to be unusual," remarked the gentleman from Richmond, Virginia, "when the menu stated that our waiter would describe all the desserts which are made fresh daily on the premises."

His wife joined in, "I knew it was something special when I realized that our table water had little slices of lime in it."

We had just finished a positively sumptuous dinner at the Inn For All Seasons and had moved from our table in the white brick Garden Room to some very comfortable chairs in the Victorian parlor.

This inn, in the harbor town of Scituate, (by the way, it is pronounced as if it had no "c") is indeed an Inn For All Seasons, since both the menu and the decor change four times a year. "Everything has to be pleasing," explained Elaine, who is one of the Wondolowskis involved in the inn. "We try to have the colors and mood of

43

the season reflected in the atmosphere and food at the Inn. The room accents are fresh greenery, autumn leaves or pines. We serve heartier meals in fall and winter, and light, more delicate foods in spring and summer.

I discovered that the cuisine is Continental which allows plenty of opportunity for imagination with Spanish, French, Italian and other European dishes.

The menu on my visit featured Veal Oscar with Bearnaise sauce, chicken Kiev, and sweetbreads Financiere. These are generously augmented by American and New England offerings, like scallops, beef Wellington, and fresh fish which are caught by the fishermen of Scituate, and complimented by the fantastic dessert list.

"We do all our own cooking here with only the finest ingredients," asserted Elaine. "We don't serve ice cream because it isn't convenient to make it here."

Ed, Elaine and Dorothy took some of us on a tour of the bedrooms upstairs. They were all attractive with highly individualized furnishings. Some rooms have a view of the water. On the house tour, Ed gave us a running account of some of the many scenic and historical attractions in the vicinity. I learned that Scituate has six miles of excellent beaches. Sailing and fishing are a must, with clamming thrown in for fun. There are also many preserved and restored historical sites, including the famous Lighthouse which is open at various times during the summer.

In January 1977, The *Boston Globe* honored the inn as having one of the 10 best dining rooms in eastern Massachusetts.

An imaginative menu, attractive, homelike bedrooms, the beckoning sea, historic sites, and plenty of activities—that is the Inn For All Seasons. As that lady from Richmond said, "I would call it the 'Inn For All Reasons.'"

*INN FOR ALL SEASONS, 32 Barker Rd. Scituate Harbor, Mass. 02060; 617-545-6699. An 8-room inn in a picturesque south shore sea town, 32 mi. from Boston. Shared baths. European plan. Continental breakfast, lunch and dinner served to travelers daily except Mondays. Open year-round. Children over 12 years old and attended pets allowed. Bicycles, fishing, golf, swimming, tennis, antiquing, and deep-sea fishing nearby. The Wondolowskis, Ed, Elaine, Stan and Dorothy, Innkeepers.*

*Directions: From Boston, take Southeast Expressway south to Rte. 3. Continue south on Rte. 3 to Exit 31. Turn left at bottom of ramp and take right on Rte. 123 at traffic light. Go approximately 8 mi. to traffic lights intersecting Rte. 3A. Come across Rte. 3A and bear right. Follow signs for Scituate Harbor. At end of town take a right turn at set of traffic lights on to Jericho Rd. Take second left after Pier 44 on to Barker Rd. The inn is two blocks up on the right.*

## LONGFELLOW'S WAYSIDE INN
### South Sudbury, Massachusetts

It was my pleasure a few years ago to teach American history to a group of 8th grade students, and in my endeavor to stay at least one chapter ahead of the class, I found myself once again exploring the fascinating events that preceded the American Revolution. Of course the ideal procedure to follow was to visit the scene of these remarkable events, and this trip took me to Boston, Cambridge, Concord and other eastern Massachusetts communities which were the sites of so many of the events of 1775 and 1776.

In pursuit of these earlier times I left the well-traveled roads to search for old buildings, mildewed markers, and ancient trees which might indeed have been witnesses to events of history. In this way I eventually arrived at Longfellow's Wayside Inn in South Sudbury.

In my wildest hopes I couldn't have expected to find a more ideal setting. Built of red clapboard with white trim, the inn sits off the winding country road which once was the stagecoach route between Boston and Albany.

The inn was built around 1702 and originally was called Howe's Tavern. In 1775, the Sudbury farmers, led by Ezekiel Howe,

innkeeper of the inn, were among the men at nearby Concord. Revolutionary War soldiers found sustenance at the inn's tables. Today all musters of the Sudbury Minutemen take place at the inn as preparations are made for their annual reenactment of the march from Sudbury to Concord on April 19th.

Henry Wadsworth Longfellow immortalized the inn in 1863 with his *Tales of a Wayside Inn,* and thereafter it was known by its new name. Thanks to a grant from the Ford Foundation, the buildings and priceless antiques have been preserved as an historical and literary shrine. The inn is filled with pewter, old china, and preserved and restored antiques. It combines being a museum with the more practical function of providing lodging and food.

Just up the road there is a reproduction of an 18th century grist mill that is in operation and grinding flour. Also, just a stone's throw away is the famous Martha-Mary Chapel, a reproduction of a classic New England church which is the setting for many a marriage these days.

Although the 200th anniversary of the Battle of Lexington and Concord was celebrated in 1975, I must echo the advice of innkeeper Frank Koppeis that anyone who is expecting to visit Longfellow's Wayside Inn either for a meal or lodgings within the next few years should be sure to make a reservation in advance.

Here is an excerpt from a letter I received recently: "The Wayside Inn was as good as ever. It's got to be the classic in country inns. Probably its only fault is that it is too popular — especially on Sunday afternoon. Our first evening there we tried something new, a swordfish dinner. It was pretty darn good. When we had retired to our room for the evening we heard bagpipes and got up to see what was going on. Unbelievably, a parade of pipers dressed in complete Scottish uniform was marching through the inn. Quite a treat."

*LONGFELLOW'S WAYSIDE INN, Wayside Inn Rd., off Rte. 20, South Sudbury, Mass. 01776; 617-443-8846. A 10-room historic landmark inn, midway between Boston and Worcester. Within a short distance of Concord, Lexington, and other famous Revolutionary War landmarks. European plan. Lunch and dinner served daily except Christmas. Breakfast served to overnight guests. Francis Koppeis, Innkeeper.*

*Directions: From the west, take Exit 11A from I-95 to Rte. 495 N. Proceed north on 495 to Rte. 20. Follow Rte. 20 east to inn. From the east, take Exit 49 from Rte. 128. Follow Rte. 20 west to inn.*

## ANDOVER INN
### Andover, Massachusetts

The sun was brilliant, the snow was deep, and the air was brisk and New Englandy. As I walked across the campus of Phillips Academy in the lovely town of Andover I saw students with cross-country and downhill skis across their shoulders on their way to the Boston Hill ski area nearby. Behind me was the Georgian facade of the Andover Inn where I had spent a most interesting few hours discussing American and Continental innkeeping with the two innkeepers, Henry Broekhoff and John Oudheusden, both of whom are Dutchmen.

It is very interesting that the Andover Inn, on the campus of a traditional New England preparatory school should now be kept by these two men trained in Continental innkeeping who bring to it a feeling of innovation and excitement.

Some of the excitement is provided by the Indonesian "Rijsttafel," which is translated from the Dutch literally as "rice table." It is served every Sunday from 4 to 9 p.m.

Henry explained it to me like this: "Indonesia was a colony of the Netherlands for 350 years and during that time many Indonesian dishes became popular in the Netherlands. Rijsttafel is rice with anywhere from ten to twenty-five side dishes."

Rather than note the Dutch names I'll list the contents of a few of these side dishes: seasoned coconuts and peanuts, cold marinated vegetables, batter fried bananas, liver with coconut sauce, shrimp

47

and string beans, chicken and curry, fruit in hot sauce, a very hot relish, fresh salad with peanut sauce, shrimp, celery and corn pancakes, and beef strips in hot sauce.

"Rijsttafel is eaten from a soup plate with a large spoon in the right hand and a fork in the left," John explained. "You start by taking a little of the hot rice and surrounding it with the side dishes. The flavor is brought out because each side dish has a special taste of its own."

I first enjoyed Rijsttafel during my trip to Amsterdam, but I must say that this sedate New England inn was the last place where I expected to find it in the United States. Other innovative dishes from John's kitchen are Dutch beefsteak, tournedos flambe, which are pan fried at each table, and many delicious desserts including Black Forest cake and Dutch apple torte. The service is most attentive.

Many of the lodging rooms at the inn are in the process of being redecorated and both of the innkeepers were very enthusiastic about the new color schemes and fabrics.

Phillips Academy is the oldest incorporated school in the United States, established in 1778. Its companion school, Abbott Academy, was founded in 1829 and was the earliest incorporated school for girls in New England. On the campus there are beautiful buildings including the Addison Gallery of American Art which houses collections ranging from Colonial times to the present. Among the artists are Copley, Homer, Wyeth and Hofmann.

The campus is surrounded by beautiful old white New England clapboard houses and much history. The Stowe House is located behind the inn and was the residence of Harriet Beecher Stowe. The American House on Main Street was where Samuel F. Smith at the age of 24 wrote the hymn "America." There is a bird sanctuary located on the campus next to the inn. I could see it from my bedroom window.

Yes, in a corner of New England where tradition is intertwined with ivy, the Andover Inn looks to both the past and future.

*THE ANDOVER INN, Andover, Ma. 01810; 617-475-5903. A 33-room village inn 23 mi. from Boston, on the campus of America's oldest preparatory school. European Plan. Breakfast, lunch, dinner served daily except Christmas. Special Indonesian Rijsttafel served on Sunday from 4 p.m. to 9 p.m. Children welcome. Small trained pets only. Tennis, swimming, skiing, nearby. Henry Broekhoff and John Oudheusden, Innkeepers.*

*Directions: From Boston take Rte. 93N Exit 15 (Rte. 125). Proceed to Rte. 28N for 3½ mi. Inn on right hand side. From the west: Exit 29 South from Rte. 495. Go 3 mi. on Rte. 28.*

## RALPH WALDO EMERSON
## YANKEE CLIPPER
### Rockport, Massachusetts

No one appreciates country inns more than country innkeepers themselves.

In previous editions I have written of the fact that innkeepers included in CIBR have gathered together once or twice a year to have an "Innkeepers Holiday" where they exchange ideas, talk over new developments, enjoy good food and socialize.

A few years ago we had a meeting in Rockport, distributing the innkeepers and their wives among the facilities of these two inns, both of which are owned by the Wemyss family. When the decision was made to revisit Rockport again for another meeting in the fall of 1976, many innkeepers made immediate reservations because they enjoyed themselves so much at Rockport the last time.

I thought it was very interesting that innkeepers expressed preferences for one or the other of these two inns. They have much in common but maintain distinct personalities.

The three-story gleaming white Emerson is a traditional north shore hotel with an expansive view of the ocean. The Yankee Clipper sits back in the shelter of some great trees and was once a late 19th century mansion. One of the buildings was originally designed by the 19th century Boston architect Bullfinch who is highly praised in New

England. (There is a group of Bullfinch houses in Orford, N.H.) Both inns have swimming pools, but the grounds of the Emerson also provide the opportunity to play croquet, horseshoes and badminton. The Clipper has less emphasis on active sports but there are nature trails that start at the inn and wind back through the wooded hills.

It is possible to sit on the big terrace at the Emerson and gaze at the ocean for hours on end. At the Clipper guests can either sit on the grassy section of the low cliffs and watch the boats in Rockport Harbor, or climb to the top of the great granite boulders and find their own private ocean viewing point.

Both inns have a profusion of flowers including roses, tulips, pansies, spirea, rhododendrons, dahlias, petunias.

Some innkeepers said they liked the Clipper because it gave them more of an opportunity to talk to Fred and Lydia Wemyss, while others enjoyed chatting with Gary Wemyss, their son, who is the innkeeper at the Emerson. Several of them mentioned the whirlpool bath and sauna at the Emerson.

All were enthusiastic about Rockport itself, which has so many engaging qualities. The town has many late 18th and 19th century homes with narrow clapboards, wooden shutters and fan doorways which are to be found on beguiling lanes and winding elm shaded streets.

The harbor has elements of ocean and sky that have drawn artists to Rockport for over 100 years. Fishing boats and luxury yachts are moored side by side with a generous sprinkling of fisherman's dinghies, dories and lobster boats.

To add further to the ambiance, Rockport has dozens of galleries, studios, and interesting shops which include places specializing in pottery, weaving, basketry, gems and jewelry and both soft and hard sculpture.

A great many of these shops are open year-round, although I have always found that spring and fall were excellent times to visit this community which is close enough to Boston to be an afternoon's excursion.

The innkeepers meeting was a huge success, with the staff of both inns doing an incredible job of keeping everything running smoothly. Since we were there for two days, everyone had the opportunity to visit both inns and sample the offerings on the two menus. The Emerson has such things as Yankee pot roast, native lobster and fried filet of sole. The Clipper features fish chowder, steamed lobster, chicken Yankee Clipper and blueberry pancakes among many other offerings.

It is to the credit of both inns that many innkeepers and their wives said when our two days came to a close, "Let's come back here again in a few more years. We always have a good time."

*RALPH WALDO EMERSON, 1 Cathedral Ave., Rockport, Mass. 01966; 617-546-6321. A 36-room oceanside inn, 40 mi. from Boston. Modified American and European plans. Breakfast and dinner served to travelers daily. Snack bar luncheon in season. Season: July 1 through Labor Day. Open Memorial Day through Nov. 1. No pets. Pool, sauna and whirlpool bath on grounds. Tennis, golf nearby. Courtesy car. Gary Wemyss, Innkeeper.*

*Directions: Take I-95 to Rte. 128 to 127 (Gloucester). Proceed 6 mi. on Rte. 127 to Rockport and continue to Pigeon Cove.*


*YANKEE CLIPPER, Rockport, Mass. 01966; 617-546-3407. An intimate 26-room inn on the sea, 40 mi. from Boston. European plan available year-round; Modified American plan from May 15 to July 1 and Sept. 5 to Nov. 1. Breakfast and dinner served daily. Lunch served during July and August. Meals served to travelers by reservation only. No pets. Ocean view, shoreline walks, many antique shops and other stores nearby. Fred and Lydia Wemyss, Innkeepers.*

*Directions: Take I-95 to Rte. 128 to 127 (Gloucester). Proceed 6 mi. on Rte. 127 to Rockport and continue to Pigeon Cove.*

## YANKEE PEDLAR
**Holyoke, Massachusetts**

Bess Stathis, the innkeeper of the Yankee Pedlar, Virginia Rowe, and I were having a bite of lunch in the Oyster Bar, and catching up on the events at the inn since my last visit.

"You remember you wrote about a wedding we had in the Opera House," she said, as we helped ourselves to some appetizers and relishes from the array of silver dishes. "Well, that same couple came in just a short time ago to have their first anniversary dinner here. In fact, I remember they sat in the Colonial dining room, you know the one with the old barnboard siding."

Bess and I joined Virginia at one of the round tables in this attractive reproduction of a turn-of-the-century dining room. There are old-fashioned Victorian-style lamps which once were gas and converted to electricity, green upholstered chairs, handsome walnut paneling and a great collection of pewter platters and teapots, all of which came from another era.

"Most of the Victorian decorations and furniture here at the Pedlar are from Kenilworth Castle which was a landmark in the area. The Tiffany lampshades and stained glass window panels came from old houses in nearby communities as well as from Kenilworth. Gene Tamburi, who is the owner, has been an enthusiastic collector for many years."

As we were talking, more and more people were coming in for lunch on this Saturday afternoon and ordering the open sandwiches which are served with lettuce and tomatoes. These include roast beef, tuna, cheese and turkey. Virginia had the oyster stew and announced that it was perfect.

After lunch we took another tour of the inn and saw some of the recently redecorated lodging rooms in the main building and in the

1850 House annex next door. One of them has a corner room with its own sitting room and twin poster beds. Next door to this room is a room with a canopied bed. "Oh, so many people love to sleep in a canopied bed," said Bess.

Before we left the Yankee Pedlar, which is located at the crossroads for both east/west and north/south travel in New England, I shared with Bess a letter that I had received from one of our readers:

"My husband and I stayed at the Yankee Pedlar for one night on a two-week vacation. We are both in our mid-twenties but we enjoy old-fashioned inns and antiques. We read about the Pedlar in *Country Inns and Back Roads* and we want to tell you how much we loved the food there and the lovely room we had in the Carriage House. We really felt we were treated like special people. The food was delicious and prepared with care. The people serving were attentive and we have never been to such a wonderful place. Our room was so lovely looking, especially the four-poster bed, so colorful. It was the cleanest room we have ever come upon. We had breakfast the next day and it was delicious. We could tell from the people working there that they really cared. It was just perfect. We hope to go back to the Yankee Pedlar again some day."

Bess said, "Oh, I think I remember those people. I remember chatting with them about the fact that the next time they came they could stay a little longer and perhaps visit Deerfield or Sturbridge or take a ride up to Mt. Tom which is our local ski area. How nice of them to write you a letter."

*YANKEE PEDLAR, Holyoke, Mass. 01040; 413-532-9494. A 36-room village inn with antiques, 8 mi. north of Springfield. Breakfast, lunch and dinner served to travelers daily except Christmas. Oyster Bar open until 12:30 a.m. Historic 19th century mill town with unique canal system. Mt. Tom ski area, golf, tennis nearby. Bess Stathis, Innkeeper.*

*Directions: From I-91 take Exit 16. The inn is located at junction of Rtes. 202 and 5.*

## RED LION INN
### Stockbridge, Massachusetts

For many people the Red Lion Inn is a "first" country inn experience. When traffic is reasonable it is about a three-hour drive from New York City via Route 22 or the Taconic Parkway. Some people prefer to turn east from Rte. 22 to Rte. 55 at Wingdale, N.Y., and then turn north on Route 7 through the Connecticut villages of

Gaylordsville, Kent, Cornwall, and Canaan. This is a beautiful road running along next to the swiftly flowing Housatonic River.

Lunchtime at the Red Lion invariably draws a great number of travelers from many states. I can see from the expression on the faces of some travelers that it is the first time that they have visited a country inn. I was having lunch there recently with a friend of mine from the village who happened to remark that he thought it was wonderful the way the owners, Jack and Jane Fitzpatrick have turned the inn into a real living thing. "They have put so much of themselves into it."

I agreed instantly because the Red Lion has many things that I look for in a country inn. For example, there is a wonderful feeling of personal warmth. Although Jack and Jane are both very busy (he is our state senator), when they are not in Boston, they are very often found at the inn talking to guests and making them feel at home.

The low-ceilinged lobby with the usually ever-present fire in the fireplace and seasonal decorations make everyone feel at home almost immediately. Let me share with you an excerpt from a letter I received recently from a reader in Atlanta, Georgia:

"What struck us at once about this place, apart from its architectural interest, was the attractive lounge, the sizzling fire, and the 19th century earthenware teapots and platters arranged around the walls and on tall shelves. We loved the dining room with its fresh damask linen. We were also impressed with the courtesy of the staff. We opted for a room in the quietest location and were assigned a charming, freshly decorated room. As we did not have advance reservations, we were allowed only one night at the Red Lion, but I would love to have a chance to repeat it."

Stockbridge is a very pleasant town with a wide main street with many trees. There is much to do at the height of the summer, winter, and fall seasons with Tanglewood, the Berkshire Theatre Festival,

Jacobs Pillow Dance Festival and other musical and theatrical offerings nearby. In winter there is downhill and cross-country skiing, and walking the streets of the village which is especially beautiful when the snow falls.

In the "off season" it is a quiet pleasant experience and there are always quite a few guests at the inn 'tween seasons, who enjoy a quiet respite from a world that gets rather hectic at times. Incidentally, the Norman Rockwell Museum, just down the Main Street from the inn, is open year-round.

Like many other country inns, the Red Lion is also a family affair with the Fitzpatricks' daughter, Nancy, very much involved with the hospitality of the inn. Their other daughter, Ann, has gained well-deserved plaudits for her candy sculpture which can be seen at Gumdrop Square, a small shop located in the former village fire station.

There has been a tavern or an inn on this site for more than 200 years. In keeping with that tradition, the Red Lion continues to supply excellent food, lodgings and entertainment for travelers and townfolk alike.

*RED LION INN, Stockbridge, Mass. 01262; 413-298-5545. A 90-room historic village inn in the Berkshires. Adjacent to Tanglewood, Norman Rockwell's Old Corner House Museum, Berkshire Playhouse, Jacob's Pillow, Chesterwood Gallery and major ski areas. European plan. Breakfast, lunch, dinner served to travelers daily. Open year-round. Outdoor pool on grounds. Tennis, golf, bicycles, swimming, and Alpine and xc skiing nearby. Jack and Jane Fitzpatrick, Owners.*

*Directions: From the Taconic State Pkwy. take Exit 23 (N.Y. Rte. 23) to Mass. Rte. 7. Proceed north to Stockbridge. From the Mass. Tpke. exit at Lee and follow Rte. 102 to Stockbridge.*

## STAGECOACH HILL
### Sheffield, Massachusetts

"Which of the English and Scottish inns that you visited in the British Isles was closest to being like Stagecoach Hill?"

Scottie Burns was taking a few minutes between greeting guests, seating them, and attending to their dining needs. Once again I was at Stagecoach Hill, "the English inn of the Berkshires" with a Scottish flavor.

This time, after my recent trip abroad, I saw more than ever the strong Scottish and English influences at the inn. For example, there

are pictures of the English Royal Family including Queen Victoria, Queen Mary, and King George. There are some English hunting prints and Scottish scenes as well. The Union Jack and the bonnie blue flag of Scotland were displayed side by side.

The old red brick building, part of which used to be the town poorhouse over 100 years ago, looks like it had been transplanted from the Cotswolds or the Lake District and dropped here at the base of a mountain in Sheffield, Massachusetts. The cover on the 1977 edition of CIBR is a watercolor painting of Stagecoach Hill by Jan Lindstrom.

The entrance is through huge doors and up the stairs to a lounge where there are usually a number of people seated in romantic semi-darkness which is lighted by the glow from two fireplaces and candles in red hurricane lamps. This time there was soft piano music coming from one corner of the room.

Stagecoach Hill is a wee bit on the intimate side. The local guests find its atmosphere most congenial and those who come up from the city appreciate the fact that it is somewhat small and really quite cozy. For winter fun, there are several south Berkshire ski areas nearby and in summer, it is within easy drive of Tanglewood, summer theatres, and other seasonal attractions.

Good food with an English and Scottish flair is one of the main reasons why Stagecoach has so many devoted followers. Wilbur Wheeler, Scottie's partner, is the chef and the menu includes such original ideas as the Alderman's Carpetbag, which is a sirloin steak lined with oysters, Blackbird Pie, many veal dishes, chicken livers Rumaki, and some rather luscious desserts including an English trifle.

In answer to Scottie's question, I ruminated for a moment or two thinking about inns I had visited in Rye, Chiddingfold, Broadway and Grasmere in England, and the Isle of Skye, Isle of Mull, Inverness and Nairn in Scotland.

I finally decided that Stagecoach Hill had a remarkable resemblance to the Tullich Lodge in Ballater, which is located in the Grampian section of eastern Scotland. It too, is run by two gentlemen and is situated in a very distinguished, turreted manor house. Among the specialties on the menu are steak and kidney pie, roast beef, and delicious homemade paté. These are on the Stagecoach menu, also.

"Well, they do have a lot of things in common with us," said Scottie. "I must make a point to visit them on my next trip back home."

*STAGECOACH HILL INN, Undermountain Road, Sheffield, Mass. 01257; 413-229-8585. A British inn with Scottish overtones on Rte. 41 midway between Salisbury, Conn. and Great Barrington, Mass. Motel accommodations available. European plan. Dinner served nightly and all day Sunday. Closed Christmas Eve, Christmas Day and Wednesdays. Near South Berkshire ski areas, Tanglewood, Jacob's Pillow and all summertime attractions. Scottie Burns and Wilbur Wheeler, Innkeepers.*

*Directions: From Mass. Tpke., take Exit 2 and follow Rte. 102 west to Stockbridge. Take Rte. 7 south to Great Barrington, then follow Rte. 41 south to inn.*

## THE VILLAGE INN
### Lenox, Massachusetts

It was a cold, bright January day when I drove the few miles from Stockbridge to Lenox, taking the winding road which goes up Prospect Hill past Lake Mahkeenac and enters Lenox through the woods from the south. I was about to meet my friends John and Peggy Rogers and Mary and Harry Harrison for lunch at the Village Inn, a place where we frequently enjoy the midday meal.

As many times as I have driven this road it always gives me a real lift to see the lake, mountains and open marshes where so many birds reside in all seasons. It is a reminder of a sustaining gentle mood of New England.

This same gentle mood is preserved on the elm-shaded streets of Lenox, a village with some interesting history dating from colonial days through the 18th and 19th century. In many ways the Village Inn reflects quite a few of these historical ages. The building, itself,

dates back to the early 19th century and curiously enough the entrance is at right angles to the street. It is a two-and-a-half story yellow clapboard building with a basic Federal design that has been adapted to meet various needs over many years. One of these adaptations is an addition which creates an L-shaped sheltered terrace and lawn on which there are a number of beautiful maples, a small fountain and an American flag. Plantings of iris, daffodils, tulips, peonies, roses, and petunias brighten the picture throughout the warmer weather.

The fact that there has been an inn here for a great many years reflects the resort nature of the town of Lenox. Since the early 1800's the natural beauty of the area has attracted vacationers, some of them quite notable, many of whom became seasonal residents. Nathaniel Hawthorne, Edith Wharton and Fanny Kemble all were visitors to Lenox.

I walked through the porch area of the inn which is very popular for summer dining and went through the big door into the hallway. There is a very snug feeling in the inn because of the low ceilings, flowered wallpaper and many old Victorian prints and photographs. The inside parlor where the front desk is located has white paneled ceilings, a brick fireplace and a most inviting air. The inn also has a front parlor where there are attractive groupings of furniture, an organ, and still another fireplace.

Today the Village Inn is kept with love and care by Richard and Marie Judd whose objectives are to preserve the traditions of American innkeeping.

"What I hope we are doing here is combining the best part of the past with today's conveniences," said Richard. "We've tried to furnish our lodging rooms with comfortable homelike furniture. We are very flexible, providing meals and accommodations for a few permanent residents as well as travelers and vacationers. We are never closed. I could never imagine a Colonial inn closing its doors at anytime."

"The meals are my department," said Marie, "and we have a great many dishes prepared from scratch like Yankee pot roast, chicken fricassee, braised short ribs of beef, barbecued spareribs and a New England boiled dinner. Our menu is basically American. We almost always have hot apple pie and Indian pudding for dessert."

The Village Inn is a quiet New England experience.

*THE VILLAGE INN, Church St., Lenox, Mass. 01240; 413-637-0020. A 25-room inn in a bustling Berkshire town 4 mi. from Stockbridge, 8 mi. from Pittsfield, and 1 mi. from Tanglewood. Lenox is located in the heart of the Berkshires with many historical, cultural and recreational features. (See special note on Berkshires.) All plans available. Breakfast, lunch and dinner served daily to travelers. Open every day of the year. Eleven rooms with shared baths. No pets. Swimming pool privileges across the street from inn. All seasonal sports available nearby. Richard and Marie Judd, Innkeepers.*

*Directions: Lenox is on route 7A, one of the principal north-south routes in New England.*

# Rhode Island

*The first time visitor to Rhode Island is bound to be in for a tremendous surprise. The smallest state in the Union can stand right up to its larger New England neighbors in the categories of historic interest, culture and natural beauty. For example, one visit to Newport is never enough to absorb its many different facets. The restored section of Providence has buildings which date back to Colonial times. Rhode Island beaches, which traverse almost the entire southern stretch of the state are warm and inviting in the summer, and quiet and moody the remainder of the year.*

*Rhode Island also has offshore islands including Block Island which is reached only by ferry or air service. A car isn't necessary but the island has some of the best bicycling roads I have ever seen. Incidentally, a great many motorists are carrying bicycles on their cars these days. It's one of the best methods for getting around the back roads of any state.*

## INN AT CASTLE HILL
**Newport, Rhode Island**

"I'm surprised," said Paul McEnroe, the innkeeper at Castle Hill, "that so many people are still writing me in care of the DeLaVergne Farms Inn in Amenia, New York. I'm still getting reservations through the mail from CIBR readers," he said. "I'm happy to tell them that after the fire in 1974 which completely destroyed the inn, I'm relocated here and I invite them to come and visit me in Newport."

Paul and I, who have known each other for more than ten years, were walking through the many bedrooms in this Newport mansion which has a most fascinating past, a highly enjoyable present, and a future with much promise.

Alexander Agassiz, the famous 19th century naturalist, built Castle Hill a hundred years ago as a summer residence. It has remained unchanged in character and many of the original furnishings including Oriental rugs and the handcrafted oak and mahogany paneling are still there.

"This is the room that Thornton Wilder stayed in several times," said Paul. "In fact, he describes it in his book, *Theophilus North*." We were on the top floor of the inn enjoying a fantastic view of the Atlantic approaches to Newport, Narragansett Bay, the Newport Harbor and the great Newport Bridge.

"When the Tall Ships were near this point in 1976," he said, "it was just the most awesome sight that can be imagined. I suppose we will never see anything quite like that again. However, the America's Cup Races will be in Newport in 1977 and to see all of those great yachts with full running gear is a tremendous experience."

To my mind Newport is one of the great places to visit in the United States. Sometime I would like to be there during Christmas for the ceremonial lighting of the community tree and walk around Newport. During that season of the year, 7½ watt lights are placed in the windows of the Colonial and Federalist homes in the downtown area. Christmas lasts for thirty days during which time there are many church choirs and choruses making appearances and several orchestra concerts and readings. Many of the 17th and 18th century homes are open to the public and there are tours to old business buildings and houses.

Newport has fascinating historical sites including Touro Synagogue, the oldest in the United States built in 1763; the 96-year-old Newport Casino which has the National Lawn Tennis Hall of Fame and Tennis Museum; attractive waterfront shops on Owen's Wharf, the famous Newport Mansions along the Ocean Drive, and frequent programs of music. (Remember Newport was the location of the first Newport Jazz Festival.)

Accommodations at the inn vary from mansion-like rooms, all with a view of the water and some with really enormous bathrooms, to housekeeping cottages which are rented by the week during summer and fall.

Dinner at Castle Hill is quite continental in nature and many of the dishes are prepared with a flourish at the table.

The Inn at Castle Hill is a country inn that looks to the elegance of Newport's past.

*INN AT CASTLE HILL, Ocean Drive, Newport, R.I. 02840; 401-849-3800. A 20-room mansion-inn on the edge of Narragansett Bay. Near the Newport mansions, Touro Synagogue, the Newport Casino and National Lawn Tennis Hall of Fame, the Old Stone Mill, the Newport Historical Society House. European plan. Continental breakfast served to house guests only. Lunch and dinner served daily to travelers. Possibly closed from January to end of April. No pets. Swimming, sailing, scuba diving, walking on grounds. Bicycles and guided tours of Newport nearby. Jens Thillemann, Manager. Paul McEnroe, Innkeeper.*

*Directions: After leaving Newport Bridge follow Bellevue Ave. which becomes Ocean Dr. Look for inn sign on left.*

## LARCHWOOD INN
**Wakefield, Rhode Island**

Frank Browning looked up from the open grill on the patio with a twinkle in his eye. "This," he said, "is yours," indicating with a long-pronged fork one of the steaks on the charcoal fire.

The lady standing next to me asked, "Which one is mine?" Frank said, "The one up in the corner is yours. You said you wanted medium, didn't you?"

I was at the Larchwood Inn during Memorial Day weekend, and the spring flowers and flowering fruit trees were in their most delightful profusion. The red maples and pine trees were shimmering in the afternoon sun. There were both steaks and lobsters being done on the grill, and although there was no hint of rain in the air, the blue and white striped cover overhead would certainly protect us in case of a shower.

While we were watching Francis being happy in his work, I discovered that this lady was part of a family of four who had sailed up the Connecticut and Rhode Island coast from Greenwich, Connecticut, and were now enjoying a treat of a dinner ashore. "We just love this section of Rhode Island. The countryside is so pretty and there is a great deal of history to poke into."

The Larchwood, itself, reflects these engaging features of Southern Rhode Island. Actually, it is a large mansion dating back to 1831 with conservative lodging rooms and food that reflects the off-shore fishing as well as the hearty farm products. Among the bounty of the sea are lobster, native scallops and bluefish.

The interior has many Scottish touches, including quotations from Robert Burns and Sir Walter Scott, and photographs and prints of Scottish historical and literary figures. One of the dining rooms has wall paintings showing farms and seascapes of Southern Rhode Island.

Rhode Island is a state of stone walls. They come in various heights, thicknesses and conditions of repair. The back roads, which are most numerous for a state that is reputedly small, often offer some interesting historical sites as well as beautiful homes. There is much to see and do, I discovered, within a short distance of the Larchwood. The nearby south shore beaches are often favorably compared with others elsewhere in New England.

The inn building has a fascinating history that has its roots in Indian raids in Nebraska, the discovery of gold in California and the continuing saga of a restless New England family. It became an inn in 1926. I first visited it in 1968 and it's been a regular stop ever since.

In the conversation following dinner, the boating family invited me to sail to Nantucket with them the next day. It sounded like a great idea. I could hardly wait to see Phil Read's expression when he would look out from the Jared Coffin House and see me walking up the street with a seabag over my shoulder.

*LARCHWOOD INN, 176 Main St., Wakefield, R.I. 02879; 401-783-5454. An 11-room village inn just 3 mi. from the famous southern R.I. beaches. Some rooms with shared bath. European plan. Breakfast, lunch, dinner served every day of the year. Swimming, boating, surfing, fishing, xc skiing and bicycles nearby. Francis Browning, Innkeeper.*

*Directions: From Rte. 1, take Pond St. Exit and proceed ½ mi. directly to inn.*

### 1661 INN
**Block Island, Rhode Island**

As I noted in the 1975 edition, the 1661 Inn, which is kept by Justin and Joan Abrams along with their daughter, Rita, and two sons, Mark and Ricky, is in an old white house partially hidden from the road by thick hedges. There are 21 rooms in this inn on Block Island which can be reached by ferry from Providence, Point Judith and Newport, R.I., and New London, Conn., and also by air.

I have given you this background because I am sure that Joan Abrams will not mind if I share the contents of a letter she sent me early in January, 1977. I think it provides a great deal of insight into country innkeeping.

63

"We have removed the gift shop and turned it into a small lounge called the Settlers Pub. It is probably the smallest lounge in the world. We have decorated some of the walls with American prints including some of the nicest Winslow Homer woodcuts from our own private collection. We put books and plants in the rooms, all new carpeting in the hallways, and wallpapered two rooms that had been painted. We're quite pleased with our new colonial guest rooms.

"We have a brand new kitchen from floor to ceiling with all new equipment. We really did spend a fortune, but I feel it was very worthwhile. We will have teams in the dining room, each waitress with her own bus person. We're planning a very large garden this year. Almost every night last summer we served something that was grown in the garden, and I can count the nights we used other than our garden vegetables for our main vegetable. Rita, who is our assistant manager and strong right arm, will again serve as dining room hostess.

"Our menu will continue to feature Block Island seafood, including flounder, scallops, swordfish and lobster. Our johnny cakes and Indian pudding which are from an old recipe, are always very popular.

"Rick is our second chef and he also designed the layout for our kitchen. Mark runs the Sandwich Shoppe down at the foot of the hill in the village. The waitresses have new patchwork uniforms — they're red, white, and blue with a little yellow in them. Oh yes, before I forget, we have increased the number of our three-speed Schwinn bikes. That's one thing that everyone loves to do here on Block

Island. It is the best way to get around, since you can leave your car at the ferry terminal on the mainland.

"We are all hoping to see you during the summer of '77. Come out for the races, if you can."

I think that that letter from Joan Abrams conveys the warmth and concern that is expressed at the 1661 Inn much better than anything I could write. I will certainly be there in the summer of '77, if possible, for the Block Island Races.

*THE 1661 INN, Box 367, Block Island, R.I. 02807; 401-466-2421 or 2063. A 21-room island inn off the coast of R.I. and Conn. in Block Island Sound. Modified American and European plans. Most rooms with shared baths. Open from Memorial Day through Oct. 4. Breakfast and dinner served to travelers daily. Lawn games on grounds. Tennis, bicycling, ocean swimming, sailing, snorkeling, diving, salt and fresh water fishing nearby. Block Island is known as one of the best bird observation areas on the Atlantic fly-way during migrations. The Abrams Family, Innkeepers.*

*Directions: By ferry from Providence, Pt. Judith and Newport, R.I. and New London, Ct. By air from Newport, Westerly and Providence, R.I., New London and Waterford, Ct., or by chartered plane. Contact inn for schedules.*

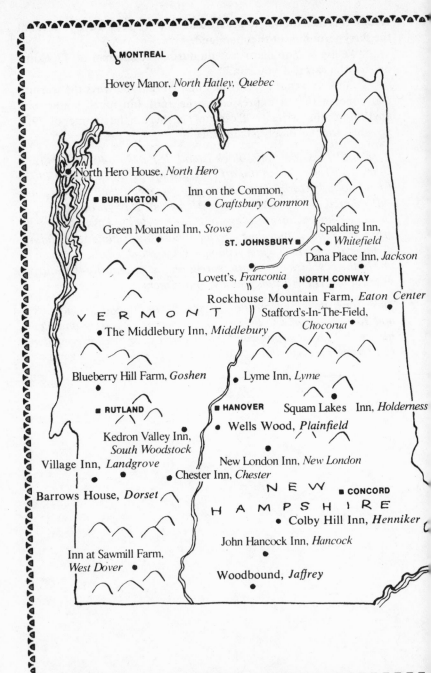

MONTREAL

Hovey Manor, *North Hatley, Quebec*

North Hero House, *North Hero*

BURLINGTON

Inn on the Common,
*Craftsbury Common*

Green Mountain Inn, *Stowe*

ST. JOHNSBURY

Spalding Inn,
*Whitefield*

Dana Place Inn, *Jackson*

Lovett's, *Franconia*

NORTH CONWAY

Rockhouse Mountain Farm, *Eaton Center*

V E R M O N T

Stafford's-In-The-Field,
*Chocorua*

The Middlebury Inn, *Middlebury*

Blueberry Hill Farm, *Goshen*

Lyme Inn, *Lyme*

RUTLAND

HANOVER

Squam Lakes Inn, *Holderness*

Wells Wood, *Plainfield*

Kedron Valley Inn,
*South Woodstock*

New London Inn, *New London*

Village Inn, *Landgrove*

Chester Inn, *Chester*

N E W

CONCORD

Barrows House, *Dorset*

H A M P S H I R E

Colby Hill Inn, *Henniker*

John Hancock Inn, *Hancock*

Inn at Sawmill Farm,
*West Dover*

Woodbound, *Jaffrey*

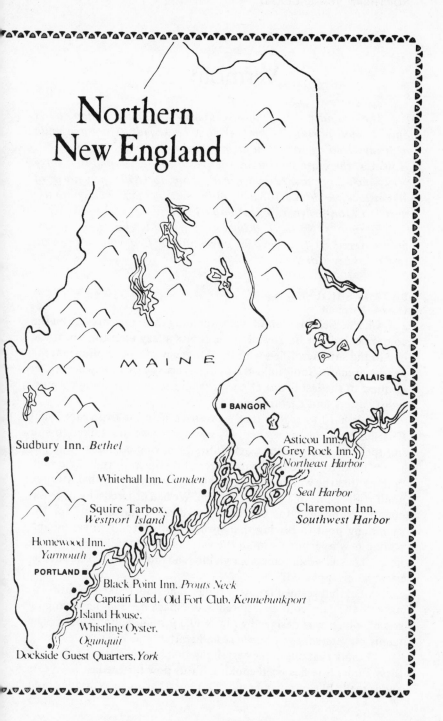

# Northern New England

MAINE

CALAIS ■

■ BANGOR

Sudbury Inn, *Bethel*

Asticou Inn,
Grey Rock Inn.
*Northeast Harbor*

Whitehall Inn. *Camden*

*Seal Harbor*

Squire Tarbox,
*Westport Island*

Claremont Inn,
*Southwest Harbor*

Homewood Inn.
*Yarmouth*

PORTLAND ■

Black Point Inn, *Prouts Neck*
Captain Lord, Old Fort Club, *Kennebunkport*
Island House,
Whistling Oyster,
*Ogunquit*
Dockside Guest Quarters, *York*

# Vermont

*The ordinary three-state Northern New England map shows only a small portion of the Vermont backroads. The three main highways leading to Vermont are Route 7, Route 100 and I-91. However, there are several alternatives to these. A road that I like very much is Route 12 which runs from Taftsville, just north of Woodstock, to Route 107 just south of Bethel and then continues north to Montpelier, running parallel to I-89.*

*Vermont's Northern Kingdom has roads that seem almost undiscovered. It is always an adventure to find your way north to Craftsbury Common.*

## BARROWS HOUSE
### Dorset, Vermont

Charlie Schubert and I were watching the tennis players on the courts behind the Barrows House. It was a lazy afternoon near the end of the summer, filled with the pungency of ripe apples from the nearby orchard. Some industrious honeybees occasionally buzzed by in quest of the last drops of nectar from the late blooming cosmos, phlox, asters and nasturtiums.

"It is hard to realize that we've been here for five years," said Charlie, "and I guess it's actually seven since we first talked to you in Stockbridge about the possibilities of having a country inn.

"Oh, there have been some interesting times all right," he said. "I think that the winter of the gas shortage was the year that Marilyn and I really came of age as innkeepers. We had ordered a lot of cross-country equipment for the ski shop, made arrangements for the swimming pool to be dug that spring, and started renovating and adding new apartments in all the various old outbuildings we have here. Then, as we all remember vividly, the snow didn't come and the gasoline disappeared!"

All of that seemed far away today. The pool looked beautiful to me with the gaily colored umbrellas, the snack bar and the "changing room" which was designed to look like a small country barn. The tennis players changed partners and started another set.

"I think that one of the best things that happened to us was when Sissy came. She has been cooking for us now for the last few years and is really like our own family. Our guests are always raving about

all of the different things that she loves to prepare. You know she makes everything—soups, meats, vegetables and desserts— from scratch."

Charlie excused himself for a few moments to greet some arriving guests and I sat there in the early twilight enjoying the quiet and peace of this Vermont country town. Dorset has always been a town in which I feel at home. I have been well acquainted with it for more than thirty years. The streets are tree-shaded, the houses are traditionally late Colonial and early Victorian, there is a village green, a post office and general store. I have played many a round of golf on the rather sporty course and enjoyed many an evening of theatre at the Dorset Playhouse. Incidentally, Charlie Schubert himself is an actor and during the winter he has appeared in quite a few plays given by the local company.

I have received many letters from readers who say that they enjoyed their stay at the Barrows House very much, particularly the lodging rooms with flowered wallpaper and country furniture. Many mention the views of the garden and the comfortable living room with the fireplace where everybody seems to gather after dinner.

There is indeed a spirit at the Barrows House which I find so frequently among people who have left the city to take up a new life as country innkeepers. As busy as Charlie and Marilyn are in this thriving inn, they always seem to have time to stop and pass the time of day with their guests, help them plan an antiquing trip through the Green Mountains, arrange for a fourth at doubles or even accompany them out on the cross-country ski trails.

"Sometimes," Marilyn Schubert says, "this can be deceiving. It looks like the life of a country innkeeper is all fun and games. Believe me, maintaining 26 rooms in 6 houses, a ski shop, swimming pool, tennis courts, a full service dining room, and keeping up with all of our guests is a time-and-a-half job. Don't get me wrong, I'm not complaining. It is great fun, but there are lots of times that Charlie and I never even see each other during the day. But we love it and we wouldn't do anything else."

*BARROWS HOUSE, Dorset, Vt. 05251; 802-867-4455. A 26-room village inn on Rte. 30, 6 mi. from Manchester, Vt. Modified American plan omits lunch. Breakfast, lunch and dinner served daily to travelers. Swimming pool, tennis courts, bicycles, xc skiing facilities, including rental equipment and instruction, on grounds. Golf, tennis, paddle tennis, trout fishing, and Alpine skiing nearby. Charles and Marilyn Schubert, Innkeepers.*

Directions: From Rte. 7, proceed north on Rte. 30 at Manchester to Dorset.

## BLUEBERRY HILL
### Goshen, Vermont

I really had no way of knowing what great changes would be forthcoming when I made my first trip to meet Tony and Martha Clark at Blueberry Hill in mid-December of 1972.

I remember stopping the car for just a moment at the bridge over the brook. The sign "Blueberry Hill Farm" pointed to the left and I thought that I had really accomplished something by following Tony's directions on the snowy mountain roads from the village of Brandon without making a mistake. He had explained that if there were snow on the road I should go "straight" at this point and use the long way around to get to the inn. If the roads were clear, I should make a left turn at the Civil War monument in the middle of the woods and follow that road.

There was fresh snow, so I went the long way around and found my way to the top of the mountain and Blueberry Hill.

There I met Tony and Martha Clark, an energetic and inventive young couple who had purchased this old farmhouse in the late sixties. After living in it for a couple of years, they decided to do something innovative for that time—open an inn devoted to cross-country skiing!

Cross-country skiing at that time was being enjoyed by comparatively few people. Now it has really captured the imagina-

tions of outdoor-minded people everywhere. I'm certain that Tony Clark, with his far-sightedness and high standards has really made a significant contribution to the sport. On a visit a few years later, Tony told me that while a lot of places were called "ski touring centers," at Blueberry Hill they feel that a ski touring center should be so named because it devotes itself entirely to cross-country skiing, keeps a fully equipped shop and supplies instruction. "We supply complete maps of all of the trails and make sure that everyone signs in and out. People are not allowed to ski alone on the trails."

The Blueberry Hill Inn, the cross-country skiers inn, is very definitely family style. Everyone sits around the big dining room table and there is one main dish at each meal which Martha prepares in the farmhouse kitchen. She is a country cook with gourmet tendencies, so sometimes these main dishes can be exotic. One of my most recent meals offered beef Bourguignonne, spinach soufflé, cheese soup and apple pie. All the breads, cakes and pies are baked in the cozy kitchen.

From the very start the lodging rooms were "real Vermont farmhouse." For example, there are hot water bottles on the backs of the doors, down comforters and country furniture. But things have changed in recent years, and Tony and Martha who always lived in the inn, have moved out making more room. Six rooms in the back of the house have been made into three rooms with balconies. Each room sleeps four people.

From the very start families with children have found a vacation at Blueberry Hill a very happy experience. Tony and Martha's two

71

young sons Timothy and Christopher have grown up on skis and set an example for novice skiers.

Incidentally there are no facilities for babysitting really young children. Reservations for winter accommodations begin the previous winter and the inn is often booked solid for weeks at a time. The inn accommodates 18 guests.

What about visiting Blueberry Hill when there is no snow on the ground? It sits on the top of a mountain right next to the Green Mountain National Forest and in September and October, when the Vermont Mountain air and foliage are so glorious, it is really a very special place. As Tony says, "We can always use help clearing the trails."

*BLUEBERRY HILL FARM, Goshen, Vt. 05733; 802-247-6735. A 9-room mountain inn passionately devoted to cross-country skiing, 8 mi. from Brandon. Modified American plan omits lunch. All rooms with private baths. Meals not served to travelers. Open from September to April. Closed Christmas. Swimming, fishing, and xc skiing on the grounds. Indoor tennis, Alpine skiing and bicycles nearby. Tony and Martha Clark, Innkeepers.*
*Directions: At Brandon, travel east on Rte. 73 through Forrestdale. Then follow signs to Blueberry Hill.*

## CHESTER INN
### Chester, Vermont

Tom and Betsy Guido acquired the Chester Inn in late Spring of 1976, and by the time I visited them in September they had already endowed it with some of their personal belongings and their own brand of enthusiasm.

"Tom and I came to Vermont from Cleveland, Ohio, where he had been in the executive branch of an insurance company," explained Betsy. "While neither of us had prior experience in the food service or hotel management business, we did come armed with a lot of nerve and the determination to do well.

"Tom took a crash gourmet cooking course from Audrey Patterson, who with her husband, Jim, had owned the inn for a number of years. Our guests tell us that Tom is doing very, very well. Our dinner menu will remain essentially the same but Tom will be adding specials of his own.

"While Tom dons his chef's cap, I act as hostess in the dining room. People especially like to have the personal touch of the owners being intimately involved. We feel that this also affords them the opportunity to talk and ask us questions about the inn.

"We're making many changes in the lodging rooms. Our pride is our new Victorian suite which has only the authentic furniture and accessories of that period, from heavy brocade swag draperies to frivolous grass reeds in gaudy vases. We will also be personalizing other rooms."

Among changes in the inn is the fact that the mirrors have been moved from either side of the big fireplace in the living room up to the second floor and have been replaced by some very bright paintings. There are quite a few watercolors on display throughout the inn as well. There is also a Florentine Renaissance settle which came out of a doctor's office in western Pennsylvania. The tapestry was done by Betsy's great-grandmother and there is also a wooden bench from Berks County, Pennsylvania, with unicorns on it and a date of 1845. On the landing to the second floor there is a brass rubbing that Tom and Betsy did when they lived in England.

How are Betsy and Tom doing? Well, here is one opinion from a man in Harrisburg, Pennsylvania, who visited there in the fall of 1976.

"While we ate dinner we kept saying to ourselves, 'this is absolutely the best veal we have ever tasted.' In fact the entire meal was just terrific as was the service.

"The escargot was as good as any appetizer we've ever been served and we enjoyed dipping bread into the leftover garlic butter. Another appetizer, the eggplant Caponata, was wonderful.

"The salad was mixed at tableside. After dinner we spent a long time talking with Tom and Betsy, in fact until after midnight. We were quite impressed with their obvious dedication to serving and pleasing their customers.

"The next morning at breakfast we helped ourselves to orange juice, bacon, scrambled eggs and muffins. Looking out the window we saw Tom Guido at 8:30 a.m. cleaning the lovely swimming pool."

Sometimes when an inn is sold the new innkeepers find that the previous innkeepers are a "hard act to follow." I think that Tom and Betsy Guido, the new headliners at the Chester Inn, have already proven that they also have star quality.

*CHESTER INN, Chester, Vt. 05143; 802-875-2444. A 30-room village inn on Rte. 11, 8 mi. from Springfield, Vt. Convenient to several Vt. ski areas. Lodgings include breakfast. Lunch and dinner served to travelers daily except Mondays. Closed from late October to late November and April to mid-May. No children under 5 in dining room. No pets. Pool, tennis and bicycles on grounds. Golf, riding, Alpine and xc skiing nearby. Tom and Betsy Guido, Innkeepers.*

*Directions: From I-91 take Exit 6. Travel west on Rte. 103 to Rte. 11.*

## GREEN MOUNTAIN INN
### Stowe, Vermont

A few years ago, I received one of the funniest letters ever from my friend, Parker Perry, the host at the Green Mountain Inn. The essence of it was his experiences with the state of Vermont in adding ten more lodging rooms in the area immediately behind the inn. He illustrated the point that Vermont has the toughest environmental restrictions of all fifty states and proved the point well.

I first visited Green Mountain Inn in March of 1967, and it has been on my schedule every year since. One visit is always in the summertime, when I enjoy Stowe for its quiet mountain atmosphere. It has a reputation for being a rather mad place in the winter, and this is justifiable because the skiing on Mt. Mansfield, Spruce Peak, and Madonna is first rate. But, it is in the summertime that I can really appreciate its peaceful, country tranquility.

At the inn I always start my day with a wondrous Vermont breakfast which includes sausage and is topped off with a piece of apple pie! Food has always been an important factor at this Vermont inn which was built in 1833. There is a great deal of emphasis on New England food with hearty fare that includes pork chops, ham steak, fresh calves liver, and much more. I have seldom seen a larger selection of desserts, and Parker never fails to remind me that deep

fat fried foods are never served at the GMI.

The red clapboard GMI is a New England village inn that "puts on airs." Dottie Perry is responsible for the most impressive flower arrangements—real in summer and dried in winter. There are ample books in the second floor library and rooms. Air conditioning is never needed, and there is a blessed absence of mosquitoes.

When it comes to back roads, crafts, antique shops, and gift shops, Lamoille County has more than its share. The Stowe Area Association Office which is right across the street from the GMI has directories to all of these, as well as a complete map of roads and tours of the area. This includes 11 suggested circle tours.

The GMI, with its additional facilities, is very popular with bus tours. Parker Perry meets about every new group and gives them a warm welcome talk. "We love them," he said, "and they love us."

I'm glad that Vermont has such tough environmental restrictions, and I am also sure that now that Parker has gotten everything squared away, he would agree with me. It is a state well worth preserving.

*GREEN MOUNTAIN INN, Main St., Stowe, Vt. 05672; 802-253-7301. A 61-room village inn on Rte. 100, 36 mi. from Burlington, 6 mi. from Mt. Mansfield, Vermont's highest peak. Modified American plan omits lunch. Breakfast, lunch, dinner served to travelers daily. Open mid-December to mid-April, late May to late October. Golf, tennis, riding, hiking, bicycles, Alpine and xc skiing nearby. Parker and Dorothy Perry, Innkeepers.*

*Directions: From I-89, take Exit 10, and proceed north on Rte. 100 to Stowe.*

## INN AT SAWMILL FARM
**West Dover, Vermont**

"They said we couldn't grow roses in Vermont, but just look at those!"

Rodney Williams pointed to some gorgeous rose bushes of many varieties which line the pleasant little terrace of the Inn at Sawmill Farm. Three sides of this secluded little enclave with a tidy swimming pool are formed by a farmhouse and a series of connecting barns, some of which were moved into place by Rodney and Ione Williams when they escaped Atlantic City, New Jersey, to open a country inn a few years ago.

"The early Vermont settlers tried to build their houses in little green valleys beside a stream with an apple orchard on the southern slope," he said. "That is why there are so many beautiful houses with beautiful surroundings." Even as Rod was expounding on this idea I realized how closely this description fits his country inn. Looking south across the swimming pool past the picturebook Christmas tree, I could see the white spire of the West Dover church. Just below the swimming pool and past the Spring House I caught a glimpse of the two-acre pond that provides ice skating in the winter and trout fishing and boating in the summer. The warm sunshine (on the south side, naturally) also provides perfect light for the profusion of apple and maple trees. It is a scene that has been photographed and painted quite a few times during the past few years.

At dinner, Rod explained that his son, Brill, was the chef and that the menu frequently contained such non-Vermont items as crepes Maison, frogs legs, Imperial crab meat soufflé, steak au poivre, beef tenderloin with Bearnaise sauce, roast duck, backfin crab and rack of lamb.

When Rod and Ione Williams made the "big break" from the pressures of urban life, they brought their own particular talents and sensitivities to this handsome location, and it is indeed a pleasing experience. There was plenty of work to do—a dilapidated barn, a wagon shed and other outbuildings all had to be converted into lodgings and living rooms. However, over the years, the transition has been exceptional. The textures of the barn siding, the beams, the ceilings, the floors and the picture windows combine to create a feeling of rural elegance.

The newest of the lodging rooms is to be found in the Cider House Studio which has been redecorated. It has a bedroom, living room and a fireplace, as well as bath and dressing room. The king-size bed is in an alcove facing the fireplace. It has sliding glass doors that overlook the pond. Sounds like a wonderful place for a honeymoon.

The living room contains a superb conversation piece that perhaps symbolizes the entire inn. It is a handsome brass telescope mounted on a tripod providing an intimate view of Mt. Snow rising majestically to the north.

*INN AT SAWMILL FARM, Box 8, West Dover, Vt. 05356; 802-464-8131. A 15-room country resort-inn on Rte. 100, 22 mi. from Bennington and Brattleboro. Within sight of Mt. Snow ski area. Modified American plan omits lunch. Breakfast and dinner served to travelers daily. Closed Nov. 7 through Dec. 7. No children under 8. No pets. Swimming, tennis, and trout fishing on grounds. Golf, bicycles, riding, snowshoeing, Alpine and xc skiing nearby. Rodney and Ione Williams, Innkeepers.*

*Directions: From I-91, take Brattleboro Exit 2 and travel on Vt. Rte. 9 west to Vt. Rte. 100. Proceed north 5 mi. to inn. Or, take US 7 north to Bennington, then Rte. 9 east to Vt. Rte. 100 and proceed north 5 mi. to inn.*

## KEDRON VALLEY INN
### South Woodstock, Vermont

Early in December I received a letter from Paul and Barbara Kendall, my good friends, who with their sons, Chip and Dane, have been keeping one of my regular stops on the country inn trail since the mid-sixties.

"Well now that winter is here, we have closed the 1828 main

building until next May and are busy serving fireside meals in the cozy Tack Room Lounge of the 1822 Tavern building. Our winter activities include paddle tennis, riding and driving the horses, ice skating, cross-country skiing and downhill skiing. Everyone enjoys relaxing in the lounge and playing darts.

"Dane, whom you have known ever since he was a small boy, will be 18 later this month. He graduated from high school last June and has been doing post-graduate work at Woodstock Country School. He has caught the travel bug, which is something you ought to understand, and has been to Texas and New Mexico. Chip, who will be 19, graduated from Woodstock Country School this past June. He is interested in maple sugaring and is working for us at the stables. He is at the "Just A Plain Farm" in Coltsville, Pennsylvania, for the winter and took his new three-year-old bay mare with him.

"Our stables were very busy this past year with breeding, training, buying and selling as well as the trail rides, lessons, surrey rides and sleigh rides. We ran a 50-mile competitive trail ride in September and I think it will become an annual event."

In a great many respects the Kedron Valley Inn is quite similar to one of our new inns in this edition—the Rockhouse Mountain Farm in Eaton Center, New Hampshire. Both are most interesting places for families to vacation and both have horses, trail rides, skiing and swimming nearby or on the grounds.

The main house of the Kedron Valley Inn dates back into the 19th century and has typical country inn rooms and furniture. A few years ago the Kendalls built several lodging rooms in a modern log cabin just a short distance from the main house. These fit the needs of people who feel they are happier in a more conventional motel room.

"Hearty Vermont" is one way to describe the food. Breakfasts include corn muffins, griddle cakes with Vermont maple syrup and country sausages. Dinners offer baked brook trout, a New England boiled dinner and sugar-cured ham. Indian pudding and strawberry shortcake frequently round out the picture.

The Kedron Valley Inn is a traditional Vermont inn that reflects the changing vacation interests and enthusiasms of America. Many guests who visit and revisit enjoy the quiet atmosphere, beautiful mountain scenery and opportunity to sit in the rockers on the big front porch and watch an occasional car pass by. They are just as happy as guests who spend their days in the saddle or on the ski trails.

*KEDRON VALLEY INN, Rte. 106, South Woodstock, Vt. 05071; 802-457-1473. A 34-room rustic resort-inn, 5 mi. south of Woodstock. Near Killington, Mt. Ascutney ski areas. All plans available. Breakfast, lunch and dinner served daily from May to November. Closed Sundays from November to May. Closed Christmas and month of April. Swimming, riding, sleigh rides and carriage rides, hiking, and xc skiing on the grounds. Tennis, golf, and bicycles nearby. Paul and Barbara Kendall, Innkeepers.*

*Directions: Take Exit 1 from I-89 and follow Rte. 4 to Woodstock. Proceed south on Rte. 106 for 5 mi. Or, take Exit 8 from I-91 and follow Rte. 131 for 8 mi. Proceed north on Rte. 106 for 12 mi.*

## MIDDLEBURY INN
### Middlebury, Vermont

I have found quite a few inns closely associated with colleges and secondary schools. There are inns of this nature in Granville (Ohio), Andover (Massachusetts), New London and Henniker (New Hampshire), Berea (Kentucky), Cazenovia (New York), St. Stephen (New Brunswick), and New Wilmington (Pennsylvania).

A classic example is the Middlebury Inn in Middlebury, Vermont, which is almost an adjunct to Middlebury College. The intermingling of town, gown and inn creates an atmosphere that is complementary to all three.

The three come together in the geographical center of this small town. Recently David Beach, the innkeeper at the Middlebury Inn, wrote me a letter to bring me up-to-date on what's going on in that beautiful part of the world: "The band concerts still echo from the village bandstand in the summer and people enjoy walking on the green. Other seasons offer different types of recreation including hockey games, football, basketball, art shows, musicals and skiing.

The college, of course, goes full tilt for most of the year. It is one of the most famous language schools in the world and, among other things, it requires a year in Europe for all Master's degrees.

Many of our guests enjoy the college drama group and a visit to Meade Chapel. The Frog Hollow Craft Center is within walking distance of the inn and the Shelburne Museum is within convenient driving distance.

"You may recall that 1977 will be Vermont's Bicentennial year and also happens to be the Middlebury Inn's 150th anniversary. Needless to say the present structure is quite different from 1827 but we believe its character continues. Each year many people return to relive a honeymoon journey or a college experience.

"Most of the remodeling work at the inn is complete. We have many new beds, a new private dining room and extensive painting and redecoration in the bedrooms. We are making good progress in spite of the fact that the building itself is so old that everything has to be done with extreme care. It is wonderful to receive so many complimentary letters indicating interest in our old inn.

"Our meals continue in the New England tradition with popovers for dinner, blueberry pancakes for lunch with Vermont maple syrup, oyster stew in season, Vermont apple pies, and Vermont ham and roast turkey.

"Middlebury was described by author William Hazlett Upson (the real Alexander Botts) as follows: Here is a lovely old town whose people are as adept at getting their monies worth as they are at getting along with one another. And if it snows, they let it."

Congratulations in 1977 to the Middlebury Inn on its 150th anniversary, and to its enthusiastic and conscientious innkeepers, David and Jean Beach. Now let's look forward to another 150 years!

*MIDDLEBURY INN, Middlebury, Vt. 05753; 802-388-4961. A 75-room college town inn midway between Burlington and Rutland in the Champlain Valley. Convenient drive to Lake Dunmore, Lake Champlain, historic Fort Ticonderoga, the Morgan Horse Farm and Shelburne Museum. European plan. Breakfast, lunch and dinner served daily to travelers. Open year-round. No recreation facilities on grounds, but golf, tennis, swimming, bicycles, alpine and xc skiing nearby. David and Jean Beach, Innkeepers.*

*Directions: Middlebury is accessible by major highways from all directions. The inn is located at junction of Rtes. 7, 125, and 30.*

## NORTH HERO HOUSE
### Champlain Islands, North Hero, Vermont

The North Hero House is the summertime endeavor of Dr. Roger Sorg, a dentist from Flemington, New Jersey, his wife Caroline, their son David and daughter Lynn. Together they run this island country inn for twelve weeks each summer. I visited first in July of 1972 at which time the Sorgs had been involved in it for two years.

It was a family project from the very beginning and Lynn and David even as small children had their chores. As a result it has become a wonderful place for families to visit. Many of the same guests have been returning year after year.

Vacation activities at or near the inn include boating, water-skiing, sailing, snorkeling, fishing, tennis, bicycling, golf, and horse-back riding. The inn is also in a great location for backroading, antiquing, and just simply rocking on the porch gazing at Lake Champlain.

Something new has been added or restored each year, and here is a letter from Roger and Caroline which summarizes some of the activities during 1976 and what they look forward to in the summer of 1977:

"We had a very pleasant and busy summer season with great fishing, the best we've ever known for years and years. Our larder was full and our guests thrived on freshly caught fish. Our new sauna provided many enjoyable hours for our guests who cool off with a refreshing plunge in the lake right outside the door.

"The 'Carrie,' a launch built in 1899 by Caroline's grandfather, Everett H. Kennedy, and named for Caroline's mother, was completely restored and much to everyone's surprise won first prize in the Lake Champlain Bicentennial Antique and Classic Boat Review. The silverplate trophy now resides in the North Hero House.

"Our new 24-foot float-boat provided an enjoyable vehicle for guests' touring, snorkeling and scuba expeditions to various reef areas and last but not least, moonlight excursions on warm summer nights."

Most guests ask the Sorgs how they happen to be keeping a country inn on Lake Champlain. Caroline explains that Roger used to come to North Hero Island during the summer when he was a boy. "Even then the inn was old," she said, "dating to the 1880's." Many years later he and Caroline came here for vacations and she and the children loved the island. "When the inn went up for sale we decided to buy it and become summer innkeepers."

"It has been a great adventure," said Roger, "and I am sure we will be coming here for many years to come."

In the 1976 edition I explained that although Roger had beaten me at several of the sports at the inn including sailing and swimming, I was finally successful in taking two sets of tennis from him. The account ended with his demand that we "play three out of five after dinner." Some people have written to inquire about the results of the rematch.

He won it in straight sets.

*NORTH HERO HOUSE, Champlain Islands, North Hero, Vt. 05474; 802-372-8237. A 22-room New England resort-inn on North Hero Island in Lake Champlain, 35 mi. north of Burlington and 65 mi. south of Montreal. Modified American plan. Luncheon a la carte only. Breakfast and dinner served daily to travelers. Open from late*

*June to Labor Day. No pets. Swimming, fishing, boating, water-skiing, ice house game room, bicycles and tennis on grounds. Horse-back riding and golf nearby. Roger and Caroline Sorg, Innkeepers.*

*Directions: Travel north from Burlington on I-89, take Exit 17 (Champlain Islands) and drive north on Island Rte. 2 to North Hero. From N.Y. Thruway (87 north), take Exit 39 at Plattsburg and follow signs "Ferry to Vermont." Upon leaving ferry, turn left to Rte. 2, then left again to North Hero. Inn is 15 min. from ferry dock on Rte. 2.*

## THE VILLAGE INN
### Landgrove, Vermont

"There isn't a paved road in Landgrove." Jay and Kathy Snyder were showing me around the Village Inn in Landgrove, and as we were walking around the outside of the old inn with its red clapboards, I had remarked about the beautiful dirt road which runs directly in front. "Yes," continued Kathy, "Vermont is one of the few states that's doing its best to preserve its country roads rather than pave every single one of them. This section of the state has quite a few."

The Village Inn, formerly called the J-Bar Lodge, has been owned and operated by the Snyders for 16 years. It first opened its doors as an inn in 1939 and for many years the main interest was skiing. However, in recent years the Snyders have made it an all-season resort-inn, which is particularly attractive to families with children of all ages.

When I paid my first visit there were many active young people around, most of them in the Rafter Room which has a big fireplace, log beams across the low ceiling, and plenty of games like Ping Pong, skittles and bumper pool.

In the winter the outdoor-minded guests can enjoy downhill skiing at five major areas nearby plus cross-country skiing, snow-shoeing, and sledding in the woods right behind the inn. There is also an ice skating pond.

Summertime activities on the grounds include tennis courts, a nine-hole pitch and putt golf course, a heated pool, hiking trails, volleyball and fishing. There is a wealth of Vermont fun nearby including horseback riding, indoor tennis, summer theatre, hiking, auctions, music festivals, country fairs, barn dances and church suppers. The inn accepts a few swimming pool and tennis member-ships which means there are local people meeting inn guests at this friendly inn.

If I seem to be emphasizing the outdoor activity which may appeal to young people, it's because it's a joy to find a place where families can simply relax and enjoy good times together.

There is a wide variety of lodging facilities including everything from bunk rooms to rather luxuriously furnished new rooms which were just being completed at the time of my visit. The lodgings include a hearty breakfast. Dinner is offered during the winter, and in summer, lunch is also available to guests.

Along with Jay and Kathy and their two young daughters, both of whom are active participants in just about everything, are Jay's father and mother who are very much involved with the guests, and Lois MacArthur who has been doing the cooking at the inn ever since the Snyders came.

At dinner, the dining room was buzzing with people who had been having a good time all day long. Dinner consisted of a loaf of homemade bread right out of Lois' oven, a salad with an interesting house dressing, a baked potato, green peas and slices of rare roast beef. The strawberry shortcake was made the old-fashioned way.

At the next table there was a Dutch family who had lived in this country for two years. They were from a small town near Amsterdam and were familiar with many of the places I had written about in Holland. We had a very nice chat. They said they had been here several times because, "their children enjoyed it."

And, there are no paved roads in Landgrove, Vermont. Isn't it wonderful!

*THE VILLAGE INN, Landgrove, Vt., 05148; 802-824-6673. A 21-room rustic resort-inn in the mountains of central Vermont, approximately 4½ mi. from Weston and Londonderry. Lodgings include breakfast. Breakfast, lunch, and dinner served to travelers during the summer except Wed. dinner. Open from Nov. 15 to April 15; July 1-*

*Nov. 15. Children most welcome. No pets. Swimming, tennis, volley-*
*ball, pitch and putt, xc skiing, fishing on grounds. Downhill skiing,*
*riding, indoor tennis, antiquing, backroading, summer theatre*
*nearby. Jay and Kathy Snyder, Innkeepers.*

*Directions: Coming north on I-91 take Exit 2 at Brattleboro, follow*
*Rte. 30 to Rte. 11 and turn right. Turn left off Rte. 11 at signs for*
*Village Inn. Coming north on Rte. 7 turn west at Manchester on Rte.*
*11 to Peru. Turn left at signs for Village Inn.*

## INN ON THE COMMON
### Craftsbury Common, Vermont

I was singing in the shower after a beautiful afternoon in Craftsbury Common in the middle of Vermont's Northeast Kingdom. I
polished off my last bass arpeggio, turned off the shower and slipped
into one of the golden terrycloth bathrobes which are supplied to
each guest at the inn. "In lieu of private baths for each room,"
explained Penny Schmitt "we felt that these bathrobes would give a
homey feeling. There's one for every guest."

This feeling is reflected in every aspect of this unusual, personal
country inn. There are six guest rooms, each of them furnished
individually with gay country furniture and a daily supply of fresh
flowers. Flowers are definitely one of the big things here with
trillium, iris, crocus, peonies delphinium, roses, monkshood, phlox
and many others. They grow in deliciously colorful beds between
broad stretches of lawn and tall trees. The rose garden, a prelude to
the side entrance to the inn, has dozens of varieties.

Although Innkeepers Penny and Michael Schmitt are both from
New York, they are longtime summer residents of this top portion of
Vermont. Like many other innkeepers, opening the inn three years
ago was the realization of a dream that had been cherished for many
years.

Craftsbury Common is a well-named town dominated by a
huge open space in its middle which dates back to the late 18th
century. It was cleared to provide grazing areas for oxen and horses.
Today many of the village houses are built around it and each
property owner is responsible for painting a section of the considerably large enclosing fence. It is inside this common that so many
exciting things happen every summer including a fiddlers contest, an
antiques and uniques festival, a banjo contest and Old Home Day.

The active sports to enjoy at the inn and nearby are swimming,
canoeing, horseback riding, fishing and hiking. A superb clay tennis
court was added just beyond the vegetable garden during the summer

of 1976, and a croquet court has been constructed in the second flower garden. The Schmitts went to Bermuda and fell in love with the game as it is played with English equipment and rules. As Penny says, "Guests need a bit of instruction, but seem to love it. We have a very good English croquet set." On the skiing scene the Schmitts have three excellent cross-country instructors and can outfit just about anyone who shows up. Snowshoes are available for people who would like to try them as well.

When I came downstairs for dinner I admired the antiques, oil paintings and general appointments of this lovely Vermont house, and Michael introduced me to the other guests. Penny came sweeping into the room wearing a beautiful long skirt. After a leisurely chat with everyone she took her place at one end of the oval dining room table, Michael took his place at the other end, and we all enjoyed dinner together.

I asked Penny how it was that she was able to prepare dinner and still join her guests. She explained that it was done with the cooperation of her daughter, Liz, and other young women of the village. "I plan it well in advance, and they take over. After all, one of the reasons we opened an inn is to enjoy people, and having dinner with them is one of the most enjoyable parts of our innkeeping experience."

Penny proudly pointed out that the vegetables served at the inn are grown right in their own garden. "Sometimes guests prefer to choose them themselves and they are cooked to order. Virtually everything is homemade: pies, soups, breads, salad dressings, and desserts," she explained. "We just do not use things out of cans."

It seems to me like an ideal way to keep a country inn.

*INN ON THE COMMON, Craftsbury Common, Vt. 05827; 802-586-9619. A 6-room inn in a remote Vermont town 35 mi. from*

*Montpelier. Shared baths. Modified American plan omits lunch but snacks are available. Breakfast and dinner served to house guests only. Open from May 15 to Oct. 20 and Dec. 20 to Mar. 31. Attended pets allowed. Tennis, croquet, xc skiing, snowshoeing, on grounds. Golf, tennis, swimming, sailing, horseback riding, canoeing, xc and downhill skiing, skating, hiking, and nature walks nearby. Michael and Penny Schmitt, Innkeepers.*

*Directions: From Exit 7, I-89N, take Rte. 2 east to Rte. 14 north until 8 mi. north of Hardwick. Watch for marked right hand turn, go 2 mi. to inn. From Canada and points north, use Exit 26 on I-91 and follow Rte. 58W to Irasburg. Then Rte. 14 southbound 12 mi. to marked left turn, 3 mi. to inn.*

# New Hampshire

*The fastest way from Boston to New Hampshire is to take Route 3 or I-95 North. However, I would like to suggest taking Route 119 from Concord, Mass., and proceeding through Littleton, Groton and Townsend, crossing over into New Hampshire near East Rindge. Follow the route through Fitzwilliam, Richmond and on into Winchester, Jaffrey Center, Swanzey, Hancock, Antrim and similar secluded New Hampshire towns and villages.*

*I-89 is now the quickest way to go from Concord diagonally across New Hampshire, through New London, up to Lebanon and across into Vermont. However, an alternate way would be to follow Routes 4 and 4a which run somewhat parallel to I-89 and provide a look at little towns such as Andover, and Wilmot.*

*One of my personal favorites is to turn off I-93 at Ashland and then go north on Route 113 through Holderness, Center Sandwich, Whitefield, Wonalancet, Tamworth and into Conway.*

## COLBY HILL INN
### Henniker, New Hampshire

The Glover Family, Don and June (classmates of mine at Bucknell University) and their son, Don Jr., his wife Margaret, and the Glovers' daughter Sally O'Donnell and her husband, Roger, have all had a most enjoyable time being innkeepers at Colby Hill. Don Jr., with considerable restaurant experience behind him, does the cooking and everyone pitches in with the bedmaking, waitressing and chores.

I understand that Christmas and Thanksgiving dinners are quite an occasion and are served to inn guests only. "We all sit down at the table with our guests," said Don, "and it is like being one big family. We always have turkey with all the trimmings." I was very glad to hear this, because every year when the frost is on the pumpkin I receive letters from readers who are particularly interested in knowing where they can go for a family Thanksgiving or Christmas.

Here is an excerpt from a letter I received from a guest who had stayed at the inn. "The Colby Hill Inn was just as you described it. The house, the furniture, the paintings, the wide floor boards were all a feast to the eyes. We all especially enjoyed looking out the dining room window watching the silhouettes of two large birds roosting in the doorway of the barn. Then we realized that they were live turkeys!"

"I took a swim after dinner while my wife watched the sun set behind the mountains. As I swam back and forth, the mist rose out of the lower field and gradually enveloped the bottom of each of the hills so that only the top edge was clearly visible, just like in a Japanese print."

The inn, built around 1800, is rather small, and the dining room with its pewter serving plates and gay linen is a popular dining place for people from the surrounding countryside and towns. There are many country antiques, a group of old post office boxes, a solemn grandfather's clock, and a handsome fireplace and baking hearth in the living room.

Country inn hospitality continues at the Colby Hill Inn. This part of southern New Hampshire has many lakes, state parks, golf courses, summer theatres, antique shops and skiing which add to the attraction for vacationers or weekenders.

The little New Hampshire town, home of New England College, with church spires rising into the blue sky, and white clapboard houses, is an ideal location for this trim little inn. "It's just what I expected," said my correspondent.

*COLBY HILL INN, Henniker, N.H. 03242; 603-428-3281. An 8-room inn on the outskirts of a New Hampshire college town. European plan. Some rooms with shared baths. Breakfast served to house guests only. Dinner served to travelers Tuesdays through Sundays. Open year-round. No children under 6. No pets. Swimming pool on grounds. Alpine and xc skiing, tennis, golf, canoeing, hiking and bicycling nearby. The Glover Family, Innkeepers.*

*Directions: From I-89, take Exit 5 and follow Rte. 202 to Henniker. From I-91, take Exit 3 and follow Rte. 9 through Keene and Hillsborough to Henniker, on Western Ave., one half mile west of the center of town.*

## JOHN HANCOCK INN
### Hancock, New Hampshire

For the past few years I have had a great deal of fun sharing some of my letters from Pat Wells with the readers of CIBR. Pat and Glynn bought the lovely old John Hancock Inn (the oldest in New Hampshire) in 1972, packed up their two children and moved from New Jersey to southern New Hampshire.

Over the years I've passed along Pat's description of Old Home Day, the day when former residents return. What began as a family picnic over a century ago has grown to a town-wide celebration complete with parade, band concert and all kinds of sports and fun.

Pat has also written to me about how the room with the murals on the second floor attracts so much attention and admiration. "The murals are at least 150 years old," she said. "We think it is nothing short of miraculous that they have been preserved this long."

Another year I told of all of the activities at the inn over Thanksgiving including her description of the harvest time decorations and the menu and the fact that the inn has as many as six or seven entrees besides the turkey.

I have also been able to report the progress of both Andrew and Susan who have taken their place with the chores of the inn.

Here are a few excerpts from Pat's most recent letter so we can all be updated:

89

"Now that we have almost completed our fifth year, we often have return visitors and many are now old friends. We're slowly patching together the history of the inn and since the town is working on its bicentennial history for 1979 we are getting research help from that quarter as well.

"We have renovated the second floor ballroom to be living quarters for the Wells family so that we will be living in the inn. This renovation is part of what we are calling our 20-year plan. I hasten to add that we don't want to expand, but we want everything to be a part of the total plan.

"Rather than concentrate on growing, our thoughts head in the direction of providing a gathering place for the people in the village. For example we will have an 'honor' coffee pot where townfolk can come in after they have been to get their mail or the copy of the *New York Times* at the Cash market across the road, or gather for small meetings of town groups. We would like the inn to serve as a village gathering spot.

"For just two days last summer Glynn and I had a chance to do what we have wanted to do for a long time — visit some other country inns. We took along some of our brochures and brought back theirs to make available to our guests. We have met some of your inn-keepers at meetings, but it is wonderful to see them at their own inns."

Like dozens and dozens of other innkeepers in CIBR, Pat and Glynn have put their hearts and hopes into the John Hancock and have become an integral part of the village, doing what innkeepers in America have been doing for well over 200 years — providing food, lodging and comfort for traveler and vacationer alike.

One final quote from Pat: "The snowball we started almost five years ago has at times seemed to release an avalanche, but we are learning (with varying degrees of success at times) to make our peace with the all encompassing quality of innkeeping life. The friends we've made in our community and among the inn guests have been our greatest reward."

*THE JOHN HANCOCK INN, Hancock, N.H. 03449; 603-525-3318. A 10-room village inn on Rtes. 123 and 137, 9 mi. north of Peterborough. In the middle of the Monadnock Region of southern N.H. European plan. Breakfast, lunch and dinner served daily to travelers. Closed Christmas Day and one week in spring and fall. Bicycles available on the grounds. Antiquing, swimming, hiking, Alpine and xc skiing nearby. Glynn and Pat Wells, Innkeepers.*

*Directions: From Keene, take either Rte. 101 east to Dublin and Rte. 137 north to Hancock or Rte. 9 north to Rte. 123 and east to Hancock. From Nashua, take 101A and 101 to Peterborough. Proceed north on Rtes. 202 and 123 to Hancock.*

## LOVETT'S BY LAFAYETTE BROOK
### Franconia, New Hampshire

Charlie Lovett was explaining his philosophy of innkeeping which he has been practicing here at Lovett's for over 30 years: "The whole idea is to run a comfortable inn. We think ours accommodates itself to the landscape." Looking out over the striking White Mountains and then glancing back at the distinctive New England lines of the white clapboard house, I fully agreed with him.

"This is a mountain inn, and you know there are many reasons for coming to the White Mountains and especially to our little village of Franconia. We have antiquing, and flower shows and horse shows, summer theatre, auctions, and country fairs. There also is the fall foliage, good winter and spring skiing, and cross-country skiing as well. I think people like to escape here from city life.

"There are walks all over these mountains and all kinds of places to motor to as well," Charlie pointed out. "Most of the ski areas run their lifts during the summer and autumn. Shopping seems to intrigue our guests as well. We have several superior places right here in Franconia and a sprinkling of country stores and craftshops throughout the mountains."

Charlie and I were in the sitting room with its big deep couches, overhead beams and the wood burning stove. There is a painting of the inn showing Cannon Mountain in the background. I had already

been there for a day and a half, but this was the first opportunity that we had to be in the same place at the same time. He is, indeed, a very busy man because he takes complete charge of the kitchen and is constantly in the dining room.

I have always heard that Lovett's had excellent food and Hank and Mary Petteys of the Black Point Inn in Prouts Neck, Maine, have been glowing in their praise. But the extent and variety of the menu surprised me. On the evenings that I was there, there were 18 main dishes, many of them specialties of the house. Among them were braised sirloin of beef in Beaujolais, lamb with the inn's own chutney, fresh Boston scrod, and curried fresh shrimp with apple raisin chutney.

"We're particularly proud of our cold bisque of native watercress, our eggplant caviar, and our pan-broiled chicken in brandy, herbs and cream and several of our desserts," Charlie said. "Almost everything is made right here from the basic ingredients, and our guests tell us that they know the difference right away."

There are a variety of lodgings at this mountain inn including small chalets on the campus-like grounds with mountain views and living rooms, many of them with fireplaces . Then there are poolside chalets, several rooms at the inn itself, and two nearby houses that have many bedrooms as well.

Lovett's is a sophisticated country inn with considerable emphasis on excellent food and service. It is well into its second generation of one-family ownership and many of the guests have been returning for years. Their fathers and mothers came before them. There is a very definite spirit that pulls everybody together. As one guest remarked, "It's almost like a club."

*LOVETT'S BY LAFAYETTE BROOK, Profile Rd., Franconia, N.H. 03380; 603-823-7761. A 32-room country inn in New Hampshire's White Mountains. Modified American plan omits lunch, although box lunches are available. Breakfast and dinner served by reservation to travelers. Open daily between June 20 and Oct. 15 and Dec. 26 and April 1. No pets. Two swimming pools, xc skiing, badminton, lawn sports on grounds. Golf, tennis, alpine skiing, trout fishing, hiking nearby. Mr. and Mrs. Charles J. Lovett, Jr., Innkeepers.*

*Directions: 2½ mi. south of Franconia on N.H. 18 business loop, at junction of N.H. 141 and I-93 South Franconia exit. 2¾ mi. north of junction of U.S. 3 and 18.*

## LYME INN
### Lyme, New Hampshire

The bell on the church clock sedately tolled seven times. Its tone was not obtrusive or insistent. It simply stated: "It's seven o'clock in the morning in Lyme, New Hampshire, and if you have business it's time to be up, if not go back to sleep." I went back to sleep.

I awakened about an hour later, and from my advantageous position in one of Connie Bergendoff's antique beds I surveyed the scene before me. It was, I conceded, the perfect bedroom and I would love to pick it up and transport it to the Berkshires! There were the matching twin antique beds immediately on my left. My eye caught a most inviting chaise longue I'd like to have in my own bedroom. A fireplace, inactive now, but very much welcome during the chilly months, separated two side windows with a view of the inn carriage shed which the Bergendoffs have reconstructed for their expanding business.

The front two windows overlooked the villlage green of Lyme. The blue, flowered wallpaper harmoniously blended with the window curtains and the fabrics of the comfortable wingback chairs.

The Lyme Inn is a precise, antique-furnished New England gem. Bedspreads and wallcoverings, fabrics, furniture, paintings and the like have all been chosen to successfully create a New England feeling. I don't believe it is an ideal experience for children under twelve or thirteen, but it certainly is a satisfying and warming experience for a mature individual with an appreciation of fine things.

The dining room belowstairs is an attractive tavern with an open fireplace and hand-planed wide pine board paneling. The

main dining room is decorated with Connie's sampler collection and another dining room has been furnished with Shaker reproductions and decorated with antique maps of northern New England.

On the subject of food, Ray Bergendoff says that every country innkeeper should learn to be at home in the kitchen. "We never know when we are going to have to boil lobsters, bake Lyme Inn cider pie, prepare the beer barrel potatoes, or even cook the morning flapjacks."

The newest edition to the inn is a Crafts Shop on the inn property where Connie and others in Lyme offer antiques, hand-made quilts, macrame, pottery, jewelry, ironwork and paintings all by local craftsmen and artisans. It is a most appropriate addition to the inn and is a perfect match for the Granwell Bookstore next to the inn where literary and artistic teas bring well-known authors, painters, poets and even Pulitzer Prize winners together with the inn guests and residents of Lyme and nearby Hanover.

Although the inn sits on the edge of a long New England village green, it has a feeling of being rather remote. It is, nonetheless, just 10 miles from Hanover, New Hampshire, the home of Dartmouth College, and inn guests have the opportunity to share some of the sporting and theatrical events taking place at the college. It is also just a few miles from the Dartmouth Skiways, an excellent ski area, and there is plenty of cross-country skiing nearby.

Yes, in many respects, it is as Connie and Ray say on their stationery, "The kind of New England Inn you always hoped to find."

*LYME INN, on the Common, Lyme, N.H. 03768; 603-795-2222. A 15-room village inn, 10 mi. north of Hanover on N.H. Rte. 10. Convenient to all Dartmouth College activities including Hopkins Center and with music, dance, drama, painting and sculpture. European plan year-round. Some rooms with shared baths. Breakfast and dinner served daily to travelers, except dinner on Tuesdays. Closed Nov. 29-Dec. 16 and March 14-31. No children under 8. No pets. Alpine and xc skiing, fishing, hiking, canoeing, tennis, and golf nearby. Ray and Constance Bergendoff, Innkeepers.*

*Directions: From I-91, take Exit 14 and follow Rte. 113A east to Vermont Rte. 5. Proceed south 50 yards to a left turn, then travel 2 mi. to inn.*

## ROCKHOUSE MOUNTAIN FARM
### Eaton Center, New Hampshire

Rockhouse Mountain Farm really has a great story. It is a family run farm-inn that for thirty years has been a way of life for John and Libby Edge, and their now-grown son, Johnny, and daughter, Betsi Ela, who is married to Bill.

It is not only family run, but definitely oriented for family vacations. Just imagine taking young children to a place where there are riding horses, cows, ducks, geese, chickens, pigs, piglets, ponies, pheasants, guinea hens—all with their own names!

What about the chance to help with farm chores like haying, milking and grooming the horses? How about the opportunity to learn not only how to canoe, but where the best blueberries are located on Foss Mountain. Think of a barn filled with hay, with swings and tunnels, and chances for playing hide-and-seek on rainy days.

There are other things too, including the first sauna in the area. Sailboats, rowboats and canoes are at the Rockhouse private beach, located on Crystal Lake. Then think about fresh rolls or bread every day, fresh vegetables, special desserts and all that anyone can eat.

After I had seen the lodging rooms, dining rooms, parlors and 200-year-old barn, and met all the animals, Johnny Edge summed up the spirit of RMF this way. "We have tried to create an inn for families, because we believe that the family was the basis of society,

business and religion in Colonial times, and should be the basis of our life today. Families that can vacation together and spend leisure hours together have a chance to grow together and understand one another.

"We have tried to make available to our guests the simple way of life. They can enjoy things like running through the fields and chasing our dogs, cantering along a country road as the sun rises over the hills or sliding down the waterfalls of Swift River.

"I think Dad and Mother have always seen in our place the opportunity for a 'refresher' period — a chance to exchange everyday concerns over coffee at breakfast, to enjoy the quietness of dinner by candlelight, and to exercise the body with things like tennis and golf.

"You would have to stay with us for at least a year to see all there is to do in this part of New Hampshire, and to do all there is to do at Rockhouse.

"What brings our guests together even more are the Wednesday evening chicken barbecues in the Sugar House and the Saturday evening steak roasts on the north lawn. My sister Betsi is a marvelous cook."

Libby Edge told me of a very interesting tradition that has been going on for some years at the inn. "When our first guest departed thirty years ago one of us grabbed an old school bell and rang it as a farewell. We have been doing it ever since. One bell has grown to a variety of nine, and all the guests join the Edges lined up on the front driveway as the cars of guests roll away from Rockhouse. It has gathered more sentiment as the years have gone by and everyone anticipates the royal sendoff." This is quite similar to the custom of remaining guests waving good-by to departing guests at Milford.

RMF is informal, rustic and gregarious. The happiest guests are those willing to lend a hand with the chores, "do" the dozens of White Mountains things together, and sit around the table talking long after it has been cleared. Long may it prosper.

*ROCKHOUSE MOUNTAIN FARM INN, Eaton Center, N.H. 03832; 603-447-2880. An 18-room farm -inn in the foothills of the White Mountains, 6 mi. from Conway, N.H. (14 rooms without private bath). Mod. American Plan, telephone for special rates. Dinner served to travelers. Open from June 15-Oct. 31 and possibly during the winter of '77-78. Horseback riding, boating, hiking, swimming, shuffleboard, fishing on grounds. Soaring, gliding, alpine slide, and many White Mountain attractions nearby. Near 9 major ski areas and xc skiing in winter. The Edge Family, Innkeepers.*

*Directions: From I-93, take Exit 23 and Rte. 104 to Meredith. Take Rte. 25 to Rte. 16 and proceed north to Conway. Follow Rte. 153,6 mi. from Conway to Eaton Center.*

## SPALDING INN CLUB
### Whitefield, New Hampshire

Many years ago the White Mountains in New Hampshire had numerous summer resorts where "mother and children" might come up early in the season and where "father" joined them for the last four weeks or so. These resorts were wonderful, gay, places where everything that was needed for a long complete vacation was either on the grounds or nearby. The lure of the mountains drew people in great numbers from Boston and New York.

Now, with few exceptions, all of these family-run resorts have disappeared, but not the Spalding Inn Club which is thriving under second and third generation owners and innkeepers. Many of the amenities of earlier times are still preserved. For example, gentlemen wouldn't think of going into dinner without a jacket and tie, and the inn is a focal point for the sports of lawn bowling and tennis, with several tournaments scheduled from mid-June to mid-September including the U.S. National Singles and Doubles Lawn Bowling Championships.

The Spalding Inn Club is an excellent example of entertainment and hospitality that can be provided for a family with many different preferences. For example, on the inn grounds there are four clay tennis courts, a swimming pool, a nine-hole par-3 golf course, two

championship lawn bowling greens and shuffleboard. Five golf courses are within 15 minutes of the inn and plenty of trout fishing and boating, and enticing backroads nearby. The Appalachian Trail System for mountain climbing is a short walk from the inn.

There is also a well-blended balance of vigorous outdoor activity and quiet times including an extensive library, a card room and a challenging collection of jigsaw puzzles. Groves of maples, birches, and oak trees native to northern New Hampshire are on the inn grounds and there are over 400 acres of lawns, gardens and orchards.

There are real country inn touches everywhere. The broad porch is ideal for rocking, and the main living room has a fireplace with a low ceiling, lots of books and magazines, baskets of apples, a barometer for tomorrow's weather, a jar of sour balls and great arrangements of flowers.

Those country inn touches also include the traditional hearty menu items so satisfying after a day of outdoor activities in the White Mountains. Among other offerings are delicious clam chowder, oyster stew, boiled scrod, poached salmon, pork chops, roast duckling, roast tenderloin, and sweetbreads. Children love the Indian pudding. All of the pies, including hot mince, the breads, and rolls are made back in the bakery of the inn.

An innovation at the inn includes completely furnished and equipped cottages that are available for rental periods of three days or longer from December to April. This makes winter activities including downhill and excellent cross-country skiing as well as snowmobiling and snowshoeing available during the New Hampshire winter.

I am just as pleased and as proud as I can be that Ted and Topsy Spalding continue to keep their standards high and that this delightful, elegant, resort-inn continues to offer its unique White Mountain hospitality.

*SPALDING INN CLUB, Mountain View Road, Whitefield, N.H. 03598; 603-837-2572. A 70-room resort-inn in the center of New Hampshire's White Mountains. American plan only from early June to mid-October when breakfast, lunch and dinner are served daily to travelers. Housekeeping cottages only from mid-December to April. Heated pool, tennis courts, 9-hole par 3 golf course, 18-hole putting green, two championship lawn bowling greens and bicycles on grounds. Also guest privileges at 5 nearby golf clubs. Trout fishing, boating, summer Playhouse and backroading nearby. Ted and Topsy Spalding, Innkeepers.*

*Directions: From New York take the Merritt and Wilber Cross Pkwys. to Wallingford, Ct.; I-91 from Wallingford, Ct. to Wells River, Vt., Wells River to Woodsville, N.H. and Rte. 302 to intersection of Mountain View Rd. approximately 3 mi. north. The inn is located 1 mi. west on Mountain View Rd. From Boston take I-93 north through Franconia Notch to Littleton, N.H., then Rte. 116 from Littleton thru Whitefield to the intersection of Mountain View Rd. approximately 3 mi. north. The inn is situated 1 mi. west on Mountain View Rd.*

**SQUAM LAKES INN**
**Holderness, New Hampshire**
Squam Lakes Inn is a wonderful family inn located in the White Mountain foothills. It is run by Ella and John Connelly and their six sons, Ed, Jack, Paul, Jim, Bill and Joe, and their daughter, Anne,

The Connellys live in Boston. I suppose one day they counted noses and decided that the best thing to do with this many children was to buy a country inn. They found the Squam Lakes Inn, and although it needed a lot of work, after a family conference a vote was taken and everyone agreed it would be a great idea. Since that time everyone has been pitching in, exhibiting his or her own special skills.

"At a time in their lives when lots of families would be disintegrating, we think this is a marvelous way to bring us all together with a common project," explained John. "We don't expect the children to stay with us indefinitely, but the inn really has made a great difference in their lives."

The lodging rooms in the main building of the inn are for the most part much larger than one might expect. They are all very pleasantly furnished, and each has a view of the lakes and mountains.

Just before the final deadline for this edition I talked to Ella about preparations for the new season. "We have reorganized our duplex cottages," she said. "Instead of two separate guest rooms in one building, each cottage has a living room area, the much-sought-after two bedrooms, and complete housekeeping facilities. We rent these on a weekly basis, hoping to please the people who look for this type of accommodation for their summer vacation."

I think that the idea of spending an entire summer vacation at the Squam Lakes is an excellent one. For one thing, there is just about every type of summer recreation available. Just a few steps from the inn is an excellent clay tennis court, and I have enjoyed many a dip in the pool, which like the inn, offers an excellent view of the mountains. At the inn boathouse on Squam Lake there are canoes, rowboats, and a small sailboat for the enjoyment of the guests.

To make a week-long stay in the summertime even more attractive, the Squam Lakes Science Center in Holderness is open during the summer and provides entertainment and recreation for every member of the family. There are a great many different programs dealing with ecology, geology, birding and tree and plant identifications which sound most interesting. Every effort is made to bring children into contact with animals and nature. There are also programs designed specifically for adults. Besides maintaining several nature trails, the Center has a barn-auditorium, which houses indoor programs, slide shows and movies.

Last summer many people stopped for a meal or a night or two at this delightful place. But with all of the recreational facilities and the Squam Lakes Science Center, it looks to me like the perfect place to take a family for a longer stay.

*SQUAM LAKES INN, Box 28, Holderness, N.H. 03245; 603-968-3348. A 13-room mountain inn, 6 mi. from Plymouth. European and Modified American plans. Breakfast and dinner served daily to travelers. Open from late June to mid-October. Tennis, swimming, boating, and fishing on grounds. Golf, tennis and hiking nearby. John and Ella Connelly, Innkeepers.*

*Directions: From I-93, take Exit 24 and travel south on Rte. 3, 4½ mi. to inn.*

## STAFFORD'S-IN-THE-FIELD
### Chocorua, New Hampshire

Fred and Ramona Stafford joined me on the front porch of their little inn at the end of the road in Chocorua. It was mid-July and the sun in this mountainous part of New Hampshire made the fields glow at noonday. We sat on the corner of the porch to catch the light breeze that seemed to come from two directions. Fred put his finger to his lips and pointed to two birds swinging on a bough. "They're scolding us," he said. "Their nest is down at the end of the porch."

"We have a number of wild animals nearby," added Ramona. "There are deer, rabbits, foxes and game birds. Once in a while someone sees a small bear. We have our own farm animals here, which is something that delights the city children. They like to collect the eggs from our hens. They also help to collect the sap buckets."

Stafford's-in-the-Field is a real family proposition. First, there is Ramona Stafford, who, along with her daughter Momo, does the cooking. The Stafford sons, Hans and Fritz, are in charge of the grounds, cutting brush and keeping the buildings in repair. They are also the cross-country skiing instructors in the wintertime. Father Fred keeps a benign eye on everything, seeing to it that guests are introduced, organizing walks and hikes, and informal singing that frequently takes place after dinner.

Dinner is fun at this country inn within sight of Mt. Chocorua. Guests have probably been out walking in the woods and fields, perhaps visiting the nearby beaver pond or swimming in the lake. If it is winter, they probably have been trying out their cross-country skiing prowess on the many trails nearby.

It is also possible that they've been sitting on the porch or in front of the fire just enjoying the relaxation of being in the country with nothing to do.

Everybody gathers for a few moments before dinner, either on the front porch or in the living room, depending on the season. This

is a good time to get acquainted and exchange experiences of the day. Dinner is served at large tables, informally, which again is part of the New England family feeling.

The food is always a surprise to city guests, because they hardly expect to find such a sophisticated approach to dining. Ramona Stafford describes her particular approach to food preparation as "country gourmet." It varies from meal to meal, but there is a definite continental influence. Ginger chicken, chili rellenos and spare ribs cooked in maple syrup are some of the entrées.

Momo's particular specialties are desserts and bread. These include chocolate mousse, raspberry torte, blueberry pie, cheesecake and lemon cream cake.

Accommodations in the main house are comfortable rooms that have been furnished with country antique furniture. Other accommodations are found in family-style cottages which are scattered around the grounds.

*STAFFORD'S-IN-THE-FIELD, Chocorua, N.H. 03817; 603-323-7766. An 8-room resort-inn with 5 cottages, 17 mi. south of North Conway. Modified American plan at inn omits lunch. European plan in cottages. Some rooms in inn with shared baths. Meals served to guests only. No pets. Winter specialty: ski touring. Bicycles, square dancing and xc skiing on the grounds. Golf, swimming, hiking, riding, tennis and fishing nearby. The Stafford Family, Innkeepers.*

*Directions: Follow N.H. Rte. 16 north to Chocorua Village, then turn left onto Rte. 113 and travel 1 mi. west to inn. Or, from Rte. 93 take Exit 23 and travel east on Rtes. 104 and 25 to Rte. 16. Proceed north on Rte. 16 to Chocorua Village, turn left onto Rte. 113 and travel 1 mi. west to inn.*

## WELLS WOOD
### Plainfield, New Hampshire

The sounds were unmistakenly operatic. More than that, they were beautifully operatic. I followed my ear around one of the old stone walls, passed an oak tree and eventually ended up with my nose pressed against the screen of a window from which exuded some of the most enticing cooking aromas and scents that I had experienced in some time. There, amidst the skillets, whisks and saucepans, obviously having a wonderful time both singing and seasoning, was a very pretty woman.

"What," I asked, "is a girl with good looks and talent like that doing in a place like this?"

"I am, kind sir," she said, "the innkeeper's wife, and I also happen to be the chef." The year was 1974 and this was my introduction to a truly unique country inn on the Connecticut River in Plainfield, New Hampshire, just north of Windsor, Vermont.

The inn is the former home of Maxfield Parrish, one of the most popular of American artists in the early 20th century. A sort of florid ambiance usually associated with Parrish remains in the exterior and the interior of the many buildings and studios. Many people are attracted to it because of the Parrish influence. The inn has terraces, old stone walls, marvelous huge oak trees, reflecting pools, and perhaps above all, almost gilding the lily, a magnificent view of Mt. Ascutney.

Very special original main dishes include Hunter's Horn ragu which is braised scallops of beef in wine and herbs with tiny carrots and onions, potatoes and peas; chicken amandine, or baked stuffed shrimp, crab Mornay, veal piccata and shrimp Ranchipur.

The main dining room has a high beamed ceiling with a huge fireplace on one side and a stage with a small baby grand piano on it. At various times during the year there are musical evenings. "Yes, some of the friends from opera days come, and we have a marvelous time trying to outdo one another," Rosalind said.

Wells Wood is really the concept of Tom and Rosalind Wells,

originally from Chicago, who arrived here at a portentous point in time when the Parrish estate was available. It lends itself beautifully to the operation of a country inn. There were four lodging rooms, and because of Tom's background as an interior designer, everything has been well-integrated and harmonized.

Even if this were not an unmistakably unique estate with a marvelous setting and an unexcelled view of one of New England's most gorgeous mountains, Rosalind's food would be enough in itself to attract favorable attention. Wells Wood has had well-deserved write-ups in at least 25 major publications.

I'm happy that CIBR was among the very first.

*WELLS WOOD, Mailing address: R.R. #2, Windsor, Vt. 05089; 603-675-5360. A stately 4-room country inn on Rte. 12A, Plainfield, N.H. in the former mansion and studio of Maxfield Parrish. Near Hopkins Center for Performing Arts and St. Gaudens Memorial. European plan. (Continental breakfast served to inn guests only.) Dinner served to travelers daily by reservation. Winter and off-season hours and dates may vary. Please call ahead. Lunch limited to some summer months. No pets. Antique shop located in studio. Bicycles, hiking, golf, swimming, antiquing, auction gallery, riding, Alpine and xc skiing nearby. Thomas and Rosalind Wells, Innkeepers.*

*Directions: From Rte. 89, take Exit 20 and proceed south on Rte. 12A, 8½ mi. to inn. Or, from I-91 take Windsor/Ascutney Exit, cross Conn. River to N.H. Rte. 12A left (north) approximately 8 mi.*

## WOODBOUND INN
**Jaffrey, New Hampshire**

As I recall it was mid-September in 1972 when I first visited the Woodbound Inn. I was driving on a narrow woodland road which afforded an occasional glimpse of Mt. Monadnock. An early turning tree was a subtle preview of the fall colors for which this region is famous.

I came out of the woods into a clearing and there was an L-shaped three-story, clapboard New England house with green shutters and a big front porch with lawns and hedges. Across the road were some tennis courts and there was a golf tee and a fairway with a distant green. Through the trees next to the house the sun sparkled on the lake and I saw some water skiers.

The Woodbound is a genial family resort-inn. Ed and Peg Brummer started it all, their son Jed continued, along with his wife Mary Ellen, and there is a third generation of Brummers doing inn chores as well. For guests who like outdoor activities, it is a delight. The lake, the sailboat, canoes and swimming are just a step away. There are miles of hiking and walking trails, golf, tennis and shuffleboard. In the wintertime, the Brummers have two ski tows and an extensive cross-country skiing program.

To really update activities at Woodbound, I would like to share the letter I received from Ed Brummer just before we went to press: "During the coming year, along with the usual physical improvements, we will be adding some new activities to our social entertainment program. This will include handcraft classes. In the past we have had ceramics, needlepoint, metalwork and basket weaving. Incidentally, the latter is best done at the beach where the materials can be soaked in water and worked on as long as guests are enjoying the afternoon in the sun. I believe learning and self-improvement are characteristic of many Americans, and in line with New England ethics. People enjoy learning as well as playing. The handcraft and nature trail plans that we are pursuing fit in with our country Colonial atmosphere and location. We have a great deal of activity in these fields nearby, especially at the Sharon Arts Center.

"In the winter we will have a special Sunday-to-Friday rate for cross-country skiing and are adding several miles of trails by connecting our trails to those of the state forest."

Not only on that first visit but on each subsequent visit to the Woodbound I was particularly impressed by the number of happy children at the end of the day who were enjoying playing on the slides and swings in the backyard while their parents chatted or practiced putting on the lawn. "Some people have been returning here for years

with their children and grandchildren," explained Ed. During July and August guests are accepted only by the week, but during the rest of the year stays of any length are welcome.

Among the comments I have received through the mail from guests who have stayed at Woodbound, perhaps the most frequent one is "I did not know a place like this existed." Yes, there is a Woodbound and with three generations of innkeepers on the premises it looks like there will be a Woodbound for many, many years to come.

*WOODBOUND INN and COTTAGES, Jaffrey, N.H. 03452; 603-532-8341. A 40-room resort-inn on Lake Contoocook, 2 mi. in the woods from West Rindge or Jaffrey. Within walking distance of Cathedral of the Pines. American plan in summer and winter. Overnight European plan available in May, June and late fall. Breakfast, lunch and dinner served daily. Open from May 28 to Oct. 14; Dec. 26 to March 14. Par 3 golf course, swimming, beach, sailing, water skiing, tennis, hiking, children's program, ski area, touring trails, tobogganing and skating on grounds. Ed and Peggy Brummer, Jed and Mary Ellen Brummer, Innkeepers.*

*Directions: From Boston, follow Rte. 2, then Rte. 119 to Rindge where there are directional signs to inn. From New York, follow I-91 to Bernardston, Mass. Proceed on Rte. 10 to Winchester, then Rte. 119 to Rindge and watch for signs to inn.*

## NEW LONDON INN
### New London, New Hampshire

John and Sally Biewener and their daughter, Cathy, and I were seated in front of the fireplace at the New London Inn exchanging "country inn experiences."

"This has been absolutely wonderful," said Sally. "We've met some of the most delightful people and each day brings new people and new experiences."

"I was in the corporate world for most of my adult life and this is a marvelous change," said John. "After looking at several country inns, we fell in love with this one as soon as we saw it. The longer we are here the more admiration we have for the outstanding restoration job that Frank and Lois Conklin performed in 1967.

"We've been enthusiastic collectors of antiques and old houses for a good many years, and many of the pieces in the lobby and living room came from our home. Actually they belong here, since the inn is, in fact, our home at this time."

I thought that was an interesting statement because to me a country inn is the extension of the personalities, aspirations and dreams of the innkeepers. I could already sense a subtle change in the New London Inn as this new family of innkeepers become established and gain new experience with each passing day.

"Oh, we have developed some new ideas already," said John enthusiastically. "We're not going to make any major changes in what has been a most successful country inn under the Conklins for the past several years, but naturally we have got to do 'our thing.' Fortunately, we have Cathy and our other daughter, Judy, with us to share in all the fun. Cathy is a dancer and actress 'on leave' from Manhattan, but I can already sense our considerable number of younger guests identify readily with both her and Judy who is still in high school."

The New London Inn has seen changes of owners and innkeepers many times since it was built by Ezekiel Sargent in 1792. After several additions, today it is a three-story white clapboard town landmark with a long two-story porch on the side facing the main street in New London, New Hampshire. The lobby and parlor, each with its own fireplace, provide homelike surroundings, and in warmer seasons the porch, lawn and gardens provide pleasant places for relaxation.

Winters are even more enjoyable in this college town especially now that cross-country skiing is such a popular sport. "There are many trails nearby," said Cathy. One of the unusual family

attractions is King Ridge where there is limited downhill skiing on crowded weekends but the New London Inn can reserve a place on the slopes for their guests.

Lodging rooms in this old inn are interesting and inviting. Up on the second floor landing there is an old Morris chair, other comfortable chairs, and a carved bench. The corner bedroom, which is in the oldest part of the inn, has paneling on the wall and overlooks the Common. Another corner bedroom with green flowered paper and rose covered chintz chairs has twin beds, one with a firm mattress and one with a soft mattress. This is true of all rooms with twin beds. Each room is individually furnished and has its own private bathroom.

I had a nice long visit with Sally, John, Cathy and Judy and enjoyed a dinner of baked stuffed pork chops. When I complimented Sally, she responded: "Oh, we are very much involved with the preparation and serving of our food. After all, the four of us love to eat. That's how we became interested in country inns in the first place."

*NEW LONDON INN, New London, N.H. 03257; 603-526-2791. A 24-room village inn in a college town, 35 mi. from Hanover and Concord N.H. Near Lake Sunapee and King Ridge and Mt. Sunapee ski areas. European plan. Breakfast, lunch and dinner served daily to travelers. Open year-round. Closed Christmas Day. Swimming, boating, climbing, hiking, bicycles, snowshoeing, Alpine and xc skiing nearby. John and Sally Biewener, Innkeepers.*

*Directions: From I-89, take either Exit 11 or 12 and follow signs for New London. Inn is in the center of town.*

## DANA PLACE INN
### Jackson, New Hampshire

I was out for an early morning stroll beside the gurgling waters of the Ellis River which runs right next to the Dana Place Inn. The path is also used for Nordic skiing in wintertime. This beautiful early Fall day was filled with yellows, russets, and greens, and I could see Mt. Washington through the trees. Only the sounds of water and wind and an occasional bird call broke the total silence of being alone in the woods.

However, I soon realized that I was not completely alone when I saw one of the other guests coming toward me with a stout walking stick in hand. He picked up our conversation where we left off last night at the inn: "I think this is a place for people who love mountains," he said. "Their presence gets hold of you and compels you to get out and walk. My wife and I have been coming here for the past six years, and as well as we know these White Mountains in both winter and summer, they constantly amaze me. We see something new on each visit.

"I just walked down to the village and picked up a ski touring folder," he continued. "They have really developed this area as far as cross-country skiing is concerned. Do you know that it's possible to tour the entire Jackson Valley on skis? You can go as near or far as you wish, stopping off at different places. I think it is one of the best-maintained and most carefully marked Nordic systems anywhere. They've been skiing cross-country up here for forty years, although people think it's something new."

As we neared the inn, Innkeeper Mal Jennings was just helping a departing guest with some bags and suggested that we get in a little tennis later that morning. "You can go swimming if you want. The pool is heated or you can try the river." He said the last with a twinkle in his eye because the river is really cold in the Fall.

Mal and Betty Jennings are old friends and delightful innkeepers. I've known them for many years at other inns. The Dana Place represents their dream come true—an inn of their own!

"It's an historic inn as well," said Betty. "There has been an inn here since the late 1800's. At one time it was a farm, as you can see with all these apple trees."

Although the Dana Place is "into" ski touring, the great downhill ski areas still attract great numbers. Wildcat is just up the road opposite Mt. Washington, and other areas are within an easy drive. The lifts run in all seasons which means that all of this great scenery can be enjoyed throughout the year.

Rooms at the inn are pleasant and homey. There's a guest living room with a great fireplace and lots of comfortable furniture.

The food—ah the food. Bob Earle does the cooking, and among the specialties are chicken sauteed in apricots and brandy, saltimboca, and fresh veal sauteed in mushrooms. Three separate dining rooms lend a feeling of intimacy to the dining experience.

For vacationers and travelers who like the presence of mountains, the Dana Place has them in all sizes.

*DANA PLACE INN, Route 16, Pinkham Notch, P.O. Box 157-B, Jackson, N.H. 03846; 603-383-6822. A 14-room resort-inn, 5 mi. from Jackson, N.H., in the heart of the White Mountains. European plan includes complimentary breakfast. No lunch served. Dinner served to travelers daily from late-May to late-October and from mid-December to late April. Closed Thanksgiving Day. No pets. Heated pool and Ellis River for swimming, 2 tennis courts, trout fishing, xc skiing on grounds. Indoor tennis courts, downhill skiing, soaring, hang gliding, 5 golf courses, hiking nearby. Malcolm and Betty Jennings, Innkeepers.*

*Directions: Follow Rte. 16, north of Jackson village toward Pinkham Notch.*

# Maine

*In the past I have talked about US-1, which follows the coastline from Kittery clear up to Calais. An alternate route east of Ellsworth*

*is 182 which avoids some of the traffic on Route 1 to the west of*
*Machias north to Calais where it joins Route 9 near Baring. The*
*really fast way to go from Bangor to New Brunswick is on Route 9,*
*a road called the Air Line. I believe it has sufficient ups and downs*
*and turns to satisfy even the most avid backroad enthusiasts.*

## ASTICOU INN
### Northeast Harbor, Maine

The Asticou is a luxurious summer resort-inn in the now rare
tradition that was popular for so many years in the White Mountains
of New Hampshire, the Berkshires, the Maine coast and certain
resort areas in West Virginia, South Carolina and Palm Beach.

These were the small, extremely well-run resorts where guests
would spend a great deal of the summer, reaching it by train and
making a trip back to the city at the "end of the season." Now, there
are very few of these medium-sized resort-inns that have the many
little touches that make them so special such as beautiful table linen,
fresh flowers and turn-down service. Even today, many guests stay
for as long as three or four weeks, but just a few for the entire season.
In *Country Inns and Back Roads* I think these beautiful little jewels
are typified by the Asticou, the Black Point, Stafford's Bay View,
the Spalding Inn Club and the Brazilian Court.

I'm not really sure how long the Asticou has been in Northeast
Harbor, but a rough guess would be fifty years. In 1976 came a most
dramatic addition to the entire environment—the construction of a
swimming pool. In a conversation I had with George Stiles who is the
manager of this inn, he said, "The swimming pool was an idea whose
time had come. We've had the same people coming back here for
many years and now their children and grandchildren are returning.
The Asticou is going to grow with the times. The former guests used
to go swimming in the harbor waters but today's guests enjoy the
opportunity to swim just a few steps away from the deck of the inn.
I can also tell you that we have tennis courts in our plans."

These are the changes at the Asticou, but it is the enduring
tradition and the beautiful situation of the inn which make it such a
joy. For the most part, because this is an older building, the
bedrooms are larger than usual and many of them have a view of the
harbor which is one of the most exciting and dramatic in the
Bar Harbor area.

The furnishings in the dining room and the various sitting rooms
are very gay with bright summer colors that offer an immediate

holiday atmosphere. The inn is a friendly and relaxing place with backgammon, jigsaw puzzles, many books and perhaps best of all, the sundeck which offers everyone an opportunity to sit outside and enjoy the panorama of sky, water and trees.

"I think today's guest at the Asticou is a much more active person," explained George, "We have so many things here on Mt. Desert that attract outdoor-minded people with natural curiosity about ecology and nature. Our guests stay here on the modified American plan which omits lunch and allows everyone to be at one of 100 different places in the Mt. Desert area all day long. It's fun to see them come back in the evening and sit around exchanging their adventures of the day."

For me, George and his wife, Esther, personify the new spirit of the Asticou. I have known him for quite a few years because during the wintertime he is at the Lakeside Inn in Mt. Dora, Florida. He seems to be everywhere at once, filled with good humor and genuine concern for his guests.

"It's a funny thing," said George as we were saying good-by after a short visit, "the Asticou has been here since the days of the Bar Harbor 'cottages' when it was considered a leisure class summer resort. Now it is being discovered by more and more people every year who are looking for the elegance of those days."

*ASTICOU INN, Northeast Harbor, Me. 04662; 207-276-3344. A 60-room elegant resort-inn on the northern coast of Maine. Near Acadia National Park, Cadillac Mountain, Abbey Rockefeller Gardens, Thuya Lodge and Gardens, and Jackson Laboratory. Modified American plan omits lunch. Breakfast, lunch and dinner served daily to travelers from late June to mid-September. Swimming pool and extensive gardens on the grounds. Bicycles, golf, tennis, sandy beaches nearby. George M. Stiles, Innkeeper.*

*Directions: Exit Maine Tpke. (Rte. 95) at Bangor. Follow Alt. Rte. 1 to Mt. Desert Island.*

## THE CLAREMONT
**Southwest Harbor, Maine**

At the very last minute before going to press, I learned that the main building of the Claremont was being completely renovated and that only cottages would be available during the summer of 1977. Breakfast and dinner will be available to American Plan cottage guests only. The beauties of Somes Sound and Mt. Desert Island with the cruises among the islands, walking and hiking through Acadia National Park, and just the fun of finding where the twisting and turning roads may lead, remains the same.

Accommodations in the cottages are limited, so I would recommend a prompt reservation. For further developments see the 1978 edition of *Country Inns and Back Roads*.

*THE CLAREMONT COTTAGES, Southwest Harbor, Maine 04679; 207-244-5036. Cottages open from June 1st through October 15th. Tennis, dock and deep water moorings on grounds, fresh water swimming, golf, bicycles, riding, boating and sailing rentals nearby. The McCue Family, Innkeepers.*

*Directions: From Maine Tpke. exit at Augusta and proceed east on Rte. 3 to U.S. 1. At Ellsworth pick up Rte. 3 again and follow Rte. 102 on Mt. Desert Island to Southwest Harbor. Follow inn signs approaching Southwest Harbor.*

## GREY ROCK INN
### Northeast Harbor, Maine

Rummaging through some old letters recently, I ran across the original letter of recommendation that directed me to the Grey Rock Inn. I'd like to share it with you:

"On Mount Desert Island we found an inn that you may want to visit. Grey Rock Inn is in Northeast Harbor not far from the Asticou and Claremont inns. It is located up a steep rocky hill from the road (Route 198) and overlooks the sailboats of Northeast Harbor. It is an 1890's Philadelphia doctor's vacation house. The dimensions of most of the rooms upstairs and down are generous. The bathtub adjoining our bedroom was big enough for President Taft. It has six or eight rooms and is owned by Janet Millett, a young English woman who grew up in London and has lived in this country for nine years.

"Although the design of the house is what some people call 'Teddy Roosevelt,' under Janet's care it has taken on a look of English domesticity, with white painted furniture, pink flowered wallpaper and lampshades with bows.

"Seated on the second floor porch of Grey Rock Inn on a rainy day, talking with Janet Millett, we felt like we were in the Lake District of England. There was a fire for us to sit by in the morning when we came down to breakfast and in the evening when we returned from dinner. When we went to our room at night each of our beds had been turned down, just so. We were sorry to leave Grey Rock Inn and more, to say goodby to Janet Millett. I hope you will like her and her inn as much as we did."

Well, of course, I found the Grey Rock Inn a very happy experience. Apparently many other guests have also because I have received quite a few letters. These letters also mention the brass beds, the four-poster and the beautiful old wicker furniture which is very much in evidence. I should also mention that each of these bedrooms faces the harbor and has its own bath. Five fireplaces provide a warm welcome.

The reference to an English Lake District inn is well made. Janet's father, by the way, lives in a small cottage in one of the unspoiled villages of the Cotswolds.

Janet serves a continental breakfast to her guests in the sunny living room and on the front balcony. She is happy to suggest luncheon and dinner possibilities and also to alert her guests to the many cultural and recreational opportunities on Mount Desert Island.

Throughout eleven years on back roads and in villages in both North America and Europe in search of warm, personal, country inn hospitality, I've eagerly welcomed letters of recommendation and receive many each year.

I am particularly grateful for this one that sent me to the Grey Rock Inn.

*GREY ROCK INN, Harborside Rd., Northeast Harbor, Me. 04662; 207-276-9360. A 10-room village inn in the town of Northeast Harbor, Me. European plan. Continental breakfast served to house guests. No other meals served. Season from early spring to Nov. 1. No pets. Grey Rock is adjacent to Acadia National Park and all the attractions of this unusual region. Janet Millett, Innkeeper.*

*Directions: Located on the right-hand side of the road approaching the town of Northeast Harbor. Note sign. Do not try to make a right-hand turn. Proceed about one block, turn around and head the other way. Then turn left going up hill.*

## BLACK POINT INN
### Prouts Neck, Maine

Ever since 1972 I have kept a small egg-shaped rock on the sill of my picture window. I mentally refer to it as my Prouts Neck talisman. The rock was picked up on a walk next to the sea. No doubt the action of the water had bounced it around, grinding it against rocks and sand, until it had been worn smooth and soothing to the touch.

I'll never forget that morning. Under a brilliant mid-August sun, I set out after breakfast to walk the Prouts Neck Path, winding my way among the beautiful trees and cottages that make up this

unusual community. The same families have been coming here for generations. The area is private and its beauty is well protected.

I cut through to the ocean at a point where I could see the Winslow Homer studio, and then started winding my way back inland. George Collier, the owner of the inn, had told me at dinner the previous night that the first settlement of Prouts Neck was about 1630, but in 1690 the trouble with the French and Indians caused the colonists to abandon it for twelve years. In 1702 they started a new trading post. However, in 1773, nineteen men were ambushed and killed by the Indians at the southern end of Massacre Pond, which is just across the road from the Prouts Neck golf course.

In the middle of the 19th century it became popular as a summer resort and a number of hotels were built. In 1886 there were a half dozen summer "cottages," one of them occupied by Charles Savage Homer, whose son, Winslow, became one of America's best known artists. Winslow Homer spent the last twenty-five years of his life at Prouts Neck. His finest oil paintings, including the *Fox Hunt, Fog Warning, Eight Bells, Canon Rock* and the *Wreck of the Nor'easter* were inspired by his studies of the coast and seas in both summer and winter.

The Black Point Inn fits perfectly into the ambiance of Prouts Neck. Gentlemen wear coats for dinner, and there is a small orchestra for dancing after dinner and at the poolside for noontime buffets. The quiet dignity, personal service, attention to detail, excellent tennis courts, a good golf course, exceptional food and excellence in general make the Black Point one of the really impressive resort-inn experiences on the Maine coast.

*BLACK POINT INN, Prouts Neck, Me. 04070; 207-883-4311. A 76-room luxury resort-inn on Rte. 207, 10 mi. south of Portland. American plan. Breakfast, lunch and dinner served to travelers. Open late-June to early-September. No children under age 12. No pets. Pool, bicycles, sailing, dancing, golf, tennis and ocean bathing all within a few steps. Henry Petteys, Innkeeper.*

*Directions: From Maine Tpke. take Exit 7. Turn right on Rte. 1. Proceed 2.7 mi. to Rte. 207. Turn left. This is the road to Prouts Neck.*

## CAPTAIN LORD MANSION
### Kennebunkport, Maine

"How is the snow in Kennebunkport?" Shirley Throumoulos' voice was filled with expectancy and enthusiasm as she answered, "It's marvelous. We've got about two feet and the entire village looks wonderful!"

It was mid-January and the snows of early 1977 that blanketed the Northeast made a weekend in Kennebunkport a delightful prospect. I'd been there in all seasons, therefore an opportunity to get away from it all and just spend a couple of days on the Maine coast in the dead of winter when it was so quiet and peaceful was something that sounded very attractive.

"Are the roads all clear?" Shirley answered, "Oh yes, the plows are out on the day it snows. In fact, we are never really troubled by snow. By the way we have some people you met here last year who are coming this weekend and I know it will be a really wonderful time."

"A wonderful time." That's exactly what I had in mind when I thought of waking up in the morning in my usual corner room at the Captain Lord, with the fireplace all laid, and the view of the beautiful Kennebunkport houses and lawns all laden with snow. What I wanted to do was to join the rest of the guests in the kitchen at breakfast with some of Shirley's steaming muffins, hot tea and hard-boiled eggs, and then, maybe possibly, just possibly, go back upstairs, stoke the fire and get out the book I'd been saving. If not that, I could don my coat and mittens and take a walk all around the village and even down on the seashore which during the summer has so many bathers delighting in the warm waters, but now would belong only to me and the seabirds.

It was too good an opportunity to miss. I made my reservation and on Friday evening arrived just as two other cars pulled into the parking lot which Jim had already cleared of snow. The steep

roof of the old barn which was being remodeled by Jim and
Shirley was covered with snow and everything was glistening in the
light of the half moon. Jim was helping with bags and we had a
hearty greeting, and soon I was in the house standing by one of the
downstairs fireplaces already feeling thawed out and very much
at home.

The weekend turned out to be all that I had anticipated. With
the aid of some advice from Shirley and Jim, some other guests and I
chose a good restaurant on the beach where we all enjoyed dinner
together. During the weekend we roamed a lot of the back roads
which gave us a real old-fashioned winter feeling. From somewhere,
somebody found some cross-country skis and I even managed to
find a trail handy to enjoy about two hours of quiet and exercise.
There was also a handful of shops open.

The Captain Lord Mansion is a large yellow building with a
lookout cupola (a perfect place for really getting above it all) with
larger-than-usual lodging rooms, many with a working fireplace. It
was built during the War of 1812 and additions and subtractions
have been made over the years. Now it is not only a quiet guest house
but a way of life for Shirley and Jim. "Many guests stop over for a
day or two en route to Grey Rock in Northeast Harbor," said Shirley.

Late Sunday morning we all separated to return to Boston, New
York, and the Berkshires, convinced that while Kennebunkport,
Ogunquit, the shore roads and beauties of coastal Maine were hard
to match in summer, there was something wonderful about being in

these old villages in the dead of winter along with the year-round residents. Fortunately, the Captain Lord Mansion is there whenever anyone needs it.

*THE CAPTAIN LORD MANSION, Box 527, Kennebunkport, Me. 04046; 207-967-3141. A 10-room seacoast village inn, 3 tenths of a mi. from Dock Square in Kennebunkport, off Ocean Ave. Near Rachel Carson Wildlife Refuge. Shaker community and Alternative Energy Research Structures open to the public. Lodgings include breakfast. No other meals served. Some rooms with shared bath. No pets. Open year-round. Bicycles, hiking, xc skiing, deep sea fishing, golf and indoor swimming and tennis nearby. Shirley and Jim Throumoulos, Innkeepers.*

*Directions: From Boston follow I-95 into Maine. Take Exit 3 and follow signs to Kennebunkport.*

## DOCKSIDE GUEST QUARTERS
York, Maine

Every year I receive letters from people asking if I can help them locate a country inn for either a vacation or a honeymoon. Most of them inquire about rooms overlooking the water, preferably in New England. Well the Dockside Guest Quarters is one that fills the bill.

It is located on Harris Island in York Harbor, Maine, and almost every lodging room has a beautiful view of the ever-changing mood of the harbor.

The innkeepers are David and Harriette Lusty. David is a real "State of Maine" man complete with a wonderful down-East accent. They met in college and were themselves married at Dockside Guest Quarters so the precendent for honeymoons has been well established.

The inn includes the original New England homestead of the 1880's which is called the Main House, and other cottage buildings of a contemporary design, each with its own porch and water view. Some have a casual studio feeling.

The traffic on York Harbor begins at dawn with the lobster and fishing boats headed out to the ocean, guided by hundreds of shore birds. Other feathery inhabitants walk near the water's edge scavenging for breakfast. Sailboats and dories which provide pleasure jaunts are gently rocking in the wash created by the outgoing boats.

This scene is constantly enlivened by convoys of small ducklings, a part of the regular harbor contingent of mallards. All of this is to the intermittent cacaphony of cries, screeches, peeps, and calls, a fitting paean to the morning.

119

The Dockside season is from May 27 to October 11, and I find that fall is an ideal time to visit this section of Maine. It is fun to be awakened by the October sun peeking into the east window and illuminating the trees along the shore—the white pines, firs and native spruces which remain green throughout the year. These are intermixed with the yellows, oranges, and the rusty greens of the hickories, sumac and beeches.

Late September and early October days in York can be spent in many different ways. There are a number of sandy beaches in the vicinity including the famous York beach, and swimming can be excellent when the sun is highest at midday and early afternoon. At other times it is great fun to wander along these stretches of beach and have them almost entirely to one's self. Golf and tennis are available at the golf club where Dockside guests are introduced. The marina has rental sailboats and outboards. Something else that autumn guests enjoy is picking their own apples at a local orchard farm. There is also off-season antiquing and backroading.

A few years ago David and Harriette added the Dockside Dining Room now managed by Steve and Sue Roeder, serving luncheon and dinner with a great many seafood specialties including lobster, baked sole, halibut and swordfish. One of the features of the menu is roast duckling a la Hickory Stick which comes to the table at just the perfect degree of crispness. Incidentally, Steve Roeder is a birdwatcher and can give local pointers to any interested guest.

After I described the inn to one young man on the telephone he was so enthusiastic that he asked me whether I thought arrangements could be made to have the wedding on the lawn overlooking the harbor. I referred him directly to Harriette and David, but I felt certain that being sentimentalists, they would look with favor on the idea.

*DOCKSIDE GUEST QUARTERS, Harris Island Rd., York, Maine 03909; 207-363-2868. An 18-room waterside country inn 10 mi. from Portsmouth, N.H. Some larger quarters in newer multi-unit cottages. York Village is a National Historic District. American plan available. Continental breakfast served to houseguests only. Dockside Dining Room serves lunch and dinner to travelers daily except Mondays. Open from May 27 to Oct. 11. Fishing, sailing and boating from premises. Golf, tennis, hiking and swimming nearby. David and Harriette Lusty, Innkeepers.*

*Directions: From US 1 or I-95, take Exit 1 at York to Rte. 1A (the main street of York). Take Rte. 103 (a side street off Rte. 1A) and follow signs to Harris Island Rd.*

## HOMEWOOD INN
### Yarmouth, Maine

It was a neat little map. As he handed it to me Fred Webster explained, "This will tell you about all of the changes which will be in effect in 1977. First of all, the dining room has been moved from the Maine House to the Lodge and that space has been turned into three more guest rooms on the first floor, each with a bath and a fireplace, and one room upstairs with a bath.

"In the Lodge, the area that was formerly used for shops and reception will become the restaurant. The Lodge will also continue to have our famous Maine Craft Shop and the game room. It will be very convenient to have the major function of the inn under one roof."

The Homewood Inn, operated for a number of years by the Webster Family, is on the shores of Casco Bay with a view of some of the 365 Calendar Islands. Many of the single and double cottages which make up most of the inn complex have fireplaces and are set among the juniper, cedar, maple, and Norway pine trees. There is a multitude of flowers including roses, phlox, snapdragons, marigolds and petunias and dozens of other flowering plants and bushes.

Guests are frequently delighted to discover that they are sharing their waterside environment with dozens of varieties of land and shore birds.

On one of my trips, Fred, Colleen and I walked around the grounds to the edge of the seawall to look at the dozens of boats. "We

have many families with children and everyone seems to get enjoyment at being next to the water," explained Colleen. The property also has a meadow and hay field, and it is possible to walk quite deep into the fields and get a feeling of being close to the land.

I enjoy being at the Homewood on a Monday night so that I can have fun at the regular Monday night summer clambake. This consists of a real "down East" feast with lobster, steak, clams, and chicken served outdoors at rustic tables and presided over by Col. Bob Young, who is famous in the Yarmouth region for these Maine cookouts. It occurs to me that no one can go to a Maine clambake and feel left out. It is the kind of experience that brings everybody together.

On other nights the restaurant menu has a great many items that reflect both the agricultural and water-oriented location of the inn. These include many chicken and beef dishes and the lobster, scallops and broiled fish native to Maine waters.

The Homewood is certainly well named. It's very homelike and looks happily settled among the woods, fields and harbor. Its informal atmosphere invites vacationers, especially those with children, to enjoy a real country resort-inn experience. Sooner or later everyone meets at the Lodge, around the pool, or at the tennis courts.

I'll be back visiting the Homewood during 1977 and am looking forward to a night at one of the new rooms in the Maine House. Then I'll be ready for another breakfast with all the Websters and more blueberry pancakes.

*HOMEWOOD INN, Drinkwater Point, Yarmouth, Me. 04096; 207-846-3351. A 46-room waterside inn on Casco Bay north of Portland. European plan. Breakfast and dinner served to travelers daily except Mondays when Continental breakfast and steak or lobster cookout at night available (by advance reservation). Open June 10 through Oct. 10. (Some rooms and cottages with kitchenettes available from May 1 and after Oct. 10.) Bicycles (incl. tandems), pool, tennis, croquet court, boating, hiking, salt water swimming on grounds. Golf, riding, fishing, state parks, theatre nearby. Fred and Colleen Webster, Ted and Doris Gillette, Innkeepers.*

*Directions: From the south, take Exit 9 from Maine Tpke. (I-95) to Rte. 1-N and follow signs to inn. From the north, take Exit 11 from I-95 at Gray and follow Rte. 115 to Yarmouth. Follow signs to inn.*

## ISLAND HOUSE
### Ogunquit, Maine

I've been writing about my visits to the Island House for quite a few years, so now I'd like to share a letter from some readers who tell of their experiences:

"For pure relaxation and feeling at one with the sea while at the same time enjoying charming, comfortable lodgings, one can not do better than to go to the Island House. We enjoyed our well-furnished bedroom overlooking the sea; sat on the rocks for hours photographing breakers, gulls and even a seal; drove into Perkins Cove and found some surprisingly sophisticated crafts and prints; walked to the Whistling Oyster for dinner; sat on the Island House porch in the afternoon watching the water; and talked into the night with some of the other guests in the sitting room before the fire. There is a very lighthearted atmosphere here and no phoniness."

Here is another letter which said in part:

"The next day was stormy and, if we hadn't already made a deposit at the Island House, we probably would have driven on, but we were richly rewarded.

"Although it was rainy that evening we went outside to watch the surf pound the rocks around the Island House. The spray of the ocean shot many feet into the air and was really quite a sight to see. There was an English girl staying at the inn who was having the time of her life—all bundled up in her raincoat—dripping wet—and watching the surf while collecting rocks. We had breakfast with her the next morning and it was quite delightful listening to her enthusiasm and English accent.

"The sun was shining brightly and it was a perfectly lovely day.

But I am sure that the sun shines even on the cloudy days—as it did for us the night before.

"I really enjoyed the evening before sitting in the Laurents living room beside the fireplace and reading old *National Geographics*. I felt sorry for a young man who came in soaking wet, looking for lodging, but of course with no reservation he was out of luck. I felt extremely lucky to have such good accommodations on a cold and rainy evening."

There is really very little that I can add to these two accounts of visits to this small, tidy inn by the sea in Perkins Cove, Ogunquit. The only meal served is breakfast, but the Whistling Oyster, now with a brand new building after the fire, is open for lunch and dinner.

*ISLAND HOUSE, Ogunquit, Me. 03907; 207-646-8811. A 6-room oceanside inn overlooking Perkins Cove, 15 mi. from Portsmouth, N.H. Lodgings include Continental breakfast, served daily except Sundays to house guests only. (Lunch and dinner available at the Whistling Oyster nearby.) No children under 12. No pets. Open from early June to Oct. 1. Advance reservations necessary. Golf, swimming, fishing, scenic walks, interesting shops and art galleries, all within walking distance. Paul and Marge Laurent, Innkeepers.*

*Directions: From Maine Tpke., exit at York or Wells. Follow US #1 to Ogunquit. Go 1 mi. on Shore Rd. to Perkins Cove. Inn is last house in Perkins Cove.*

## OLD FORT CLUB
### Kennebunkport, Maine

Yale Brass and I had just finished two sets of tennis and were seated at courtside enjoying the sunshiny weather in mid-June and discussing different types of vacations.

"As you know, I'm an airline pilot and I've seen a great many parts of the world," he said. "However, Kennebunkport is really 'home' for us. I guess it is a second home to many of our guests who return each year. We have people here from all over the States, but did you know that this part of the Maine coast is also very popular with Canadians? We have guests from Quebec and Ontario every year. Kennebunkport is a focal point for Canadians. Everybody loves the beach, and it's only a short walk from here.

"There used to be a hotel on this property, but Marjorie and I had it torn down. We converted one of the buildings into twelve efficiency apartments which include daily maid service and an enclosed garage. We also converted the Carriage House, part of which has Marjorie's antique shop and gallery. In the section overlooking the swimming pool she designed a club room with a big fireplace, large terrace and a separate kitchen for entertaining. It makes a very nice place for our guests to have lobster and steak cookouts."

The apartments Yale mentioned are meticulously designed in decorator colors. There is every effort made to harmonize the drapes and the slipcovers. All of them have fully equipped kitchen facilities.

Just before this edition went to press I received a letter from Marjorie Brass:

"We are now going to include 'Spruce Tops,' our own 20-room estate, which is also on the grounds, as part of the Old Fort complex. It is really a beautiful, huge Newport cottage which has been lovingly restored. It will offer six beautiful rooms, all with working fireplaces, and Continental breakfast will be included for house guests. It also has a 3-room apartment with its own kitchen. We have added a 2-room apartment with an efficiency kitchen in our Carriage House overlooking the pool. Therefore we will now have 14 apartments and six guest rooms. The main house will be for adults only, but with the same maid service, use of pool and tennis courts, as the rest of the club. When we showed our home to Isobel MacAulay of the Inverary Inn in Nova Scotia, her first comment was, 'Has Norman seen this?' Isobel was enthralled and said it would be a beautiful country inn.

"I forgot to mention the guest house has a beautiful living room, a dining room, a butler's pantry and two huge porches."

125

So, I think that our readers can see that the Old Fort Club is an ideal place for families or couples who wish to vacation in Kennebunkport.

*OLD FORT CLUB, Old Fort Ave., Kennebunkport, Me. 04046; 207-967-2709 or 3980. A 12-apartment resort-inn on Cape Arundel within walking distance of the ocean in an historic Maine town. No meals are served but a full kitchen is provided with each apartment. Daily maid service. Balconied club room. Open from Memorial Day to Oct. 1. No pets. Heated pool, tennis court, shuffleboard on grounds. Bicycles, golf, salt water swimming and boating nearby. Yale and Marjorie Brass, Innkeepers.*

*Directions: Use Exit #3 (Kennebunk) from Maine Tpke. Turn left on Rte. 35 to Kennebunkport and follow signs to inn.*

### SUDBURY INN
**Bethel, Maine**

I clomped up the steps into the front door of the Sudbury Inn making a great show of getting the snow off my parka and ski boots and then stepped inside to the cheerful warmth. Sure enough, there was Bev Gasser waiting for me with a broom in her hand and a stern look in her eye. I know that it was all part of the good-natured kidding I would get about bringing more snow inside than I left on the slopes.

"Where did you ski today," she said. I wrenched off my ski boots and staggered over to the fireplace. "Today I went up to Sunday River," I said. "That 3½ mile run was great and the lift lines weren't long at all. Tomorrow it's Mt. Abram.

She handed me a cup of tea and sat down on the couch. "I told you that the best ski secret in New England is that we have skiing earlier and longer here." From the number of other skiers who were drifting in, I could see that the secret of the Sudbury Inn was fast becoming unguarded.

The inn dates back to 1873 when Bethel was a busy lumbering town in western Maine. It has flourished even more as four-season vacationers have learned about the beauties of inland Maine.

The inn is homey and unpretentious. The lobby has a rack of paperback books and current magazines and very comfortable chairs which invite plenty of reading and conversation. There is an old wind-up Victrola in one corner, a big bowl of apples on the table, and countrified touches like dried flowers on the mantelpiece and kerosene lamps.

Upstairs there are more books and magazines on a big table in the hallway in case the guest runs out of reading material. The rooms are simple. They have what I call "country inn" furniture — good and solid. On each successive trip I find that five or six more rooms have been redecorated. The towels for each guest are piled up on the bureaus in the old-fashioned way. Seven of the rooms have private baths and there are ten others with shared baths.

Almost everybody wanted to know what was going to be served for dinner that evening, so the menu was posted. It offered roast beef, lamb chops, chicken Yankee-style (this is cooked with maple corn fritters, bacon strips and cranberry sauce), scallops and rainbow trout. Desserts included Indian pudding, maple rum parfait and cheescake. It all sounded pretty good especially to skiers with Gargantuan appetites. One couple with two children noted that there were special children's prices — which, of course, pleased them to no end.

In 1976 a new roof was added to the inn. Beverley was able to do more gardening out in front and everything bloomed very nicely. "We started many things from seed," she said. "It's a real challenge with our short growing season. We still receive many compliments on our plants indoors."

Although this account tells of my visit in January, western Maine is a most attractive location for a summer or fall vacation. The region abounds with beautiful lakes and many almost undiscovered

backroads. New Hampshire's White Mountains are just a few miles away and the region has long been famous for its beautiful resort facilities. The fun and good times to be had at John and Bev Gasser's tidy inn in Bethel goes on twelve months of the year.

*THE SUDBURY INN, Box 65, Bethel, Me. 04217; 207-824-2174. A 17-room village inn on Main St., 70 mi. northwest of Portland, within sight of Mt. Washington. Near the Sunday River, Mt. Abram ski areas. Some rooms with shared baths. European plan includes Continental breakfast. Dinner served to travelers daily except Mondays. Lunch and dinner served daily to travelers in July and August. No pets. Closed Christmas Day. Bicycles available. Golf, tennis, swimming, Alpine and xc skiing nearby. John and Beverley Gasser, Innkeepers.*

*Directions: From the south, take Exit 11 at Gray from I-95. Follow Rte. 26 to Bethel.*

## SQUIRE TARBOX INN
### Westport Island, Maine

Elsie White and Anne McInvale are the new innkeepers at the Squire Tarbox Inn. Elsie wrote to me about some of the joys and trials of being a country innkeeper.

"As you know, Anne and I began our experience at a very busy time at the inn, on July 1st. Our goal was to have as little interruption as possible in the transition from Eleanor and Mary. We both have wanted to have a country inn for many years and this represents the culmination of a three-year search. Anne has enjoyed cooking and she is the one who creates the gourmet fare that we serve. We have a limited menu with a choice of two entrees daily and a set menu for the other courses of soup, salad, vegetables and dessert. All of our soups are homemade as are our breads.

"Among our main dishes are beef bourguignonne, beef stroganoff, roast or curried lamb, chicken breast baked in wine, fillet of sole and finnan haddie. Soups include French onion, celery, potato and some more unusual ones such as eggplant and cucumber.

"We now enjoy serving in the 200-year-old Pine Room with the huge fireplace. That was the room Eleanor used as a sitting room.

"Our summer was very exciting. We had guests from Hong Kong, Milan, Israel, Latvia, Netherlands, Denmark and Capetown, South Africa, and many from Canada as well as the U.S. Many of our guests were lovely people who shared their interests with everyone at the dinner table and other times which, of course, makes for lively conversation.

"Everyone shared our enthusiasm in our new venture and many, in their own ways, made suggestions and contributions. For example, a park planner from North Carolina redesigned our problem parking area, drawing plans to scale to correct the problem. Another couple with an advertising agency in Wisconsin are doing our brochure, so it will reflect what they feel we have to offer.

"We hope by next season to improve the trail through the woods to Squam Creek and erect some comfortable benches on the water's edge.

"We don't plan any changes in the bedrooms because they seem

ideal. Many of our guests describe them as being 'just like home, and with very comfortable beds.' "

And so the order changeth but the tradition of personal innkeeping continues. The warm, friendly, white clapboard Squire Tarbox Inn on Westport Island is in excellent hands. Stewart McBride of the *Christian Science Monitor* visited there at my suggestion in the fall of 1976 and wrote a most complimentary article about his stay.

*SQUIRE TARBOX INN, Westport Island, R.D. #2, Box 318, Wiscasset, Me. 04578; 207-882-7693. A restored Colonial home on Rte. 144 in Westport, 10 mi. from Wiscasset. European plan. 6 rooms with shared baths; one with private bath. All lodgings include Continental breakfast. Breakfast served to house guests only. Lunch and dinner served to travelers by reservation. Open from May 1 to Oct. 31. No pets. Golf, tennis, pool, sailing nearby. Anne McInvale and Elsie White, Innkeepers.*

*Directions: From Maine Tpke. take Exit 9 and follow Rtes. 95 and 1 to Rte. 144, 8 mi. north of Bath. Follow Rte. 144 to Wiscasset-Westport Bridge. Inn is located 6 mi. south of bridge on Westport Island.*

**THE WHISTLING OYSTER**
**Ogunquit, Maine**

The late afternoon sun, reflecting the still waters of Perkins Cove, created dappled patterns on the walls and ceilings of the Whistling Oyster. The lobster boats were coming in under the drawbridge and the smaller boats darted among the pleasure craft. Ogunquit's love affair with the sea has been continuous. Now I was sitting on the upper deck dining room caught in its magic spell.

It was dinnertime and the staff were already briskly preparing for the diners who were waiting patiently or browsing at the Oyster's famous gift shop.

A glance at the menu indicated such interesting offerings as Captain Blight's Delight, a truly remarkable seafood chowder, filet of haddock, swordfish steak, lobster Provencale, and many other offerings for which the Oyster has been famous for many years. I watched a sailboat run a slalom course among the lobster boats and sightseeing craft as I lingered over my dessert of fudge cake. The recipe is included in the *Country Inn Cookbook.*

*I wrote that description of a visit to the whistling Oyster in the mid-60's in an early edition of* Country Inns and Back Roads. *Since*

*that time I have visited this exceptional restaurant many times and have enjoyed my friendship with John Parella, the innkeeper. However, in the late summer of 1976 the Whistling Oyster was completely destroyed by fire. John Parella told me on the telephone at the time, "It is absolutely devastating and I am heartsick, but we have got to go to work immediately and rebuild and start all over again."*

In February of 1977, just days before the final deadline for this edition, I visited John and the new Whistling Oyster, built on the same spot overlooking Perkins Cove. When I saw what had been accomplished and listened to John explain all of the new concepts that were emerging, it was really exciting. "We've designed a new building, with some of the best concepts of the old," he said.

In the half-finished building he pointed out where the new dining rooms, lounge areas, kitchen and gift shop would be situated within almost a matter of weeks. In fact, John was so optimistic about the progress that he and I scheduled a meeting of nearby New England CIBR innkeepers to be held at the Oyster late in April.

As for what I wrote years ago, much is exactly the same. The sun still reflects the waters of Perkins Cove, the lobster boats are still running under the drawbridge and the pleasure craft are gathering. The Whistling Oyster menu with perhaps a few new touches by Chef Bill Cardwell continues to delight guests, the flower garden blooms and the Whistling Oyster Gift Shop has re-opened.

Jan Lindstrom's sketch of the new Oyster from the cove shows many new levels and architectural features which blend with the ocean, sky, and low hills.

Congratulations to John and everyone concerned on the new Whistling Oyster.

*WHISTLING OYSTER, Perkins Cove, Ogunquit, Me. 03907; 207-646-9521. A waterfront restaurant in Perkins Cove at Ogunquit. No lodgings. Lunch and dinner served daily. Closed Jan. 19 through March 16. Reservations advisable. (For accommodations: the Island House just a few steps away.) John Parella, Innkeeper.*

*Directions: From the south, take the York exit from I-95. Turn north on Rte. 1 to Ogunquit Square. Proceed south on Shore Rd. for about 1 mi. to Perkins Cove turnoff.*

## WHITEHALL INN
### Camden, Maine

In the past eleven years that I have been writing *Country Inns and Back Roads*, I have received countless letters from readers telling me of their experiences at staying at inns that I have visited, or recommending inns that I haven't discovered. Sometimes these letters are the best way to convey the individually unique experience to be found in each inn. Here are excerpts from three guests at the Whitehall Inn:

"We traveled to Camden, Maine, via New Brunswick (explained this gentleman from the Midwest). Although we had not planned on staying at the Whitehall Inn we were intrigued by your description of Camden. We wanted to see the town, and we checked the Whitehall to see if there were any rooms available. Luckily there were. That is why we always travel in September — it is not as crowded — it is still warm and quite often we get off-season rates. We had a very enjoyable stay there. The next morning, while packing, I discovered that I had left my camera in the dining room. I was sure it was gone forever, but Mr. Dewing had found it and locked it in his safe overnight. I thanked him wholeheartedly and now realized the kind of service and hospitality I could expect in country inns and, most certainly, at the

Whitehall in particular."

Another guest wrote: "We found Camden a most delightful spot and its people charming. We feared it would be rather 'touristy' but this was not the case at all. The Whitehall was a gracious example of the white clapboard buildings so prevalent in New England, and was different from our own type of building in Kansas. Mr. Dewing was most helpful and Mrs. Dewing appeared to be a tower of strength in the dining room. The Maine lobster we had there more than repaid the effort needed to eat it!"

The final letter is from a gentleman in Vermont: "Because I have been connected with the food industry most of my life, stateside and abroad, I instinctively noticed the small considerations that lift an establishment head and shoulders above the rest. We found the Whitehall Inn to be one of these outstanding establishments. During the past few years we enjoyed a few meals at the inn and this year we were guests for a delightful week. Hosts Jean, Ed, Chip, Jonathan and Heidi made us feel right at home as soon as we arrived.

The Dewings seem to accomplish something new every year. The latest good news is the purchase of an island in Penobscot Bay and running luncheon cruises to it all summer.

The family aspect of innkeeping continues with daughter Heidi attending the Culinary Institute of America. She went to Germany for the Culinary Olympics in the Fall of 1976. Jonathan is the first cook and also the breakfast cook, and Chip continues as the host in the lounge.

The Edna St. Vincent Millay collection, a tribute to the American poet who lived in Camden, is always of great interest to inn guests. And that's the report from Camden, Maine, and the Whitehall Inn. Such popularity must be deserved.

*WHITEHALL INN, Camden, Me. 04843; 207-236-3391. A 38-room village inn in a Maine seacoast town, 75 mi. from Portland. Modified American and European plans. Breakfast and dinner served daily to travelers. Light lunch served to houseguests in annex across from inn overlooking Penobscot Bay. Open June to late October. Tennis, bicycles, shuffleboard, day sailing, harbor cruises on grounds. Own island in the bay for picnics. Golf, hiking, swimming, fishing nearby. Jean and Ed Dewing, Innkeepers.*

*Directions: From Maine Tpke. take Exit 9 to coastal Rte. 95. Proceed on 95 to Rte. 1 at Brunswick. Follow Rte. 1 to Rte. 90 at Warren, to Rte. 1 in Camden. Inn is located on Rte. 1, ¼ mi. north of Camden.*

# Mid Atlantic

Grandview Farm, *Huntsville*

ONTARIO

TORONTO

LAKE ONTARIO

Clarkson House, *Lewiston*

Oban Inn, *Niagara-On-The-Lake*

Asa Ransom House, *Clarence*

NEW

Holloway House *East Bloomfield*

Glen Iris Inn, *Castile*

LAKE ERIE

NEW

PENNSYLVA

INTERSTATE 80

Tavern, *New Wilmington*

PITTSBURGH

PENNSYLVANIA TPK.

Century Inn, *Scenery Hill*

Fairfield Inn, *Fairfield*

MONTREAL

ngside Inn, *Auburn*

Lincklaen House,
*Cazenovia*

Bull's Head Inn,
*Cobleskill*

ALBANY

Almshouse Inn, *Ghent*

Greenville Arms, *Greenville*

Swiss Hutte, *Hillsdale*

Redcoat's Return, *Tannersville*

Oliver House, *Ancram*

Y O R K

Inn at Starlight Lake,

Beekman Arms, *Rhinebeck*

*Starlight*

Old Drovers Inn, *Dover Plains*

Sterling Inn,
*South Sterling*

Overlook Inn,
Pump House, *Canadensis*

Bird & Bottle, *Garrison*

ine Barn Inn, *Danville*

The Algonquin Hotel,
*New York City*

Three Village Inn,
*Stony Brook*

Moselem Springs Inn,
*Moselem Springs*

NEW YORK CITY

1740 House, *Lumberville*

Candlewyck Inn, *Green Lane*

PHILADELPHIA

Accomac Inn, *Wrightsville*

N E W

J E R S E Y

The Mainstay, *Cape May*

# New York

*In the past I have shared my enthusiasm for Route 20 which runs east and west in New York, parallel with the New York State Thruway. It has several advantages, not the least of which is that it is a toll-free road.*

*Route 20 has an alternate that starts near East Aurora and runs through Varysburg, Orangeville Center, Warsaw, Geneseo and Livonia, and according to my map disappears somewhere north of Canandaigua.*

*Someone must have been impressed by Greek and Roman names, because central New York State abounds in them. I found Aurora, Scipio, Fabius, Delphi Falls, Manlius, Pompey and Cincinnatus.*

### THE ALMSHOUSE INN
**Ghent, New York**

In the summer of 1976, a gentleman from Brush Valley, Pennsylvania, wrote me a letter about the Almshouse which said in part:

"I recently visited an old college friend in Ghent, N.Y., and discovered that he and three associates are involved in an exciting venture that may be of interest to you for *Country Inns and Back Roads.*

"My friend, Mr. Robin Litton, Dr. and Mrs. Cullen Burris, and Joseph Leon have purchased the old Columbia County Poorhouse and restored it to a delightful bed-and-breakfast inn. Prix-fixe dinners of English and French cuisine are carefully prepared by Shirley Burris. Guests gather earlier in the pub and parlors which are furnished with antiques, or they browse through the antiques shop in the basement. The building has charm and history and comes equipped with amusing anecdotes which the owners love to share at after-dinner conversations. The guest rooms are also furnished in antiques and all feature working fireplaces. One room even has a fireplace in the bathroom!

"I returned from my visit with much enthusiasm for the inn and the attention to detail with which all aspects are being considered. Incidentally all four owners have very interesting backgrounds. Mr. Litton is a former TV producer, Dr. Burris is currently chief of psychiatry at Albany's V.A. Hospital, his wife Shirley was a well-

known Chicago interior designer, and Joe Leon is a professional actor with a long list of credits. I urge you to look at the Almshouse."

I needed no further urging. I made the short trip from Stockbridge to Ghent and arrived on a beautiful late fall afternoon.

I found that my informant, if anything, had understated the elegance and care displayed at this beautiful country inn. The parlors, lodging rooms and dining rooms were all beautifully furnished, and the fireplaces were blazing.

Shirley was already at work on dinner, so to get better acquainted I spent some time seated at the kitchen table while she prepared the evening meal which that evening was leg of lamb with vegetables. Robin, Joe, and Dr. Burris all were in and out of the kitchen setting the tables, and preparing the dining room.

"We couldn't do it except by 24-hour reservation," explained Shirley, "because I like to prepare everything very thoughtfully, just as I would if they were guests in my home. We have one entree that serves 30 people and dinner is at 8 o'clock. There's only one sitting."

Because Robin and Joe have many show business friends from New York, they quite often have informal singing and entertainment after dinner.

Dinner also consisted of a broccoli-filled crepe, and salad with a dressing made with walnuts. Shirley's specialties also include duck English-style, fillet of beef served with Madeira sauce, Beef Wellington, and veal served in many different ways with various sauces.

There are only three lodging rooms and they are frequently spoken for in advance, so as with dinner, reservations are not only advisable, but usually mandatory.

*THE ALMSHOUSE INN, Rte. 66, Ghent, N.Y. 12075; 518-392-5242. An elegant 3-room inn, 30 mi. southeast of Albany, N.Y., and approximately 30 min. from the Berkshires. European Plan. Lodgings include breakfast. Dinner served at 8 p.m. by reservation except Mondays and Tuesdays. (Inn is open for overnight guests on these days. Closed Christmas and probably during March. Sunday Brunch, 1 p.m. No pets. 7 mi. from Lindenwald, home of Martin Van Buren; 30 min. from Tanglewood, 90 min. from Saratoga, summer theatres in Chatham, N.Y., and Stockbridge, Mass. Tennis, swimming, riding, skiing nearby. Dr. & Mrs. B. Cullen Burris, Joseph Leon, Robin Litton, Innkeepers.*

*Directions: Follow Taconic Parkway to Rte. 203, Chatham. Stay on Rte. 203, 2 mi. to intersection with Rte. 66. Turn left on 66, proceed 2 mi. to inn.*

## ALGONQUIN HOTEL
### New York, New York

I have always had a great deal of fun writing about my experiences at the Hotel Algonquin in New York City.

The first time I mentioned it it was in the 1971 edition when I explained how it really came to my attention when so many people following *Country Inns and Back Roads* felt the need of a place to stay in New York City. One recommended the Algonquin and after a long visit, I agreed that it was the closest thing to a country inn I'd found yet in Fun City.

In the 1972 edition I spoke about seeing a well-known French movie actor having tea in the lobby, and about riding up in the elevator with a famous stage actress who announced in the glorious tones of a French horn: "Fifth Floor, please."

Andy Anspach, the innkeeper, explained that people like actresses, diplomats and internationally famous people deserved a private life, and the Algonquin attempts to provide it while they are in New York. As he said, "We are terribly conservative by inclination. We've tried not to change too many things around here since the early 1920's, when it was famous as a meeting place for the Algonquin Roundtable Wits. People seem to enjoy our accommodations which include oversized bathtubs, and meticulous room service."

In 1974 I spoke at length about the friendliness of the staff and how guests are quite likely to be remembered even though the Algonquin is, in truth, a very busy place.

In 1975 I did a long piece on the late evening supper buffet where guests come in after the theatre, the opera, or basketball or hockey

games to enjoy Welsh rarebit, salad, fluffy cakes, apple pie, ice cream and lobster Newburg.

In 1976 I luxuriated in having breakfast in bed at the Algonquin and described the browned corned beef hash with a poached egg, warm Dutch coffee cake and, above all, the superb Algonquin hot chocolate!

This year I would like to share a letter with you from one of our readers who travels quite a bit both in the U.S. and abroad:

"The Algonquin is my favorite hotel in the country because they genuinely seem to be concerned with each guest's comfort and well-being. The suites are comfortable and offer good value. The food in the restaurant is superb and the room service is amazing. The staff makes the guests aware of only being comfortable and not being the recipient of attention from well-trained personnel. The location is good because it is in easy walking distance to the theatres and the garage is across the street. It is where we always stay when in New York, and staying at another hotel is like being in exile. In fact my idea of heaven would be a suite at the Algonquin and unlimited room service."

O happy day!

*ALGONQUIN HOTEL, 59 W. 44th St., New York, N.Y. 10036; 212-687-4400. A quiet, conservative 200-room country inn in the heart of Manhattan. Convenient to business, theatres and shopping. European plan. Breakfast, lunch, dinner and late supper buffet served to travelers daily except Sunday dinner. Open year-round. No pets. Very near bus, rail and air transportation. Garage directly opposite entrance, with complimentary parking for weekend visitors arriving after 3 p.m. Fri. or Sat. for minimum 2-night visit. Andrew Anspach. Innkeeper.*

*Directions: 44th St. is one-way from west to east; 43rd St. from east to west. Garage is accessible from either street.*

## ASA RANSOM HOUSE
**Clarence, New York**

In just a short time since it originally opened on Thanksgiving Day in 1975, the Asa Ransom House, which is a dream-come-true for Bob and Judy Lenz, has already established itself as a most satisfying country inn experience.

I have received letters of praise from a great many people including Jim Mellow of St. Louis who spoke glowingly of the dinner which was a most succulent smoked beef with a raisin apple sauce.

After a brief visit, John Tovey, the innkeeper at the Miller Howe House in Windermere in the English Lake District, wrote a letter of commendation for just about everything.

However, I would like to quote from Marthe Lane's column in the *Buffalo Courier Express* which tells about some of her adventures in visiting the Asa Ransom House for the first time:

"This is not the kind of place for restaurant-goers seeking a nightclub atmosphere or the currently fashionable 'eclectic' look. Tranquility, Early American decor, and country style cooking are the theme. It is all done in as simple and genuine fashion as feasible.

"The center staircase leads to four upstairs bedrooms providing lodging. Bedrooms can be seen if unoccupied. At the left, past the old grandfather's clock, is the library furnished with antiques, bookshelves brimming with reading material and a partially assembled 500-piece puzzle.

"Our table was in an inviting, cheery dining room near a glowing fire. In the non-smokers dining room, hurricane lamps, fresh flowers and ironstone table settings as well as ball fringe tieback curtains and flowered carpets contributed to the Early American atmosphere. The waitresses were smiling, pleasant and unhurried. All wore black skirts, white blouses, calico pinafores and white dust bonnets. The customers, too, fitted the mood. All were 'properly attired' as required by the framed notice at the entrance. The menu includes the Asa Ransom News: an explanation of what country inns stand for; information about Clarence—the oldest town in the county of Erie; and good health—'everyone's heritage.' "

Marthe Lane went on to explain that the vegetables were the freshest obtainable, meats flavored only with herbs and no MSG, cream is whipped on the spot, and all bottles and glass used are taken to recycling centers. She was most glowing in her admiration of the potato chowder soup, the salmon pond casserole and Caesar salad. She commented at length about the homemade breads served in a calico chicken basket and the homemade desserts offered on a tray which included peach soufflé pie, pudding parfaits and fresh fruits.

The Asa Ransom House is closed on Fridays and Saturdays because of the religious beliefs of the innkeepers who are members of the World Wide Church of God. As I have pointed out in the past, Walter and Madeline Stoudt of the Moselem Springs Inn in Pennsylvania are also members of this religious faith, and their inn is also closed on those days.

There are two new additions to this inn—a complete gift shop which I am sure reflects Bob and Judy's admiration of the useful and beautiful, and an herb and flower garden on the west side of the inn where Judy tells me that they will grow a wide variety of herbs using them in the kitchen and selling many in the gift shop.

My thanks to Marthe Lane for permission to quote her column. I am delighted to have my original impressions confirmed by such a knowledgeable and well-informed food editor.

*ASA RANSOM HOUSE, Rte. 5, Clarence, N.Y. 14031; 716-759-2315. A 4-room village inn approximately 15 mi. from Buffalo near the Albright Knox Art Gallery, the Studio Arena Theatre and Niagara Falls. European plan. Dinner served Mondays through Thursdays, 4:30 p.m. to 9 p.m.; Sundays, 12:30 to 8 p.m. Closed Fridays and Saturdays. No pets. Tennis, golf, fishing and swimming nearby. Bob and Judy Lenz, Innkeepers.*

*Directions: From the N.Y. Thruway east (Exit 48A—Pembroke) Turn right to Rte. 5 and proceed for 11 mi. to Clarence. From the N.Y. thruway west (Exit 49) turn left on Rte. 78, 1 mi. to Rte. 5 and then proceed on Rte. 5 for 5½ mi. From the east via Rte. 20, just east of Lancaster, N.Y. turn right on Ransom Rd., go to end and turn left.*

## BEEKMAN ARMS
**Rhinebeck, New York**

I awakened from a deep slumber aware of voices raised in anger from belowstairs. Their intensity mounted and with some alarm I fumbled for the lamp next to my bed. However, there was only the stub of a candle. I groped in the darkness, struck a light and then crept down the stairs in awe, if not complete fright, of two gentlemen facing each other.

"By God," said one shaking his fist at a pretty young girl, "you are not too good to bring me a bootjack!" Immediately the other man sprang up and shook his fist and cried, "By God, Sir, she is too good to bring you a bootjack and if you say that again, I'll knock you down, Sir!" The first man backed away and went to a table to sit by himself. The onlookers broke into small knots whispering agitatedly.

Knees quaking, I went upstairs to my room. The door was locked and I stood outside in some consternation banging on it with my fists, calling out, "Let me in, let me in." The next thing I knew, I woke up sitting bolt upright in my bed. I had dreamt the entire episode.

It all started earlier that night at dinner at the Beekman Arms when Chuck LaForge told me the true story of the confrontation between Aaron Burr and General John Armstrong in 1813. The pretty young girl (who bore a striking resemblance in my dream to our waitress dressed in a Colonial costume) was the innkeeper's daughter whom Burr was trying to intimidate into fetching a bootjack. The General had faced him down.

We had eaten dinner in the Pewter Room where Sue LaForge

said the episode had taken place. The 8x12 oak beams and the massive 14-inch-wide floor planks are still there, and much of the original paneling as well.

Of course, Sue and Chuck had dozens of stories about generals, Presidents and foreign dignitaries who had partaken of the inn's hospitality over the years.

The Beekman Arms shares with Longfellow's Wayside Inn in South Sudbury, Massachusetts, the reputation of being the oldest, continuously operating inn in America. When the episode between Burr and Armstrong took place it was already 113 years old! Quite naturally, there have been some changes but basically the inn has remained the same for well over 250 years.

The exterior of the inn has recently been repainted and the shutters are now a very attractive Williamsburg gray.

After dinner, when the three of us walked next door to the 19th century fire station which is now the Beekman Arms Fire House Gift Shop, I saw many counters of attractive gifts where old pumpers used to await the alarm.

But I didn't see any bootjacks.

*BEEKMAN ARMS, Rhinebeck, N. Y. 12572; 914-876-7077. A 13-room village inn with 4 guest houses, 1 mi. from Penn Central Station at Rhinecliff. Short drive to F.D.R. Library and Home in Hyde Park. European plan. Lunch and dinner served to travelers daily. Closed Christmas. Open year-round. Golf nearby. Charles LaForge, Innkeeper.*

*Directions: From N.Y. Thruway, take Exit 19, cross Rhinecliff Bridge and pick up Rte. 199 south to Rte. 9. Proceed south on Rte. 9 to middle of village. From Taconic Pkwy. exit at Rhinebeck and follow Rte. 199 west 11 mi. to Rte. 308 into village.*

## BIRD AND BOTTLE INN
### Garrison, New York

Tom Noonan was at the top of his game. It was obvious that he was doing one of the things he enjoys most—preparing dinner at a guest's table.

When I mentioned this to him, he replied, "You're absolutely right. This is my idea of great fun."

A few minutes earlier he had wheeled a cart over to my table at the Bird and Bottle and began to form two very thin crêpes in a chafing dish. "You've got to flip them over at the precise second," he said, deftly tossing the first one and then the other into the air. In

what seemed like just a few seconds, he filled them with a seafood melange that contained bits of lobster, crab, scallops and shrimp.

"This is almost as much fun as flying my airplane," he said, carefully transferring the crepes to a warm plate and then placing them in front of me with a flourish.

Tom and Nancy had flown up to Stockbridge to have lunch with me just a few weeks previously. He's one of several innkeepers who fly their own airplanes. "Yes, Nancy and I frequently fly to one of your inns on Mondays when we are closed. It's a good way to keep in touch."

The main dish was fresh trout baked in white wine and stuffed with mushrooms. A great many of the menu offerings are Continental and French although oyster stuffed chicken is one of the specialties. "It's about as American as apple pie," explained Tom.

The Bird and Bottle goes back to the mid-1700's when it was a stagecoach stop on the New York to Albany route. Its nearness to West Point undoubtedly made it a meeting place for Benedict Arnold's emissaries to the British, prior to his defection.

Today that colonial atmosphere is preserved with narrow clapboards (quite unusual), low ceilings and rich paneling. The wide floor boards gleam in the candlelight. The inn is beautifully decorated with duck decoys, period wallpaper, pewter, old paintings and many wooden accessories.

The building hasn't always housed an inn, although it was built in 1761 and called Warren's Tavern. Like many Colonial buildings it has seen a variety of uses and owners. This makes the fact that it has retained its Early American contour and feeling quite remarkable.

Warren sold the inn in 1832, and it was a farm for three generations. In 1940 it regained its original inn status, and in recent years Tom and Nancy have added their own variety of "country chic." It is a surprisingly traffic-free ride from Manhattan, if one follows Tom's directions via the George Washington and Bear Mountain Bridges. There are no lodgings.

After dinner I went for a walk on the terrace and into the meadow which is reached by a rustic bridge over a gurgling stream.

The bridge had a magic of its own, no doubt explained by the fact that it was the exact spot where many people have been married over the past few years. I could almost hear Mendelssohn in the musical waters.

*BIRD AND BOTTLE INN, Garrison, N.Y. 10524; 914-424-3000. A country restaurant rich in antiquity located on Rte. 9, a few miles north of Peekskill, N.Y. A short distance from Boscobel Restoration, U.S. Military Academy at West Point and Sleepy Hollow Restorations. No lodgings. Lunch and dinner served daily except Mondays and Tuesdays. Closed month of January. Thomas and Nancy Noonan, Innkeepers.*

*Directions: From N.Y.C., cross George Washington Bridge and follow Palisades Pkwy. north to Bear Mtn. Bridge. Cross bridge and travel on Rte. 9D north 4½ mi. to Rte. 403. Proceed on Rte. 403 to Rte. 9, then north on Rte. 9, 4 mi. to inn. From I-84, take Exit 13 and follow Rte. 9 south for 8 mi.*

## BULL'S HEAD INN
### Cobleskill, New York

Shirley Allen pointed to the oil painting and said, "That is Timothy Murphy." I had to confess that I had never heard of Timothy Murphy. "Oh," she said, "he figured prominently in the history of the Schoharie Valley during the American Revolution. The area is filled with legends of him. You really ought to find out more about him."

Thus far, my visit with Shirley and Monty had been both an historical and gastronomical success. In fact, I've always found it difficult to separate the two, realizing, for instance, that the building which houses the Bull's Head Inn had been burned by hostile Mohawks three times within thirty years.

During the American Revolution, central New York State was literally the breadbasket for the American army and the British incited the Indians to rise up, burn and plunder. At one point, on October 17, 1780, all the people in the valley took refuge in the Old Stone Fort in Schoharie when it was attacked by a force of 800 Tories

and Indians under the leadership of Sir John Johnson and the notorious Joseph Brandt.

I was getting all this from Monty and Shirley between bites of sliced beef tenderloin with an excellent sauce bordelaise. The Bull's Head is best known for its numerous varieties of hearty beef dishes, many of which are prepared at the open hearth at one end of the rustic dining room. At various times I have had strip sirloin, prime ribs of beef and even tiny bay scallops. Today I had another one of those wonderfully crisp salads served in a chilled bowl garnished with a slice of anchovy. Monty pointed out that he had a couple of additions to his collection of bull's heads.

The other guests didn't look like Tories, or even Indians, although it is quite possible that their ancestors could have been either. They were, in fact, the hardworking folk from the heartland of New York State, which is still a granary for much of the east. The farmlands around Cobleskill and the Schoharie Valley abound in rich orchards, lowing herds and golden grain. The region is replete with thriving middle-size farms. The walls of the Bull's Head reflect the agricultural nature of the region, decorated with a collection of old farm tools.

Once again, I made a tour of the kitchen with its beautiful tile floors, banks of ovens and spotless tables. Monty pointed out that all of the baked goods are made here including the small loaves of bread.

"So, you've never heard of Timothy Murphy," said Monty. "Well, have another dessert and let me tell you about him."

*BULL'S HEAD INN, 2 Park Pl., Cobleskill, N.Y. 12043; 518-234-3591. A country restaurant, 5 mi. west of Howe Caverns and 30 mi. from Schenectady. No lodgings. Lunch served Tuesdays through Fridays; dinner served Tuesdays through Saturdays and Sundays from 1-8 p.m. Closed Christmas Day. Monty and Shirley Allen, Innkeepers.*

*Directions: Restaurant is 40 mi. southwest of Albany on N.Y. Rte. 7.*

## CLARKSON HOUSE
### Lewiston, New York

A light snow was falling on an early December evening when I first visited the Clarkson House in Lewiston, New York, a number of years ago. The Christmas tree lights were already blinking out their happy message, and there was a small group of figures depicting the Holy Family across from the inn. I ventured down the street to see the appealing miniature Christmas tree lights draped around each of the trees in the business district. It all made a very happy holiday effect.

This was my first visit to this corner of New York State dominated by the presence of Niagara Falls. I learned about the Clarkson House from my good friend, Robert Lenz, now the innkeeper of the Asa Ransom House in Clarence, New York. Bob said that it was very special, and he proved to be right.

I found the Clarkson House to be an excellent restaurant — something I knew the moment I smelled a most delicious aroma. I discovered that the reason for the enchanting aroma was the charcoal grill right in the middle of the dining area, and the filets and lamb chops were sizzling away merrily. Around it, there is an unusual arrangement of booths and tables, and on the walls a collection of tools and gadgets used more than 100 years ago. "They haven't discovered the use for some of them!" said Marilyn Clarkson. There are old-fashioned kerosene lamps on the tables, and the walls have several good paintings interspersed with wall lamps.

On that first trip I discovered that Bob Clarkson is a great believer in having things under control. For example, there are 22 tables, all carefully spaced out on the wooden floor which is scrubbed every day. This means that reservations are most advisable as there are a limited number of diners that can be accommodated.

Secondly, the menu has been carefully limited to a few entrees which are very carefully prepared and most tastefully arranged on the plates. There is an emphasis on beef, including sirloin, filet and prime rib. There are also delicious French-cut lamb chops. A combination of beef filet and lobster tail, or half of a Maine lobster (flown in fresh) are also offered. That, plus four desserts, including cherries jubilee and baked Alaska, is the menu. I mustn't forget to mention that there was a little sign on one of those delicious-looking baked

potatoes that said: "Eat all of me if you like, I've been scrubbed and tubbed."

I've revisited the Clarkson House several times since then and noted with great satisfaction the continued growth of the Niagara Falls area with the addition of the Artpark—a parkland and theatre devoted to the arts, the continuing Shaw Festival at nearby Niagara-on-the-Lake, Ontario, and the continuation of many other area recreational and cultural activities.

*THE CLARKSON HOUSE, 810 Center St., Lewiston, N. Y. 14092; 716-754-4544. A country restaurant, 7 mi. from Niagara Falls and Olde Fort Niagara. No lodgings. Dinner served daily except Mondays. Closed Christmas. Bob and Marilyn Clarkson, Innkeepers.*

*Directions: From I-90, exit at Lewiston and follow Rte. 104E for 1½ mi. Turn right on Rte. 18F and travel 2 blocks west to restaurant.*

## GLEN IRIS INN
### Castile, New York

"It's hard to imagine a more marvelous setting for a country inn," I remarked as Peter Pizzutelli and I walked back to the broad green lawns from the lookout point in front of the Glen Iris Inn where the Genesee River falls are 107 feet high.

"Well at least today you can hear yourself," said Peter. "Sometimes after a heavy rain the sound is positively thunderous."

We threaded our way through the tall pine trees and now and then the morning sunlight caught a flash of color, as birds flitted from tree to tree. Everything in and around the inn was beautifully attended with evergreens, shrubs, ferns and brilliant flowers.

I have visited the Glen Iris Inn in Letchworth State Park many times. It is very well run and has excellent food and most comfortable lodgings. It is a part of this truly beautiful state park which never fails to invoke a feeling of wonder because of its great natural beauties. The park is located in western New York, south of Rochester, and is a patch of green about 18 miles long and a few miles wide on most of the gasoline company maps. The original 1000 acres was donated by William Pryor Letchworth whose home in the early 1900's was in the building which is now the inn.

Cora Pizzutelli told me that they had some guests in the inn recently who stayed at Letchworth, England, near London. "It is the home of William P. Letchworth's ancestors," she said. "They described an English inn nearly as gorgeous, with many lovely rooms." I made a mental note to visit it on my next trip to England.

For thousands of years the Genesee River has been slicing its way between high banks creating deep channels. The entire region is rich in geological lore, and was also a significant location of the Six Nations, a group of Indian tribes in western New York state.

The park is traversed north and south by a road which comes very close to the high cliffs next to the river, and in several places extremely well-designed lookout points have been established. It abounds in small game and one of the oddities is that woodchucks are protected by law because the Park Commissioners feel that this was the most accessible animal for small children to see in their natural habitat.

There is a natural affinity between honeymooners and country inns and each year I receive letters from people who are looking for an unusual setting for their wedding ceremony. The lawn next to the

Falls is very popular, especially in June. Guests then go to the inn for the wedding breakfast.

Just before this edition went to press, Cora Pizzutelli wrote me as follows: "Each year we have an increasing number of guests who visit us through *Country Inns and Back Roads*. They are always lovely, gentle, interesting people who are very enthusiastic about the inns that they have been to, and they intend to visit many more. We enjoy having their comments and descriptions. They seem to be a part of the Berkshire Traveller family.

"Don't forget to remind your readers that because so many people want to visit Letchworth State Park, advance reservations for the Glen Iris are an absolute necessity, and we hate to turn people away."

*GLEN IRIS INN, Castile, N.Y. 14427; 716-493-2622. A 20-room country inn located at the Middle Falls of the Genesee River in Letchworth State Park. European plan. Breakfast, lunch and dinner served to travelers daily. Open from Easter Sunday to Nov. 6. Footpaths, swimming, and bicycles nearby. Historical sites in Park and spectacular views within walking distance. Peter and Cora Pizzutelli, Innkeepers.*

*Directions: Inn is located off Rtes. 436, 19A and 39 in Letchworth State Park, 55 mi. from Buffalo and Rochester.*

**GREENVILLE ARMS**
**Greenville, N.Y.**

Ruth Stevens carefully set my plate down saying, "Be careful, it's hot." I expected it to be hot because I could tell almost from the first moment of my visit to this Catskill mountain inn that certain things had always been done in a most particular manner like fresh hot rolls, recipes from scratch, very clean, crisp white sheets and good hefty towels.

I had already enjoyed a fresh fruit cup and now generous slices of baked ham, zucchini squash and scalloped potatoes were awaiting my pleasure. Scalloped potatoes! Boy, how I love scalloped potatoes, and it's something that I'm not often served.

Meanwhile in another corner of the tidy dining room, Ruth's married daughter, Barbara, was busy serving a group of approximately 18 rural mail carriers who were enjoying their yearly dinner. Barbara recently moved back to Greenville to join her mother in operating this old inn which had been in the Stevens family for 25 years. Another daughter, Laura, joins the family during the summer months.

In many ways, what I had seen so far was typical of a country inn: Warm friendly people who still liked to do things in the old-fashioned way. The inn is within walking distance of churches, movies and shopping, and Mrs. Stevens or her daughters will explain the many historical places of interest that are just a short distance away.

There is still another dimension to be found in the fact that the Greenville Arms is also a very comfortable resort-inn. Behind the main house which has homey, comfortable rooms with private baths or shared baths, the Carriage House has many more contemporary rooms all with private baths. There is a large beautiful lawn with shuffleboard, ping pong, horseshoes, badminton, lawn bowling, and a swimming pool.

"Oh, yes," said Ruth, "there are all kinds of things to do here. In the winter there is skiing at Hunter Mountain and Windham Mountain. In spring, we have trout fishing and hiking and there are many historical houses and places of history nearby. In the summer and fall, guests can go horseback riding, play golf or spend the day in the mountains if they like."

I could see that many of the guests could also enjoy sitting quietly on the front porch, reading a good book or watching the robins and bluejays flit among the maples, birches, and pines.

"Memorial Day is fun here," she said. "We always have a local parade, and there's a Naval ceremony at the village pond that has become quite a tradition. But we are a small town and far enough off the main roads to be quiet and unhurried."

Quiet and unhurried—those are two excellent words to describe this country inn which is a surprising resort-inn in the northern Catskills.

*GREENVILLE ARMS, Greenville, N.Y. 12083; 518-966-5219. A 20-room country inn with many resort features 20 miles from Catskill, N.Y., on Route 32. Modified American or European plans. Breakfast and dinner served to travelers by reservation only. Open every day; no meals served Thanksgiving and Christmas. Children most welcome; cribs, cots and highchairs available. Pets accommodated in nearby kennels. Pool and lawn sports on grounds. Riding, golf, skiing, hiking, backroading, antiquing nearby. Ruth Stevens, Innkeeper.*

*Directions: Exit N.Y. Thrwy. at 21B. (Coxsakie-New Baltimore). Turn left on 9W South 2 mi. to traffic light. Turn right on Rte. 81W 13 mi. to Greenville. Turn left at traffic light. Inn is second house on right. Via Taconic Pkwy., exit at Ancram on Rte. 82W over Rip Van Winkle Bridge and follow Rte. 23 to Cairo. Turn right on 32N, 9 mi. to Greenville.*

## HOLLOWAY HOUSE
### East Bloomfield, New York

I was headed west on Route 20 toward Buffalo and Niagara Falls. I had just visited the Sonnenberg Gardens in Canandaigua where there are over 5000 rosebushes set against a background of evergreens and a gleaming white Grecian temple—quite unusual for central New York State. Passing through the little town of East Bloomfield, I was attracted to a beautiful white clapboard house set back among large old maple trees. The sign told me that it was Holloway House, a country restaurant.

I pulled into the parking space, walked up the stone steps into the front hallway, and found myself in what resembled a most gracious home. There were several fireplaces and lots of comfortable furniture. Lunch was still being served, so I decided to remain and asked for a table by the window.

An attractive woman came over and introduced herself. That's how I met Doreen Wayne. She and Fred are the keepers of the Holloway House, and both of them were kind enough to give me a tour after lunch and explain how all of this came about.

"Peter Holloway, the village blacksmith, built this house in 1808 and operated it as a tavern," explained Doreen. "You can still see the many hand-hewn beams and square nails.

"In those days cooking was done in the cellar and as a kind of reminder this large open fireplace with a Dutch oven was built. In reconstructing our Country dining room, old homemade bricks were used, and we have tried to preserve the early 19th century feeling."

I found that the Waynes have been at the Holloway for 17 years and have a marvelous reputation for serving delicious and interesting food. Among the items on the menu is Killarney Kress, a sweet pickle sauerkraut which is green in color. They also serve homemade Sally Lunn bread every day. "The original recipe came from Bath, England," Doreen explained. "It's cooked with a great many eggs and has a cake-like texture. It's made daily by our baker who has been with us for twelve years."

The menu has unusual depth. It includes fried chicken and biscuits, baked ham and turkey. Fred said that turkey is the most popular item on the menu. There is also a choice of beef and seafood dishes as well. "Lots of people come on Sundays because that's when we serve black bottom pie and creamed mushrooms."

The kitchen at Holloway House is absolutely immaculate, roomy, and cool, and anyone is welcome to look in on it at any time. The kitchen floor and varnished tables are shining clean. I would feel at home dining there myself.

Still another interesting sidelight is the fact that there are many signature water glasses. These are fine grade glasses in which the customers names have been etched. "It is one of our ways of saying 'thank you' to people who have become such good friends," explained Doreen.

*HOLLOWAY HOUSE, Rtes. 5 & 20, East Bloomfield, N.Y. 14443; 716-657-7120. A country restaurant 8 miles west of Canandaigua, N.Y. No lodgings. Lunch and dinner served daily except Mondays. Open April 1-Dec. 1. Golf courses and Finger Lake Racetrack nearby. Fred, Doreen and Mildred Wayne, Innkeepers.*

*Directions: From N.Y. State Thruway take Exit 45, follow Rte. 96E 3 mi. to Victor N.Y. Go south on Victor-Holcomb Rd. 5 mi. Turn right at light in Holcomb then second left to Rte. 5 & 20.*

## LINCKLAEN HOUSE
### Cazenovia, New York

I was back at the Lincklaen House. The hour was 11:15 p.m. I had arrived at approximately 10 o'clock and found the ubiquitous Helen Tobin still at the inn. We sat in front of the parlor fireplace for a nice hour-long chat. One of the things that she mentioned was that people using Exit 34 on the New York State Thruway had the advantage of coming up Route 13 past Chittenango Falls which is just a few minutes away from Cazenovia.

"They are actually higher than Niagara," she said, "and it is such a beautiful spot. During the wintertime the ice formations are spectacular."

Guests staying at the Lincklaen House and meeting Helen for the first time frequently say, "Oh, I feel as if I have known you for a long time." This is because Helen has genuine warmth and consideration and the Lincklaen House reflects this feeling. It's this feeling, also, that keeps the paneled walls and ceiling as gleaming as the white tablecloths. She also insists on fresh flowers, crisp vegetables, hot popovers, hearty portions, lots of bath towels and, above all, a feeling of rapport with her guests.

"I try to talk with everyone while they're here," she said. "Many become good friends and I hear from them at Christmas." Speaking of Christmas, Helen has framed many of the Christmas cards from the Golden Lamb Inn in Lebanon, Ohio, and they hang in the lobby.

Helen was bubbling over with the news that her daughter, Barbara, was going to be married in April, and, of course, the reception would be at the inn. Still another daughter is in the hotel business and her son, Edward, is now at the University of Pennsylvania.

Cazenovia is one of the attractive towns along Route 20 in central New York state and its situation on a beautiful lake is an added attraction for Lincklaen House guests. The inn has been called the best example of the architecture of the first part of the 19th

century. Fortunately the classic Greek Revival lines have been well preserved.

The area has recreation for outdoor-minded guests in both summer and winter and there is especially good downhill and cross-country skiing nearby.

"Being an innkeeper is so much fun," Helen said as we walked through the dining room, faintly lighted by the last glow of the fireplace. "It's taken quite a while to have things right, but returning guests make it all worthwhile. Some say they were here the day the deer came through the side door; others remember the day that Ann was accepted at Cornell. It's just great."

I planned on being up and away before breakfast but Helen assured me that some provision would be made for me to have at least a bite before leaving.

"It's something we try to do for everyone who has to leave early in the morning," she said.

The "bite" proved to be warm rolls, fresh juice, eggs and coffee. Quite a send off!

*LINCKLAEN HOUSE, Cazenovia, N.Y. 13035; 315-655-3461. A 27-room village inn, 20 mi. east of Syracuse. Near several state parks, the Erie Canal Museum and the Canal Trail. European plan. Modified American plan upon request. Breakfast, lunch and dinner served to travelers daily. Open year-round. Tennis, golf, bicycles, Alpine and xc skiing nearby. Helen Tobin, Innkeeper.*

*Directions: From west on N.Y. Thruway, take Exit 34A, follow Rte. 481 south, take Exit 3E and follow Rte. 92 east to Cazenovia. From east on N.Y. Thruway, take Exit 34 and follow Rte. 13 south to Cazenovia. From Rte. 81, take Exit 15 (LaFayette) and follow Rte. 20 East, 18 mi. to inn.*

## OLIVER HOUSE
**Ancram, New York**

While I usually associate the Victorian style with a slightly overdone period of Americana, I found that the Oliver House had a refreshing spirit of modesty about it. True the porches, doorways and interior had the familiar embellishments, but they all seemed quite natural.

The entrance hall is flanked on the left by the Palm Room for dining which has several gorgeous chandeliers imported from Europe, bentwood chairs and two handsome potted palms reminiscent of the '90's. To the right there is a small sitting room with deep cushioned chairs and sofas and a welcome fireplace.

There are five Victorian-furnished bedrooms at the inn which share one large bathroom. Each of these rooms has been furnished individually in Victorian furniture of varying designs.

The menus from the Oliver House make most interesting reading. There is usually only one entree for dinner (two on weekends). The most popular ones are roast leg of lamb Bordeaux and breast of chicken roasted in champagne. This is a prix-fixe dinner which includes soup, some delicious homemade bread, and a choice of heavenly looking cakes which are offered on a teacart. There is no tipping permitted at the Oliver House.

However, all of these things only begin to tell the complete story about what is really going on in this interesting New York State village which is known as the Ancram Restoration. It is a new concept in historic preservation.

Along with the inn, there is the Ancram Opera House which is the home of the Gotham Light Opera Guild where live concerts and recitals are offered throughout the year. Across the village street is the Johann Strauss Atheneum which, among other things, contains the only operetta museum in the world. Here I found posters, playbills and photographs depicting the works of the great operetta composers such as Victor Herbert, Johann Strauss, Franz Lehar and many others. The second floor gallery is the scene of frequent frolics and balls throughout the year. I attended the Twelfth Night Frolic on January 8th which starred the Broadway entertainer Anne Francine. It was a gala evening with everyone in formal dress. The Atheneum also offers a film festival each weekend. Some of the upcoming films were "Sweet Adeline," the "Singing Marine," "Colleen," and "Madame Du Barry."

At the crossroads in Simon's General Store which dates back to 1874, and today has all kinds of beautiful china, sachets, soaps, elegant gifts, homemade apple and blueberry bread, date and nut bread, cheeses, candies and artificial flowers.

There is also Vauxhall, a restored Greek-Gothic villa complete with the beautiful period furniture and decorations.

The Ancram Restoration and all of the ideas, designing, innovations and inspiration come from two men, John-Peter Hayden, Jr. and Donald Richard Chapin. They are indeed lighted from within to restore and preserve an elegant Victorian way of life. Both Messrs. Chapin and Hayden are very much in evidence, and with all that they have to plan and supervise they still have time to chat with inn guests and share their enthusiasm.

For up-to-date information about the many different events at Ancram, I suggest that readers send their name and address to the Ancram Standard in Ancram, N.Y. 12502 for a complimentary copy of a sprightly eight-page paper which has it all.

*THE OLIVER HOUSE, Columbia County, Route 7 and N.Y. Rte. 82, Ancram, N.Y. 12502; 518-329-1166. A 5-room restored Victorian village inn midway between Salisbury, Conn., Hudson and Rhinebeck, N.Y., and Gt. Barrington, Mass. European Plan includes continental breakfast. Lunch and dinner served daily to travelers. Not especially for children. Small well-trained pets welcome. Ice skating and fishing on grounds, swimming, horseback riding, skiing, antiquing and backroading nearby. J.P. Hayden, Jr. and Donald Chapin, Innkeepers.*

*Directions: From New York City, Exit Taconic Parkway North at Jackson Corners, turn east and follow the signs 7 mi. to Ancram. From Massachusetts: turn west from Rte. 22 into Copake and turn right at the village clock following signs to Ancram.*

## SPRINGSIDE INN
### Auburn, New York

Barbara Dove and I were standing in front of the long list of things to do in the Finger Lakes District, all within a reasonable drive of the Springside Inn.

"Oh our guests seem to just love this," exclaimed Barb, "and everyone is grateful for the assistance." The list was on a wall-mounted scroll about four-feet long and included places to go antiquing, to rent boats, to bird watch, to rent bicycles, where to find churches, golf courses, museums and glass factories, how to reach the nearby Indian village, and 10 colleges in the area, where to play tennis, and a list of shops with unusual gifts and crafts.

It also listed trips to nearby wineries and many interesting activities for any season of the year.

We walked up the red-carpeted stairway to the second floor to look at several of the rooms which had been redecorated since my last visit. "Here's one that we finished last summer," she said, "and it has been occupied most every night. Would you believe we hung pictures and mirrors ten minutes before the first occupants arrived? It was sheer madness, but we made it."

Each of the lodging rooms is decorated to give a different feeling. One is in shades of pink with a pink bedspread and matching curtains. A friendly rocking chair is in front of the window overlooking the lake.

Another room has twin beds, Victorian furniture, and lamps

with red bows. By way of contrast, a room on the top floor is done in shades of tan and yellow with formal valances on the window, a Tiffany-type lamp, hooked rugs and twin beds.

We walked back down the stairs to the first floor pausing for a moment where the open staircase is L-shaped, and once again talked about how many weddings are held at the Springside and how many bridal bouquets have been tossed from this particular point in the stairway.

Barbara explained that about 85% of their overnight guests were traveling with *Country Inns and Back Roads*. "They seem to enjoy the food, our summer dinner theatre and, of course, our ducks," she said. "We've had comments about the comfortable mattresses, and quite a few guests have left notes praising our "breakfast-in-a-basket."

"We enjoy meeting so many people from all over the United States and Canada. Many of them came from Toronto and Montreal. They seem especially pleased to get a jar of our homemade salad dressing to take home."

We walked through the veranda on the front of the inn. "Oh, this has been a marvelous success," she said. "We really celebrated the Bicentennial here with red, white and blue flowers and were written up in the local newspaper. When you are recognized locally, you know you've arrived. However, we were much too busy to let it go to our heads."

I think that that last statement typifies the Springside Inn. It is one of the busiest places I have ever seen and Barbara and Bill Dove and their family and staff keep things humming at all times.

The Springside Inn, on the northern end of Owasco Lake, is one of the most beautiful spots imaginable in autumn. It is particularly enjoyable to drive along the lakeside roads where there are many farm stands offering apples, pumpkins, pears and other Finger Lakes fruits and vegetables.

"There aren't nearly as many people in the region at that time either," explained Barbara. "We like it because we have more of a chance to spend some time with our guests and take some day trips ourselves."

*SPRINGSIDE INN, 41 West Lake Rd., Auburn, N.Y. 13021; 315-252-7247. A 7-room country inn, 1 mi. south of Auburn with a view of Owasco Lake. In the heart of the historical Finger Lakes. Lodgings include Continental breakfast. Some rooms with shared baths. Dinner served to travelers daily except Mondays and Tuesdays. Closed Memorial Day, July 4th, Labor Day, Christmas and New Year's Day. Boating, swimming, bicycles on grounds. Golf, riding, Alpine and xc skiing nearby. Bill and Barbara Dove, Innkeepers.*

*Directions: From N.Y. Thruway, take Exit 40 and follow Rte. 34 south through downtown Auburn to Rte. 38. Follow Rte. 38 south to traffic circle at Lake and take 2nd exit right at West Shore of Owasco Lake. Drive ¼ mi. to inn.*

## OLD DROVERS INN
### Dover Plains, New York

It was a real country inn kind of evening in mid-October—just chilly enough to make a fire welcome. We were as hungry as bears. My son Keith came home from college, and the two of us drove down Rte. 22 through Millerton and Amenia. We turned off at a sign a few miles below the village of Dover Plains that said "Old Drovers Inn" and proceeded half a mile to a lovely inn built in 1750. Outside on the sheltered porch, there were piles of wood for the many fireplaces inside. A small blackboard informed us that the old inn was open for lunch and dinner from Thursday through Monday and that jackets for gentlemen were requested.

We stepped into a low-ceilinged dining room, and warmed ourselves by the delightful fire. The first things I noticed were the handsome hurricane lamps on each table. Innkeeper Trav Harris came forward, we talked for a minute, and because some of his guests for the night had not checked in as yet, we decided to make an immediate tour of the lodging rooms.

A succession of staircases took us to the top floor. Each bedroom had a different name which in some way described the room itself. For example, the Cherry Room had handsome antique cherry wood furnishings, and the Sleigh Room had a big 19th-century sleigh bed. There were designer sheets and fluffy down comforters on all the beds. On the walls were authentic period prints, and each bedroom had a wood-burning fireplace.

The second floor had a room set aside as a breakfast room for the inn's overnight guests. On the walls was a most distinguished group of murals.

Because there are just a few rooms at this inn, its real reputation, which is considerable, is based on food. With this in mind, we were happy to return below stairs and take a good long look at the menu which is written in chalk on a blackboard and hung up conveniently for every guest to peruse.

"There are several things we have been serving here for the past

30 years," said Trav. "Among them are the Old Drovers cheddar cheese soup, shrimp rarebit, partridge with stuffing, prime sirloin steaks, Indian curries and pheasant."

The other menu offerings that evening included chicken tarragon, calves sweetbreads, Norwegian river trout, casserole of Alaskan crabmeat Mornay, curry of turkey, steak and kidney pie, browned turkey hash with mustard sauce and roast duckling with Dutchess apple stuffing. By the way, their popovers were terrific. Reservations are advised on Saturday nights.

The Old Drovers Inn is an elegant and luxurious inn, and the tariff reflects this. A great deal of care is taken with the food, drink and table settings, and anyone dining here should set aside sufficient time to absorb the atmosphere and dine in a leisurely fashion. This is an intimate little inn, and Trav Harris personally oversees the service of each meal. I enjoyed the food and accommodations tremendously. It is a great country inn experience.

*OLD DROVERS INN, Dover Plains, New York 12522; 914-832-9311. A 3-room country inn midway between New York City and the Berkshires just off Rte. 22. European plan. Breakfast available to house guests. Closed on Tuesdays and Wednesdays and for 3 weeks prior to Dec. 30 each year. Luncheon served weekdays from noon to 3 p.m. Dinner served weekdays from 6-9 p.m., Saturdays and holidays from noon to 9:30 p.m., Sundays from 1-9 p.m. Located in historic Dutchess County in the scenic foothills of the Berkshires. Travis Harris, Innkeeper.*

*Directions: From New York follow I-684 which leads into Rte. 22. Go north to Dover Plains.*

## SWISS HUTTE
**Hillsdale, New York**

Jack McWilliams and I were returning from an innkeepers' meeting in the Poconos and decided to stop off at the Swiss Hutte for dinner. We found Tom and Linda Breen seated by the window with a view of the lighted Catamount Ski Area making plans for the summertime activities.

"We're going to have gardens everywhere," said Tom. "We'll have a garden of perennials, a wildflower garden and a rose garden. I'm planting flowers up and down the banks of the brook and we'll have them from early spring through late fall.

"We are also going to have an English croquet course which will be ready by July." I told him about the croquet course that is used by Michael and Penny Schmitt at the Inn on The Common in Craftsbury Common, Vermont. "Well, we will have to get together and have an inter-inn match," he said.

The Swiss Hutte is a continental-type inn in a hidden Berkshire valley right on the New York-Massachusetts line. It is actually in Hillsdale, New York but part of it is in Massachusetts.

There are two types of accommodations available. One is in the main building of the inn where there are country inn-type rooms. The other 15 rooms are in chalet-type motel units, each with its own balcony and with an excellent view of the mountains.

In spite of all the natural beauty of its surroundings the Swiss Hutte is probably best known for its food. Lunch and dinner are leisurely affairs with individually prepared dishes. Guests can choose from the menu written on large blackboards. On this particular visit these offerings included French pancakes filled with chicken, wiener schnitzel, sauerbraten, chicken diable, roast pork and sauerkraut, veal chops Normande, roast duckling a l'orange and sweetbreads in Bearnaise sauce.

The desserts, which by the way are included with the cost of the entree, had such temptations as creme caramel, meringue glace, French apple torte, cheescake, raspberry cream pie and chocolate mousse.

The cool fresh salad is delicately bathed in a perfect combination of oil, vinegar and condiments and the fresh French bread comes right from the oven.

In summer the Swiss Hutte has icy cold swimming in the mountain brook which flows through the property, and also provides a swimming pool with more temperate water. There are two all-weather tennis courts, a golf putting green and many opportunities to walk in the nearby forest.

It is an easy drive to Tanglewood and all the Berkshire summer attractions and is simply glorious during the fall foliage season. In winter, skiers can walk out of their room and in two minutes can be on the lift line in Catamount!

We had a very wonderful evening with Tom and Linda with lots of kidding about the flower gardens. We also arranged for a regional meeting of innkeepers to be held at the Swiss Hutte early in March, 1977. We would then enjoy lunch and a day-long discussion of innkeeping problems.

But Tom's mind was really on his flower garden."Do you realize that we were going to have over 300 different varieties of perennials? And we will also have Oriental poppies in many different colors. There will be three or four varieties of veronicas and many alpine flowers and phlox in all colors."

Linda, Jack and I just threw up our hands and agreed that there was nothing you could do with a man who was that crazy about flowers.

*SWISS HUTTE, Hillsdale, N.Y. 12529; 518-325-3333. A 21-room Alpine country inn overlooking Catamount ski area, 6 mi. from Gt. Barrington, Mass. Modified American plan omits lunch. Breakfast, lunch and dinner served to travelers daily. Closed month of April and from Nov. 15 to Dec. 15. Pool, tennis, putting green, Alpine and xc skiing on grounds. Tom and Linda Breen, Innkeepers.*

*Directions: From Boston, travel on Mass. Tpke. and take Exit 2. Follow Rte. 102 to Rte. 7. Proceed on Rte. 7 to Rte. 23. From New York City, follow Taconic Pkwy. and Rte. 23. From Albany, follow N.Y. Thruway and Taconic Pkwy. Inn is 10 mi. east of Pkwy. on Rte. 23.*

## THREE VILLAGE INN
### Stony Brook, New York

Whitney Roberts, resplendent in his Colonial costume, and I were enjoying a leisurely walk through and around the "3VI" late in the afternoon before the arrival of the many expected dinner guests.

"Well, we have made a few changes since you were last here," he said. "For one thing, as you see, we have redecorated the lobby and the main dining room and we've taken the small parlor, the one with the original old fireplace, and turned it into a Common Meeting Room for our guests. Now that we have a total of twenty-two rooms, we find our guests need a room for getting together among themselves."

We paused for a moment at the front desk where there is a display of Berkshire Traveller books. "A great many people from overseas come to stay here," he said. "Many of our Chinese, Japanese and German guests are here to visit our State University. They are all delighted to find our quiet little inn, and a great many of them follow your suggestion about going to the post office at noon to watch the wooden eagle flap its wings.

"Last winter we did something almost by accident and it turned out to be a wonderful idea. We pushed the snow away on the lawn in front of the inn and made our own ice skating pond. The young people from the village skated here almost everyday and evening, and our guests enjoyed watching them from the dining room windows. In warmer weather, as you can see, we have quite a few geese on the lawn and they are always popular."

The Three Village Inn is located in one of the most interesting, well-preserved towns on Long Island, about 60 miles from New York. It has a natural little harbor and is, today, a model village dominated by an architectural style called "Early Republican," which is characteristic of this section of Long Island.

The inn is located in a house originally built about 1785 by Jonas Smith, a man who made a million dollars in shipping and ship building. In recent years some very attractive cottages have been built facing the yacht club and marina, bringing the total of rooms available for guests to 22. Whitney explained that the modernization of these small cottages is now complete and they are available in both summer and winter

From the very beginning Nelson and Monda Roberts have placed a great deal of emphasis on the food they serve at the inn. They are very particular about some things including not using foil for baked pototoes and baking them in rotation through the evening, and using fresh vegetables whenever they are available. The menu is quite extensive and includes a great deal of fresh seafood as well as generous helpings of beef, pork, veal and lamb. The extra touch of serving fruit sherbet with the main meal is something that I have always enjoyed.

Desserts are always interesting with such things as apple crisp, homemade cakes, Indian pudding, and delicious fruit pies and tarts. They are all made in the inn's kitchen.

Besides walking the sandy beach behind the inn and watching the boats in the marina, there is a great deal to do in this area of Long Island which is very rich in Colonial history. A most interesting afternoon can be spent at the Suffolk Museum and Carriage House which contains a fine collection of horse-drawn vehicles.

Whitney and I finished our tour including my first glimpse of the newly decorated small cottages and returned to the front terrace. "I'm happy to say that my mother and father took a couple of days off last year, drove up to Massachusetts, and had lunch at Longfellow's Wayside Inn. They enjoyed meeting Innkeeper Frank Koppeis very much and I am hoping that there will be more time for them to travel to CIBR inns this year."

With Whitney taking to the country inn business like one of those famous Stony Brook ducks takes to water, I'm sure that Nelson and Monda will have time for many more visits.

*THREE VILLAGE INN, Dock Rd., Stony Brook, L.I., N.Y. 11790; 516-751-0555. A 7-room village inn with 15 adjacent cottage/motel accommodations, 5 mi. from Port Jefferson, N.Y., on Long Island's*

*historic north shore. Near Suffolk County Museum, Craft Center and Carriage Museum. European plan. Lunch and dinner served to travelers daily. Closed Christmas. No pets. Golf, swimming and boating nearby. Nelson and Monda Roberts, Innkeepers.*

*Directions: From L.I. Expressway, take Exit 62 and travel north on Nichols Rd. to Rte. 25A. Turn left on Rte. 25A and proceed to next light. Turn right on to Main St. and travel straight ahead to inn. Available from New England via L.I. ferries from Bridgeport during the summer. Ferry reservations advisable.*

## REDCOAT'S RETURN
### Tannersville, New York

The Redcoat's Return. I wondered what the significance of the name could be. I was on my way from the Berkshires to Tannersville, New York, in the nearby Catskill mountains. At the village of Catskill I turned west on Route 23A and immediately entered a land that reminded me of the Austrian resort village of Semmering with chalets and houses clinging precariously to the sides of cliffs, and deep gorges and waterfalls next to the road. In the winter it was spectacular with great sheets of ice hanging down from the rock ledges. I could imagine how beautiful it would be in summer.

Turning left at the traffic light in Tannersville I followed Greene County Route 16 past some old mountain resorts and eventually found my way to the intersection at Dale Lane. There on my right in the fields against a mountain backdrop was the four-story Redcoat's Return. It was a white clapboard building in excellent repair with a friendly porch on two sides.

As I parked my car, an Irish setter and a collie bounded up to make me feel welcome. I felt even more welcome when I stepped inside the front door and found a roaring fire and an imposing moose head hanging over the mantelpiece. "Welcome to Redcoat's Return," said a voice on my left and there was Peggy Wright. She and her husband Tom are the innkeepers of this rather fascinating country inn.

The first thing I did was to drop into a deep comfortable chair next to the fire and request a cup of tea. This gave me a chance to look around at this large living room which also doubles as a portion of the dining room. There were wooden shutters at the windows and a great many old prints, paintings and photographs on the walls. Overhead the beams were exposed and it was a perfect place to be on a cold winter afternoon. Rex, the Irish setter, apparently felt that way because he came in and was snuggled down already.

A tall sandy-haired man came striding into the room with his hand outstretched and said, "Hello, I'm Tom Wright. We're certainly glad to see you." I began to get a clue about the name of this inn from his very definite British accent, and when I inquired about it, he laughed and replied, "Oh, it is just our sense of humor. As you can see, I'm British, but I have been in this country a long time. Peggy and I thought this would be a great name for an inn in the Catskills. A lot of people comment on it."

There is another great innkeeping-family story here. Tom and Peggy and their children—Christine, 17, Max, 12, and Alex, 14— have put all of their hearts into keeping this inn.

"We were looking for a country inn to buy and came up here. We knew this just had to be the place," said Peggy. "We're 2000 feet high here and this section of the Catskills has some beautiful old homes and a private park nearby. When we saw the building and realized its potential, we all agreed we would leave the city and become country innkeepers."

While innkeeping may have been a new experience for the Wright family, Tom brings some very real experience as a chef. He was with the Cunard Line for a number of years and on the Queen Mary. He was brought up in England and did his apprenticeship at the Dorchester Hotel in London. He does all of the cooking and some of his dishes include prime ribs with Yorkshire pudding, poached fillet of sole, roast duck in orange sauce, steak and kidney pie and English style fish and chips. Desserts include chocolate mousse, sherry trifle and cheese cake.

There are 12 rooms in this inn, all of them with wash basins. Only a few have private baths. Tom and Peggy went over the redecorating plans which were going into effect in the spring of 1977. "We're going to preserve the best of what is really appropriate for the building," explained Peggy, "and make a few major changes that will provide more bathrooms." These lodging rooms are rather small and cozy and definitely of the country inn variety. There is an unusual sitting room on the first floor that has a very impressive collection of Hogarth prints including the "Rakes Progress" and other well-known works. It is a little room that inspires comment and conversation.

Comment and conversation are characteristic of the Redcoat's Return. After a day in the Catskills, walking, hiking, skiing or fishing, guests enjoy sitting on the porch in warmer weather or around the fire in cooler times and getting acquainted. Both Tom and Peggy are lively conversationalists and their interests are broad and varied.

I am mighty happy that that "redcoat" returned!

*REDCOAT'S RETURN, Dale Lane, Elka Park, N.Y. 12427; 518-589-6379. A 12-room English inn approx. 4 mi. from Tannersville, N.Y., in the heart of the Catskill Mts. Within a short drive of several ski areas and state hiking trails. European Plan. Lodgings include breakfast. Dinner served daily except Thursdays. Open from Memorial Day to Easter. No pets. Hiking, nature walks, trout fishing, croquet, skiing, swimming, ice skating, riding, tennis nearby. Tom and Peggy Wright, Innkeepers.*

*Directions: Exit 20 or 21 from N.Y. Thwy. Follow 23A to Tannersville; turn left at traffic light onto County Road 16. Follow signs to Police Center 4½ mi. Turn right on Dale Lane.*

# Pennsylvania

*I have always felt very close to Pennsylvania. Actually I was born in New York State just a few miles from the northern Pennsylvania border and the many relatives on my mother's side lived in places like Gillett, Jobs Corners, and Mansfield, Pa. What great family picnics we had on their farms. My maternal grandfather was a baggage master on the Tioga Point Railroad and often I have heard the story of how he jumped in a water barrel on a railroad bridge one freezing night, in order to avoid being hit by a train.*

*One of my most poignant memories of Pennsylvania goes back to the time when my father and I left about midnight in an old 1926 Buick to go across New Jersey, through the Delaware Water Gap and up through Scranton and Towanda to visit in Elmira. In Stroudsburg, Pennsylvania, we had a flat tire about 3 a.m. We changed it as fast as you could change an old rim tire, and then proceeded on down the road and blew another tire in about ten minutes. At that point we had to wait for the tire store to open up so he and I sat in the car and talked until dawn. In those days motoring was really motoring.*

## ACCOMAC INN
**Wrightsville, Pennsylvania**

Except for a brief interruption, there has been an inn operating on the banks of the Susquehanna River at this spot since 1775. It was originally known as "The Inn at Anderson's Ferry" and entertained many distinguished travelers throughout its long history. Samuel Adams, General Horatio Gates and Philip Livingston paused here on their way to and from meetings of the Continental Congress at York, Pennsylvania. Lafayette referred to Anderson's Ferry in a letter written in 1778 in which he said that he crossed the Susquehanna River at that point and that the river was full of ice.

After 160 years, on May 16, 1935, a fire that started in a pavilion nearby spread to the inn and unfortunately left only a smoldering foundation and memories of an historic past. Norman Pickle, the proprietor at that time, started to rebuild immediately, using fieldstone from the old Witmer Bridge in Lancaster County. By fall of that year the Accomac Inn was able to resume operations. Today, a plaque outside the restaurant describes the history of Anderson's Ferry.

The Accomac Inn is best described as an elegant country restaurant. It has no lodgings available. The menu is French, and everything is served with a most unusual and gracious flair. The offerings include fresh trout in puff pastry, breast of chicken served with prosciutto and artichokes, roast duckling in an orange sauce with wild rice, roast pheasant with chestnuts, steak Diane, and roast filet of beef stuffed with paté de fois gras with truffle sauce.

The waiters, in elegant black-tie attire which complements the 18th-century decor, prepare a great many dishes right at the table. The salads are made with fresh scallions and spinach, mushrooms, romaine lettuce, and other ingredients while the guests look on. Many of the entrées are cooked in the dining room in chafing dishes; and their most famous dessert, Bananas Foster, is prepared with great flair by the headwaiter.

The Sunday brunch menu includes crepes stuffed with creamed seafood and mushrooms, omelette provencale, eggs Benedict and chicken in puff pastry.

Lunch is served from mid-May to mid-September, and dinner is served year-round. Sunday brunch is one of the special events of the week.

Today the Accomac Inn is carrying on in the tradition so well preserved by the Inn at Anderson's Ferry, with the addition, of course, of quite a few sophisticated touches.

*ACCOMAC INN, P. O. Box 126, Wrightsville, Pa. 17368; 717-252-1521. An elegant country restaurant on the banks of the Susquehanna River 1½ mi. north of Wrightsville. No lodgings. Lunch served daily from mid-May to mid-September. Dinner served daily year-round from 5:30-10:30 p.m. Mondays through Saturdays and from 5-9 p.m. Sundays. Sunday brunch served from 12-3 p.m. Closed Christmas Day. Ernest Wickey Helmick, Innkeeper.*

*Directions: From Pa. Tpke., exit at Reading-Lancaster and follow Rte. 222 south to Rte. 30. Proceed on Rte. 30 west and exit at Wrightsville. From the south and west, travel on Rte. 83 to York, exit at number 9E. Proceed on Rte. 30 east and exit at Wrightsville. Turn north and follow the signs to inn.*

*Pennsylvania Dutch barn*

## CANDLEWYCK INN
### Green Lane, Pennsylvania

In last year's edition I wrote about attending a boys' preparatory school near Green Lane and how some of us used to leave after "lights out" via the fire escape to visit the local towns. I thought that the statute of limitations made my secret safe to reveal but I got a letter from the current headmaster jokingly calling me to task.

Some years after my escapades, Bob and Dorothy Smith and their son, Bob Jr., and daughter Barbara saw wonderful possibilities in making a country inn out of a very old farmhouse in Green Lane. They set about creating Candlewyck which takes its name from both the huge silo which is lit up like a candle at night and the dozens of candles which illuminate the interior.

Many wonderful things have happened for both the Smiths and their guests over the years.

For one thing, Barbara Smith became Barbara Schwind and in due time Bob Sr. and Dorothy had a grandson, Brian, who is very popular with inn guests and is a great conversationalist.

Barbara and Bob are very much a part of all of the activities at the inn and in a recent letter Dorothy spoke glowingly of what a boon Bob Schwind has been since he acts as maitre d' and host. He has also taken on the gardening chores.

After a few years of learning about other methods of cooking at other restaurants, Bob Jr. has rejoined the family as head chef. He has added many specials to the regular menu including beef Wellington, veal maison, fresh filet of sea trout St. Milo, frogs legs in wine sauce, and many other delicious entrees. Bob Jr.'s new wife,

Caroline, has also become part of the team as waitress and hostess.

In 1976 the waitresses donned Colonial dresses in honor of the bicentennial and I understand that they will continue to wear them in 1977.

The lodging rooms in Candlewyck are on the austere side, but many travelers, including myself, found them most welcome after a long day on the road. It is both the decor and the food which have made the inn extremely well known. Just imagine 135 candles casting their soft flickering glow in the twilight.

Candlewyck is quite close to Valley Forge and other historic places and many guests take day trips during their stay at Candlewyck. It is a fifty-minute drive from the center of Philadelphia. The Green Lane Reservoir is just a few minutes away where inn guests can rent boats and buy bait. It is stocked with trout and muskies and occasionally Bob Jr. cooks the day's catch for the lucky fisherman.

Among the letters I have received from guests visiting the Candlewyck is one from England which said in part: "The highlight of our tour during our visit to the United States was a few days of hospitality which we enjoyed at the Candlewyck Inn. This was increased as we got to know all the members of the family. We look forward to paying a return visit and I have suggested to my son, John, who lives in the United States, that he would be sure of a welcome should he decide to follow in our tracks. I think that a few lines from a little poem on innkeeping by Alfred Starratt might not be out of place: 'It is not the chairs and tables nor the shingles on the roof, but the wanting others happy, that furnishes the proof.' "

*CANDLEWYCK INN, Green Lane, Pa. 18054; 215-679-2998. A 9-room country inn, 17 mi. from Allentown. European plan. Lunch and dinner served to travelers daily except Mondays. Closed Christmas Day and New Year's Day. Bicycles on grounds. Tennis, fishing and Alpine skiing nearby. The Smith Family, Innkeepers.*

*Directions: From the Northeast Extension (Rte. 9) of Pa. Tpke., exit at Lansdale and turn right after toll gate. Follow Rte. 63 north to Rte. 29. Proceed north on Rte. 29 to Green Lane.*

### CENTURY INN
#### Scenery Hill, Pennsylvania

During the past few years as I have been visited and written to about the Century Inn, I have had a lot of fun talking about the French fried asparagus. Almost every year some reader writes and suggests I have made a printing error. Others say that they were so

intrigued with the idea they tried it at home themselves with varying results.

Nancy Scheirer said with a twinkle in her eyes, "I think that many of our guests think that it's the only vegetable we have. So I have prepared a list of vegetables for you to pass along for your readers. It includes corn or fruit fritters, brandied carrots, carrot pudding, scalloped cabbage, glazed stewed tomatoes and red cabbage. We also have French fried cauliflower, zucchini squash and green tomatoes as well as asparagus. Of course these are not all served on the same day but they are frequently the 'vegetable of the day.' "

The bicentennial celebration of the historic events that took place near the Century Inn will not take place until 1994, 200 years after the Whiskey Rebellion. The original Whiskey Rebellion flag is now framed and hanging over the mantelpiece at the Century Inn.

The inn is a beautiful old stone building with top floor dormers and, as far as I know, was built sometime prior to 1800. It was one of the famous inns on the National Pike which was a road authorized and financed by Congress to connect the East and West. This section which crossed Pennsylvania began in Cumberland, Maryland, thus earning the title of the Cumberland Road. It ends in Wheeling, West Virginia, which at that time was part of Virginia. Most of it is now U.S. 40.

The interior of the inn is filled with rare antiques and there is a story behind almost every piece. Most of them have been collected by Nancy Scheirer's mother and father, Mary Harrington and her late husband, Gordon. In the years that Nancy was growing up many inn guests made presents of their precious antiques to the Harringtons because the inn seemed to be the most appropriate place for them. Visitors always marvel at the Chippendale highboy which was brought from Carlisle, Pennsylvania, probably by Conestoga Wagon in the late 18th century. The carved shell at the top is upside down!

Today the Century Inn with its ten lodging rooms is best known by the people in western Pennsylvania as being an exceptional place to have lunch or dinner. People drive many miles to enjoy the roast turkey, spring chicken, roast stuffed pork chops, baked ham and breaded shrimp. They also favor the sweet potatoes, applesauce, whipped potatoes and even the crispy, tender waffles. Desserts include a varying selection of homemade pies as well as frozen pecan balls with butterscotch sauce and fresh strawberry shortcake.

But remember, French fried asparagus is not offered every day!

*CENTURY INN, Scenery Hill, Pa. 15360; 412-945-6600 or 5180. A 10-room village inn on Rte. 40, 12 mi. east of Washington, Pa., 35 mi. south of Pittsburgh. European plan. Breakfast served to house guests only. Lunch and dinner served to travelers daily. Closed approximately Dec. 21 until April 1. Contact inn for exact opening and closing dates. No pets. Nancy and Bob Scheirer, Managers, Mary W. Harrington, Innkeeper.*

*Directions: From the east, exit the Pa. Tpke. at New Stanton. Take I-70W to Rte. 917S (Bentleyville exit) to Rte. 40E and go 1 mi. east to inn. From the north, take Rte. 19S to Rte. 519S to Rte. 40E and go 5 mi. east to inn or take I-79S to Rte. 40E and go 9 mi. east to inn. From the west, take I-70E to I-79S to Rte. 40E and go 9 mi. east to inn.*

### FAIRFIELD INN
#### Fairfield, Pennsylvania

"I've simply got to tell you about what happened the day the wagon train came through Fairfield and stopped off long enough to have a meal." Nancy Jean Hammett and I were taking a few moments during one of our innkeepers' meetings in Rockport, Massachusetts, to catch up on all of the things that had been going on at the Fairfield Inn since my last visit. She and her husband, "Dr. Jim," and their five children have been lovingly restoring their beautiful stone inn, a portion of which dates back to 1757.

When I asked her about the family she replied, "Oh, everybody is just fine. It's great to have a family that pitches in and enjoys something exciting like keeping an inn. At the moment we are still busily painting the exterior stone walls. We are going to construct an old-fashioned shed as soon as possible, so that we can remove my garden tools from the last room to be redone on the first floor. We're planning to restore that to be a small dining room."

Since there are presently only two lodging rooms available (most of the time occupied by CIBR travelers), breakfast, lunch and dinner are the main activities at the Fairfield Inn. Chicken and biscuits, special apple dishes, fresh vegetables from the garden, frizzled "city" ham, crab cakes, fresh batter-dipped shrimp, fantastic homemade desserts including deep dish apple pie made with local apples, and served with a wedge of sharp cheese or a pitcher of cream are typical of the country menu.

The inn building has a long and fascinating history. The Miller family settled in this section in 1757. The front stone section was built in 1801 when Squire William Miller laid out the town of Fairfield. It became an inn in 1823, and has been one ever since.

Now this impressive, beautiful stone building is a landmark, not only for its esthetic and historical importance, but for country inn hospitality.

"But let me tell you about the wagon train," she said. "It stopped here for lunch. As you know, we call it 'dinner' here in southern Pennsylvania. We had all the plans made ahead of time. The townspeople were to open their homes to the people on the wagons and serve them a cold drink. Then they sent them over to our inn for their midday meal. We served hot chicken sandwiches, relishes, chips and homemade fresh cherry pie. We served 307 people in 45 minutes! The train included 57 wagons! It was a huge success in every way and everyone had such fun."

It looks to me that fun is one of the main features of Nancy Jean Hammett's Fairfield Inn.

*FAIRFIELD INN, Main St., Fairfield, Pa. 17320; 717-642-5410. A country restaurant near Gettysburg with 2 lodging rooms available. Breakfast, lunch and dinner served daily. Closed on major holidays, Sundays and last week in August. Dinner reservations advised. No pets. Nearby region is rich in history including Gettysburg Battlefield. Nancy Jean and Jim Hammett, Innkeepers.*

*Directions: Fairfield is 8 mi. west of Gettysburg on Rte. 116.*

### INN AT STARLIGHT LAKE
#### Starlight, Pennsylvania

"We think that being in show business has provided us with an excellent background for becoming innkeepers," said Jack McMahon. "We're certainly sensitive to the moods and needs of our guests, and after all, running a country inn is something like putting on a show — a different show every day, bringing all of the parts together into one continuous production."

The Inn at Starlight Lake is situated on a back road in the rolling hills of northeastern Pennsylvania. It has been in operation since 1909 and originally was intended to be a summer refuge for people living in New York and New Jersey. In May 1974 Jack and Judy McMahon bought it and resolved to preserve the character of the early period when it flourished.

The inn is a rambling, old-fashioned, comfortable place reflecting the accumulated furniture of years. The lobby is a big room with a fireplace in one corner and a piano and guitar in another corner. It looked like a good place for children. There's an indoor game room and four McMahons for company.

Along with the usual sports offered at resort-inns such as swimming, boating, canoeing, sailing, tennis and hiking, there is another family-type activity that I was glad to see. The inn has an extensive cross-country ski program with trails that run two, five and six miles into the natural forests of the area. The well-equipped cross-country ski shop can outfit anyone.

"We also have one of the largest wild deer herds in the area," said

Judy. "We often see deer from our front porch and from the dock in front of the lake. Many of our guests love the idea that the wild creatures are so close."

The food is most interesting. There are a number of German specialties including a Jager Schnitzel and Weiner Schnitzel. Some other dishes I sampled were cream of cauliflower soup, Hungarian goulash, sauerbraten, buckwheat cakes, and blueberry pie. "We like holidays here," said Judy, "when families gather for Thanksgiving and Christmas. We're open and everyone's welcome."

There is also great emphasis on serving only fresh meats and vegetables and homemade breads. Even the coffee is freshly ground before each pot is brewed.

I remember on my first visit we all sat around the fire vying with each other for points in a game of nostalgia. We began with old popular songs. Jack picked up the guitar and sang a few bars. Soon everyone was joining in.

The McMahons may no longer be in show business, but they are a smash in Wayne County, Pennsylvania.

*THE INN AT STARLIGHT LAKE, Starlight, Pa. 18461; 717-798-2519. A 35-room resort-inn (25 rooms in winter) located 5 mi. from Hancock, N.Y. Modified American and European plans available. Breakfast, lunch, dinner served daily between May 15 and April 1. Closed Easter if it falls within above dates. Swimming, boating, canoeing, sailing, fishing, hunting, tennis, hiking, bicycling, horseback riding, xc skiing and lawn sports on grounds. Canoeing, hunting, fishing, golfing nearby. Judy and Jack McMahon, Innkeepers.*

*Directions: From N.Y. Rte. 17, exit at Hancock, N.Y. Take Rte. 191S over Delaware River to Rte. 370. Turn right, proceed 3½ mi., turn right, 1 mi. to inn. From I-81, take exit 62 and go east on Rte. 107. Turn left on Rte. 247 to Forest City. Turn left on Rte. 171, go 10 mi. to Rte. 370. Turn right, proceed 12 mi. Turn left, 1 mi. to inn.*

## MOSELEM SPRINGS INN
### Moselem Springs, Pennsylvania

As I look back on the years that I have been writing this book, one of my happiest memories is of the day I met Walter and Madeline Stoudt, the innkeepers at Moselem Springs Inn. The three of us instantly became friends, and I am happy to say that the friendship has continued to grow over the years.

The Stoudts both have Pennsylvania Dutch backgrounds, and they and the Moselem Springs Inn are the antitheses of the commercialism and exploitation that I sometimes see in southeastern Pennsylvania. There is enough of an accent in their speech to make it distinctive, and their good humor and boundless optimism are most infectious.

These were a few of the reasons why I was anticipating my visit with them with such pleasure. I drove east from Harrisburg on Route 22 shortly before lunch time on an early fall day. I turned off the Interstate at Shoemakersville (Route 61) and continued south to Route 662 where I made a left turn. Route 662 is one of Pennsylvania's most pleasant back roads. It winds among sprawling farmhouses, orchards, grazing cattle, and marvelous barns. It drops down out of the hills and comes to the four corners where the inn is located.

There were corn stalks tied around the inn's pillars and pumpkins on the porch. The many cars in the parking lot indicated that quite a few people had stopped there for lunch.

The Moselem Springs building has stood at the four corners since the mid-1800's. It has served a number of purposes over the years, but certainly none more noble than its present one of providing excellent food for travelers and local people. There are no lodging rooms available, but the Stoudts can recommend nearby accommodations if necessary.

At luncheon Walter was full of new ideas. "You know, we have a great many friends, and people come here for lunch or dinner frequently, so naturally we can't rest on our laurels. We've got to keep adding new dishes to the menu and new ideas for serving the food. We try to do as many extra things as possible."

Madeline joined in, "These squares of cinnamon graham crackers spread with whipped lemon butter are a good example. Serving these started as an extra, but they are now included as part of every meal."

Walter said, "Another one of our unusual offerings is Dutch pickled tripe which you don't find very often. We also have smoked beef sausage served with apple fritters and horseradish, and corn pie served with hot buttered milk."

"Some of the foods we serve are sold in our meat shop including the smoked meat, cheese, molasses, ham and sausages," added Madeline.

"Many of our guests who come here for the first time are surprised that we are not open on Fridays and Saturdays, but after we explain that it is because of our religious persuasion, they always understand, and our business on other days is fantastic," said Walter. This is also true of the Asa Ransom House in Clarence, New York.

My lunch, fresh flounder amandine, was finished, the Stoudts had to get back to work, and I had to continue on my way. I promised to return next year. After 11 years it has become a delightful habit.

*MOSELEM SPRINGS INN, R.D. #3, Box 10, Fleetwood, Pa. 19522; 215-944-8213. An historic country inn restored to 19th century opulence on U.S. 222, 13 mi. from Reading and 18 mi. from Allentown. No lodgings. Lunch and dinner served daily except Fridays and Saturdays. Full dinners served all day Sundays. Closed Christmas. Open year-round. Walter and Madeline Stoudt, Inn-keepers.*

*Directions: From I-76 and Rte. 22, exit at Rte. 100 and travel south to Rte. 222. Follow Rte. 222 south to Rte. 662. Inn is located at this junction.*

## OVERLOOK INN
### Canadensis, Pennsylvania

Right from the very start I have always maintained that one of the things that sets country inns apart from other accommodations and restaurants is "people"—people who keep country inns, and guests who enjoy being in country inns.

This time the combination was absolutely perfect. The inn-keepers of the Overlook Inn are Bob and Lolly Tupper who purchased the inn relatively recently, and brought with them not only

some experience as innkeepers, but also a tremendous amount of concern and involvement with their guests.

During the weekend of my visit, four of the guests were Mr. and Mrs. Conrad Arensberg of Harrisburg and Mr. and Mrs. Jerald Roeder of Pittsburgh.

The Arensbergs and Roeders were old friends and visiting country inns, especially those in CIBR, was one of the things they had in common. This time they had arranged to meet at Overlook and spend the weekend trekking about the Poconos and looking for old railroad bridges.

As soon as Bob and Lolly introduced all of us, everybody started talking at once about country inns that we had visited or would like to visit, and the conversation carried well through the afternoon, dinner, and into the evening.

I was thoroughly familiar with all the physical features of the Overlook Inn since I had included it in CIBR a few years ago. However, it had been omitted in recent editions because of the change in ownership. This was my visit to meet the new owners, Bob and Lolly, and it was a success from start to finish.

The location of the inn in the fragrant pine, blue spruce and locust forests of the Poconos was as beautiful as I remembered. The cardinals, quail, and robins still flitted about and the rhododendron and mountain laurel, famous in the Poconos, seemed even more prolific than ever.

The very pleasant, typical country inn rooms were much the same with their crocheted bedspreads and homey type furnishings. The Victorian antiques which were generously placed throughout the inn, had been augmented by Bob and Lolly's own collection, which was considerable.

I think it is fair to say that all of us rhapsodized about the food prepared by Chef Joseph Vibercik, an Americanized Czechoslovakian who speaks five languages. In a conversation I had with him after dinner he said, "I love to cook, and I love to cook here because people who come here seem to have such big appetites and therefore appreciate my food that much more."

Chef Vibercik seems to have an unending supply of menu ideas. When I asked him what he liked to cook the most he reeled off everything from duckling with French orange sauce to marinated chicken. He has a considerable assortment of desserts including homemade cheesecakes and fresh fruit pies. There is, wonder of wonders, a delicious rice pudding which is very hard to find these days.

Though it rained from Friday night to Sunday morning, all the guests seemed to have a most enjoyable time. It was a little too chilly to go swimming in the pool, but as one couple said, "We love to walk in the rain, especially in the forest." The antique shops in the vicinity were open and some people sat by the fire reading books, doing puzzles, or playing cards.

I left early Sunday morning to a quasi-tearful waving of handkerchiefs by my new-found friends, plus Bob and Lolly. I couldn't have asked for a better country inn experience.

*OVERLOOK INN, Dutch Hill Rd., Canadensis, Pa. 18325; 717-595-7519. A 28-room resort-inn in the Poconos, 15 mi. from Stroudsburg, Pa. 17 rooms without private baths. Mod. American Plan. Dinners served to travelers. Open every day of the year. Not ideal for children. No pets. Pool, archery, shuffleboard, bocci, hiking on grounds; golf, tennis, ice skating, downhill and xc skiing, indoor tennis, antiquing, backroading, summer theatre nearby. Bob and Lolly Tupper, Innkeepers.*

*Directions: From New York City take George Washington Bridge to I-80, west to Exit 52, follow 447 North through Canadensis to first traffic light. About ½ mi. past traffic light, turn right on to Dutch Hill Rd., 1½ mi. to inn.*

## THE PINE BARN INN
### Danville, Pennsylvania

"Pleasantly surprised," is one of the most frequent comments I have received from readers who have stopped at the Pine Barn Inn located in the middle of Pennsylvania. Another comment is that it is very unusual to find fresh seafood being served this far from the sea. "Well, fresh it is," said Shube Walzer. "It is delivered fresh twice a week and we never offer frozen seafood items on our menu."

The Pine Barn is another family-oriented country inn, and both Shube and his son Marty realized a dream when they completed the restoration of a large 19th century Pennsylvania barn in 1967. A considerable amount of the original heavy stone walls were preserved, as well as the exposed beams and pillars. Today the dining room has handsome reproductions of Pennsylvania Windsor chairs, candles on each table and a scattering of old country furniture to add to the atmosphere. One dining room has wooden shutters on the inside, polished stone floors and heavy wooden pillars and posts to continue the Pennsylvania barn theme.

The accommodations at the Pine Barn are quite unusual. Although somewhat motel in style, the rooms are furnished with attractive cherry reproductions and there are many thoughtful touches which I always enjoy finding in a country inn including magazines and books for guests to read. There are also plants in the rooms.

The menu at the inn includes homemade pies, breads and rolls, and other dishes such as roast beef, roast leg of lamb, and salads that are large enough to actually be a whole meal.

The last time I saw Marty he told me about a marvelous party they had the night after Thanksgiving. "Since we are close to Penn. State and they were playing number one-ranked Pittsburgh, we rented two sets of bleachers from our high school and set them up in one dining room with a television suspended from the ceiling. On the porch we had a Dixieland Band and three more televisions in the main dining room. For non-football fans we kept one quiet dining room. Waitresses wore cheerleader outfits and bartenders had football jerseys. About 300 of us had a great time and at midnight we invited everybody into our kitchen for mushroom omelets."

One of the memorable features about the Pine Barn is the unusual number of flowers. When I mentioned this to Marty he laughed and said "I tell people that this is one of the few inns with an outside horticulturist (my father), and an inside one (my wife, Barb). Dad's planning is a study of timing. From tulips and daffodils in the spring, to our fall marigolds, we are a virtual blanket of color with Dad out early each morning urging roses and peonies to fill the gaps. Our guests were amused to find tomatoes and brussel sprouts outside their door intermingled with snapdragons, dahlias, zinnias and four o'clocks.

"Barbara keeps the sun porch and all the tables filled with plants

and flowers from the garden, and the plants in the rooms seem to do very well."

Another real country inn touch at the Pine Barn is the Barn Swallow Gift Shop. It is now two years old and guests "ooh and ah" over the unique gifts, especially those that represent the nearby central Pennsylvania crafts. It began with only a few handmade dolls, wreaths and candles, and has been growing steadily. I bought two very attractive dolls on my last visit and also a jar of local honey.

Located just off I-80, Danville is a convenient distance from the Tavern in New Wilmington, Pennsylvania, near the Ohio border and several other country inns in this book in the Pocono Mountains. It's also a very short, pleasant drive to the Inn at Starlight Lake to the north. Danville is close to three colleges, Bucknell, Susquehanna, and Bloomsburg.

Incidentally the Pine Barn Inn shares with the Bay Hill Club in Orlando, Florida, a CIBR "first." They are brother and sister inns. Marty is the innkeeper for the Pine Barn and his sister, Winnie, is at the Bay Hill. Shube who has a winter home at Bay Hill says, "It certainly is a full-time job keeping my eye on both of them."

*PINE BARN INN, Danville, Pa. 17821; 717-275-2071. A picturesque country restaurant with 45 attractive motel rooms in central Pennsylvania. European plan. Breakfast, lunch and dinner served daily except Christmas, July 4th and Memorial Day. Pets allowed in some rooms. Near several colleges and historic sites. Golf, tennis, water skiing, sailing, and canoeing nearby. Martin and Barbara Walzer, Innkeepers.*

*Directions: From Exit 33 of I-80, go south 3 mi. to Danville. Take a left at the first traffic light. Proceed 10 blocks and follow signs to Geisinger Medical Center. Pine Barn adjoins the Center.*

## THE PUMP HOUSE
### Canadensis, Pennsylvania

Twelve years ago the Drucquer Family, who had lived and worked in New Jersey for a number of years, were touring the Poconos looking for some property for a second home. As they came up the road near Skytop they saw a farmhouse for sale. It sat on about seven acres of rolling land. There were huge trees, a sizable lawn, and, as an extra bonus, a view of the mountains from the front porch.

"As I think back now," explained Todd Drucquer, "the idea came to almost all of us at the same time. What a wonderful place for a country inn!"

To make a long story short, they purchased the property, refurbished it, decorated it with loving care, and the Pump House Inn is now a way of life for all Drucquers including Todd and his wife, Penny, his brother Mark, his father Henri and Todd's two growing sons, Chris and Cole.

Almost from the start the Pump House has had a reputation for innovation. For example, the first menu reflected the Drucquer family's French heritage, and even today the day's specials listed on the blackboard are written in French. Another novel idea was to create a dining room that actually had a waterfall in it. "This came about because there was one large rock that we just couldn't move," said Todd. "So we decided to make it into a waterfall. It is called the 'Thirsty Deer Room.' "

Other changes came with the passing years, and I've been sharing them with readers since my first visit in the late sixties.

In 1976 the Pump House established the Saturday night fixed-price dinner. They offer a choice of entrees including roast rack of lamb Persille, roast tenderloin Chasseur, duckling Normande and red snapper poached in leeks and wine. There is a wide choice of appetizers including shrimps in beer batter served in a pungent fruit sauce, fresh artichokes and smoked trout. All of the soups are homemade and there is a large assortment of fresh vegetables.

This year's innovation involves Thursday evenings during winter until the middle of March. Todd explained that that's when they have Epicurean evenings. We take only twelve people, and all bookings have to be made by the previous Monday night so that Mark Kaplan, our chef, can plan the meal in the best possible way. We serve two hors d'oeuvres, one cold and one hot. It might be cold salmon aspic and stuffed mushrooms with lobster and crabmeat. Then there is a soup course which is sometimes lobster bisque or pumpkin soup. This is followed by a fish course, something simple like filet of sole. Then there is a meat course which is usually a steak, tournedos of beef, or rib eye steak with green peppers and onions that is prepared in a chafing dish at the table. We round the meal out with fresh vegetables, homemade bread, a salad, dessert and coffee. There are eight courses in all and everything is done in a leisurely elegant manner. It's more expensive than the average country inn dinner."

Although the emphasis at the Pump House is on the menu, there are four very pleasant country inn bedrooms on the second floor, some of which are suites with baths. When all the rooms in the inn are booked, Todd directs people to the Overlook Inn which is just around the corner or to the Sterling Inn which is just a few miles away. Both of these are also in CIBR.

The Pump House is a sophisticated country inn in the Poconos. Its food and ambiance have received accolades from many well-known publications including *Gourmet Magazine* and the *New York Times*. One reporter said that the cuisine outranked any other resort-dining room in the Poconos.

*THE PUMP HOUSE INN, Canadensis, Pa. 18325; 717-595-7501. A 4-room country inn high in the Poconos, 1½ mi. north of Canadensis village and 16 mi. northeast of Stroudsburg. European plan. Sophisticated country dining. Dinner served to travelers daily. Closed Mondays in summer and Mondays and Tuesdays in winter. Closed Christmas and New Year's Day. Bicycles and golf nearby. The Drucquer Family, Owners. H. Todd Drucquer, Innkeeper.*

*Directions: From the north, follow I-84 to Rte. 390 south. Inn is located 13 mi. south on Rte. 390. From the south, follow I-80 to Rte. 191. Travel north on Rte. 191 to Rte. 390 north. Follow signs to Canadensis. Inn is 1½ mi. north from light in Canadensis.*

## 1740 HOUSE
### Lumberville, Pennsylvania

I've just found a new word to include among the adjectives describing Harry Nessler and his little inn on the banks of the Delaware just above New Hope, Pennsylvania. It's "fastidious."

The 1740 House is one of the "most discovered" country inns. Guests send him dozens of letters each month and Harry's scrapbook has a truly impressive number of excellent notices from national and international newspapers and magazines.

I've culled a few of the many complimentary phrases: "He (Nessler) combs the grounds with the magnifying glass eyes of a protective owner"; "The nicest place to be is in that room with the view"; "Big beds, thick towels"; "You can sit with your feet up on the railing and watch the river lazing by"; "He is a perfectionist"; "Chocolate mousse with real whipped cream"; "Nothing ersatz"; "Food painstakingly prepared resulting in Cheshire grins on the faces of the guests."

But Harry will be the first one to say that you cannot live on press notices alone. It's performance that counts.

And performance is one thing that Harry understands. I've received dozens of letters about the 1740 House since my first visit many years ago, most of whom praise Harry for his ability as a raconteur and host. Readers tell me that they are entranced with Harry's stories and his courtly manner.

However, not everyone appreciates Harry. Some people find

that his single-minded approach to running a country inn doesn't fit in with their preconceived notions. "We have no radios, no clocks, no telephones in our lodging rooms," he says, somewhat dogmatically, "and we expect our guests to behave like ladies and gentlemen at all times. This is my house and I consider people who come to the inn as my house guests."

Harry is also very firm on the subject of reservations. For one thing, weekend reservations must include two nights. Usually these are booked well in advance. It is also necessary to have dinner reservations in the rather tiny dining room.

In many ways, Harry Nessler and Rush Wray, the indomitable innkeeper at the Nu-Wray Inn in Burnsville, N.C., are very much alike. Both of them march to the beat of their own drum.

Lodging rooms at this canal and riverside inn are in barns and stables which were part of a farm until a few years ago. There are original paintings on the wall, extremely tasteful furnishings and a remarkable blending of fabrics and textures. Each room has air conditioning and its own balcony or patio facing the beautiful Delaware River. There is also a small but welcome swimming pool.

From among the many letters that Harry receives, here is one with much originality:

*"Your country inn is sure perfection,*
*Its slightest flaw defies detection.*
*And you, sir, host extraordinaire,*
*Delight your guests with talents rare.*
*Our memories which serve us well*
*Recall no finer three-day spell*
*Than that just spent in quarters fair*
*Beside the dark, sparkling Delaware!"*

*1740 HOUSE, River Rd., Lumberville, Pa. 18933; 215-297-5661. A 24-room riverside inn, 6½ mi. north of New Hope, in the heart of historic Bucks County. Lodgings include breakfast which is served to house guests daily; dinner served daily except Sundays and Mondays, by reservation only. Open year-round. Pool and boating on grounds. Golf and tennis nearby. Harry Nessler, Innkeeper.*

*Directions: From N.Y.C., travel south on N.J. Tpke., and take Exit 10. Follow Rte. 287 north to Easton exit. Proceed west on Rte. 22 to Flemington, then Rte. 202 south over Delaware Toll Bridge. After an immediate turn onto Rte. 32N, drive 5 mi. to inn. From Pa. Tpke., exit at Willow Grove and proceed north on Rte. 611 to Rte. 202. Follow Rte. 202 north to Rte. 32 and turn north to inn.*

## STERLING INN
**South Sterling, Pennsylvania**

"Do country inns change very much?" That is a question that I am frequently asked. The answer is that of course they have to make progress with the times but hopefully there are some things which never change. To show what I mean I would like to share with you a letter from a gentleman who lives in Ambler, Pennsylvania:

"I was surprised and delighted to read about the Sterling Inn in your book. Because I have such an intimate connection with the inn I hope you will forgive what may turn out to be a rather long letter.

"I went to the Sterling Inn every year from 1917 to the late 1930's. My father was a notable dry fly trout fisherman and South Sterling was about 50 miles from our Wilkes-Barre home.

"The inn was an old-fashioned country boarding house frequented by a number of fishermen and their families as well as the usual William Dean Howells kind of front porch sitters. The food was plentiful and the rooms were comfortable. The place was pleasant, peaceful and quiet except for the presence of noisy little boys having fun, especially on the Fourth of July. The air was pure, the Wallenpaupack Creek was fast and clear, the fishing was good. We swam in what had been an ice pond behind the house (it is still there) fed partly by the stream and partly by springs. We built rock dams across the stream and walked for miles in all directions. Sometimes as a special treat we were allowed to walk a mile or so to the post office. The local churches had fairs where hot dogs were sold and 50¢ was all a boy needed to be reduced to a pauper in less than an hour. It was a great place for a kid.

"I remember it as the only place in the world that made oatmeal that I liked. It was cooked all night on an old coal stove and covered with real cream that came from the morning's milking.

"We were still going to the Sterling when Mrs. Julian took over and I have known Carmen Arneberg for a long time.

"Excuse this flow of nostalgia. Only iron self-control keeps me from amplifying it beyond all decent limits. I simply had to respond to you about a place that we both like and about which you have written so charmingly. Many thanks for the happy remembrances you have stirred up."

I think that that summarizes the continuing good things about the Sterling Inn, except that I don't think they cook the oatmeal on a coal stove!

The accommodations, of course, are one of the things that have changed and the rooms and sitting rooms are all attractively furnished. They are mentioned frequently in letters to me.

There is also considerable amount of attention given to entertaining guests. There is something happening almost every night such as singing, movies or lectures.

However, there are no changes in the really important things like the clear air, the gurgling creek, rock dams, the quiet Pocono walks, plentiful food and even some noisy little boys!

*STERLING INN, Rte. 191, South Sterling, Pa. 18460; 717-676-3311. A 69-room secluded Pocono Mountain Inn, 8 mi. from I-84 and 12 mi. from I-380. American plan. Reservation and check-in office closes at 10 p.m. Breakfast, lunch and dinner served to travelers daily. Breakfast served 8-9 a.m.; lunch served 12:30-1:30 p.m.; dinner served 6-7:15 p.m. No liquor served. Open from May 1 through Oct. 26. No pets. Swimming, putting greens, shuffleboard and woodland walks on grounds. Golf courses and horseback riding within short driving distance. Henry and Carmen Arneberg, Innkeepers.*

*Directions: From I-80, follow I-380 to Rte. 940 to Mount Pocono. At light, cross Rte. 611 and proceed on Rte. 196 north to Rte. 423. Drive north on Rte. 423 to Rte. 191 and travel ½ mi. north to inn. From I-84, follow Rte. 507 south through Greentown and Newfoundland. In Newfoundland, pick up Rte. 191 and travel 4 mi. south to inn.*

## THE TAVERN
### New Wilmington, Pennsylvania

The year was 1973. For years I had been fascinated with the "plain people" who live in eastern Pennsylvania. These include the Amish, Dunkards, Moravians and Schwenkfelders. I had always enjoyed the back roads of Lancaster and Berks counties and admired the picture-book farms and industrious people.

Now at the western end of Pennsylvania, I was once again in "Dutch Country." I had heard there was a sizable community of Amish here but I was surprised at the scope.

The purpose of my visit was to meet Mrs. Ernst Durrast and visit The Tavern in New Wilmington. When I drove through the town, I saw the familiar black buggies and plain dress of these pious folk who originally fled from Europe in the 18th century to obtain religious freedom.

"Oh, yes," Mrs. Durrast explained over a cup of tea, "this is Amish country, and they are a people who are quite proud of their ancestry. I hope that while you're here you'll drive out to the countryside to see those neat farms and spotless buildings." We talked about New Wilmington and Westminster College and some of the joys of living in western Pennsylvania. "Well, I've had this inn for forty-two years," she said. "and I just can't imagine living anywhere else. This is a lovely little town. I like it especially because there's a constant flow of young people from the college."

The talk then shifted to the startling number of entrees on the luncheon menu. Just for fun, I counted twenty-seven, plus an appetizer, vegetables, fritters, salad, rolls, dessert and a beverage. It was real country fare including gourmet beef balls, creamed chicken on a biscuit, cabbage rolls, grilled smoked pork chops, ham steaks, cheese and cheese souffle with creamed chicken.

On the dinner menu I found even more entrees including roast leg of lamb, stuffed pork chops, lamb kabob, red snapper and a surprising amount of fresh fish for an inn so far from the ocean.

Lodgings at the Tavern are rather simple, but very clean.

"It wonders me," said Mrs. Durrast, borrowing a quaint Amish saying, "why it has taken you so long to find us."

Well, thanks to Clare and Lucy Dee Dee of Grand Rapids, I did find the Tavern back in 1973.

*THE TAVERN, Box 153, New Wilmington, Pa. 16142; 412-946-2020. A bustling country restaurant on the town square with 5 sleeping rooms in a lodge directly across the street. European plan. Lunch and dinner served daily except Tuesdays. Reservations required. Closed Thanksgiving and Christmas. Sports and cultural events at Westminster College nearby. Mrs. Ernst Durrast, Innkeeper.*

*Directions: From I-80, take Exit 1-S, and follow Rte. 18 south to Rte. 208. Proceed east on 208 to town square. From I-79, follow Rte. 208 west for 14 mi. to New Wilmington.*

# New Jersey

*The Visitors Guide to Cape May, New Jersey written by Jane and Donald Timmons says that "if the visitor has been to Cape May before, their return is no accident. It is the first visit, the visitor should be advised that Cape May can become habit forming. However, it is in no way hazardous to health. Many visitors have made it a lifetime habit."*

*The discovery of Cape May as a resort for people from nearby Philadelphia and Baltimore began in 1840 and 1850. Steamboat travel from Philadelphia became so popular that runs were being made daily, and trains began to compete with the boats after 1833.*

*Five presidents and one president-to-be resorted here when Cape May's fame was at its height. Abraham Lincoln may have started the trend some twelve years before he was to become president. Subsequent Presidents included Grant, Chester A. Arthur and Benjamin Harrison.*

*Biking began at Cape may in the Gay Nineties. Bikes were so prevalent here by 1896, that the City Council adopted regulations to control the situation. Along with ocean swimming, it is the principal recreation.*

*Today Cape May is probably best known for its famous Historic District and the Visitors Guide includes a map and many pictures of the beautifully preserved and restored Victorian homes and "gingerbread castles."*

## THE MAINSTAY
Cape May, New Jersey

Now here is a CIBR "first." Inns have changed hands or gone out of business, but here is an inn where the location was changed but not the name.

I've written about Tom and Sue Carroll and their rambling old house in Cape May, New Jersey. Now the Mainstay has moved a few blocks away, still in the heart of Cape May's Historic District, one block from the beach and two blocks from the shopping mall. Here is what Tom and Sue have to say about the new Mainstay:

"The building is an Italian villa built in 1856 by wealthy Southern planters to serve as a very elegant gambling club. The first operator of the club, a Mississippi River showboat minstrel, employed a lady to rock on the front porch and watch for the police. If she rocked violently the gamblers inside would quickly stash their evidence and when the police arrived they would be having a harmless musicale.

"About 1896 the house was sold to a wealthy Philadelphia family who added a wing off the back to house six maids. During their ownership, John Wanamaker often dined at the house and James Cardinal Gibbons, the first American Cardinal, spent an entire summer.

"We bought it from a retired Baptist minister who has run it as a guest house for nearly thirty years.

"Many of the furnishings are original pieces, custom-built for the house. A pair of matching loveseats and two brass chandeliers are identical to those found in a plantation in Natchez, Mississippi. The copper bathtub framed in wood is like one in Washington Irving's home which we have visited.

"In addition to the ten-foot mirrors, ornately carved head-boards, and marbletop dressers, there are some most unusual Victorian features. Under the beds are chamber pots which roll out on wooden trays! We also have the original mosquito nets which attach to small pulleys in the ceilings.

"We'll serve breakfast in our grand dining room except in summer when we will use the broad veranda. We will also serve afternoon tea at 4 p.m. For those who aren't staying with us, we have a tour of the first floor at 3:30 each day and then visitors may join the house guests for tea.

"We will be able to offer a variety of guest rooms; some of them are most elegant and spacious with 12 foot ceilings, and others in the maid's wing are small and cozy. We think our guests will enjoy using the parlor which extends the full length of the house and boasts a marble fireplace and a huge Chickering piano. The veranda will have rocking chairs and baskets of flowers and we will probably set up a croquet game in the garden. We have great plans for the cupola. Those brave enough to ascend the ladder will be rewarded by a grand view of the town and the ocean."

Congratulations, Tom and Sue. I greatly enjoyed the old Mainstay, but the new one is terrific!

*THE MAINSTAY INN, 635 Columbia Avenue, Cape May, N.J. 08204; 609-884-8690. A 10-room inn in a well preserved Victorian village just one block from the ocean. Modified American plan. Breakfast served to house guests. Open every day of the year from March to December. No pets. Bicycles on grounds. Boating, swimming, fishing, riding, golf, tennis and hiking nearby. Tom and Sue Carroll, Innkeepers.*

*Directions: From Philadelphia take the Walt Whitman Bridge to the Atlantic City Expy. Follow the Atlantic City Expy. to exit for Garden State Pkwy., south. Go south on the Pkwy. which ends in Cape May. The Pkwy. becomes Lafayette St.; turn left at first light onto Madison. Proceed 3 blocks and turn right onto Columbia. Proceed 3 blocks to inn on right side.*

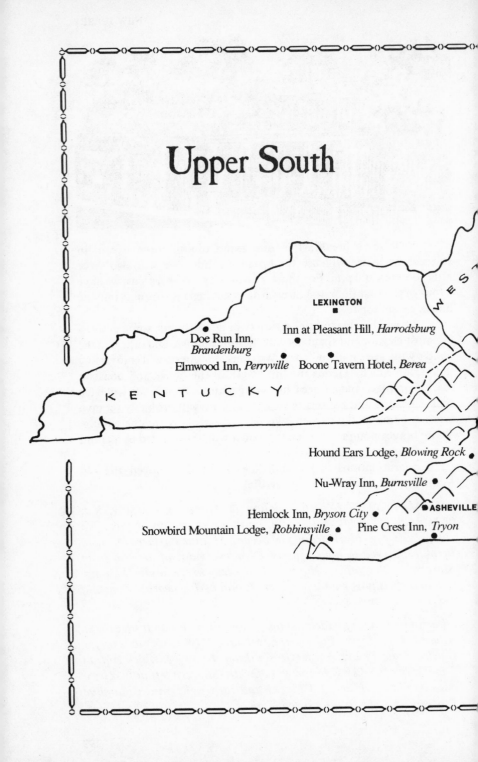

# Upper South

LEXINGTON

Doe Run Inn, *Brandenburg*

Inn at Pleasant Hill, *Harrodsburg*

Elmwood Inn, *Perryville*   Boone Tavern Hotel, *Berea*

WEST

K E N T U C K Y

Hound Ears Lodge, *Blowing Rock*

Nu-Wray Inn, *Burnsville*

Hemlock Inn, *Bryson City*   ASHEVILLE

Snowbird Mountain Lodge, *Robbinsville*   Pine Crest Inn, *Tryon*

Drovers Inn, *Wellsburg*

MARYLAND

Wells Inn, *Sistersville*

Country Inn,
*Berkeley Springs*

Wayside Inn,
*Middletown*

**WASHINGTON**

Old Club Restaurant,
*Alexandria*

Maryland Inn, *Annapolis*

Robert Morris Inn,
*Oxford*

VIRGINIA

Graves Mountain Lodge, *Syria*

■ **CHARLOTTESVILLE**
Hollymead Inn, *Charlottesville*

General Lewis Inn,
*Lewisburg*

Alexander-Withrow House, *Lexington*

Gristmill Square, *Warm Springs*

erside Inn,
*ce Springs*

VIRGINIA

■ **RALEIGH**

NORTH

CAROLINA

# Maryland

*Although the road was narrow, unobtrusive signs kept re-assuring me that I was indeed going in the right direction. Here and there I passed a country store and a house or two but it was mostly Maryland woods and open fields. There were quite a few pheasants and ducks. Just at a point when I thought I would be in somebody's backyard, there was a little wooden trestle. At one end of it was Captain Bill Benson's Tred Avon Ferry.*

*It held all of three cars on one trip!*

*Since there were no other cars waiting we started right across and Bill asked me into the wheel house and was very friendly and patient with all of my questions. The ferry, he explained, is believed to be the oldest one in the nation— it was started in 1760. Bill had it for about thirty-five years. At that time he was the owner, captain, crew, collector and tour director. He showed me a photograph of the ferry which was taken seventy-five years ago with the Robert Morris Inn in the background. He also had photographs of boatyards, docks and shops which he said used to be along the Bellevue side, many years ago. Changing times have apparently moved them to other locations because now there is just high grass and a pair of whistler swans floating about. Bill shook his head with a touch of sadness and said, "It's hard to believe that it's all gone."*

*The ferry is still there. Captain Bill has retired although his old friends still see him quite frequently riding a bicycle down to the ferry slip and he still makes many trips.*

*The ferry, of course, continues to run as it has since 1760.*

*We said good-by and I promised to ride back with him the next morning on the return trip.*

## ROBERT MORRIS INN
### Oxford, Maryland

I can remember back in the early seventies when Ken and Wendy Gibson were the youngest innkeepers in *Country Inns and Back Roads*. They had been married about a year and had just taken over managment of the Robert Morris Inn after they had worked in a Montreal restaurant to learn something about the business.

*Captain Bill Benson's Oxford-Bellevue ferry*

Now, about seven years later, there have been many wonderful changes and some great progress. In February, 1975, Ken and Wendy became sole owners of the inn, which now probably makes them the youngest inn proprietors in the book.

Another indication of the passage of time, is the fact that Benjamin and Kent, the Gibsons' sons, are now in school and Wendy will have more time to herself. "Whether to play tennis or work at the inn remains the question," she says.

I visited the Robert Morris in the fall of 1976 and was delighted to see many new things. For example, the Robert Morris Lodge, located just a few paces from the main inn on a very picturesque point of land in Chesapeake Bay, was getting new siding in a color Wendy referred to as "prestige creme."

Rooms in the lodge were also being redecorated including new wallpaper and curtains. Wendy and her mother have been making all new curtains for the main inn as well and there are beautiful new lamps in almost every room. There are potted plants in most of the inn rooms except for a few that some guests drown by zealous overwatering.

The Robert Morris Inn is located on the banks of the Tred Avon River in the small town of Oxford which has been there since the early 18th century. It is one of those places on Chesapeake Bay that is "discovered" periodically, and I am sure that if there were 50 more rooms at the inn, they would be filled every weekend. Reservations for lodging are made six to eight weeks ahead of time.

In the past I have stayed in one of the rooms where the bed is so high that a small set of steps has been supplied to reach it. However, this time I stayed in #17, a corner room on the third floor, a part of the original 1710 section of the inn. A unique feature of this room is that it has a closet with a window and a window seat overlooking the waterfront. During the oyster season there are often six to ten boats in the bay, and the quaint Eastern accent of the oystermen can be heard rather clearly as the voices carry over the water. The room has a three-quarter sized Jenny Lind bed and Wendy says that they only rent it to small people. I had to sleep on an angle.

Oysters, prepared in many ways, as well as a wide variety of Chesapeake Bay seafood dishes are just two of many reasons why people drive from Baltimore and Washington to enjoy dinner at the Robert Morris. The seafood platter, including crabmeat, shrimp, small crab Imperial, rockfish, clams and oysters, is one of the most popular menu items. Oysters a la Gino are so distinctive that even the local fishermen say they are the best. There are several desserts that deserve attention, but my favorite is always the home-made strawberry pie. Breakfasts include scrapple and homefries as well as omelets and blueberry pancakes.

Robert Morris, wherever you are, I can assure you that the inn that bears your name is in good hands with Ken and Wendy Gibson.

*ROBERT MORRIS INN, Oxford, Md. 21654; 301-226-5111. A 29-room village inn in a secluded Colonial community on the Tred Avon, 10 mi. from Easton, Md. European plan. 4 rooms with private baths; 25 rooms with shared baths. Breakfast, lunch and dinner served to travelers daily. Closed from mid-January to first weekend in March. No pets. Tennis, golf, sailing, swimming and bicycles nearby. Kenneth and Wendy Gibson, Innkeepers.*

*Directions: From Delaware Memorial Bridge, follow Rte. 13 south to Rte. 301 and proceed south to Rte. 50, then east on Rte. 50 to Easton. From Chesapeake Bay Bridge, follow Rte. 50-301 to Rte. 50 and proceed east to Easton. From Chesapeake Bay Bridge Tunnel, follow Rte. 13 north to Rte. 50 and proceed west to Easton. From Easton, follow Rte. 333 to Oxford and inn.*

## MARYLAND INN
### Annapolis, Maryland

My choice of rooms at the Maryland Inn? .. I paused, considering the intimate rooms where the building is just one-room wide overlooking the rooftops of the Colonial town, and those giving a glimpse down Church Street to the 18th century waterfront where white sails sparkling on the bay invite all for a sailing vacation. This is also a place to share the feeling of the working watermen on the fleet of skipjacks or bugeyes who bring in the day's "dredge" of oysters.

I was visiting Annapolis, a town whose vivid history I value because we all have so much to learn from the past.

In the 1770's when the Maryland Inn was built, the innkeeper or Ordinary Keeper, as he was then called, was required to provide stabling for at least ten horses plus a store of oats and hay. Although the hitching post no longer flanks the front entrance, the inn still retains that refreshing warmth and strong spirit which characterized the Colonial period.

Thomas Hyde built the inn and advertised it as "an elegant brick house in the dry and healthy part of the city . . . one of the first houses in the state for a house of entertainment."

Entertainment today, is being carried on in a very exciting way as a result of the energetic efforts of the present proprietor, Mr. Paul Pearson, and I would imagine Ordinary Keeper Hyde would approve of such festive occasions as the Dickens' Christmas, Thanksgiving, Bastille Day, Heritage Weekend, and the First Annual Freakers Ball on Halloween.

Furthermore, today's entertainment features weekly appearances of great jazz artists of the caliber of Charlie Byrd, (who makes the inn his second home), Ethel Ennis, Earle "fatha" Hines and Dizzy Gillespie. A big band series has also proven very popular including the orchestras of Woody Herman, Tommy Dorsey, and Count Basie. The inn sponsors a Jazz Festival at Annapolis during the month of May, with the very finest jazz groups and big bands in concert.

Meanwhile the private restoration of the inn which began in a dramatic way with the restoration of the King of France Tavern, is continuing. For example the iron railing on the main entry porch has been replaced with a wood railing and banjo boards, duplicating the original wood and banjo boards of the Victorian period that remain in their pristine condition on the second floor porch. In addition, the main entry door has been replaced with a handsome double door which is also designed to conform to the Victorian period.

Before I get lost in the architectural styles of the inn which are themselves a subject of great interest, let me make a point that one of the main reasons to visit the inn these days is the food and it can best be described as French-American. Main entrees include crab Imperial, flounder stuffed with oysters, whole baby flounder stuffed with crabmeat and cream of crab soup. One of the most popluar entree offerings is Tournedos Chatham Shores, two pieces of tenderloin stuffed with sauteed oysters and wrapped in bacon.

Well, Ordinary Keeper Hyde, your original inn has had a variety of owners and probably what best could be described as a chequered career. However, I'm certain that you would recognize certain old portions of the building today, and you would certainly savor the food. You'd find the beds very comfortable, and your foot will probably beat time to the likes of Basie and Woody Herman. I believe you would find the rather audacious blend of the old and new entirely to your satisfaction.

*MARYLAND INN, Church Circle, Annapolis, Md. 21401; 301-263-2641. A 44-room 18th century village inn in a history-laden town, 20 mi. from Baltimore and Washington, D.C. Near U.S. Naval Academy and Chesapeake Bay. European plan. Breakfast, lunch and dinner served to travelers daily. Sunday brunch served year-round. Jazz Club, music nightly except Mondays. Sailing, swimming and tennis nearby. Side trips to historic and scenic points of interest. Special holiday rates and tennis and sailing school arrangements. Paul Pearson, Proprietor; Peg Bednarsky, Innkeeper.*

*Directions: From Baltimore, take Rte. 2 south to first directional turnoff "Washington/Annapolis." From Washington, take Rte. 50 east to exit "Annapolis, Naval Academy."*

# Virginia

*When I was first married, we lived for about five years in Lynchburg, Virginia. My two sons were born there and although they can't claim any Confederate heritage, and we didn't stay long enough for them to acquire a southern accent, nevertheless we all learned to love the many features of the state.*

*Virginia is particularly pretty when the dogwood is in bloom, during Annual Garden Week which is usually the last week in April. During that week privately owned houses built in the Georgian tradition and a number of beautiful gardens are open to visitors by their owners as a courtesy to the Garden Club of Virginia, who sponsors this annual event. Fine antique furniture, china, art, silver and glass are featured in many homes. Flowering shrubs and evergreens of unusual interest may be seen in many of the gardens.*

## GRISTMILL SQUARE
### Warm Springs, Virginia

Here is what Cathy Hirsh has to say about her part of southwestern Virginia:

"Springtime in Warm Springs brings out a beautiful array of dogwood and red bud with its lovely mauve color. In June we have laurel and rhododendron in the mountains, and in the woods we have trailing arbutus, which is really quite rare. Lady slippers, trillium, blood root, dog tooth violets and wild azaleas abound.

"In the little stream just in front of Gristmill Square we often have tiny native trout and there are wildflowers throughout the summer. Once a young man from the National Geographic stood in midstream with his tripod and camera taking pictures. He later told me he had taken pictures of thirteen varieties of wildflowers within four feet of where he was standing.

"Bird-watchers love us because we have so many varieties of birds," Cathy continued. "I have identified over 100 species in the last 12 years by just looking out my dining room windows.

"The Cowpasture River or the Jackson River can be followed by foot and offer good fishing with all kinds of river fish such as bass, pickerel, red eyes and rainbow trout. Our region still abounds in foxes, deer and wild turkeys.

"We raise our own vegetables for the restaurant and I raise all the flowers in my garden on our farm. I arrange them daily for the restaurant and art gallery. We are 2,500 feet up in the Allegheny Mountains. This means good skiing and generally plenty of snow in winter."

Cathy and Philip Hirsh began the restoration of Gristmill Square in the Bath County seat in 1973. Decay and dilapidation in the center of this little town were replaced with a complete refurbishing of several buildings including a mill which has been turned into a rustic yet elegant restaurant. All around the square are

found small shops including an art gallery, a country store and an antique shop. There are two two-bedroom apartments on the second floor, each with a bath or baths, kitchen, living room, balcony or sundeck, and a woodburning fireplace. The ground floor accommodations are double rooms or small suites, some with a fireplace. The furnishings are extremely tasteful with a number of the rooms done in authentic antiques. In the spring of this year new tennis courts and a swimming pool will be available to guests, making it a complete small resort-inn. There are two golf courses nearby.

Gristmill Square must be viewed with a different perspective. It is not a large tourist attraction and will never become one if Philip Hirsh can avoid it. For example, the entire square complex is closed on the Fourth of July which is ordinarily a big tourist time.

Since it first opened, the food at the Waterwheel Restaurant has attracted people from some distance. Philip Hirsh is in complete charge of the kitchen and many of the dishes are his recipes (quite a change from being a corporate executive just a few years ago). Some of his specialties include curried chicken, fresh rainbow trout from the hatchery in the next county, veal dishes, shepherd's pie, and really super chili.

Sunday brunch may well include eggs Benedict, roast beef hash, creamed chicken on toast and several fish dishes.

There are many more things about this most unusual restoration in the heart of the Allegheny Mountains. Everything is done with style and grace and not a small amount of whimsy. It will really take me several visits to put it all together, and I'm looking forward with a great deal of anticipation to every one of them.

*GRISTMILL SQUARE, Warm Springs, Va. 24484; 703-839-2231. An unusual restoration which includes a restaurant, accommodations, small shops and many resort attractions, in a small country town approx. 19 mi. from Covington in the Allegheny Mts. European Plan. Lunch and dinner served daily except Mondays. Closed Christmas Day, Thanksgiving Day, July 4th. Many different types of accommodations available. Suggest telephone for details. Children welcome. Pets allowed but not permitted loose on grounds. Tennis, swimming pool on grounds. Golf, skiing, skating, riding, hiking, fishing, hunting, antiquing, back roading nearby. Philip and Catherine Hirsh, Innkeepers.*

*Directions: From Staunton, Va., follow Rte. 254 to Buffalo Gap, Rte. 42 to Millboro Spring, Rte. 39 to Warm Springs. From Lexington, take Rte. 39 to Warm Springs. From Roanoke, take Rte. 220 to Warm Springs.*

## GRAVES MOUNTAIN LODGE
### Syria, Virginia

The night I had my first dinner at Graves Mountain Lodge I shared the family-style table with four teenagers and three other adults. The only generation gap I felt was that I knew the teenagers would out-eat me! It happened to be Potluck Night which falls between Monday and Wednesday, so oddly enough we were having pot roast! I later discovered that Thursday it's roast beef; Friday, rainbow trout; Saturday, sirloin steak and Sunday, from 1 to 2 p.m., fried chicken and, from 6 to 7:30, country ham.

Every time they passed the pot roast around and the platter was empty a young waitress would appear with another platter. And there was a steady stream of bowls and plates of string beans, corn, hot bread, mashed potatoes, peas, lima beans, pitchers of milk, relish, jams, ad infinitum.

I noticed that total strangers at all the tables had already introduced themselves and the atmosphere was one of real country congeniality. Many of the license plates were from Washington, D.C., which is within reasonable driving distance. Some of the diplomatic-types had shed their coats and settled down to the real business of eating and visiting.

Even though the porches and dining rooms can serve a great number of people (832 last Thanksgiving), reservations are always advisable.

There is a fascinating story connected with Graves Mountain Lodge. I got part of it from seventy-two-year-old Jack Graves, the head of the clan, who was born here and owns three thousand surrounding acres of farm and orchard land. He told me that the tradition of innkeeping here in "the Hollow" dates back to when the road which now stops in Syria at the foothills of the Blue Ridge, used to go across into West Virginia and this was a "way station" for wagons and coaches. It was the last stop on this side of the mountain on the way back.

Mr. Graves, along with all of the family, came right off the farm changed into spotless overalls and helped to dish the food out to all of the hungry guests. The lodge is a family affair with much of its operation supervised by Jim and Rachel Graves.

My accommodations were in the old Farmhouse (there are several different cabins and houses available). My room had the ambrosial scent of applewood. The windows looked out over the valley through the fields to the nearby mountains. The shower was in the adjacent Wash House, reached by a covered porch. I wish I could have remained a week, swimming in the lovely pool, playing tennis (there are eight courts), tramping the hills and maybe even working on the farm.

But now, back to that first meal . . . country baked apples, hot beets, sliced home grown tomatoes, homemade cole slaw, corn bread, apple butter, apple pie with vanilla ice cream . . . what a way to go!

*GRAVES MOUNTAIN LODGE, Syria, Va. 22743; 703-923-4231. A 21-room secluded resort-inn on Rte. 670, off Rte. 231, 10 mi. north of Madison, Va., 38 mi. N.W. of Charlottesville, Va. American plan. Rustic lodgings including 11 cottages and cabins. Breakfast, lunch, dinner served to travelers by reservation only. Closed Dec. 1 to late March. Swimming, tennis, riding, fishing, basketball on grounds. Golf nearby. Jim and Rachel Graves, Innkeepers.*

*Directions: Coming south from Wash., D.C., take I-66 to Gainsville. Follow Rte. 29 south to Madison, turn right onto Rte. 231 West, go 7 mi. to Banco, turn left onto Rte. 670 and follow 670 for 4½ mi. to lodge.*

## HOLLYMEAD INN
### Charlottesville, Virginia

"And here, sir, are your choice of desserts."

Right there on a gleaming silver tray just a few inches from my nose were three fantastic looking confections that defied description.

"This is chocolate mousse, and this is rum pie, and here's a chiffon cheesecake."

Hobson had an easier choice.

I had left Washington, D.C., a few hours earlier, after lunching at the Old Club in Alexandria. It was like old times for me to be on Route 29 through Warrenton and Culpeper. It was rolling country with many impressive, typically Virginia homes and markers from Civil War battlefields.

The directions said to watch for the sign for Hollymead on the east side of the road just 6 mi. north of Charlottesville. And there it was.

Innkeepers Peg and Joe Bute were both at the door to wish me welcome, and the fun of visiting a country inn for the first time began. Each of them bubbled over with information. "The floors and beams are original," said Peg. "It was built by Hessian soldiers taken prisoner at Saratoga during the Revolutionary War. They were housed nearby but, when conditions became overcrowded, they constructed the first part of the house, which we call the Hessian Room.

"The center part of the house was built around 1815 and used for a while as a private boys' school. The boys lived in two rooms on the third floor. They had their lessons in this room which we now keep as a private dining room."

There is a great deal more, including a radio program every week from the inn in which guests and well-known people visiting the nearby University of Virginia are interviewed. Peg explained that she used to be a cook at one of the fraternities and the boys from that fraternity are now waiters at Hollymead.

One of the unique features is a country butcher shop, The Hook and Cleaver, which is located in the basement where Virginia hams and beef are sold. There is also a sportswear and gift shop.

I was delighted with the atmosphere, cleanliness and really crisp look of Hollymead, and the food was equally exciting.

Dinner started with a relish tray that had beets, beans, creamy cucumbers, apple butter, and cranberry sauce. These were served with homemade muffins and a very good garden salad. I ordered the baked chicken with Hollymead sauce served over rice. It was so delicious, I wish I had some right now.

Peg explained that besides the steaks, seafood, and the fresh batter-fried mushrooms which are available with every meal, there are daily specials which might be Beef Wellington, trout stuffed with crabmeat, flounder stuffed with shrimp, ribeye steak, scallops in mushrooms and wine, or country stuffed pork chops.

While I was eating, a number of tweedy faculty-types from UVA popped in for dinner as well as some blue-jeaned students. "Oh yes, everyone comes here," said Peg.

This brings me back to where we started. I was really going to fend off the desserts with regret but the chocolate mousse was too much for me. And, like the man in the television ad, I can't believe I ate the whole thing!

It didn't hurt a bit.

*HOLLYMEAD INN, Rte. 8, Box 367A, Charlottesville, Va. 22901; 804-973-8488. A country restaurant a few minutes north of Charlottesville on Rte. 29. Near Monticello, Ash Lawn, University of Virginia and Skyline Drive in Blue Ridge Mts. No lodgings. Dinner served Tuesdays through Saturdays. Open year-round. Closed Christmas Eve, Christmas Day and New Year's Day. Mr. and Mrs. Joseph Bute, Innkeepers.*

*Directions: Proceed 6 mi. north of Charlottesville, Va., on Rte. 29 North.*

## WAYSIDE INN
### Middletown, Virginia

The Wayside Inn dates back to at least 1797. It is quite correct to refer to it as an "historic restoration." This restoration began in 1960 when Leo Bernstein, a lawyer and banker from nearby Washington, happened to drive down the main street of Middletown and saw the inn's tremendous possibilities.

Since that time he has filled all of the inn's lodging rooms and public rooms with a remarkable group of antiques from his private collection, many from the Colonial period. This collection also reflects Leo's taste for the unique and unusual from all parts of the world.

The first guests at the Wayside Inn undoubtedly came by foot and on horseback. Travel by stagecoach was replaced by train and car, and the Wayside has been called America's first "motor inn."

This famous landmark in the Shenandoah Valley of Virginia quartered American leaders in the Revolutionary War and was used by both sides during the War between the States. It's just a few miles from the Battle of Cedar Creek and undoubtedly General Sheridan passed by the inn at the end of his famous ride from Winchester in October 1864.

In the past, I have always enjoyed having dinner in the Slave Kitchen. This was a room that was discovered by accident during the restoration of the inn a number of years ago. It has the original brick walls and the beams have adz marks on them. Presently it is adorned with an excellent group of Early American tools.

The food prepared by Anna Rose includes authentic Southern dishes such as lightly salted sugar cured baked ham served with raisin sauce, famous Virginia ham served with redeye gravy, Southern fried chicken, duck a l'orange and spoon bread. And now there is apple strudel, German chocolate cake and lemon ring cake which are all made from scratch from Anna's own recipes.

In the summertime, Middletown also hosts the Wayside Summer Theatre with a professional company of actors and every effort is made to coordinate dinners with curtain time.

Belle Grove, an outstanding restoration of the National Trust is located nearby. This beautiful house, built in 1794 with architectural refinements suggested by Thomas Jefferson, has survived the ravages of time, and is a graceful reminder of another age.

The Wayside Inn offers an interesting combination of history, comfortable accommodations, good food, and a countryside that has dozens of attractive back roads. It is just a short drive to the northern entrance of the Blue Ridge Parkway. It is also the only inn of my acquaintance that has its own FM radio station, WFFV-FM 99.3, which the traveler to the Shenandoah Valley can tune in approximately 25 miles from the inn.

*WAYSIDE INN, Middletown, Va. 22645; 703-869-1797. A 21-room country resort-inn since 1797 in the Shenandoah Valley. About 1½ hrs. from Washington, D.C. European plan. Breakfast, lunch and dinner served daily to travelers. Open every day of the year. Professional summer stock theatre and arts center, Belle Grove, Cedar Creek Battlefield, Blue Ridge Parkway, Crystal Caverns and Shenandoah Valley historical sites nearby. Bill and Cathy Castro, Innkeepers.*

*Directions: Take Exit 77 off I-81 to Rte. 11. Follow signs to inn.*

## ALEXANDER-WITHROW HOUSE
### Lexington, Virginia

I first saw the Alexander-Withrow House on a beautiful, sunny June afternoon and was immediately impressed with its unusual design. I was amazed to learn that such a sophisticated structure was built in 1789, just two years after the original founding of the town. It has four corner chimneys and a most elaborate brickwork, which innkeeper Carlson Thomas said was known as "diapering." Another unusual feature is the Italianate roof.

Today this historic house, which is now included in the National Register for Historic Places, is an exquisite guest house. Its preservation was the first chapter of an extensive and exciting restoration in Lexington.

It was in the mid-sixties that historic preservation began coming into its own in Lexington. In 1966 the Historic Lexington Foundation (HLF), a non-profit organization, was established. Its main purpose was to guard Lexington's achitectural heritage.

The first property was the Alexander-Withrow House which was one of the few structures to survive a fire in 1796. It would serve as an inspiration and direction for future properties in the town.

The HLF engaged Thomas Craven of Charlottesville, a distinguished preservation architect, and the restoration work was begun. In 1971, Carlson Thomas and his wife, Patty, bought the house and redesigned, restored and decorated the interior.

Patty and Carlson showed me through every room in the house. There are five suites, each with its own sitting room, bedroom and small refreshment center. The furnishings are beautiful antiques and reproductions.

There are no meals served at the AW House. However, there is an arrangement with the pastry shop next door to deliver pastries, breads, sticky buns and coffee in the morning. Guests can enjoy these right in their own suite. Patty and Carlson have many suggestions for area restaurants for lunch and dinner. They also see to it that their guests are deluged with material about Lexington, including a 26-stop walking tour. Many people come for one night and stay longer because there is really so much to offer the vacationing traveler. Lexington is also the home of Washington and Lee University and Virginia Military Institute.

During 1976, another section of I-64 was completed, so that it intersects I-81 just north of the town. This means no more 10-ton trucks driving through the quiet streets.

*ALEXANDER-WITHROW HOUSE, 3 W. Washington St., Lexington, Va. 24450; 703-463-2044. An elegantly restored, 5-suite guest house. Lodgings only. No meals served. Room service Continental breakfast available. Advance reservations recommended. Open year-round. No pets. Lexington is the home of Virginia Military Institute, Washington and Lee University, and the George C. Marshall Research Library, Natural Bridge, Blue Ridge Parkway nearby. Carlson and Patty Thomas, Innkeepers.*

*Directions: Any Lexington exit from I-64 or I-81.*

## OLD CLUB RESTAURANT
### Alexandria, Virginia

"The food must be good," I thought, "because the natives eat here."

In this case, the "natives" whose cars were in the Old Club's parking lot, were the business people of Alexandria and nearby Washington. I learned this from looking at the license plates of the cars in the parking lot.

I stopped long enough to look at the very well-kept grounds. I was looking, in particular, for the English walnut tree and the black walnut tree that are said to have been given to General Washington by the Marquis de Lafayette. Although we were just a few squares from downtown Alexandria, the white fence and high hedges provided an attractive cushion against the urban intrusions. I

particularly liked the terrace with lush grass growing between flagstones.

A few years ago I stopped here with my son, Keith, and we both enjoyed the Virginia country ham served over cornbread and covered with maple syrup. This time, however, I resisted this in favor of Allegheny mountain trout, which was boned and stuffed with mushrooms and rice. A good tartar sauce was the topper. I might have ordered chicken Laura Lee, which is a chicken breast on hickory ham with a mushroom sauce. Both of these are really something!

The oldest part of this Colonial house was built by George Washington and his friends as a private club. The little brick building on the north is said to have been young Washington's office while he was surveying this area. There are dozens of little stories connected with this place, including the fact that during the War of 1812 when the enemy was at the gates of Alexandria, all the good furniture was buried in the vegetable garden.

When Keith visited with me, it was for him, as it is for so many people from the north, the first time that he had ever experienced real Southern food. One of the things that he simply couldn't resist was the peanut soup which is a feature of this historic restaurant. I am very fond of it myself and have found that a cup is the perfect amount. After lunch, I drove down the George Washington Parkway and parked at a convenient distance enabling me to spend part of the afternoon at the Washington Monument and the Lincoln Memorial.

They are both just a few pleasant moments from Alexandria.

Many guests visiting "DC" (as the city of Washington is known in the area) for the first time are impressed with the beautiful and well-preserved Colonial and Federalist buildings in Alexandria. To me they are reminiscent of those in Charleston, South Carolina; Providence, Rhode Island; and Nantucket, Massachusetts. I found a booklet at the Old Club with an extensive walking tour of Alexandria that included 27 locations just minutes away.

*OLD CLUB RESTAURANT, 555 So. Washington St., Alexandria, Va. 22314; 703-549-4555. Just across the river from Washington, D.C. in one of the country's best preserved Colonial cities. No lodgings. Lunch and dinner served daily except Mondays and Christmas. Convenient to Christ Church, Robert E. Lee House, Gadsby's Tavern, Old Apothecary Shop, and Potomac River. Mt. Vernon and Gunston Hall nearby. Lee Palmer, Innkeeper.*

*Directions: North and south bound traffic on 495 take Exit #1 North to Rte. 1. Turn right on Franklin St. and left on Washington St., 1 block to inn. (Mount Vernon Memorial Hwy. is Washington St. in the city.)*

# North Carolina

*The best way to describe the Great Smokies is "spectacular." The mountains are the highest in eastern America and as I understand it the oldest in the world. There are more varieties of flowers and trees than anywhere outside of China. There are marvelously fantastic roads and backroads twisting up, down, over and between these mountains which live up to the name given them by the Indians because of the almost constant cloud formations above them. The area has the largest birch, spruce and hardwood forests in the United States. It is the scene of the original home of the Cherokee Indians before they were unmercifully uprooted and taken further west. In fact, the Cherokee Reservation still occupies a tremendous number of acres.*

### NU-WRAY INN
**Burnsville, North Carolina**

"Rush," I inquired, "what makes the ham here taste so different?" Rush Wray's dinner bell had rung a few moments earlier, and all the members of the "Nu-Wray Inn Admiration Club"

dutifully filed in on time to take their places at the long tables. Rush then introduced all of the newcomers, we took our places in the bentwood chairs and set about the pleasant task before us.

Large platters of homemade baked beans, fried ham, hot breads, corned beef, fried chicken, green beans, corn on the cob, and many other good things were passed from hand to hand, and the room was filled with the laughing and talking of undeniably happy people.

Rush turned to answer my question. "First of all, you've got to have a genuine iron skillet, very hot. Then put in one teaspoon of grease, place the sliced ham in the pan and allow it to remain long enough to heat thoroughly. Be certain to cook it on both sides. Then add a small amount of water which makes the gravy, pour this over the ham after it has been removed to the platter, and, by all means, be sure to serve it hot."

While I have written extensively in previous editions about the ringing of bells to awaken everyone and to call them to breakfast and dinner, there's a great deal more to the Nu-Wray Inn than bells. For one thing, it's in the beautiful high country of North Carolina, and Mt. Mitchell, the highest mountain east of the Mississippi, is nearby. In fact, the flora and birds attract a great many visitors to Burnsville each year, and quite a few of Rush's regular guests bring their binoculars, cameras, sketch pads, oils and water colors.

The Nu-Wray dates back to 1850 when it was established by Garrett D. Ray. His daughter, Julia Ray, married William B. Wray and in time they became the owners and operators. The building was modernized, and the name was changed to the Nu-Wray Inn, spelling it with the "w." Rush is the third generation of innkeepers.

The inn is exactly what you would hope to find in a bustling village in the North Carolina highlands. It is furnished with antiques and family heirlooms. The sitting room has a welcome fireplace against chilly highland mornings and evenings, and dozens of books and magazines are scattered around. It's impossible to sit there for very long without meeting other guests.

The rooms are the type I call "old-fashioned country inn." Most have private baths, but there are a few on the third floor with the bath "down the hallway." However, these have lavatories in the rooms.

As we finished off our dessert of apple cobbler, Rush pushed his glasses down on his nose and said, "There's one thing I forgot to tell you about cooking a Nu-Wray ham."

"What is that?" I asked expectantly.

"First you've got to catch a Nu-Wray pig!"

*NU-WRAY INN, Burnsville, N.C. 28714; 704-682-2329. A 35-room village inn on town square on Rte. 19E, 38 mi. north of Asheville. A few miles from Mt. Mitchell. Modified American plan omits lunch and Sunday night supper. Breakfast and dinner served every weekday to travelers. Noon dinner served on Sundays only. Open every day of the year. Golf, swimming, hiking and skiing nearby. Rush T. Wray, Innkeeper. Mrs. Annie Wray Bennett, Hostess.*

*Directions: From Asheville, go north on Rte. 19-23 for 18 miles, then continue on 19. Five miles from Burnsville, 19 becomes 19E. From the north via Bristol or Johnson City, Tenn., take Rte. 19-23 to Unicoi. Turn left on 107 to N.C. State Line. Take 226 and turn right on Rte. 197 at Red Hill to Burnsville.*

## HEMLOCK INN
### Bryson City, North Carolina

Ultimately the reason for writing and rewriting a book on country inns is to share my experiences with readers to enable them to see the enduring qualities of inns and innkeepers.

In the search of these enduring qualities, I frequently quote from conversations I have had with innkeepers or from their letters to me. For example, there is no way that I could truly describe Ella Jo and John Shell. Yet I feel that this letter from Ella Jo not only tells us something about the Hemlock Inn, but gives us an insight into the kind of people they really are:

"Our guests traveling with CIBR not only have been great in

number this year but great in person. People have come from all over the world. A German family with two teen-age sons asked somebody in New York City how to 'see' America for the first time. That 'somebody' introduced them to CIBR and they have been happily following the book. In fact, they stayed two days longer with us than they had planned.

"Our people are generally young, well-educated, interesting, mannerly, and looking for the kind of place we have. We find this very gratifying since we don't have TV, swimming pool, or planned activities.

"Things are going to be just the same for next year. We'll continue to serve breakfast and dinner around our lazy Susan tables, and while we are always redecorating rooms, adding new curtains, recovering furniture and replacing rugs, the nicest compliment we have is when a guest says, 'It looks fresh but not changed.' This is our aim.

"Our daughter, Lainey, is a lifesaver when she is home from college. She gives everyone a day off and does everything from waiting on tables to cleaning rooms.

"Last fall we trimmed trees, cleared out trails and also opened up the view, for it doesn't take many years of growth to have it obscured—and it is so pretty. One of our guests said, 'Your delicious food feeds my body; your peaceful, beautiful mountains rest my body, and John's blessings at dinner feed my soul.'

"John and I feel so lucky to be on a mountaintop with 65 acres just two miles from the Smoky Mountain boundary. Yet we are within half an hour to an hour's drive of many activities and trails in Cherokee, Gatlinburg, Asheville, Highlands, Fontana Dam and the national park and national forest.

"We loved Mary-Virginia and Jim Mellow. Thanks for introducing us—they really are our kind of folks. We hope to see them often for their daughter is at Emory College, just four hours away."

I can truthfully say that I bless the day a few years ago when I turned off the main highway (Rte. 19) just east of Bryson City and drove to the top of the mountain to find Ella Jo and John Shell and their Hemlock Inn.

Here's a card I got from Jim Mellow after his first visit: "Ella Jo and John Shell are perfect innkeepers. Personable, friendly, and always looking for ways to make their guests comfortable. My, what great food. We met some wonderful people around the dining tables. Mary-Virginia and I hiked up the mountain—a perfect inn. Best regards, MV and Jim."

*HEMLOCK INN, Bryson City, N.C. 28713; 704-488-9820. A 25-room Smoky Mountain inn 4 mi. from Bryson City and 60 mi. from Asheville. Near Fontana Village, Cherokee and Pisgah National Forest. Modified American plan omits lunch. Breakfast and dinner served to travelers by reservation only. Sunday dinner served at noontime. Open from early May to early November. No pets. Shuffleboard, skittles, horseshoes, hiking trails on grounds. Tubing and golf nearby. Ella Jo and John Shell, Innkeepers.*

*Directions: Located 1 mi. off Rte. 19 between Cherokee and Bryson City, N.C. Take paved road to top of mountain.*

## SNOWBIRD MOUNTAIN LODGE
### Robbinsville, North Carolina

"That is Lake Santeetlah, about 1000 feet below us." Mary Williams and I were standing on the terrace at Snowbird Mountain Lodge deep in the heart of the Great Smokies. In front of us, so close that I wanted to reach out and touch it, was a ring of mountains ranging from 4000 to 5400 feet in height. At this time of day they were gloriously lighted by the noon sunshine. Later they would take on new shades and shadows, until at dusk they would be silhouetted against the deepening blue of the North Carolina skies.

Snowbird is literally a paradise for hikers and birders. It is located just two miles from the Joyce Kilmer Memorial Forest which

is 3800 acres of magnificent hardwoods that have never been cut over. "It is one of the few stands of virgin timber remaining in the eastern part of the United States," explained Mary. "There are trails leading from Snowbird in almost every direction and we supply our guests with box lunches. These are good walking and hiking trails rather than mountain climbing expeditions."

"In the springtime," she continued, "the trailing arbutus, laurel, violets and dogwood are gorgeous. In mid-summer we have cardinal flowers, the crimson bee balm, Turks cap, Carolina lilies, and rhododendron which reaches peak bloom about the 4th of July.

"Don't forget that there are more than 110 birds that have been sighted nearby," said Ed Williams, who had joined us for a few moments. "Some of our guests are really experts, and hardly a week goes by that someone doesn't gleefully announce they have seen a bird that has been previously unreported."

As I recall, I first visited Mary and Ed and the Snowbird Mountain Lodge a few years ago, right after they had left New Jersey and decided to take up the innkeeping life on a North Carolina mountaintop. Over the years I believe I have managed to keep up-to-date on the many developments and I was delighted to learn that ·their daughter Merrilee Williams Barlow and her husband, John, will be joining the Snowbird staff in the summer of 1977 and it will be assuming the traditions of a family-operated inn.

The glorious nature-filled days of Snowbird result in hearty appetites. Among the tempting main dishes are roast beef, fresh ham, steaks and fresh mountain trout almandine. All the baking is done right in the kitchen. Breakfasts are also a highlight with delicious coffee made with spring water. Although the building has a distinctive rustic style, the interior is completely finished and each of the lodging rooms is paneled with woods native to the Great Smokies. The atmosphere is quite informal and sports clothes are the order of the day. However, I was glad I had some warm clothes because, even in the summer, the temperature average was about 70 degrees.

"It has been wonderful and we are both so terribly happy that we gave up life in the suburbs and came down to where everything is relatively calm and peaceful," said Mary. "I think one of the greatest rewards is having guests who are happy and who return year after year. *Country Inns and Back Roads* people frequently say that it is just like it says in the book."

As we left the terrace to take a walk out to the Point, Ed once again indulged in his favorite one-liner: "Up here on the terrace, we always advise our guests not to take a step backward to get a better look."

*SNOWBIRD MOUNTAIN LODGE, Joyce Kilmer Forest Rd., Robbinsville, N.C. 28771; 704-479-3433. A 16-room inn on top of the Great Smokies, 12 mi. from Robbinsville. American plan. Lunch and dinner served to travelers by reservation only. No children under 12, no pets. Open May 20 through Oct. 30. Swimming, fishing, hiking nearby. Mary and Ed Williams, Innkeepers.*

*Directions: Approaching from the northeast or south, take U.S. 19 and 129; from the northwest, take U.S. 129.*

## PINE CREST INN
### Tryon, North Carolina

I asked Innkeeper Bob Hull about the famous Tryon "thermal belt."

"This is caused by a temperature inversion," he explained, "resulting in a temperate zone which escapes the frost of the valley and the deep freeze of the mountains. The foliage here is fresh and green compared with that above and below. Scientists have studied this unusual condition for years. We love it."

Bob and I were sitting on the side terrace of the Pine Crest Inn with some other keepers of country inns included in this book. We were all gathered for one of our frequent meetings in which innkeepers come together at one of the inns to exchange ideas and enjoy each other's company.

Every visiting innkeeper was unstinting in his praise not only of the accommodations at the Pine Crest, but of the food and service as well.

"When I walked into my bedroom," said Helen Tobin of the Lincklaen House in Cazenovia, New York, "I was just enchanted. Everything was perfect. I had a fireplace with the fire already laid and I could have had breakfast in bed if I wished."

In the dining room there are beautiful oak tables which need no tablecloths to enhance them. There is a big stone fireplace at one end, flowers and candles on the tables, and as everybody agreed, marvelous food.

"Fran, of course, does all the cooking," said Bob. The other innkeepers gasped. They could hardly believe it. "Well it is something that she really likes to do. She wouldn't feel right unless she knew what was going on. Our guests seem to expect it. She makes practically everything from scratch including bread, rolls, desserts, pies and cakes.

"We have our own ways here," Bob continued. "We like jackets and ties on the gentlemen at dinner, although ties can be eliminated in warm weather. We provide a great many of the little touches that we think are important, such as having the morning paper at your table at breakfast and a delivery of ice to your room late in the afternoon. Most of the time we have a single entree for dinner, although some nights we have two. Our staff has been here for an average of about twenty years and we feel like one big family."

Our meeting at the Pine Crest, which started on Monday evening and lasted through Wednesday morning, was a huge success.

219

There were other guests in the house at the time, and we were happy to have them join some of our meetings.

The nicest part of it all was that each of the experienced innkeepers from all over the east agreed that the Pine Crest Inn got the highest marks in every single innkeeping department—especially in that of genuine concern and involvement with their guests.

I think we would all like to go back again.

*PINE CREST INN, P. O. Box 1030, Tryon, N. C. 28782; 704-852-2135. A 34-room resort-inn midway between Asheville, N. C. and Greenville, S. C. All plans available. Breakfast, lunch and dinner served daily to travelers. Closed Jan. Attended leashed pets allowed. Golf, tennis, and swimming at nearby country clubs. Riding, nature walks, rock hunting, nearby. Robert and Fran Hull, Innkeepers.*

*Directions: From Asheville, take I-26 to Tryon exit, then 108 to Tryon. Go through town. Do not cross railroad tracks but bear left to Pine Crest Lane. The inn is at the end of the lane. From Spartanburg/Greenville take I-85 north to I-26. Exit at Columbus, N. C. Take Rte. 108 toward Tryon—go through town. Do not cross railroad tracks but bear left to Pine Crest Lane. The inn is at the end of the lane.*

## HOUND EARS LODGE
### Blowing Rock, North Carolina

The balcony of my room at Hound Ears almost seemed to rest in the top branches of an oak tree. By now the sun was directly overhead casting a dappled pattern on the floor of the porch. In the distance, Grandfather Mountain was shimmering and to my left, perched on various levels of the lower mountains, were the attractively designed homes of the Hound Ears community.

Below, in the foreground, were some young people walking to the swimming pool, which I intended to visit shortly. However, dominating the valley floor, with many of the trees and greens visible from my vantage point, was the Hound Ears Golf Course.

Perhaps it was this picture of verdant greens and fairways punctuated by clear, white, menacing sand traps that momentarily made it difficult to realize that there had been eight or nine inches of snow here last Christmas and that the other face of Hound Ears, the winter visage, is one that includes spectacular skiing, roaring fireplaces and the exhilaration of pure winter air.

After a cool night's sleep, I strolled across the flower-lined walk

to the main lodge for breakfast and was on the first leg of the Hound Ears tour.

As I moved from the accommodations in the main lodge to the chalets, and from the swimming pool to several of the private homes of native stone and wood, I found excellent taste everywhere.

The furnishings, appointments, and interior and exterior were carefully harmonized. For example, my room was done in compatible shades of brown; I had yellow sheets on my bed. All of the buildings were set among rhododendrons and evergreens and in many places huge handsome boulders were allowed to remain where they rested. The road was built around them, curving and twisting and climbing.

Hound Ears is a luxurious American Plan resort-inn, and the rates reflect the additional services and elegance.

The whole concept of Hound Ears which, by the way is named for a rock formation on the mountain behind the lodge, is the inspiration of the Robbins brothers, all of whom were born and raised in this part of North Carolina. They saw the marvelous possibilities of making a resort-inn to which were added skiing and golf facilities.

Other resort-inns with championship golf facilities include the Bay Hill Club, Ojai Valley Inn and the Inn at Rancho Santa Fe.

*HOUND EARS LODGE and CLUB, P.O. Box 188, Blowing Rock, N.C. 28605; 704-963-4321. A luxurious 25-room resort-inn on Rte. 105, 6 mi. from Boone. Near natural attractions. American plan. Meals served to houseguests only. Open year-round. 18-hole golf course, swimming and tennis on grounds. Skiing nearby. Charlie Elliott, Jr., Innkeeper.*

*Directions: From Winston-Salem, follow Rte. 421 west to Boone, then travel south on Rte. 105 to inn. From Asheville, follow Rtes. 19 and 19E to Pineola, then Rte. 181 to Linville and Rte. 105 north to inn. From Bristol, Va., and I-81, follow Rte. 421 east to Vilas (mountainous), then Rte. 321 east to Boone. In Boone, pick up Rte. 105 and turn on Shulls Mills Rd.*

# West Virginia

### THE COUNTRY INN
### Berkeley Springs, West Virginia

About twelve years of searching for country inns has made me a firm believer that inns take on the character traits and personalities of their innkeepers. For that reason, in my search for inns I am as keenly interested in the innkeepers themselves, as I am in the food, accommodations and atmosphere.

The warm-hearted hospitality and good humor in this inn located in the northeast corner of West Virginia, about 100 miles from Washington, are extensions of the genuine interest and concern of innkeepers Jack and Adele Barker. I first met them in the fall of 1972 when my son Keith and I were on a trip through Maryland, West Virginia and Pennsylvania in search of country inns.

When a guest walks in the front door and Jack Barker comes forward with the strong, firm handshake and says, "Welcome to the Country Inn," it creates a wonderful feeling. He has a booming voice with a marvelous Tennessee accent that lets everyone within earshot know that he loves life and wants others to enjoy it with him.

Adele, on the other hand, imparts a very gentle feeling of concern for her guests. She has a wonderful laugh.

I enjoy sitting with Jack, Adele and other guests in a corner of the parlor. Jack's stories complement the picturesque Potomac country of Maryland and West Virginia, where the river winds back and forth among the hills and forests, and where folks are sincere and don't "put on airs."

At one time Berkeley Springs was the closest "spa" to Washington and three trains came back and fourth everyday on the B & O. There have been springs here long before the white man. George Washington paid a visit, and as legend has it, planted a tree.

The springs however, are still very much in evidence, and it is possible to use the baths, which are just a few paces from the inn, and enjoy a vapor bath, a hot tub and a massage at most reasonable rates. They are maintained by the state.

The exterior of the inn is red brick with white columns extending two stories on both the front and the sides. It is immediately adjacent to the village park and the bandstand. It is surrounded by sycamore and oak trees and flowering hedges. Even though it is in the middle of the town it is necessary to cross a small brook to reach the front door.

"We are trying to recreate the gracious colonial style of living," explained Jack, "and for that reason the name was changed to 'The Country Inn' a few years ago because it more closely expressed our conviction about what an inn should be."

Letters from readers indicate that guests enjoy the homey atmosphere and the cooking, especially the country ham, smothered chicken, salmon soup, duckling with orange sauce and the home-made hot breads.

There is much to see and do in the vicinity of Berkeley Springs. For example, there is an 18-hole Robert Trent Jones golf course nearby and good cross-country skiing in the Cacapon State Park. Of particular interest are a great many circle tours which direct guests to some of the interesting towns and hamlets of West Virginia and southern Pennsylvania.

Jack and Adele Barker are just the kind of people who should be keeping country inns. They bring a genuine concern for guests' comfort, a wealth of experience, generous amounts of intellectual curiosity and practicality, and a good sense of how to run a very demanding business.

If country inns hadn't been invented, they would have invented them.

*THE COUNTRY INN, Berkeley Springs, West Va. 25411; 304-258-2210. A 37-room resort inn on Rte. 522, 34 mi. from Winchester, Va. and 100 mi. from Washington, D.C., or Baltimore, Md. Berkeley Springs Spa adjoins inn. European plan. Most rooms with private baths. Breakfast, lunch, dinner served to travelers. Open every day of the year. Hunting, fishing, hiking, canoeing, antiquing, championship golf nearby. Jack and Adele Barker, Innkeepers.*

*Directions: Take I-70 to Hancock, Md. Inn is 6 mi. south on Rte. 522.*

## GENERAL LEWIS INN
### Lewisburg, West Virginia

"Yes, things in West Virginia have changed and they are continuing to change. West Virginians couldn't be happier." Innkeeper Larry Little and I had just returned from a ride around the beautiful countryside near Lewisburg, which prompted my remark on the beauty of this section of the state. "Well, we think the whole state is coming into its own and down here we call West Virginia 'almost heaven.' "

We re-entered the town and Larry pointed to one of the roads saying, "That's the way to the golf courses. A lot of people come down here in early spring to get a jump on the season. The Greenbrier is one of the most famous courses in the world."

He swung the car into the curved driveway in front of the General Lewis Inn with its stately pillars, sprawling lawns, and plantation veranda. As I stepped inside the entrance hallway, I stepped back in time.

There were white plaster walls and low ceilings with dark beams. Old maps, a collection of rifles and guns, powder horns, and many ancient tools and artifacts were hung on the walls of the hallway and large sitting room. As might be expected in an area where an important action of the Civil War took place in 1862, there were many Confederate flags. The old stone church directly across the street from the inn was used as a hospital during the war. Earlier that afternoon Larry had pointed out the spot where the bridge was located. "It was burned by the Yankees before their retreat," he said.

In terms of time, the building housing the General Lewis has

seen much history. The dining room, which is part of the original building, dates back to 1798. The town, itself, began in 1750. Andrew Lewis and some pioneers built Fort Savannah for protection against the Indians, and the fort was located in the center of what is now Lewisburg.

Surprisingly enough, I learned that this small city in the heart of the Allegheny Mountains is 2300 feet above sea level. That's higher than the mountain tops in my Berkshire Hills.

When it comes to regional dishes the General Lewis dinner menu has an appealing variety. For example, there are grilled pork chops served with fresh applesauce, golden brown pan-fried chicken, West Virginia country ham, and desserts made with fresh berries and fruits—all from a truly southern kitchen.

Everywhere I turned in the inn I found beautiful antiques including spinning wheels, chairs, lamps, clocks, jugs, cabinets and corner cupboards. My bed was a canopied four-poster with a tufted spread. There was a fireplace, a cozy hooked rug and a beautiful old clock on the mantle.

The rugged hills and magnificent scenery of West Virginia, its history and its warm friendly people are bringing this state into its own. And here and there, a country inn like the General Lewis is making the experience more and more enjoyable.

*GENERAL LEWIS INN, Lewisburg, W. Va. 24901; 304-645-2600. An antique-laden 30-room village inn on Rte. 60, 90 mi. from Roanoke, Va. European plan. (Modified American plan only during*

*W. Va. State Fair) Breakfast and evening meal served daily with an additional meal on Sundays at noon. Dining room closed Christmas Day. Famous golf courses nearby. Laurence Little, Innkeeper.*

*Directions: Take Lewisburg exit from I-64. Follow Rte. 219 south to first traffic light. Turn left on Rte. 60, two blocks to inn.*

### RIVERSIDE INN
**Pence Springs, West Virginia**

Ashby Berkley, wearing a leather vest and knee britches and sporting a well-trimmed beard, showed me to a heavy oaken table set with pewter plates and pistol-handle knives and said, "Welcome to our house."

The light from the big fireplace at one end of the low-ceilinged log room was reflected in the candelabra of handcrafted tin. I felt as if I had stepped into Jamestown, Virginia, in the early 1600's, which is exactly the period which Ashby and Kelly Berkley have succeeded in creating. Here was the intimacy of an old English variation of the roadside tavern where travel-weary guests refreshed themselves with the table fare of their host.

It was the table fare that next commanded my attention. It is a six-course dinner served at a lovely pace not often found in these times. In fact, Ashby frequently suggests that his guests at dinner allow at least two hours. "We have two sittings for dinner, one at 7 and one at 9:30," he said, "except in June, July and August when we have sittings at 5, 7, and 9:30. This still affords our guests a leisurely pace for dinner."

Here are just a few things that are frequently served: English mulled cider; shrimp wrapped in bacon; fresh tomato soup; bean and

226

bacon soup; scalded English slaw (this is a house specialty which consists of hot cabbage salad served with a dressing of bacon, sugar and vinegar). The vegetables served are determined by the choice of meat. Other offerings include a whole roast chicken for two served with wild rice, a stuffed duckling for two roasted in an orange glaze, chicken amandine on a bed of wild rice, rainbow trout, shrimp, frog legs, hen and hare, and a succulent game pie. Kelly explained that almost everything is made from the basic ingredients, and that includes the bread which is baked by Ashby's mother.

My dinner took more than two hours. There was a continual parade of dishes and surprises coming from the kitchen, each with its own fanfare and ruffles.

I think the Riverside Inn can best be described as an elegant West Virginia country tavern. There are no rooms here at the moment, and reservations for dinner are most advisable.

Kelly and Ashby took me on a tour of the Pence Springs Water Company which is an old mineral spa where naturally carbonated spring water bubbles up out of the ground. There is a flea market held every Sunday which often attracts as many as two thousand people. "There's everything from junk to antiques. It's a real country tradition," explained Ashby who is from Pence Springs, although he has had some interesting adventures in other parts of the world. There is also an impressive antique shop specializing in glass items. I could have spent a day just finding things such as candlesticks. lamps, tools and old bottles. "We have a stable and extensive riding trails into the mountains and rustic campgrounds along an isolated section of the Greenbrier River," Ashby continued.

*RIVERSIDE INN, Rte. 3, Pence Springs, W. Va. 24962; 304-445-7469. A country restaurant 12 mi. from Hinton, W. Va., on the banks of the Greenbrier River, 12 mi. from Lake Bluestone. No lodgings. Dinner served daily except Mondays. Lunch served by special reservation only. Open from February through Dec. 31. Closed Thanksgiving, Christmas and Easter. Located in the beautiful West Virginia mountains. Horseback riding, skiing, boating, hiking, swimming, spelunking, white water canoeing nearby. Ashby and Kelly Berkley, Innkeepers.*

*Directions: From the east, take Alta exit off I-64, follow Rte. 12-S to Alderson then Rte. 3-W 8 mi. to Pence Springs. From the west, from W. Va. Tpke. follow Rte. 3 from Beckley through Hinton to Pence Springs. The inn is located in Pence Springs on Rte. 3 between Hinton and Alderson.*

## DROVERS INN
### Wellsburg, West Virginia

Mary Marko and I had driven over to Meadowcroft Village for a few moments because she wanted to show me some of the newly restored buildings. We stopped at the one-room schoolhouse which was built in 1834, and I took the opportunity to pull the rope and toll the old school bell.

Meadowcroft in Avella, Pennsylvania, is just a few miles from the Drovers Inn in Wellsburg, West Virginia, where Mary is the innkeeper.

The history of the inn goes back to 1848 when it was built by John Fowler. At that time it was certainly one of the most auspicious structures in that part of the country. For many years it housed Fowler's General Store and the town post office. Fowler's General Store has been reproduced at Meadowcroft Village.

Over a century ago the road in front of the inn was the principal route for drovers moving their stock across the toll road from Pennsylvania and Ohio. At the Drovers Inn they could obtain lodging and food for themselves, and fodder for their livestock which were kept in pens adjacent to the inn.

Today, the inn reflects Mary's faithful restoration to a 19th century atmosphere. On the main floor are two contrasting dining rooms, one informal with interesting bric-a-brac, advertisements, old calendars, pictures and posters. It has red-checkered tablecloths. The other dining room is a more formal Victorian room, with handsome tables, each with its own individual set of matched chairs.

The mellowed red brick building is set back from the road among trees.

Mary takes great pride in showing her guests through the inn, and she has left one room exactly the way she found it seven years ago when she took over the inn.

I found the best way to get to Wellsburg from Washington, Pennsylvania is on Rte. 844 which passes through Wolfdale, Buffalo and Middletown. At the Pennsylvania border it becomes West. Va. Rte. 27. The Drovers Inn has no lodging rooms and serves dinners only from Wednesday through Sunday. It is quite an experience.

*DROVERS INN, Washington Pike, Wellsburg, W. Va. 26070; 304-737-0188. A country restaurant in a historic building on W. Va. 27, 16 mi. north of Wheeling and 18 mi. from Washington, Pa. Near Meadowcroft Village, Avella, Pa. No lodgings. Dinner only served daily Wednesdays through Saturdays from 5-10 p.m. and Sundays from 1-10 p.m. Closed Christmas. Mary Marko, Innkeeper.*

*Directions: From east on I-70, take exit 6 at Washington, Pa., follow Rte. 18 to 844 which becomes W. Va. 27. From west, exit I-70 at Wheeling, W. Va., follow Rte. 2 north to Wellsburg. Turn right on Rte. 27.*

## WELLS INN
### Sistersville, West Virginia

The newspaper was the *Daily Oil Review,* dated January 16, 1895. The big news that day was that the Hotel Wells had opened the previous night with a reception, banquet and ball. The reporter waxed eloquent over "the most successful social event in the history of the city."

The news item went on to describe the building as "three-story, brick, situated on Charles Street within easy distance of the depot, the boat landing, and the center of town. It has two fine verandas, one on the first story and one on the second. The latter is supported by columns of the Colonial period.

"The interior is a marvel of richness and good taste. In the main hallway an artistic piece of mosaic floor tiling strikes the eye, in the center of which are the words 'Hotel Wells.' "

The article speaks of the sleeping rooms "all furnished in first class style with gas and steam heat from the radiators. The house throughout is furnished with hot and cold running water."

Well, it was fun reading about the Hotel Wells which was the forerunner of today's Wells Inn, and a great deal of the description of the original hotel would certainly apply today, except of course there

are modern conveniences behind the Victorian facade and furnishings.

All the dining rooms and lodging rooms have been redecorated and furnished to create a turn-of-the-century atmosphere.

Jack Kinkaid, the innkeeper, is very proud of the fact that the Wells Inn is right in step with the rest of downtown Sistersville. It has a bronze plaque on the front of the building indicating that it has been placed on the National Register of Historic Places by the United States Department of the Interior.

Sistersville has a large group of unusually well-preserved Gothic, Greek Revival and Romanesque buildings which are most unusual considering the fact that many towns have torn down most of these old business blocks. This section of Sistersville has remained virtually unchanged since the 1900's.

Anyone planning on visiting Sistersville, should plan to spend part of the day on a walking tour that would include St. Paul's Episcopal Church, the Henderson Hotel building, the Sistersville High School, and the bank buildings at the corner of Wells and Diamond Streets.

Sistersville was a sleepy little town until early in the 1890's when gas and oil were discovered beneath the surface, and almost overnight the community became a boom town. Oil and gas created instant riches for some of the townspeople. The buildings are an outgrowth of that sudden prosperity.

Construction on West Virginia Route 2, north and south of Sistersville, is, as I understand it, virtually completed and access to the town using this route is unobstructed. However, it is also possible to reach it from the Ohio side by taking the small car ferry which crosses the river at this point.

I have, in the past, enjoyed the scenery on the Ohio side heading west toward the Buxton Inn in Granville.

Because Sistersville is on the imaginary geographical border between North and South, the menu of the inn offers excellent examples of each style of cooking. Some of them, such as roast beef with mushrooms, French peas, turkey, chicken salad and fresh fruit pies were served back in the days of the Hotel Wells.

*WELLS INN, 316 Charles St., Sistersville, W. Va. 26175; 304-652-3111. A restored Victorian 36-room village inn, 50 mi. south of Wheeling, 38 mi. north of Parkersburg. Sistersville is a former oil boom town of the '90's. European plan. Breakfast, lunch, dinner served daily. Open year-round. Skiing nearby. Jack Kinkaid, Innkeeper.*

*Directions: From the south, leave I-77 at Parkersburg and proceed north on Rte. 2. From the north, leave I-70 at Wheeling and travel south on Rte. 2.*

# Kentucky

*The American expansion westward brought the pioneers over the Appalachians into Tennessee and Kentucky. Our history and literature is rich in stories of these men and women who carved their way through the wilderness. A generation of Americans have grown up with Daniel Boone as a household word.*

*The Shakers found their way from New York State to Kentucky during the latter part of the 18th century and a colony was formed near Harrodsburg around 1810. To the east at Berea, about an hour south of Lexington, I found an outstanding college based on the principles of freedom, self-help and fellowship. In many ways Kentucky was the gateway to the West.*

**DOE RUN INN**
**Brandenburg, Kentucky**

America has had many frontiers since the landings in Jamestown and on Cape Cod, but there is certainly no more colorful frontier than western Kentucky when it was fought over by Indians and settlers during Daniel Boone's time.

I was talking to Innkeeper Curtis Brown about the considerable Daniel Boone tradition that is present at the Doe Run Inn. "Well,

Daniel Boone was never here because it was built in 1816. However, his brother Squire Boone discovered the property in 1778 and was the original landowner. Patrick Henry, who was the Governor of Virginia at the time, signed the original deed. Incidentally, it was known as "Little York, Virginia."

Pioneer America lives at the Doe Run Inn. I'm sure that it has changed very little in 165 years. The building with the huge limestone blocks on the outer walls four feet thick was made to repel Indian attacks. The tremendous front door could withstand most any attempt to break in, and the huge fireplace still sends warmth radiating through the room.

Interestingly, the property has changed hands relatively few times and has remained virtually intact over the years. There has been no intrusion on the natural environment which takes in 1,000 acres. There are many walks and trails through the woods.

An early innkeeper was "Wash Coleman," the great-grandfather of Lucille Brown who is Mrs. Curtis Brown.

The building was originally a woolen mill and then a gristmill. An old record shows a payment made to Abraham Lincoln's father who worked as a stonemason on the building.

The lodging rooms are most unusual. Many have antique beds, tables and chairs that would be in place in a museum. A few have private baths. Some have little chunk stoves for heating. I found one room where the hot and cold water faucets are switched. Rooms on the third floor are being redecorated.

The food is real Kentucky. Hot homemade biscuits, vegetables served southern style. Kentucky fried ham and fried chicken and gravy. The old-fashioned lemon pie tops the desserts.

Thanksgiving Day is always special with many foods that were offered at the first Thanksgiving such as turkey, chicken, turnips, sweet potatoes and fried pies!

*DOE RUN INN, Rte. 2, Brandenburg, Ky. 40108; 502-422-9982. A 17-room country inn reminiscent of the backwoods on Rte. 448, 4 mi. south of Brandenburg, 38 mi. south of Louisville. Near Fort Knox. European plan. 5 rooms with private bath; 12 rooms with shared baths. Breakfast, lunch, and dinner served to travelers daily. Closed Christmas Eve and Christmas Day. Hiking, fishing and swimming nearby. Curtis and Lucille Brown, Innkeepers.*

*Directions: From Louisville, Ky., take U.S. 31-W south to Hwy. 1638. Take Hwy. 1638 west and turn left on Hwy. 448. Follow Doe Run signs.*

## THE INN AT PLEASANT HILL
**Shakertown, Kentucky**

The Inn at Pleasant Hill is located in a restored Shaker community in one of the most beautiful sections of central Kentucky. Although the word "Shaker" is becoming more and more familiar to us, perhaps a word of explanation would be helpful.

The Shakers were members of a religious sect, the United Society of Believers in Christ's Second Appearing. They were actually an offshoot of the Quakers. The founder was Mother Ann Lee who brought her ideas to America late in the 18th century. After many trials and tribulations, the Shakers began to prosper.

They held some advanced social ideas. They were hospitable to visitors and took in orphans and unwanted children. One of their fundamental beliefs was hard work and austere discipline that sought perfection. This sense of perfection is extended into the design of their furniture and many people learn about Shakers for the first time as a result of being attracted by the beauty and simplicity of the functional Shaker designs.

The Shakers lived in communal dedication to their religious beliefs of celibacy, public confession of sins which culminated in the frenetic dances which gave them the name of Shakers, renunciation of worldliness, and common ownership of property.

There were five "families" at Pleasant Hill which was established in 1805. By 1820 it was a prosperous colony of five hundred persons. "Family" had a particular meaning since the Shakers did not believe in marriage. Men and women, they maintained, could live more happily as brothers and sisters helping one another but living personally apart.

The Civil War plus 19th century industrialism and worldliness seeped into Pleasant Hill and the celibacy rules prevented the natural increase in their numbers. In 1910 they were dissolved.

The inn is located in the Trustees House, one of twenty-five or more buildings clustered along the single country road. To construct buildings of enduring strength some with walls three or four feet thick, the Shakers quarried limestone from the river bluffs and hauled granite slabs a mile uphill from the river. Most of the buildings are of deep red brick or limestone.

The restaurant is on the first floor of the Trustees House, and the lodging rooms on the second and third floors are reached by two marvelous twin-spiraled staircases that are unmatched for craftsmanship.

The experience of sleeping in a Shaker room is most refreshing. In my room were two single beds, each with its own trundle bed underneath. The Shaker rockers were classic and the extra chairs were hung by pegs on the walls.

Many of the tasty dishes served in the dining room are prepared from Shaker recipes. The young men and women on the staff all wear replicas of simple Shaker garb. Most of the produce has been raised on the fields of the restored community.

It is to the credit of the incorporators of Pleasant Hill that they have managed to accomplish such a great deal in such a short time, although there are still many other buildings to be restored and reconstructed.

Fortunately, some of the enduring aspects of Shaker design are being encouraged, and there is an excellent gift shop where examples of simple Shaker-style crafts may be purchased.

*INN AT PLEASANT HILL, Shakertown, Ky., P.O. address: Rte. 4, Harrodsburg, Ky. 40330; 606-734-5411. A 63-room country inn in a restored Shaker village on Rte. 68, 7 mi. northeast of Harrodsburg, 25 mi. southwest of Lexington. European plan. Breakfast, lunch, dinner served daily to travelers. Open year-round. Suggest contacting Inn about winter schedule. Closed Christmas Eve and Christmas Day. Betty Morris, Innkeeper.*

*Directions: From Lexington take Rte. 68 south toward Harrodsburg. From Louisville, take I-64 to Lawrenceburg and Graeffenburg exit (not numbered). Follow Rte. 127 south to Harrodsburg and Rte. 68 northeast to Shakertown.*

## ELMWOOD INN
### Perryville, Kentucky

The Elmwood Inn could only happen in Kentucky. Surrounded by a grove of maple and sweetgum trees alongside the Chaplin River in Perryville, the inn features traditional southern dishes in an atmosphere of Greek Revival elegance. The building was constructed in 1842 and became a field hospital following the Battle of Perryville during the Civil War.

The main entrance with its twin two-story columns faces the Chaplin River. The sloping lawns are filled with sugar maples, black locusts, hemlock, pine, ash, gingko, and willows. Next to the building there is a very large and colorful bed of tulips which must be breathtaking when in full bloom.

The inn has been carefully furnished with antiques and Kentucky and Civil War memorabilia. Each of the six serving rooms has been named for some worthy individual well known to the region or community. For example, there is the T. C. Poynter Room, named for the founder of a school which occupied the building for many years.

In early 1976 there was a small fire in the kitchen, but now that is only an unpleasant memory.

At lunch my salad looked delicious. There was a variety of fresh fruits arranged around a generous scoop of sherbet, and hot biscuits

filled with Kentucky fried ham. Ham and hot biscuits — what a treat for a visitor from New England!

I could have ordered the southern fried chicken with cream gravy. "That's what Colonel Sanders always orders when he eats here," innkeeper Gladys Coyle explained. "He loves the chicken, hot biscuits, new small potatoes, a big salad, and a huge helping of peas. He's been here and says it's the best chicken he's ever eaten."

After lunch I took advantage of a few extra moments to visit some of the important sites in Perryville. One is the restoration of the old Perryville historic district. It was here that I learned that Perryville was originally known as Harberson's Station and was founded by some settlers from Pennsylvania. Many of the buildings are being restored, including the Karrick-Parks House which is directly across the river from the Elmwood Inn. A footbridge is planned to connect this historic section of Perryville with the inn.

I also visited the Perryville Battlefield which is just a few miles from the town and was the scene of one of the most desperate battles of the Civil War. It is very popular with the tourists.

At the end of a pleasant afternoon filled with Kentucky history, I was happy to return for the evening meal at the Elmwood. Confronted with a myriad of choices including sweetbreads, fried shrimp, Florida pompano, and other tempting dishes, I decided to try the fried chicken with cream gravy.

I think I know why Colonel Sanders keeps coming back.

*ELMWOOD INN, Perryville, Ky. 40468; 606-332-2271. A country restaurant in an historically important Kentucky town on Rtes. 150 and 68, 9 mi. from Harrodsburg and Danville. Near the Perryville Battlefield State Shrine. No lodgings. Lunch and dinner served daily except Mondays. Closed Christmas Eve and Christmas Day. Open year-round. Gladys Coyle, Innkeeper.*

*Directions: Exit Bluegrass Pkwy. at Bardstown and take Hwy. 150 into Perryville. From Harrodsburg take Rte. 68 to Perryville.*

## BOONE TAVERN HOTEL
### Berea, Kentucky

Berea College serves the youth of 230 mountain counties in the region known as Appalachia. Eighty per cent of the students are from the region and are chosen on the basis of financial need, high scholastic standing and character. The other twenty per cent come from the other states and from Europe, Asia, and Africa. The Boone Tavern Hotel is owned by the college, and the students have the opportunity to work there at one of many different jobs. Many of the students major in hotel management and have been very successful in the hotel business.

A letter I received from Michigan was typical of letters that I have gotten from many other states concerning visits to Berea.

"I had never heard of Berea College or Berea, Kentucky, or the Boone Tavern Hotel. But after reading about all of them in your book, my husband and I changed our route on the way south to go through central Kentucky for a look.

"We were enchanted with all three. The campus is beautiful, the town is most attractive and the hotel is super.

"It is as neat as a pin, and those student waitresses are so sweet and appealing. They even refuse tips! The furniture in our bedroom was all made by students in their workshop—copies of authentic early Colonial furniture. We just could not get over it.

"When it came to food, we adored that southern peanut soup, baked plantation ham and escalloped okra. The spoon bread was delicious and the desserts yummy.

"We toured the campus and saw all the student industries: broom craft, weaving, ceramics, furniture making—well, everything. We were impressed beyond words."

Student-conducted tours of the campus leave the hotel twice daily and they are the best way to get the true picture of this unusual educational experience which incorporates the hotel itself.

Since my first visit in the late 1960's there have been several new

campus buildings added and the library is one of the most impressive that I have ever visited. While I was doing a little research there on the background of the college I found that one of the founders, Cassius M. Clay, had been converted to emancipation by a speech by the famous William Lloyd Garrison. This stand for racial freedom was part of the original foundation of the college. Incidentally, the name Berea comes from the Bible town mentioned in Acts XVIII:10: "Where men were open minded."

*BOONE TAVERN HOTEL, Berea, Ky. 40403; 606-986-9341. A 60-room village inn in a unique college community on I-75, 40 mi. south of Lexington, Ky. European plan. Breakfast, lunch, dinner served daily to travelers by sittings only. Dinner and Sunday noon coats required for men, dresses or pant suits for ladies. Open every day of the year. All campus activities open to guests; campus tours twice daily except Saturdays and Sundays. Tennis on grounds. Golf, pool and bicycles nearby. Berea is on Eastern Time. Curtis Reppert and Cecil M. Connor, Innkeepers.*

*Directions: Take Berea exit from I-75. One mi. north to hotel.*

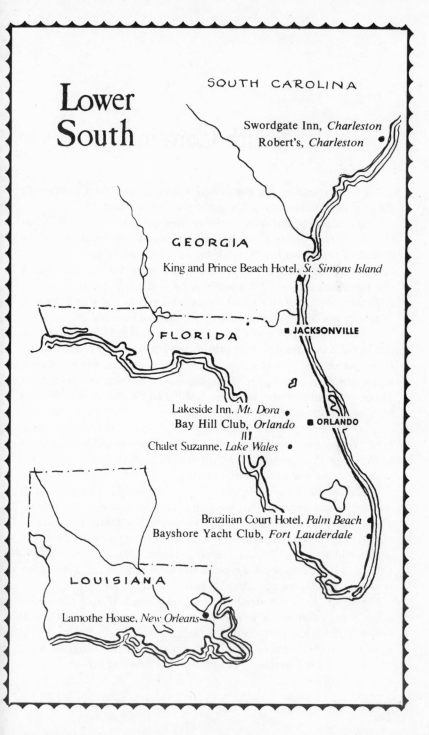

# Lower South

SOUTH CAROLINA

Swordgate Inn, *Charleston*
Robert's, *Charleston*

GEORGIA

King and Prince Beach Hotel, *St. Simons Island*

FLORIDA

■ JACKSONVILLE

Lakeside Inn, *Mt. Dora*
Bay Hill Club, *Orlando*
Chalet Suzanne, *Lake Wales*

■ ORLANDO

Brazilian Court Hotel, *Palm Beach*
Bayshore Yacht Club, *Fort Lauderdale*

LOUISIANA

Lamothe House, *New Orleans*

# South Carolina

*I was standing on the raised walkway in Old Charleston's Battery Park overlooking the panorama of the harbor.*

*Spectators might have stood on this spot on June 28, 1776, as the Americans from Fort Moultrie repulsed an invasion by the British. The British finally took the city four years later.*

*From this point also, the people of Charleston stood to watch the bombardment of Fort Sumter in 1860. Then it was occupied by Federal troops and subsequently surrendered to the Confederates. This was the first major action of the American Civil War.*

*Kerry Anderson and I had started our walking tour of Charleston in the Swordgate section (absolutely the only way to experience it) by turning off Tradd Street where the Swordgate Inn is located, to Lagare Street. The first thing he showed me was the Swordgate House. On the gate are the crossed sword and spear from which this section receives its name.*

*At 24 Legare Street there is a brass plaque next to the gate that says, "If you have a mind at peace, a heart that cannot harden, walk in this gate that is open wide, upon a friendly garden." And it is possible to take a walk in this garden.*

*This is perhaps the spirit of Old Charleston. A walk in this section would certainly put minds at peace and soften many a heart. There are, I understand, 73 pre- Revolutionary homes in this area, but actually the architecture reflects different stages of American architectural taste. The fact that this section remains preserved is a tribute to tightly controlled growth and local ordinances. Permission is needed to change the color of house paint!*

*One of the best times to go to Charleston is during the period when many of these old houses are open to the public. In 1977, this house festival took place between March 17th and April 11th. It is at approximately the same time each year. For full information write to: The Historic Charleston Foundation, 51 Meeting Street, Charleston, S.C. 29401.*

On streets like Gibbs, Lamboll, Meeting and High Battery are dozens of small hidden alleys where there are still more houses and beautiful gardens. There's also Catfish Row, the inspiration for Porgy and Bess.

Many of the houses in Old Charleston have been proclaimed National Historic Landmarks. One of them had yellow roses still in bloom during December.

Old Charleston is a place of balestrades, cupolas, dormers, galleries, fences, walls, scroll work, cobblestones, old street lamps, trees that bend over the road, gorgeous mellowed red brick walls, overhanging galleries, azaleas, camellias, cypress, and even a gazebo in the park.

At the corner of Meeting Street and South Battery it is possible to engage a horse drawn cart for a drive around the city. Of course the driver-guides know all the details about the history of the area.

Charleston has also been chosen as the American site for Maestro Gian Carlo Menotti's Spoleto Festival which arrives in May.

To really experience Charleston and the magnificent stately homes and gardens, to walk through its winding, crooked streets, to sample its theatrical, musical, architectural and natural beauty, allow at least a week.

## SWORDGATE INN
### Charleston, South Carolina

I was having breakfast in the morning sunshine on the patio at the Swordgate Inn. The muffins were hot from the oven, the Charleston grits, which had been cooking overnight, were tasty and nutlike, the jam and homemade bread continued to tempt me.

Kerry Anderson, the young, enthusiastic innkeeper, carried a pot of fresh aromatic coffee out of the little self-service kitchen and offered some to the guests. Even if we were all at breakfast at the same time, it wouldn't make much of a crowd because there are only five lodging rooms in this 18th century Charleston home.

One man from Rochester asked Kerry about the rental charge on the bicycles and he answered that there was no fee. "We just hope that you will see as much of Charleston as possible," he said. Another guest remarked that even bicycles went too fast to see the city's old beautiful homes and gardens. "The best way is by foot," he said.

"I think that's true," replied Kerry, "but be sure you get all the folders about the history tour, the historic houses and landmarks from our bulletin board in the kitchen. You can even take a horse and carriage ride to see them."

As the other guests started asking questions and exchanging experiences, I was struck by the similarity of this scene to breakfast at the Lamothe House in New Orleans. Each is a beautiful, historic, 18th century building in an old section of a beautiful American city. Each inn has true southern elegance and warm hospitality.

The five guest rooms at the Swordgate Inn are individually decorated. Each has its own distinctive sheets, pillow cases, bedspreads and ruffles. A great deal of care has been taken to make the rooms as inviting as possible. Fresh fruit and flowers are placed in the guest rooms daily and there is a newspaper at the door each morning. Four of the rooms are on the first floor of the old mansion. The fifth room on the third floor has a canopied bed and a view of the fascinating rooftops of the old city.

All of the guests are invited to view the grand ballroom on the second floor, and when my turn came, it was the first time I had ever seen what a stately old Charleston mansion really looked like. The ballroom had a handsome marbled carved fireplace at one end, and at the opposite end, a gold-leafed classic mirror that ran from floor to ceiling. I could just imagine what great parties were held there during the 19th century.

The gentle Charleston climate encourages azaleas, camellias and gardenias which are in profusion in the courtyard, as well as magnolias and holly trees.

One of the guests said that they were just going to sit in the patio and read that morning. "I think it's just lovely here," she said.

I asked Kerry whether children would find the inn comfortable, and he replied that with relatively small rooms furnished with antiques, and the absence of a swimming pool or playground, the inn would probably prove to be too quiet for the average active youngster.

When breakfast was over, Kerry made several suggestions to his guests about their day's activities. Then he said to me, "Let's take a walking tour. You know, I'm usually so busy that I seldom get a chance to do it myself. I've made reservations at Robert's for dinner, and I think you will be glad to have a good appetite."

*SWORDGATE INN, 111 Tradd St., Charleston, S.C. 29401; 803-723-8518. A quiet 5-room elegant inn located in the center of an historic area of the city, amidst distinguished 18th and 19th century homes. Within walking and biking distance of most of Charleston's cultural and historic landmarks. Bicycles furnished without charge to guests. Lodgings include informal breakfast. No other meal served. Open every day of the year. No children or pets. Beaches, sailing, and fresh water and deep sea fishing nearby. Kerry Anderson, Innkeeper.*

*Directions: Take I-26 to Meeting St. South Exit. Turn right on Meeting St., 12 blocks to Broad St.; turn right on Broad, two blocks to Legare St. Turn left on Legare for one block; turn left on Tradd St. Look for small sign that says Swordgate Inn.*

## ROBERT'S OF CHARLESTON
### Charleston, South Carolina

I had a beautiful day in Charleston wandering about the lovely crooked streets, admiring the courtyards and gardens, and touring a few of the elegant houses. What the day really needed was a finishing touch, a dinner that would be a fitting climax to my Charleston experience. When I stepped inside the front door of Robert's I knew that I had found it.

A reservation had been made three weeks earlier by Kerry Anderson of the Swordgate Inn and, even with that amount of time, I felt fortunate to have a table. This little restaurant in the Rainbow Market seats only 28 people, and there is but one serving at 8 p.m.

"Pam and I think of the restaurant as our home," explained owner/chef Robert Dickson, "and 28 people is the maximum for dinner."

I was chatting with some people at the next table while the piano played softly in the background. The menu was a polite gesture because there are no decisions to be made at Robert's. The six courses have all been chosen in advance by the chef and his staff. Waitresses with black jerseys and white aprons were serving an aperitif which is included in the six-course prix-fixe dinner.

Now the piano hit a chord, the doors into the dining room popped open, and out came the black-bearded Robert, dressed in a chef's uniform and carrying a great platter with the first course, a quiche, fresh from the oven, baked with cream, eggs, Emmenthaler cheese and spices. As if all this weren't enough, Robert was also singing one of the hit songs from "My Fair Lady" in a rich bass baritone voice. He moved from table to table graciously, still singing and welcoming guests with a smile and a nod. He disappeared back into the kitchen and there was a round of applause.

Our evening of rich food and beautiful music at Robert's had just begun.

Robert reappeared at the serving station preparing each plate himself. As the meal progressed, he produced each subsequent course with more from his varied musical repertoire which includes both opera and show music. Later on he joined our table.

"We serve quiche, a salad with an olive oil dressing, and a fish course which changes daily," he explained. Then for an intermezzo we serve fresh fruit ice made in our kitchen. The entree is a roasted whole tenderloin of beef, which is our prime offering. It is prepared in a classical way with a traditional sauce and served with fresh vegetables. There is only one entree each night.

"Dessert is always a surprise, but frequently it is crepes because I enjoy making them and our guests enjoy them. We have many different tortes and such things as pears Helene which are flambeed and topped with a rich chocolate sauce."

Well, the dining and singing went on for at least three hours, and after dinner was over, Robert came out again and did some operatic arias and even a short humorous version of "Happy Birthday."

Robert's, about which I had heard from several readers, did indeed provide a fitting climax to a day in Charleston. I left filled with Chateaubriand and joie de vivre. My dinner, including gratuity, was $20.00 and remember, reservations are needed at least four weeks in advance.

*ROBERT'S OF CHARLESTON, 42 North Market St., Rainbow Market, Charleston, S.C., 29401, 803-577-7565. Dinner served at 8 p.m. nightly except Sundays and Mondays. No lodgings. Closed Thanksgiving, Christmas, New Year's Eve and New Year's Day. One sitting. Reservations absolutely necessary. Robert and Pam Dickson, Innkeepers.*

*Directions: Once in Charleston, ask directions to the Rainbow Market.*

# Georgia

### KING AND PRINCE BEACH HOTEL
### St. Simons Island, Georgia

I awakened to the sound of the waves on the shore. It must have been about an hour after daybreak. I slipped into some swimming trunks, grabbed a jersey, and walked out of the patio door from my room at the King and Prince onto the Atlantic beach. At that moment I was sharing it with the seabirds who continued their search for food among the receding waves. The water was warm so I plunged in.

Walking back, exhilarated and refreshed, I got a good view of the King and Prince with its many verandas and patios and the luscious palm trees intermixed with oaks. Some other guests were already enjoying an early game of tennis, and I agreed to make a fourth for doubles about eleven in the morning. Others were on their way for golf at the nearby St. Simons Island Club where the King and Prince guests also have lunch and dinner privileges.

Innkeeper Baxter Webb happened to be standing on the hotel terrace as I approached and both of us had a reunion which went back to our original acquaintance a number of years ago when he was keeping an inn in western Massachusetts.

"I know you are just going to love it here," he said. "Almost everybody that comes down from the north thinks that this must be heaven. Actually we're a good mix," he continued. "People from Birmingham, Mobile, Atlanta, and Augusta are here during the summertime because this is their summer resort and, of course, you Yankees are traveling to Florida and stopping here in increasing numbers. Some are spending more time here than they are in Florida!"

Let me share a letter I had from my dear friend, Lucy Dee Dee from Grand Rapids, Michigan, who stayed here recently:

"Our suite at the hotel was beautiful, right on the ocean. The dining room was beautiful, excellent service and a gorgeous flood-lighted view of the white breakers. I had the chicken specialty with wine sauce—excellent. However, I threw all calorie watching into the ocean and ordered the Mile High Pie which was lush and similar to baked Alaska. Clare had the special for the night which was roast duckling and Harvard beets. He said it was great. His meal included nugget cake—this was unusually good as I had a taste of it. Tasted like a Christmas 'figgy pudding.' I love that Baxter."

A later visit with Clare in Grand Rapids brought out the fact that he was excited about the history of St. Simons Island. For example, it goes back to 1736 when the first fort was built, and St. Simons figured prominently in General Oglethorpe's conflict with aggressive Spanish forces in nearby Florida. They were defeated at nearby Bloody Marsh in 1742. We both exchanged notes about visiting the famous lighthouse.

At the King and Prince there is history for history lovers and birds and flowers, and there is food galore. In fact, the menus are published two weeks in advance, but we have already had a hint about them from Lucy.

I visited the King and Prince planning to spend one night on my trip north from Florida. I was so captivated with it that one night became three, and I am sure that other guests have had the same experience.

*KING AND PRINCE BEACH HOTEL, P.O. Box 798, St. Simons Island, Ga. 31522; 912-638-3631. A 94-room resort-inn, directly on the ocean; 10 mi. from Brunswick, Georgia. Near many significant natural and historical attractions. European plan. Open every day of the year. Breakfast, lunch and dinner served to travelers daily. No pets; kennels nearby. Beach, pool, tennis on grounds. Bicycles, golf, skeet shooting, horseback riding, fishing, sailing nearby. E. Baxter Webb, Innkeeper.*

*Directions: From the north, I-95 to Brunswick, take St. Simons exit to St. Simons Sea Island Causeway to the King and Prince. From the south, I-95 from Jacksonville until it ends then Rte. 17 to Brunswick, (take Jekyll Island cut-off) over the Sidney Lanier Bridge to St. Simons-Sea Island Causeway. Follow signs to hotel.*

# Florida

## LAKESIDE INN
### Mount Dora, Florida

"You're as young as you want to be." These words were firmly spoken to me by a white-haired lady wearing tennis shoes and visor out in front of the Lakeside Inn.

"Young man, I'm on my way over to the tennis courts right now," she continued. Why don't you get your racquet and join me? Mr. Edgerton told me you were a tennis player. I'm 70 years old and I play tennis every day."

While I didn't find too many senior citizens ready to challenge me on the courts at 8 a.m., I will say that the collection of grandmothers and grandfathers at the Lakeside Inn had a great deal more pep than one might ordinarily expect. I asked Dick Edgerton about this.

"We've always been popular with retired people. However, in the past few years there has been a steady increase in the number of younger guests who come with their children. I think part of this is

because we have so many facilities for everyone. There are two swimming pools and a wide variety of outdoor games. We have excellent fishing and boating, and we're not far from Disney World.

"One of the diversions which people of every age like is lawn bowling. Mount Dora has the third largest lawn bowling club in the United States, and there is nothing like good outdoor activity to keep people lively and in good spirits."

Dick could have included the fact that there are five golf courses within a twenty-minute drive of the Lakeside, including one right in the community of Mount Dora.

One of the pleasurable aspects of visiting the Lakeside is the opportunity to turn winter into summer. There are palm trees standing side by side with oaks, pines and cedars. One of the most beautiful trees in this part of the country is the serinam cherry and there are also golden raintrees and kumquat trees. The fragrance from the trees, flowers and shrubs is heavenly. This is also where migrating and resident birds meet and flit from tree to tree.

Dick and I agreed that there's a striking resemblance between Mount Dora and New England, and he said that a great many of the guests came from the Northeast. "We serve quite a few New England dishes," he said. "Clam chowder and Indian pudding are on the menu and you can even have cornmeal mush for breakfast." The rest of the menu at the inn reflects the tropical location and proximity to the Florida waters. The buffets are much admired.

My new tennis friend was getting impatient. "Well, are you going to play or not?"

"Okay," I replied, "we'll play."

"Lovely," she said. "And tonight after dinner we'll get two more people and play 'Spite and Malice.' It's an old card game. You'll love it!"

*LAKESIDE INN, P. O. Box 175, Mount Dora, Fla. 32757; 904-383-2151. A 110-room resort-inn on Lake Dora in central Florida, 30 mi. northwest of Orlando. American plan. Breakfast, lunch and dinner served to travelers daily. Open from Dec. 15 to April 15. Two swimming pools, fishing, waterskiing, putting green and shuffleboard on grounds. Golf, bicycles, lawn bowling and sailing nearby. Marie and Dick Edgerton, Innkeepers.*

*Directions: Follow I-95 south to Daytona Beach, then I-4 to Rte. 46 west to Mount Dora. Or, follow I-75 south to Wildwood, then Rte. 44 east to Rte. 441. Proceed on Rte. 441 to Mount Dora. After passing Lakeside Inn billboard on Rte. 441, turn south at first paved road (Donnelly St.) and proceed to Lakeside Inn.*

## BAY HILL CLUB AND LODGE
### Orlando, Florida

It was early December. I had left the cold, snow, fog and rain of New England, and with an excellent flight from Hartford, arrived in Orlando in less time than it would have taken me to drive from the Berkshires to New York City. Now it was about 8 a.m. in the residential community of Bay Hill and I was walking across the well-kept lawns and grounds of the Bay Hill Club. The earlybird golfers were already out in force and the pro shop, with its impressive array of golf equipment and sporting clothes, was open and doing business. I could hear the ping of the tennis balls from the nearby courts. Another great day at Bay Hill was about to begin.

Bay Hill is a place for lovers of golf and tennis, warm pleasant weather, swimming, sailing, fishing, exotic birds, beautiful plants, and relaxing sunshine.

There is an interesting story about my discovery of Bay Hill. For the past few years I have been receiving letters from readers who inquired about inns in Florida where there was a great deal of emphasis on active outdoor sports. I happened to mention this to Shube Walzer who, with his son, Marty, runs the Pine Barn Inn in Danville, Pa. He said, "I've got a great idea. Come down to Bay Hill in Florida, visit me, and meet my daughter, Winnie. She and her husband have a golf club and resort-inn that might be just what you are looking for."

Well, I visited Shube and all the lovely people at Bay Hill not once but twice, and it is exactly the kind of a place for which I was searching. The people who own the lovely houses adjacent to the clubhouse and fairways are escapees from the north.

The membership of the Bay Hill Club is made up of people from the Orlando area and many other parts of the world. The public rooms, dining rooms and lounge areas are all furnished in very attractive Florida tones and textures. On the walls of the dining room are photographs of well-known golf personalities and plaques with the names of men and women who have won the Club championships in golf and tennis. It is quite similar to my own golf club and other clubs that I have visited throughout the United States. The big difference is that the Bay Hill Club also has food and accommodations for temporary members who wish to enjoy Florida golf, tennis, and other outdoor sports in a country club atmosphere.

The lodge offers accommodations with views of either the golf course or swimming pool. Families traveling with children will find the condominiums very convenient. Speaking of children, Disney World, Sea World, Cypress Gardens and Circus World are all within a short driving distance.

Unfortunately, during my two visits to Bay Hill I didn't have time to play the 27 holes of golf, but I did get an excellent tour of the course in a golf cart and played a few holes, just enough to wish that I could spend a few days sharpening up my game.

The Bay Hill Marina is just a few steps away from the Lodge and there are some boats available for rental. Tibbett-Butler Lake is on a chain of nine lakes with 125 miles of shoreline.

We are happy to add Bay Hill to the other club-inns such as Cuttle's Tremblant Club, north of Montreal, the Spalding Inn Club in N.H., the Hound Ears Lodge in N.C., and Ojai Valley Country Club and the Inn at Rancho Santa Fe, both in California.

*BAY HILL CLUB AND LODGE, 6200 Bay Hill Blvd., Orlando, Fla. 32811; 305-876-2429. A 72-room resort-inn, 12 mi. from downtown Orlando. Near Disney World, Sea World, Cypress Gardens, ocean beaches, John Young Planetarium, Central Florida Civic Theatre, Lock Haven Arts Center and many other recreational and cultural attractions. European Plan. Breakfast, lunch and dinner served to travelers daily. Open every day of the year. No pets. 27-hole golf course, tennis, swimming pool on grounds; fishing, boating, water skiing nearby. Arnold Palmer, Owner. Bob Branson, Innkeeper.*

*Directions: Take Exit 75 from Florida Tpke. Follow I-4W to 528A, proceed west 1 mi., turn right on Apopka-Vineland Rd. to Bay Hill Blvd.*

## CHALET SUZANNE
### Lake Wales, Florida

After my first visit to Chalet Suzanne a number of years ago, I began to wonder did it really happen, or was it like Brigadoon, the fictional village that returns for one day every 100 years. This is a reaction that I frequently get from guests who visit this unusual country inn in central Florida. Sometimes they can hardly believe it.

However, there is no doubt that Chalet Suzanne is a real place and not the result of an overactive imagination. The bridges, houses, steeples, cupolas, minarets, peaked roofs, flat roofs, castles, domes, treasures, junk, antiques and pagodas are all there. It's Bavarian, Swiss, Oriental, French, English, Turkish, Chinese and anything else you can think of.

It is also a 2600-foot air strip and the home of the Chalet Suzanne Soup Factory.

In the past I have written about how Carl Hinshaw's mother, Bertha, started Chalet Suzanne in the early 1930's and how Carl and his wife, Vita, are continuing with their own touches. I have also written extensively about all of the crazy, wonderful accommodations which are available in the sugar plum rooms and fairyland castles.

This time I thought it would be fun to talk about the dining room and the food. The restaurant overlooking the lake has been enlarged over the years. It contains all types and varieties of Victorian furniture, clocks, statues, lamps, stained glass, an old piano, wrought iron tables with tile tops, and a plentiful collection of goblets and stemware. At the far end there is a little table for two set in the front window.

"That's for honeymooners," explained Vita.

Almost everyone visiting Chalet Suzanne for the first time orders the well-known Chicken Suzanne, beautifully browned and glazed. It is prepared by Carl who in addition to being the "chief pilot" of the airfield and "principal stirrer" in the soup factory, is also the chef.

Dinner also includes the original baked grapefruit centered with a sauteed chicken liver, the famed Chalet Suzanne romaine soup, hearts of artichoke salad, petite peas in cream and butter, a grilled tomato slice, deliciously hot homemade rolls, a mint ice and tiny crepes Suzanne. The chocolate cream pie for dessert is magnificent.

A gentleman from Charlotte, North Carolina, wrote me recently:

"We stayed one night at the Chalet Suzanne. Without any question we agreed that dinner there was the single best meal either of us has ever had."

Over the years many travel and food writers have raved over Chalet Suzanne, and it has caused writers to dig into their dictionaries for new and expressive adjectives.

If all of this sounds like a Disney movie, let me assure you that Chalet Suzanne is very serious about the business of hospitality. Accommodations, food and recreation facilities are all continually praised. It is not far from the real Disney World and the beautiful Cypress Gardens with waterskiing shows. It has all of the Florida resort features that encourage guests to stay on and on.

And it is real.

*CHALET SUZANNE, Lake Wales, Fla. 33853; 813-676-1477.*
*A 30-room phantasmagoric country inn and gourmet restaurant,*
*4½ mi. from Lake Wales. Near Cypress Gardens and Disney World.*
*European and Modified American plans available. Dining room*
*open from 8 a.m. to 9:30 p.m. daily. Closed Mondays June through*
*October. Pool on grounds. Golf, tennis, riding nearby. The Hinshaw*
*Family, Innkeepers.*

*Directions: From Sunshine State Pkwy. exit at Yeehaw Junction and*
*head west on Rte. 60 to U.S. 27 (60 mi.). Proceed north on U.S. 27 at*
*Lake Wales. Inn is 4 mi. north of Lake Wales on Rte. 17A. From*
*Interstate 4 turn south on U.S. 27 toward Lake Wales.*

## BRAZILIAN COURT HOTEL
### Palm Beach, Florida

I had found the other side of Palm Beach—not the glittering
social facade, but the side with more genuine people. Furthermore, I
was amazed to find a Palm Beach Hotel with the simplicity and good
taste that appealed to such people. It is called the Brazilian Court
although most everyone refers to it as the "BC."

It was built back in the 1920's, and the Palm Beach residential
area with sedate homes and beautifully landscaped gardens grew up
around it. The building is a two-story Palm Beach Mission design
with two completely enclosed patios. One patio, with several
varieties of palm trees, begonias and poinsettias, is a marvelous place
to catch the morning sun.

The other patio really sets the tone for this discreet hotel. Dis-
persed among the royal palms, orange, banana and African tulip
trees are dining tables, many with umbrellas. Weather permitting,
all three meals are served here, and each time of day has its own
captivating mood.

In the evening, small lights twinkle on the inside of each
umbrella and indirect colored lighting dramatically underscores the
trees and exotic tropical plants. As night falls the lights become more
brilliant against the dark blue sky. Now add a three-piece orchestra
playing softly in the background and you have the complete picture.

The BC is reminiscent of the Black Point and the Asticou in
Maine. And the climate brings to mind the Inn at Rancho Santa Fe,
California.

Because there are many long-staying guests, the selections on
the menu are numerous and varied. The broiled pompano amandine
is delicious. The red snapper and Florida Lobster Newburg are very

appetizing also. There are several dishes prepared with Florida fresh fruit offered at each meal.

Although the BC is two blocks from the ocean, there's a special sun deck atop one of the buildings. As innkeeper Bright Johnson explained, "This is for people who don't want to go down to the ocean every day to get a good tan."

The lodging rooms and suites are furnished with quiet elegance. They overlook the residential area of town or the attractive inner patios.

The BC is basically a conservative resort-inn with quite a few of the amenities that guests find enjoyable. There's great emphasis placed on both the food and the service. The famous Worth Avenue shops of Palm Beach are just a few minutes away.

The Brazilian Court is part of my select group of inns and hotels in larger cities including the Algonquin in New York, the Botsford on the Detroit city line, the Cheshire in St. Louis and Lamothe House in New Orleans. I think they meet a need for personal hospitality.

*BRAZILIAN COURT HOTEL, 300 Brazilian Ave., Palm Beach, Fla. 33480; 305-655-7740. A 125-room hotel in the heart of Palm Beach. A secluded patioed garden spot just a short walk from the ocean and Worth Avenue shops. All plans available. Breakfast, lunch and dinner served to travelers daily. Open from mid-December to early April. No pets. Swimming, boating, fishing, tennis, golf and bicycles nearby. Bright Johnson, Innkeeper.*

*Directions: From Sunshine State Pkwy., take Exit 40 to Okeechobee Blvd. Turn left and proceed 6 mi. to Royal Palmway Bridge. Cross bridge and take first right, then turn left after 1 block on to Brazilian Ave. Hotel is two blocks east on Brazilian Ave.*

## BAY SHORE YACHT CLUB
### Fort Lauderdale, Florida

A country inn in Fort Lauderdale, Florida? Don't even smile. I've discovered warm, hospitable inns with a feeling of personal involvement in such metropolitan areas as New York, Palm Beach and St. Louis. The emphasis is on the "inn" rather than the "country."

Baxter and Anne Webb told me about the Bay Shore Yacht Club in the spring of 1975 when I stopped at the King and Prince Hotel on St. Simon's Island in southern Georgia. "It is not exactly a New England country inn," said Baxter, who was for many years the keeper of an inn in Massachusetts, "but it is just what you would love to find in Fort Lauderdale."

"I think that is very true," said Anne, "but what really makes such a big difference to me are the innkeepers, Janet and Bert Carvalho. They are a sort of aunt and uncle to everybody that stays there, and they are such good fun to be with."

It was in late winter of 1976 when I finally made it to Fort Lauderdale and the BSYC proved to be everything that the Webbs promised and even more.

Being located on the Intracoastal Bay Shore provides three docks for convenient mooring of visiting yachts and cruisers. Although not a yacht club per se as a fun, tongue-in-cheek gesture the guests are presented with membership cards signed by the "Commodore" which entitle them to the rights and privileges of the "Club."

The BSYC is a white four-story building facing the blue waters of the Intracoastal Waterway which traverses Fort Lauderdale. A great many of the accommodations have a very impressive view of the continuous water traffic. There are over 200 feet of landscaped waterfront gardens. The tropical gardens include gardenias, ixora, crotons, dieffenbachia, schfflera, coconut and Christmas palms, fern palms and many others. In this beautiful warm climate near the ocean there are cardinals, bluejays, woodpeckers, mourning and ground doves, and spot-breasted orioles who make their homes in the trees.

Most of the accommodations are efficiencies or apartments with kitchens, so it is possible for guests to prepare their own meals or take advantage of the many restaurants in the Fort Lauderdale area. The guests' comforts are well provided for in tastefully decorated apartments furnished with fine furniture and carpeting. The cabinets are stocked with china and silverware, and the facilities include central air conditioning, heating, sheltered parking (most important with that Florida sun) and maid service.

As Anne Webb said, Janet and Bert make all of this beautiful atmosphere and sunshiny ambiance really come to life—they're the big difference that makes the BSYC an inn. I think it is a fair statement that they consider each guest their friend and do everything they can to make everybody as comfortable as possible. They introduce all the guests, and join them at the pool.

While I was there, there was a reunion between one of the guests who had been at the BSYC for quite awhile and her son who had driven down from Washington to spend a couple of days. The boy arrived while his mother happened to be out, and Janet made him feel at home immediately and took care of things until his mother returned.

Fort Lauderdale is a city that frankly awes me. Naturally, being on the sunny tip of Florida where the famous beach just stretches out for miles, there are thousands of people who visit during the cold weather in the north. I asked Burt about the best time to visit Fort Lauderdale and he said, "February and March are the popular months, but Janet and I think that April, May, September and October are ideal because it is very comfortable, not nearly as many people, and prices on everything are really much lower."

The BSYC is not Henniker, New Hampshire, but it is a place where people from Henniker, Bellows Falls, Great Barrington and Litchfield meet to thaw out.

*BAY SHORE YACHT CLUB, 341 N. Birch Rd., Ft. Lauderdale, Fla. 33304; 305-463-2821. A comfortable homelike environment with many types of accommodations, including 4 efficiencies, 2 hotel rooms, 31 apartments with kitchens and baths located on the*

*Intracoastal Waterway. Tennis, golf, sailing, ocean swimming nearby. Shuffleboard, fishing from dock, heated pool on grounds. Open year-round. Children welcome from April thru Dec. No meals served. Kitchen facilities with efficiencies and apts. No pets. Janet and Bert Carvalho, Jr. Innkeepers.*

*Directions: From Florida Tpke. exit at MacArthur Interchange, turn left (east) to Sunrise Blvd., go approx. 7½ to ocean. Turn right on Atlantic Blvd., turn right at second light to Bay Shore Drive. Proceed one block to Birch Rd. and turn left to Bay Shore Yacht Club. From I-95S exit at Cypress Creek Rd., follow Sunrise Blvd. east for 7 mi. Turn left at ocean to Atlantic Blvd. and follow directions above.*

# Louisiana

**LAMOTHE HOUSE**
**New Orleans, Louisiana**

There are special sections in many cities and towns in North America that still reflect some of the grace and style of earlier times. Fortunately, some of these have been declared Historic Districts to preserve them for generations to come. Some which come to mind are the old sections of Charleston (South Carolina), Newport (Rhode Island), Alexandria (Virginia), Sistersville (West Virginia), Boston (Massachusetts), and Cape May (New Jersey). And certainly high on everyone's list is the French Quarter in New Orleans.

That's why it has been a source of constant joy to me to have found, a number of years ago, the Lamothe House which sits on the very edge of the French Quarter and is typical of old-fashioned New Orleans hospitality.

The Lamothe House was built by two brothers from San Domingo who came to the United States to escape an uprising. They established a sugar plantation and built the house in 1800. It has the same floor plans on both sides of the center hall which divides the three floors of the house completely in half. There are two lovely winding staircases to the upper floors. The old formal parlors on the first floor have been converted into handsome suites with elegant antique furnishings. Rooms with balconies are found surrounding the flagstone courtyard on the back of the house.

Jim Mellow wrote me a short note about his last visit to the Lamothe House: "As we entered, we walked along the center hall and

emerged into the courtyard with its flowers, fish pond and banana plants. Mimi Langguth, the innkeeper, greeted us as old friends because we have been stopping at the Lamothe House for 15 years. She showed me the newly decorated Scarlett O'Hara and Rhett Butler suites. They have five beds and are great for families or can be divided for separate sleeping accommodations.

"During our three-day stay," Jim's letter continued, "I had a chance to see many of the rooms and was delighted to see the redecoration, new bedspreads and other touches which combine so well with the collection of antiques. I heard one couple say that the antique furniture of the Lamothe House rivals any they have seen in New Orleans.

"Our Landmarks Group from St. Louis had a Cafe Brulot party in the patio using Mrs. Gertrude Munson's special recipe. Mimi's husband, Ken, has enlarged the flagstone area in the back of the patio which was the perfect spot for our gathering.

"The warm, personal charm of this inn comes through at 'petit dejeuner' around the dining room table at breakfast each morning where everyone has a chance to meet. This tradition was started by Mrs. Munson and is being carried on by her daughter, Mimi.

"I have not seen the Lamothe House or the garden patio in better condition and this fine gem of an inn is continuing its warm and personal traditions."

For the benefit of many of our readers who have visited the

Lamothe House, I am happy to report that Mrs. Munson, who established this inn and, for so many years, delighted guests with her stories about New Orleans, and advice on what to see, is as indomitable as ever. She is no longer active everyday in the affairs of the inn, but is just as keen and interested as always.

For me she will always be the toast of New Orleans!

*LAMOTHE HOUSE, 621 Esplanade Ave., New Orleans, La. 70116; 504-947-1161. A small, elegant, 14-room inn in the French Quarter within walking distance of many fascinating New Orleans restaurants and attractions. European plan with complimentary petit dejeuner. No other meals served. Closed mid-July to Sept. 1. No pets. Near Lake Pontchartrain, Mississippi River, bayou and river cruises, plantations and mansions on the Great River Road. Golf, tennis, fishing and bicycles nearby. Mrs. Gertrude Munson and Mrs. Kenneth ("Mimi") Langguth, Innkeepers.*

*Directions: From the west or east on I-10, take the Orleans Ave. exit to Claiborne Ave. which runs under I-10 at that point. Proceed east for 7 blocks or until the intersection of Esplanade Ave. Turn right on Esplanade and proceed 10 blocks. Or take Esplanade Ave. exit from I-10.*

Lowell Inn, *Stillwater* ● ■ **MINNEAPOLIS**

MINNESOTA        WISCONSIN

# Midwest

ILLINOIS

MISSOURI

Cheshire Inn, *St. Louis* ●

St. Gemme Beauvais, *Ste. Genevieve* ●

Wilderness Lodge, *Lesterville* ●

Stafford's Bay View Inn, *Petoskey*

MICHIGAN

DETROIT

Botsford Inn, *Farmington*

CLEVELAND

Welshfield Inn, *Burton*

The Patchwork Quilt, *Middlebury*

OHIO

COLUMBUS

Buxton Inn, *Granville*

INDIANAPOLIS

Durbin Hotel, *Rushville*

INDIANA

Golden Lamb, *Lebanon*

CINCINNATI

New Harmony Inn, Red Geranium, *New Harmony*

EVANSVILLE

# Indiana

*I have a very warm spot in my heart for Indiana. For two years I lived near Vincennes and traveled many of the rural roads in the southwest part of the state along the banks of the Wabash.*

*Quite a while ago I found a country restaurant in the Amish country between South Bend and Elkhart and the Patchwork Quilt has been the subject of many letters of praise for more than eight years.*

*My visits to New Harmony also go back quite a few years, and once again in this edition there is news of its continuing progress.*

## HISTORIC NEW HARMONY

*Just the name "New Harmony" promises hope, peace, and progress. I have learned that these same values have played an important role in this unusual community in the past and will play an even more important role in the future.*

*New Harmony is located on the banks of the Wabash River in southern Indiana. It was founded in 1814 by a group of religious dissenters from Wurttenburg, Germany, and prospered under the leadership of George Rapp and his adopted son, Frederick. They set up what was to be the first of two experiments in communal living in New Harmony. The Harmonists, as they were known, completely pooled their assets and then shared equally from the benefits derived from their activities. They were excellent farmers and craftsmen.*

*The Harmonists remained in the community until 1824. During that short time they constructed several buildings which are standing today. When the cold winds whistled around the cabins of those early Indiana settlers they were snug in their well-insulated, uniquely constructed homes. Twenty-five Harmonist buildings remain today, many of them are restored, and not one leans with the west wind. They are scattered throughout the community and fortunately there is an excellent walking tour of the town today which includes most of them.*

*The second experiment took place when a group under the leadership of Robert Owen, a Welch social reformer, purchased the community from the Harmonists in 1825. Owen's purpose was to create "universal happiness through universal education." They chose to establish their community in America where the expression of thought was free.*

*They succeeded in attracting to New Harmony leading scientists and educators from Europe and the educational centers of the United States. The achievements of the Owenites included the establishment of the first free public school system in America, the first free library, the first free kindergarten, the first infant school, the first women's club with a constitution, the first civic dramatic club, and the site of the first geological survey in the United States. Incidentally, in New Harmony in 1825 both boys and girls had equal access to education.*

*The Owenite social experiment lasted only two years but the society remained. New Harmony became an American center of natural science for the remainder of the pre-Civil War period. The basic philosophy of the community was now well established: A combination of the thrifty, hard work ethic of the Harmonists and the intellectual and cultural objectives of the Owenites.*

*One of the most beautiful and lasting contributions of the Owenites was the importation of seeds from the Golden Rain Tree. New Harmony has been made exceptionally beautiful by the blooming of these trees in June every year.*

Another continuing monument of the two Utopian societies is the Roofless Church which is located just a few steps from the Red Geranium Restaurant and the New Harmony Inn. This contains a work by sculptor Jacques Lipchitz entitled, "Descent Of The Holy Spirit."

New shops are located in the Mews with a special emphasis on American antiques.

New Harmony is rapidly becoming an important cultural and educational center in the Midwest. Last spring the community hosted a conference of the American Academy of Arts and Sciences and also of the International Organization UNESCO.

So New Harmony continues to progress. It is everything that it ever was, plus a great deal more now under the direction of a farsighted group of people. It is one of the most exciting travel experiences in the United States.

Today the preservation of New Harmony's distinguished past, in both architecture and spirit, is being carried on at a remarkable rate. Ralph Schwarz says, "We consider New Harmony a continuing experience and not a museum village because New Harmony is as vital as it always has been. Our goal is to capture a sense of continuity and equality."

In the few short years that I have been visiting New Harmony there has been miraculous progress. For example, the Visitors Reception Area has been completed and it has facilities for arranging for tickets and tours for visitors, interpreting services, and an orientation theatre where a New Harmony film is shown.

The Murphy Auditorium, which I saw in its early stages of reconstruction, is now completely renovated and hosting a variety of concerts, lectures, and performances. Its acoustics have been praised by critics. During the summer it will house an active schedule of musical performances by the New Harmony Theatre Company featuring popular shows like, "Oklahoma,"

The New Harmony Gallery of Contemporary Art is housed in an historic building whose facade has been restored to its original beauty. It has become a gathering place for art enthusiasts in the tri-state. In 1976 an artist-in-residence created prints inspired by New Harmony, and the gallery often houses exhibits of the works of student potters, weavers, and lithographers studying and working in New Harmony.

The 12-point master tour allows the visitor to enjoy a comprehensive visit to all of the important traditional sites as well as some new additions which include the Solomon Wolfe House, a restored 1823 residence that has a scale model of New Harmony as it appeared in 1824; the 1830 Owen House which contains furniture and decorative objects of that period; and the John Beale House which is a museum of printing in New Harmony. Incidentally, the John Beale House is constructed using a very old building technique similar to the daub and wattle construction I found on St. Simons Island; and the George Kepler House, a recently restored Harmonist frame and brick residence containing a museum displaying geological specimens.

## NEW HARMONY INN
### New Harmony, Indiana

When I first visited New Harmony there were no lodging accommodations. Many people came to visit the Red Geranium Restaurant, and to see the Roofless Church and the Harmonist buildings, but there were no facilities for taking care of overnight guests. The New Harmony Inn has solved the problem and is also hosting quite a few conferences and seminars.

An unusual feature of this inn is a year-round swimming pool with a sliding glass roof to bring summer inside or keep out inclement weather.

The inn reflects contemporary influences with a generous use of stone and plaster blended with red brick walls in the rooms, hallways and reception area. The grounds are landscaped with evergreens, firethorn and Oregon holly.

I would like to share a letter from my dear friends, Clare and Lucy Dee Dee, who visited the New Harmony for the first time in July 1976:

"We arrived here around 1:30 p.m. and immediately fell in love with the place. Right now we are sitting in our very authentic room at the inn. The double French doors are open and the countryside 'rolls' down to a wee lake clearly visible from our room. The air is heavenly sans air conditioning. I don't mean to sound trite but all I can think of to say is 'it is so peaceful in the country.' I haven't felt so relaxed or contented in ages.

"I feel this is going to be a superb attraction. However, I would not hesitate to say that it is still much in its infancy. Work is going on all the time and old buildings are unique and have such great possibilities.

"When we arrived we felt like having some ice cream so we just happened to find 'The Lemon Tree' with a little sign that says 'An old-fashioned ice cream parlor.' It was! We conversed with the woman in charge and told her how much we loved the whole idea. She said, 'Have you seen Mrs. Owens? She rides all over town in her little electric car with the fringe on top.'

"We did some more sightseeing and lo and behold we saw the car standing beside a beautifully restored clapboard house. I asked someone if I could see Mrs. Owens and she came out to greet us. I told her that we were there because of you and she wished to be remembered to you. We are so happy we make ourselves known to her."

Lucy Dee Dee also added a "PS" to Clare's letter:

"We loved the Red Geranium, the food was excellent. We both had the veal Cordon Bleu. I guess we really missed something by not having one of the scrumptious desserts, but the entrees were so generous we just couldn't possibly squeeze a dessert in that evening.

"The next morning after a peaceful out-in-the-country sleep (never woke up even once) we had a neat Continental breakfast in the Entry Room. Yes, indeed, I think you can conclude we loved New Harmony."

The Dee Dees have been most generous in pointing out country inns to me, and I am delighted that I in turn was able to recommend a new country inn experience to them.

*NEW HARMONY INN, New Harmony, Ind. 47361; 812-682-4491. A 45-room village inn on the site of Harmonist and Owenite restorations. No meals served; some rooms with kitchenettes. No pets. Open every day. Year-round swimming pool on grounds. Golf, boating, tennis and riding nearby. Gary Gerard, Innkeeper.*

*Directions: Located 30 mi. northwest of Evansville. Approximately 18 mi. on Rte. 460, south of I-64.*

## RED GERANIUM AND SHADBLOW RESTAURANTS
**New Harmony, Indiana**

I had heard about the Red Geranium long before my first visit to New Harmony in 1972. Letters from avid readers praised the community, the Labyrinth, the Roofless Church, and especially the wonderful food at the Red Geranium. Many, many changes have taken place in New Harmony since then.

One of those letters said, "By all means, be sure to have the spinach salad and the Shaker lemon pie." I was prepared for something unusual on my first visit.

I remember pouring some special Red Geranium dressing on the spinach salad and my first bite convinced me. This was accompanied by the warmest homemade bread I've ever eaten—the butter on it melted instantly. I can also remember the main dish at that particular meal, it was char-prime steak. The entire prime rib is cooked rare in the oven and then sliced and put on the grill for the last few minutes. My slice was a half-inch thick and did the gravy ever taste good with that delicious bread!

Incidentally, among other entrees that require a bit more time are Chateaubriand for two, beef Wellington for two, steak and lobster combinations, veal Cordon Blue and chicken Kiev. Regular offerings include a surprising selection of seafood as well as a variety of chicken and beef dishes.

As for desserts, the strawberry pie, chocolate bavarian pie and Heavenly cake all looked good. But for me a trip to the Red Geranium is never complete without some of the Shaker lemon pie!

New Harmony, which is growing every year, also has another excellent restaurant where the pace is a bit quicker and the menu rather simplified.

The Shadblow Restaurant is located in a well-preserved 19th century block on Church St. (Rte. 60) known as The Mews. It is accessible not only through its own entrance but through a remarkably fine bookstore which features many books about the Owenites and the Harmonists.

The Shadblow is built around an open courtyard in the center of which to be sure stands a Shadblow tree. The restaurant is named for the tree whose berries and fruits delighted the early New Harmony settlers. It has a brick floor and green bentwood chairs. The menu is limited to items that can be quickly prepared. It offers tasty homemade soups and an assortment of salads and sandwiches for lunch, with most reasonably priced main dishes for dinner.

At the Shadblow the food is very homey and the service is just right for the traveler who wants to spend more time experiencing the remarkable new additions to the community.

*RED GERANIUM RESTAURANT, New Harmony, Ind. 47361; 812-682-4431. No lodgings, guests accommodated at adjacent New Harmony Inn. Open 11 a.m.- 11 p.m. Tuesdays- Saturdays; 11 a.m.- 8 p.m. Sundays. Closed Mondays. Closed July 4th, Christmas and New Year's Day. Gary Gerard, Manager.*

*SHADBLOW RESTAURANT, New Harmony, Ind. 47361; 812-682-4463. No lodgings. Breakfast served from 5:30 a.m.; lunch from 11 a.m.; dinner 4-8 p.m. Open every day except Christmas.*

## DURBIN HOTEL
### Rushville, Indiana

Wendell Willkie! What a mixture of memories that name brought to mind. The year was 1940 and I was still in college. The world was on the brink of war and Wendell Willkie was running against Franklin Delano Roosevelt. I can still remember the great Life Magazine photograph of Mr. Willkie taken in Rushville during a parade when he was standing up in the back of a car with his arms raised.

Now I was in Rushville at the Durbin Hotel which was the Willkie campaign headquarters. I could just imagine the comings

and goings that must have taken place during that eventful autumn. Now one corner of the lobby is devoted to photographs of Mr. Willkie, other state and national political figures, and people involved in the campaign. During that year Rushville was a name that most anybody could identify. After Mr. Willkie lost the election to Mr. Roosevelt things settled down a bit.

The Durbin family tradition, begun before the campaign, has continued to the present. The hotel has been in the family for fifty years. In the lobby, chairs are scattered around, for sitting, talking and reading. A grandfather clock tolls every fifteen minutes, and I have a feeling that the penny scale has been telling the weight of the residents of Rushville for at least forty years. There was one interesting change, however — one corner of the lobby has been given a French sidewalk cafe atmosphere.

This 135-year-old hotel holds a curious mixture of the tried and true and the new. For example, my bedroom had flowered wallpaper, old bureaus and tables freely mixed with contemporary pieces. Many of the beds had "Magic Fingers" mattresses. I hadn't dropped a quarter in a slot to get that fascinating vibration in a long, long time.

I found a great family story at this country hotel. It was started by Leo Durbin who was a traveling salesman from Ohio, and Mary Cain of Indianapolis. They got married and went into the hotel business in a nearby Ohio town, but soon spotted the Old Lollis Hotel in Rushville. They bought it on faith and determination, changed the name to the Durbin Hotel, and did quite a bit of remodeling so that now every room has its own bath. Originally, a four course meal was only seventy-five cents.

Over the years the Durbins had seven children. "A sort of built-in core of employees," said present innkeeper, David Durbin. It is interesting to know that some of these Durbin children are still in the hotel business. David and his wife, Jo Ellen, have seven daughters, all brought up in the hotel.

The Durbin is noted near and far for great Indiana country cooking. Everything is prepared right in the kitchen and the Durbin is famous for those homecooked meals. The homemade pies, cakes, chicken, turkey, beef and pork dishes are great attractions.

1976 was the 30th year of operation for the Durbin Hotel. To properly celebrate, the Gay Nineties Room was enlarged and redecorated with old barn beams and the original mellowed brick.

The Durbin Hotel is an excellent example of preserving some of the traditions of hotelkeeping in the Midwest.

*DURBIN HOTEL, 137 W. Second Street, Rushville, Ind. 46173; 317-932-4161. A 28-room country hotel in a bustling town, about one hour from Indianapolis. European plan. Breakfast, lunch, dinner served daily except Christmas and New Year's. Leashed pets allowed. Rushville is the home of Wendell Willkie, the 1940 Presidential candidate. Golf, tennis, swimming and boating at Brown County State Park and Versailles State Park nearby. David Durbin, Innkeeper.*

*Directions: From the Indianapolis Beltway take I-74 south to Rushville-Shelbyville exit. Or follow Rte. 52 from the Beltway directly to Rushville.*

## PATCHWORK QUILT
### Middlebury, Indiana

The man on duty at Exit 10 of the Indiana Turnpike responded quickly and with good humor to my inquiry regarding the location of the Patchwork Quilt. "Turn left at the end of the access road and then turn left at the first road on the left. Just follow it around."

This is what I was doing, and the sunset here in the heartland of mid-America was almost beyond description. There were great streaks of red in the sky. The road threaded its way between Milton and Arletta's acres and then up to the doorway of the Patchwork Quilt.

As I saw the hay rakes and farm machinery, the three new grain

271

bins, a dryer, it occurred to me that this might be one of the few times many people who live in large cities would have the opportunity to see something of a working farm. I wandered among the newly painted barns where there were chickens and pigs, and because there were great cornfields on all sides, there was a collection of corn cribs. For indeed, this is a working farm restaurant.

The kitchen is such a showplace with its many stoves and ovens, that I always walk through on the way to the dining room. Here, everyone is given a bowl of steaming homemade soup, frequently bubbling away in a large iron pot on the hearth.

Then the appetizers are served buffet style. I counted over thirty on my last visit.

A lot of us probably didn't have a grandmother that lived on a farm. But if we did, she might have served baked ham or a special chicken or one of the dozens of other outstanding dishes featured from time to time on the menu. I will say that grandmother's rolls were never like Arletta's.

And it's for certain that grandmother never had such a selection of delicious desserts. These include beautiful and delicious cakes, pies, tortes and other goodies, and they are all homemade.

The only meal served at the Patchwork Quilt is dinner, and it is always necessary to reserve in advance. They are closed on Sundays. There is a fixed-price dinner on Fridays and Saturdays.

My stay at the Patchwork Quilt is always an adventure in eating. It is the next best thing to living on a farm!

*PATCHWORK QUILT COUNTRY INN, 11748 C.R. #2, Middlebury, Ind. 46450; 219-825-2417. A working farm restaurant in the tradition of midwestern hospitality, about 20 mi. east of Elkhart. No lodgings. Dinner served daily by reservation only. Closed Sundays, Mondays, Thanksgiving, Christmas and New Year's. Arletta Lovejoy, Innkeeper.*

*Directions: From east or west, exit Indiana Toll Road at Middlebury (Exit 10) and go north ¼ mi. to County Rd. #2 and proceed west 1 mi. to inn. From Middlebury follow Indiana Rte. 13 for 8 mi. north to County Rd. #2 and west 1 mi.*

# Ohio

## BUXTON INN
### Granville, Ohio

In the 1976 edition I confessed that I had lost my heart in Granville, Ohio, and that it belonged to Amy Orr whom I first met when she was about 9½-years-old.

Amy's parents are Orville and Audrey Orr who saw great possibilities in this old building a number of years ago and in 1972 began researching, planning, redesigning and restoring.

"We discovered that the house was built on land purchased in 1806 by Orrin Granger, a pioneer from Granville, Massachusetts," explained Audrey Orr. "There has been a house here ever since. It was Granville's first postoffice and also a stagecoach stop."

"In fact, a great deal of Granville, Ohio, was settled by people from Granville, Massachusetts which is not very far from Stockbridge, is it? Orville and I have visited the Massachusetts village many times and found a surprising number of architectural similarities in both places."

On my first visit, Amy, wearing a costume reminiscent of the year 1812, showed me about the inn and introduced me to Major Buxton, whom she described at the time as 'a very intelligent cat.' "We like him so much that we even put him on the sign outside," she said.

Lodging rooms at the Buxton Inn reflect a love of color and design. Each of them is also furnished with special antiques. In fact the antiques and furnishings that are scattered throughout this inn remind me of the Alexander-Withrow House in Lexington, Virginia.

Among the menu items are roast duckling with wild cherry sauce which is a special recipe, baked stuffed pork chops with applesauce. Royal red snapper and prime ribs of beef.

The late news from Buxton Inn is that the "Tavern" has been opened in the old stagecoach driver's quarters in the cellar which is reached by a set of stairs that President William Henry Harrison rode down on horseback. The gift shop has a new look with antique cupboards, pie safes, and sideboards as display centers for copper, brass, wrought iron, tinware, glass and porcelain reproductions. A bakery wing has been added to the back kitchen which means more goodies in that department.

In a letter from Audrey she told me that many people stop off after having paid a visit to the Golden Lamb in Lebanon, Ohio, to the west and the Century Inn in Pennsylvania or the Wells Inn in West Virginia to the east.

While Amy is a year older, she still enjoys chatting with the guests and conducting mini-tours of the building. Melanie Orr, who is now 13, is enjoying her role as clerk and cashier in the gift shop on weekends. Both girls have watched the business grow and really feel a part of it.

Dennison University is located in Granville and both the town and the college were the locale used by James Thurber in his play, *The Animal Kingdom*. Jim Mellow makes the Buxton Inn a regular stop on his trip from St. Louis to Philadelphia at least twice a year. It's one of his favorites.

*BUXTON INN, 313 E. Broadway, Granville, Ohio 43023; 614-587-0001. An 8-room inn in a college town in central Ohio near Dennison University, the Indian Mounds Museum and the Heisey Glass Museum. European plan. Lunch and dinner served daily. Closed Christmas Day. No pets. Golf, tennis, horseback riding, cultural activities nearby. Orville and Audrey Orr, Innkeepers.*

*Directions: Take Granville exit from I-70. Travel north 8 mi. on Rte. 37 into Granville.*

**WELSHFIELD INN**
**Burton, Ohio**

Brian and Polly Holmes have at the Welshfield Inn, as neat and fetching a country restaurant as I have seen anywhere. Furthermore, it has a rather interesting history.

The center part of the building was built, so Brian told me, in the 1840's and was originally known as the Nash Hotel. The front addition was made by a later owner named Dr. Foster, and the name was changed to the Troy Hotel. The proprietor at that time was also the village postmaster. It was well known as a station on the Underground Railroad prior to 1860.

Polly said that during the 19th century, social affairs were held at the Nash including spelling bees, a singing school and a dancing school. A ballroom was added under Captain March as well as several other innovations.

It was a pleasure to see such well-organized food-preparing and serving areas as at the Welshfield. As Brian explained: "This type of planning allows time to be spent on such things as arranging the food on the plate, about which I'm most particular." It also provides an opportunity to prepare other special things such as homemade preserves, pickles, and soups which include a tasty New England clam chowder.

Perhaps the biggest event of the week at the Welshfield Inn is Sunday dinner. The menu I saw led off with a choice of country fried chicken, prime ribs of beef, baked ham and crab supreme. Vegetables are served in family style casseroles with mashed potatoes, gravy, relishes, salad and desserts.

Desserts include such goodies as freshly baked rhubarb, apple and lemon chiffon pies. There is also a Galliano mousse which has a special apricot sauce to enhance it. Such a feast as this ought to convince any traveler that this is, indeed, an old-fashioned Midwestern country restaurant.

There is a crazy nickelodeon which makes sounds like a piano,

275

violin, mandolin and flute. Once again I reached into my pocket and pulled out a nickel, dropped it into the slot, heard it clink and clank its way through some mysterious mechanism, and then suddenly the machine started to play. I recognized the tune immediately — "A Bird in a Gilded Cage." It was, to say the least, a triumph for my memory of trivia as I sang along with it.

Brian Holmes chuckled, "You'd be surprised how many people know the words."

*WELSHFIELD INN, Rte. 422, Burton, Ohio 44021; 216-834-4164. A country restaurant on Rte. 422, 28 mi. east of Cleveland. No lodgings. Lunch and dinner served weekdays. Dinner only served on Sundays and holidays. Closed the week of July 4th and three weeks after Jan. 1. Closed Mondays except Labor Day. Near Sea World and Holden Arboretum. Brian and Polly Holmes, Innkeepers.*

*Directions: On U.S. 422 at intersection of Ohio 700, midway between Cleveland and Youngstown, Ohio.*

## GOLDEN LAMB
### Lebanon, Ohio

A country inn at Christmas! The idea always appeals to me and I'd like to stretch the holiday season out to three or four weeks so that I could visit the many country inns where Christmas is something special.

At the Golden Lamb, for example, Christmas 1976 began on December 1st. "It was our 173rd Christmas," said Jack Reynolds, "and we took the opportunity to celebrate America's priceless Pennsylvania Dutch heritage."

"Our Christmas scene for 1976 was done in the true Pennsylvania tradition by Barbara Strawser of Stouchsburg, Pennsylvania. The painting in our lobby highlighted a sleigh of travelers bound for the inn and the surrounding countryside. We also used it in our Christmas card!

"The Pennsylvania Dutch also had a rather interesting custom called der Belsnickel. Usually a neighbor dressed as a beggar visited homes on Christmas Eve carrying candies and switches asking about the children's behavior. He rewarded good children with candy while sometimes menacing bad ones with a switch although all was in the spirit of fun. I believe that a vestige of this heritage lives today in the form of Philadelphia's famous Mummers Parade.

"In celebrating Christmas in Pennsylvania we also celebrate the heritage of the Golden Lamb. In 1821 Henry Share came to Lebanon from Marietta, Columbia County, the heart of the Pennsylvania Dutch country. As the owner of the Golden Lamb he quickly renamed the inn the 'Ohio and Pennsylvania Hotel at the sign of the Golden Lamb,' and our link to Pennsylvania Dutch was cast."

Holiday food at the Golden Lamb begins with Chef Erwin Pfiel's Frohe Weihnachten which is served during the first ten days of Christmas every year. It is a traditional German menu featuring venison, red cabbage, and a Black Forest Yule Log.

In 1976, this was followed by a week of hearty Pennsylvania Dutch Yuletide food including roast goose, krauts and other specialties. A "Christmas at Mt. Vernon" meal was served between December 20th and 23rd including turkey, and Virginia ham.

Meanwhile Dickens carolers in period costumes sang throughout the inn on several nights during the season as they do every year, and the lobby had a collection of authentic Pennsylvania Dutch candy molds, cookie cutters and Christmas folk art.

Now it so happens that Christmas 1977 will have another theme, but I was most anxious for all of our readers to know how original, gay and full of holiday spirit, the Golden Lamb is at Christmas. This is an excellent example of what has been going on at this famous Ohio hostelry for almost 200 years.

At Christmas, and throughout the year, I have always enjoyed dining and lodging at the Golden Lamb.

*GOLDEN LAMB INN, 27 S. Broadway, Lebanon, Ohio 45036; 513-932-5065. A historic 20-room village inn in the heart of Ohio farming country on US Hwys. 63, 42 and 48. European plan. 19 rooms with private bath. No pets. Breakfast served only on Sundays. Lunch and dinner served daily except Christmas. Golf and tennis nearby. Jackson Reynolds, Innkeeper.*

*Directions: From I-71, exit Rte. 48 N, 3 mi. west to Lebanon. From I-75, exit Rte. 63 E, 7 mi. east to Lebanon.*

# Michigan

*Michigan is separated into two peninsulas by the Straits of Mackeenac. The lower peninsula includes the lake plains of the eastern shore, the sand dunes of the western shore, and thousands of inland lakes. It is shaped like a mitten of the right hand, palm up.*

*At this writing I am still awaiting my first referral for inns in the upper peninsula. Perhaps they will be forthcoming this year.*

## THE BOTSFORD INN
### Farmington Hills, Michigan

John Anhut, the innkeeper, and I were standing in the attractive fully paneled private dining room of the Botsford, and I commented on the unusual patina of the walls.

"That's an interesting story," replied John. "Under Henry Ford's direction, these panels were installed carefully by expert cabinetmakers and the entire room was then sealed off. The fireplace was filled with corncobs and then lighted. Can you imagine this room filled with corncob smoke? Well, the fire burned for a long time and the wood was allowed to cure. The result is an antique finish which can only be obtained by this type of treatment. By the

way, the colonial sideboard is supposed to have come from General Lee's home in Virginia."

The Botsford Inn has a fascinating history which began 141 years ago when it was a stagecoach stop on the road between Detroit and Lansing. Like other country and village inns of the 19th century (and even today) the public room was the scene for lots of stories and jokes and probably a great deal of business. Incidentally, the doors have remained open continuously since the first day. It is Michigan's oldest inn.

The late Henry Ford became interested in its preservation in 1924 and, upon purchasing it, placed a great many of his own 19th century antiques and treasures in it. Among them are furnishings from his country home, including a beautiful little inlaid spinet, a handsome horsehair sofa, his music boxes, a Simon Willard clock, an exquisitely inlaid mahogany table and an attractive oil painting of the Botsford Inn showing people in costumes of the late 19th century.

I walked through the other rooms including one with very low ceilings and huge beams. The fireplace had mammoth andirons and there was a cross section of the wall left bare by Mr. Ford in order to show the split lathes of 150 years ago.

Innkeeper Anhut explained something else: "I think that we have many elements of a New England country inn here, but we're really a big city inn. We attempt to compensate for bucolic charm in other ways."

Later, while dressing in my room after a welcome swim, I was grateful for some modern conveniences in the Botsford Inn such as air conditioning on an afternoon of record heat. The throb of the Motor City had almost entirely receded. So near, and yet so far.

*BOTSFORD INN, 28000 Grand River Avenue, Farmington Hills, Mich. 48024; 313-474-4800. A 62-room village inn on the city line of*

*Detroit. European plan. Dinner served daily. Breakfast and lunch Tuesday thru Saturday. Sunday brunch. Closed Christmas and New Year's Day. Pool on grounds. Greenfield Village, skiing and state parks nearby. John Anhut, Innkeeper.*

*Directions: Located in Farmington Hills on I-96 which is easily accessible from major highways in Michigan.*

## STAFFORD'S BAY VIEW INN
Petoskey, Michigan

"When it comes to regional dishes," proclaimed Kathy Hart, "I think that we have more than our share." Kathy and I were taking a short walk in Rockport, Massachusetts, which is almost half-a-continent away from Petoskey, Michigan, where Stafford's Bay View Inn sits on the shores of Little Traverse Bay. I did not get the opportunity to visit northern Michigan during 1976 so Kathy was bringing me up to date on all of the exciting things that were planned for 1977. "We really had a lovely summer," she continued. "The weather was fantastic with perhaps about only one rainy day and three rainy nights and the rest just beautiful sunshine. We finished remodeling seven guest rooms and this included new baths as well. They are really great rooms and well worth all the effort.

"All the wicker in the sunroom was painted and reupholstered and many of the guests commented on it. The Garden Room was also redecorated. It's a funny thing, Stafford pointed out that we spent more on remodeling and redecorating this year then he paid for the inn originally!"

I guess this would be a good opportunity for a word of explanation. In 1960, Stafford Smith was fresh out of college and employed at Bay View. Janice was hostess there that summer and the two found many things in common. The following year they bought the inn and got married, all within two weeks. Since that time the inn has continued to flourish with a number of embellishments. One of the greatest embellishments was the arrival of Kathy Hart as manager. Stafford and Janice readily admit that her concern and involvement with the guests are responsible for the growing success of the inn.

In addition to the personal touches supplied by Stafford, Janice and Kathy, there are other explanations for the continuing progress here. For example, senior citizens are always made to feel welcome and it's a comfortable place for vacationers of all ages. I well remember a conversation I had with Janice a few years ago. "We love grandmothers and grandfathers," she said. "They are just wonderful.

They mix so well with the very young. They always have patience with little children and join in with the games. Lots of times they will walk down to the tennis courts or the beach with them and, of course, everybody knows that grandfathers have the best stories!"

But now back to my conversation with Kathy Hart at Rockport: "We're going to continue our weekly style shows in 1977," she said. "This is coordinated by one of the ladies from Bay View, and the fashions shown are from all the attractive resort shops in the Petoskey shopping area. We think it makes a really pleasant addition to our weekly inn activities."

The Bay View section of Petoskey is a summer religious, music and art center. It is quite similar to Oak Bluff in Massachusetts and Chautauqua in New York State. The entire Bay View section is removed from the commercial section of Petoskey and has many beautiful Victorian homes which were built before 1900. The mansard-roofed inn also belongs in this same area. It was opened in 1887 as the Woodland Avenue House.

"But," I asked Kathy, "what about those regional dishes you mentioned?" "Well, we have many recipes for baked apples," she answered, "and, of course cherries from this section of Michigan are highly prized. We also have corn pudding, buttermilk pancakes and biscuits, carrot cake, Michigan pea bean soup, tomato pudding, whitefish and Lake Michigan trout and hubbard squash, just to name a few."

Buttermilk pancakes! I'll certainly be at Stafford's Bay View this year.

*STAFFORD'S BAY VIEW INN, Box 3, Petoskey, Mich. 49770; 616-347-2771. A 21-room resort-inn on Little Traverse Bay in the Bay View section of Petoskey. Modified American plan omits lunch.*

*Breakfast, lunch and dinner served daily to travelers. Open daily mid-June to Labor Day and weekends through mid-October, Christmas week and long weekends during the winter sports season. Lake swimming and xc skiing on grounds. Golfing, boating, fishing, hiking and Alpine ski trails nearby. Kathleen A. Hart, Manager. Stafford and Janice Smith, Innkeepers.*

*Directions: From Detroit, take Gaylord Exit from I-75 and follow Mich. Rte. 32 to Rte. 131, north to Petoskey. From Chicago, use U.S. 131 north to Petoskey.*

# Missouri

### CHESHIRE INN & LODGE
St. Louis, Missouri

This is the story of two inns: One is one of the most prestigious and ancient hostelries in the Old World and the other is located in the heartland of the United States. One has centuries of history behind it, and the other was created for the most part within the past decade. Each is an excellent example of how good taste, good management, and dedication to serving guests can mean success. The first inn is the Lygon Arms in Broadway, England, an inn which I have written about in the European Edition of *Country Inns and Back Roads*. The second is the Cheshire Inn on the outskirts of St. Louis, Missouri.

The Cheshire Inn was constructed in Tudor style with half-timbers embedded in the plastered outer walls. The Lygon Arms, which incidentally has had several additions to it over the years, is for the most part made of red sandstone.

I have never asked Stephen and Barbara Apted whether they have visited the Lygon Arms, but since they did visit so many other English inns, manor houses, and castles, I can't help but feel reasonably certain that some of the ideas which they have incorporated into the Cheshire Inn were inspired by decorations, wall hangings, and furniture that is typical of the Lygon Arms.

Some of the lodging rooms are quite similar although there is a wide variety in both inns. I can well imagine awakening in one of the king-sized canopied beds of the Cheshire Inn and believing, at least for a moment, that I was in the heart of the Cotswolds. The hallways and lodging rooms have furniture, prints and portraits that would be equally at home in the Lygon Arms. The rooms at the Cheshire have been named after prominent English literary figures such as Galsworthy, Dickens and Tennyson. As I recall the rooms in the English inn had been named for prominent English figures as well.

Certainly the menu at the Cheshire could be served in its British cousin's dining room without raising a single eyebrow. There are main courses such as roast prime ribs of beef with Yorkshire pudding and horseradish mousse; another is roast duck which according to the menu is served in the manner "preferred by Charles Dickens." There are also glazed pork chops Buckingham with sweet and sour sauce, topped with a grilled pineapple ring. There are many more offerings including trout stuffed with crabmeat, short ribs of beef, fish, lobster tails and, of course many types of steaks. In this last respect I would imagine that the steaks at the Cheshire would probably be greater in variety because of the proximity to the great American beef of the Midwest.

Even the desserts are similar and I am sure that, as in England, in St. Louis the most popular dessert is the English trifle. However, at the Cheshire it is possible to get Missouri apple pie served with warm cheese and/or ice cream.

Speaking of cheese, there is a new cheese and wine shop at the east end of the restaurant building at the Cheshire known as the "Cheshire Cellars." There is a large selection of imported and domestic cheeses, sausages, whole bean coffee, teas and much more. I'm sure that this would include some hearty Stilton, one of the cheeses for which the Lygon Arms is famous.

There is one interesting difference between these two inns. One of them has two double-decker red London buses which are used to transport guests to various points of interest in the immediate vicinity. Is it the Lygon Arms which has these friendly means of transport? No, it is the younger American cousin, the Cheshire.

*CHESHIRE INN and LODGE, 6300 Clayton Rd., St. Louis, Mo. 63117; 314-647-7300. A 110-room English style inn, 1 block off Hwy. 40 near Forest Park. European plan only. Breakfast, lunch and dinner served to travelers daily. Accommodations available every day of the year. Restaurant closed on New Year's Day, Memorial Day, July 4th, Labor Day, and Christmas Day. Pool, bicycles on grounds. Boating, golf, tennis and riding nearby. St. Louis Art Museum, zoo, Gateway Arch and opera nearby. Mike Parker and Jim Prentice, Innkeepers.*

*Directions: Just off Hwy. 40 at Clayton Rd. and Skinker Blvd. on southwest corner of Forest Park. From the east, take Clayton Rd. exit. From the west, take McCausland Ave. exit, north two blocks to Clayton Rd.*

## ST. GEMME BEAUVAIS
### Ste. Genevieve, Missouri

I was on Interstate 55 coming south from St. Louis after a most pleasant visit at the Cheshire Inn. In a few minutes I would be turning off onto Highway 32 and paying another visit to the town of Ste. Genevieve. In 1974 I visited this historic Missouri community for the first time and met Frankye and Boats Donze and enjoyed staying in their little inn, St. Gemme Beauvais. At that time I also had a tour of the old part of the town and visited many of the carefully restored houses including the Amoureaux House and the Beauvais House, both of which are the personal projects of the Donzes.

I turned down the village street and soon found myself in front of the red brick inn with its two-story white pillars. As I approached, Frankye opened the door and said, "I'm so glad that you could come again." Boats joined us, we had a pleasant reunion, and they told me all the news.

They were very enthusiastic about the number of people who have visited the inn from reading about it in CIBR. "There are people from all over the country and our telephone is ringing constantly," exclaimed Frankye. "Travelers with the book just seem to love the inn and the town and I have taken quite a few of them on a tour. Sometimes we are terribly busy. A lot of people from St. Louis have been here who saw the picture of you in the articles in the St. Louis papers. Mike Parker, from the Cheshire inn, also recommends us to his guests."

I looked around the dining room where we were having a cup of tea. Of course, nothing has really changed. Why should it? The

beautiful walnut ladderback chairs, the Belgian lace curtains, the marble fireplace, the fine china and the graceful stemware had the elegant look of a century ago. Frankye said that because they were anxious to preserve the heritage of the town, they put great emphasis on French dishes for both breakfast and lunch. "We have crepes, French mushroom omelettes, quiche Lorraine, French toast with ginger fruit sauce, and other specialties," she explained.

The bedrooms are done in what I call "19th century Missouri" which means that they have a collection of many different kinds of Victorian antiques including marble top bureaus and high-back beds, old-fashioned flowered wallpaper. Incidentally, there are eight different suites in the inn, and each has at least two rooms. In a few instances there are two double beds. The bridal suite has an elegant crystal chandelier and big windows overlooking the main street.

During my earlier visit, I had only visited a few of the old, restored buildings, so I asked Frankye to show me more of historic Ste. Genevieve that afternoon.

It was great fun to see the Donzes again. They are two of the most sincerely involved innkeepers that I have ever met. Just before leaving, I spotted once again the little sign that expresses the philosophy of this homey inn: "There are no strangers here, just friends we haven't met."

*ST. GEMME BEAUVAIS, 78 N. Main St., Ste. Genevieve, Mo. 63670; 314-883-5744. An 8-room village inn about 1½ hrs. from St. Louis. Modified American plan includes breakfast only. Breakfast served daily. Lunch served Mon.-Sat. Open year-round. Closed Thanksgiving and Christmas Day. No pets. Golf, hunting and fishing nearby. Frankye and Boats Donze, Innkeepers.*

*Directions: From St. Louis, south on I-55 to Hwy. 32. Exit east on 32 to Hwy. 61 to the Ste. Genevieve exit.*

## WILDERNESS LODGE
**Lesterville, Missouri**

I kept hearing about Wilderness Lodge for quite a few years before I first visited it in 1975. For example, at a barbecue up in the northern section of Michigan three or four people said to me, "You've got to go to Wilderness Lodge."

"Where is it?" I inquired. "It's down in the Missouri Ozarks, south of St. Louis."

Then an interesting thing happened. When I asked what it was like, I found that I had one set of answers from people who were interested in active outdoor sports, and another from people who just preferred to find peace and quiet, fresh air and clean water.

The outdoor enthusiasts were quick to tell me about the 600-foot tram ride up the side of a hill to the tennis courts and platform tennis facilities. They loved the horseback riding and kept telling me, "You don't really have to have any experience — they will teach you how to ride." I kept hearing about Double-Up, a game played with racquets and a light sponge ball on two tables connected by a horizontal net. It combines the skills of racquet ball and tennis.

However, I think most of all I heard about floating. "Floating is the greatest," I was told. "They have over 30 canoes and they take you and the canoe up the Black River as far as you want to float back down. It can be anywhere from an hour to a full day. You can take a box lunch, if you want, and they have life jackets and inner tubes. Most of the time they take you upstream to a bridge and you float back down to the Wilderness Landing."

The people who were enthusiastic about just relaxing spoke glowingly of the beautiful log and stone cottages with the porches overlooking the river which were ideal for napping and lounging.

Some of the cottages have stone fireplaces. They also mentioned the hay rides on a wagon pulled by a team of draft horses. These are the people who also generally mention the fishing for bass, jack salmon, sunfish, perch and catfish. And, of course, everybody loves the campfire dinners down by the river on Friday evenings.

It is at these Friday evening "get-togethers" when everyone gets acquainted, and demonstrations of canoeing and trail-riding safety are given. The river is not very deep and the horses are well-trained and gentle, but many guests are having their first experiences with these outdoor sports.

I guess it is rather obvious that when I visited Steve and Barbara Apted at the Wilderness Lodge, I found that everything that I had been hearing about for years was true. I remember one incident which took place on my first evening. I heard the dinner bell which meant that I had fifteen minutes to walk down the hill to the dining room. While walking out of the cottage, I heard a young boy say to his mother and father, "I like to come here because it's so much fun."

*WILDERNESS LODGE, P.O. Box 87, Lesterville, Mo. 63654; 314-296-2011. A 24-room resort-inn located in the heart of the scenic Ozarks approximately 2½ hrs. from St. Louis. Modified American plan. Breakfast and dinner served every day of the year. Box lunches available. No pets. Tennis, platform tennis, bocci, horseback riding, canoeing, float trips, walking and nature trails, fishing, archery, and many other sports on grounds. Stephen and Barbara Apted, Innkeepers.*

*Directions: From I-244 take Hwy. 55 south and just past Festus, take Hwy. 67 south. After the junction of Hwy. 32, Hwy. 67 becomes two lanes only. Follow 67 and very shortly look for a sign: "W," Farmington. Take this exit and turn right. You'll be on W west. Remain on W for approximately 8 mi. and there will be a sign, Jct. V. Turn left onto V for 9 mi. and it ends at Hwy. 21 in Ironton, where you turn left. Follow 21 and 1 mi. past town of Hogan be careful. This is Jct. of 21 and Hwy 49. 49 will continue straight ahead and 21 will swerve to the right. No big thing if you look for it just be sure to go right toward Lesterville. As you approach Lesterville, you'll pass Lake Taum Sauk signs. ¼ mi. further, on the left, are a Dairy Queen and an old package store (both small white buildings), and a group of resort signs. Turn left, before the signs, follow the hard surface road. You'll cross over the Black River bridge and follow the road turning left at the next set of signs, and just a little further, on the right, is Wilderness Lodge.*

# Minnesota

### THE LOWELL INN
**Stillwater, Minnesota**

"Yes, including Maureen and me, there were seven Palmers working at the Lowell Inn last summer." Arthur Palmer was bringing me up to date on the activities at this remarkable inn just a few miles from Minneapolis-St. Paul.

"The seven of us," he continued, "included my youngest daughter Nelle, who is named for her grandmother. I wish that my mother had been alive to see all of us working at her inn. I'm sure she would have been very proud."

I paid my first visit to the Lowell Inn in the summer of 1975, principally as the result of considerable urging by several different readers who spoke very highly of it. From the very first moment of my visit I discovered an unusual number of unique features.

Arthur's mother, Nelle, and her husband gave up a career in show business during the 1930's to become innkeepers. "Mother was part of an act called 'The Obrecht Sisters,' " explained Arthur. "Dad was a pianist. They played Stillwater a few times and fell in love with the old inn, which was quite run-down at the time. Both of them had always wanted to be innkeepers, and after leasing it for a number of years, their dream came true when they purchased the inn in 1945. I grew up here and my family is continuing my parents' tradition."

Another most unusual feature and perhaps the most striking experience is dining in the Matterhorn Room. The room is filled from floor to ceiling with authentic Swiss woodcarvings and the staff is dressed in Swiss costume. The feature of the five-course fixed-price dinner is fondue Bourguignonne with cubes of select prime beef which each person cooks to his own taste in individual pots and dips in tasty sauces. Let me hasten to add that the Palmers, both Maureen and Arthur, have a Swiss background and when I told them that I would be visiting Switzerland in 1977, they made several suggestions about inns that I would enjoy.

In addition to the Matterhorn Room, there are two other dining rooms each with its own theme. The George Washington Room continues the exterior theme of the inn which greatly resembles Mt. Vernon. It is furnished with many antiques of the Williamsburg

period. The Colonial theme is also found in the lobby and parlors. There is a comfortable elegance about the fireplace which is augmented by a bevy of most comfortable quilted couches and blue leather chairs.

The Garden Room was originally conceived as an outdoor garden court and even has an indoor trout pool from which guests may select their own trout.

"In 1977," explained Arthur, "we will have a patio area on the south side of our front porch which will be open as a sidewalk cafe. We plan on specializing in crepes and a light lunch."

The inn has 22 lodging rooms all providing a very homey feeling. It was almost like being home in Stockbridge, Massachusetts.

I'm sure that Nelle Palmer of "The Obrecht Sisters," probably learned to "count the house" at a very early age, and would applaud the continuing innovations that are a part of her beloved inn today.

*THE LOWELL INN, 102 N. Second St., Stillwater, Minn. 55082; 612-439-1100. A 22-room village inn 18 mi. from St. Paul, near all the cultural attractions of the Twin Cities. European plan. Lunch and dinner served daily except Christmas Eve and Christmas Day. Open year-round. No pets. Canoeing, tennis, hiking, skiing and swimming nearby, including 4 ski resorts within 15 mi. Arthur and Maureen Palmer, Innkeepers.*

*Directions: Stillwater is on the St. Croix River at the junction of Minn. 95 (north and south) and Minn. 36 (east and west). It is 7 mi. north of I-94 on Hwy. 95.*

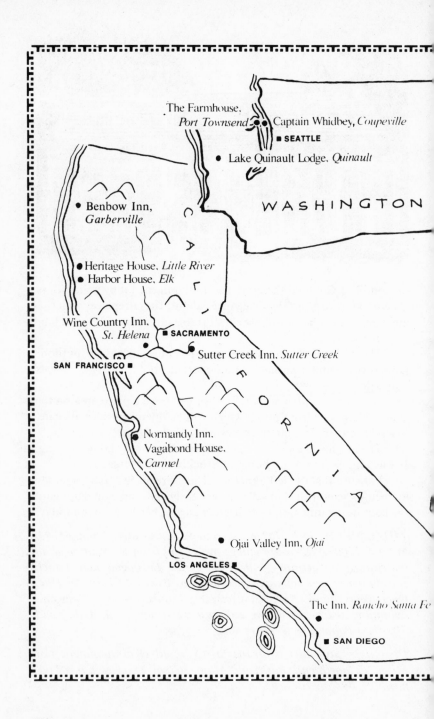

The Farmhouse,
Port Townsend  Captain Whidbey, *Coupeville*

■ SEATTLE

Lake Quinault Lodge, *Quinault*

WASHINGTON

Benbow Inn,
*Garberville*

Heritage House, *Little River*
Harbor House, *Elk*

Wine Country Inn,
*St. Helena*  ■ SACRAMENTO

Sutter Creek Inn, *Sutter Creek*

SAN FRANCISCO ■

C A L I F O R N I A

Normandy Inn,
Vagabond House,
*Carmel*

Ojai Valley Inn, *Ojai*

LOS ANGELES ■

The Inn, *Rancho Santa Fe*

■ SAN DIEGO

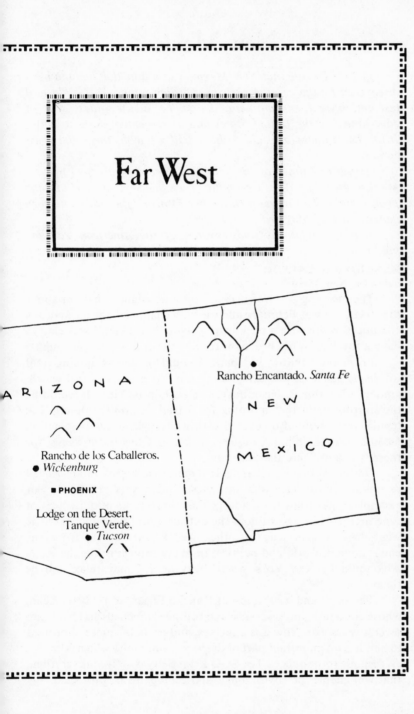

# Far West

ARIZONA

Rancho de los Caballeros,
● *Wickenburg*

■ **PHOENIX**

Lodge on the Desert,
Tanque Verde,
● *Tucson*

Rancho Encantado, *Santa Fe*

NEW

MEXICO

# New Mexico

*In 1974 I wrote that New Mexico was a state that had not been discovered by the great American traveling public. It is a place of fascination and enchantment. Santa Fe is the oldest seat of government in the United States and its settlement dates to about 1610. The Indians are said to have had a pueblo there 400 years earlier.*

*At various times of the year there are festivals held in New Mexico including San Geronimo Day on September 30th, the Procession of the Virgin on December 24th, and foot races and corn dances starting May 3rd.*

*It is still relatively undiscovered by the American traveling public.*

**RANCHO ENCANTADO**
**Santa Fe, New Mexico**

The morning sun was brilliant on a new fallen snow of about four inches. It was February and the high chapparel had a wondrous coating of white with a backdrop of azure blue skies. I was glad to have a fire laid in my bedroom to take the chill off the morning.

From my window and patio I could see the swimming pool would be active in just a few more months and the corral which, among other things, has a huge, live buffalo on view. It would be the starting point that morning for a trail ride on the desert. The tennis courts were also covered with white, but in my imagination I could hear the ping of raquet on ball in a few more weeks, for there is activity here the year-round.

One of the things that appeals to me about this mountain-ringed ranch-inn is the fact that the guests' privacy is protected. For example, a governor from a large Eastern state spent quite a bit of time here a while ago without the outside world knowing where he was. This is also true of other well-known guests from the entertainment world and politics. In many ways it is like the Hotel Algonquin in New York where busy people may relax and be themselves.

The spirit and inspiration of Rancho Encantado is Betty Egan, whose good taste, perseverance and courage launched this resort-inn several years ago. Now it is a success, and probably more important to her, it is an important part of the local community which is known as Tesuque (pronounced Tee-SOO-key). Betty is active in everything that will enable the environment and ecology to be protected.

I very much enjoyed my first visit to Rancho Encantado, and over the years I began to see it in a much broader sense. Although it is a luxury ranch-inn, it is also a meeting place for many of the permanent residents of the community, and for two nights I sat in the handsome living room well past my bedtime discussing local problems such as schools, clean water, and land development, which seem to be rife wherever I travel. The concern in this area is heightened perhaps by the fact that there is a merging of three cultures, Indian, Spanish and Anglo.

A word or two about the cuisine, which is served in an elegant dining room overlooking the Jemez mountains: It is a combination of both American and Spanish-Mexican. Many dishes are prepared from scratch and original recipes. These include heuvos rancheros, tacos, enchiladas, tostados and chili con queso. However there is a generous representation of haute cuisine offerings as well.

I also want to mention that Christmas is one of the most wonderful times at the ranch with many families and children enjoying a New Mexico holiday.

My reverie was broken by the arrival of my room service breakfast, which in a warmer month would be served on my own private patio. What a way to begin the day!

*RANCHO ENCANTADO, Rte. 4, Box 57C, Santa Fe, N.M. 87501; 505-982-3537. A 28-room luxurious ranch-inn, 8 mi. northwest of Santa Fe off Rte. 22. European plan. Breakfast, lunch and dinner served to travelers daily. Open year-round. Tennis, swimming, riding, rifle range, trap shooting on the grounds. Golf, hunting, fishing, skiing and bicycles nearby. Betty Egan, Innkeeper.*

*Directions: From Santa Fe, travel 8 mi. north on I-25 and exit at Tesuque. Drive 3 mi. to State Road 22 (Rte. 4), then 2 mi. to inn.*

# Arizona

*Arizona is a state of many contrasts. It has some of nature's most scenic attractions including the Grand Canyon, the Painted Desert, and the Petrified Forest. One-seventh of the Indian population of the United States lives here and there are 19 Indian reservations that comprise one-quarter of the state's area.*

*On the other hand, the principal cities of Arizona present a sharp contrast to these natural attractions. Phoenix and Tucson are two of the fastest-growing communities in the country, thanks to a climate that invites retirement-dwelling developers.*

*In 1866, Wickenburg, Arizona, was the third largest city in the state, and missed becoming the territorial capital by two votes. There is an old "mesquite jail tree" in the middle of the town where prisoners were chained by lawmen in the early years. This served only in the absence of a regular jail. Oddly enough the Hassayampa River running through the town was called by the Indians, "the river Which Flows Upside Down" this is because its main flow is twenty-feet below the surface of the ground.*

*In the vicinity of Tucson is the Saguaro National Monument which contains a dense stand of the Arizona state tree, the Saguaro Cactus. This tree may live to be over 200-years-old, and reaches an average height of between 25 and 36 feet. Each spring gentle white blossoms emerge from its prickly arms. One of the most impressive things about this great cactus is that it provides nesting sites for the many birds including the gilded flicker, the gilla woodpecker, and the elf owl.*

## TANQUE VERDE
### Tucson, Arizona

The postmark on the letter was "Caldwell, New Jersey." It said in part: "We've been reading about your last visit to the Tanque Verde Ranch just outside of Tucson. It sounds very intriguing. My wife and I are enthusiastic about the prospect of a new vacation experience in the desert country. The idea of staying at a ranch that may have even survived Indian raids, and your description of steak over mesquite fires, and bird-watching, are most inviting. However, it is a long way for us to go, and neither of us has ever been astride a horse. We're both about fifty years old and we'd like a little more advice as to whether we should venture forth on this trip."

Until my first visit to Tanque Verde about six years ago, horse-back riding for me consisted of a couple short hauls on a Tennessee walking horse and one or two rides on the gentlest nag in my local livery stable. When I went out to Tanque Verde I talked this over with the head wrangler, and he picked out a horse that he thought was the right size for my weight and had enough experience to guide me.

On that ride (the first of many during subsequent visits) I met a husband and wife from the Boston area, who were at a Western ranch for the first time and out on their first morning trail ride. We left the corral in single file and rode out into the desert. The entire experience was so exhilarating that by the time we got back to the ranch my Massachusetts neighbors were inquiring as to whether they could have more active horses and go for a longer ride the next day.

By the end of the week these people had purchased some blue jeans, western shirts, cowboy hats, and boots and knew all the horses by their first names.

At Tanque Verde I discovered a completely different type of country inn. I've been enthusiastic about ranch vacations ever since, and I've visited several other ranches. At Tanque Verde there are many diversions including both indoor and outdoor pools and an expanding tennis program. In 1975 I spent New Year's Eve there and had a great time with all the parents and children who had been there since Christmas.

These are some of my adventures at Tanque Verde over the years. I think that just about everyone visiting there would have the same exhilarating experience.

*TANQUE VERDE RANCH, Box 66, Rte. 8, Tucson, Ariz. 85710; 602-296-6275. A 65-room ranch-inn, 10 mi. from Tucson. American plan. Breakfast, lunch and dinner served to travelers by reservation. Open year-round. Riding, indoor and outdoor pool, tennis, sauna, exercise room and whirlpool bath on grounds. Robert and Dee Dee Cote, Innkeepers.*

*Directions: From U.S. 10, exit at Speedway Blvd. and travel east to dead end.*

## THE LODGE ON THE DESERT
Tucson, Arizona

"Schuyler," I asked, "what kind of bird is that out in the cactus garden?"

"That," replied Schuyler Lininger, "is a ferruginous owl which breeds here in southern Arizona. If you are really interested in birds," he said, "you have come to the right place. We have bird tours directed by field-experienced ornithologists from the University of Arizona graduate school. There have been over 435 species of birds recorded here. The tours are conducted with advance notice on Monday, Wednesday and Friday of each week."

I must confess that I really didn't believe that Schuyler knew the name of that bird, but when he told me about the tremendous birding program here at the Lodge on the Desert I was quite impressed. That is only one of several things that impressed me during my visit here.

Schuyler and Helen Lininger joined me for breakfast on the little patio adjoining my room. The sun was high, and we were talking about things to do in Tucson and vicinity.

On this subject, Helen provided a wealth of information. "There are so many things to do in Tucson that I don't know where to start," she said. "We have a marvelous new Art Center, the San Xavier Mission, the Arizona-Sonora Living Desert Museum, Old Tucson, the Kitt Peak National Observatory which is only 60 miles away, Colossal Cave, and, well, so much more," she said. "Mexico is only an hour away, and did you know that Tucson is one of the oldest cities in the United States? We've already had our bicentennial."

The Lodge on the Desert is a sophisticated country inn that started 40 years ago out in the desert. Gradually the city of Tucson grew to surround it. Its six acres are separated from the city's residential area by a great hedge of oleander. The lodge is a series of one-and-two-story adobe buildings built in the manner of the Pueblo Indians. The lodging rooms are tastefully designed with the small

touches that mean so much, such as very good linens and towels. Most rooms have fireplaces, and each has its own patio area. The rooms are unusually large as are the closets. Helen explained that this is because a great many of the guests stay from two weeks to three months to enjoy various seasons of the year in Tucson.

The center of inn activity is the pool area which is flanked by two great palm trees. Here guests can sit in the sun and enjoy the magnificent view of the mountains. The adjoining lounge area has a large library where many of the guests gather in the evening to play cards and socialize.

Bettie Gilbert, the former innkeeper at Colby Hill Inn in Henniker, New Hampshire, told me about her stay at the lodge and was particularly enthusiastic about the fact that the guests can order breakfast sent to their lodgings. "It was truly luxurious to have breakfast on my own patio," she said.

All around the inn are evidences of Helen Lininger's interests in furniture, art and music. There is no one particular style of decor. "If it works, we use it," she explained. "We mix traditional and modern, Indian and Colonial, although my first preference is for things of the Southwest."

All this and a ferruginous owl, too.

*THE LODGE ON THE DESERT, 306 N. Alvernon Way, Tucson, Ariz. 85733; 602-325-3366. A 35-room luxury inn within the city limits. Near several historic, cultural, and recreational attractions. American and European plans available in winter; European plan in summer. Breakfast, lunch and dinner served to travelers every day of the year. Attended, leashed pets allowed. Swimming pool and lawn games on grounds. Tennis and golf nearby. Schuyler and Helen Lininger, Innkeepers.*

*Directions: Take Speedway exit from I-10. Travel east to Alvernon Way, turn left (south) onto Alvernon. Lodge is on left side between 5th St. and Broadway.*

## RANCHO DE LOS CABALLEROS
### Wickenburg, Arizona

Boy, that sun felt good! I could just feel myself getting suntanned in December, and I could tell everyone that I had spent hours in the saddle rounding up the cattle.

Rusty Gant had a good laugh when I mentioned this. "Well, we do have cattle and this is also a working ranch, but we really don't expect any of our guests to help with the branding and roping."

At this point I was stretched out next to the pool. Los Caballeros means "ranch of the gentleman on horseback." It was a beautiful day under the clear blue Arizona sky. Some guests were gathering for the noon buffet and for the next hour or so, all of us would be exchanging experiences and enjoying an excellent lunch at the tables around the pool. The guests who had been on the 10 o'clock horseback ride through the high hills were arriving; the tennis players had walked over from the courts, and now some golfers were clattering up the stone steps.

Rusty Gant, the manager, and his mother, Edith Hayman, invited me to join them for lunch. Quite naturally the conversation led to the many things of interest on the ranch.

"Our guests seem to choose their own activities," explained Rusty. "The children's program runs all morning through lunch time. Then it has been our experience that parents and children like to do things together in the afternoon. At dinner time, the children's counselor gathers them all and keeps them until bedtime. As you know, we have a separate dining room for children."

Edie added this thought: "It has always been a tradition here for the adults to gather in our lounge before dinner. The Bradshaw Mountains across the valley change color constantly, and everyone enjoys the sunset. After dinner our social hostess arranges card games or other types of entertainment if the guests prefer. But on the whole we find that people tend to do their own thing. It's generally rather quiet because most of the guests have been pursuing outdoor activities all day."

Rancho de los Caballeros is an elegant guest-ranch in the high

desert country north of Phoenix. The horseback riding terrain has many gulches, ravines and hills. I believe it is possible to go riding twice a day for a week and never take the same trail twice. I had some excellent and patient instruction from the corral foreman, Buford Giles. I even reached the point where I was doing some pretty fast riding — at least it seemed fast to me.

Speaking of instruction, the social hostess, Ellen Kuenlen is the former tennis coach at Fairleigh-Dickinson College and not only plays a great game but offers lessons.

Most of the accommodations are built around a carefully planned cactus garden and putting green. My room was a blend of Arizona desert colors, with harmonizing hues of tan, yellow and brown. Every casita has a private patio, and many have fireplaces.

Incidentally, Christmas is always a special time here. Santa Claus visits and there is caroling, tree decorating and gifts. A great number of the guests have been returning for many years. Children have grown up and are now bringing their children. Some guests have purchased property and built homes on the adjoining land.

My Arizona tan? It was perfect. Most Arizonians say that a desert tan lasts much longer than a seashore tan. I hope they're right.

*RANCHO de los CABALLEROS, Wickenburg, Ariz. 85358; 602-684-5484. A luxury 62-room ranch-resort, 60 mi. north of Phoenix in the sunny dry desert. American plan. Rooms with private baths. A few with shared baths. Breakfast, lunch and dinner served to travelers daily. Open from mid-October to early May. No pets. Pool, corral of 75 horses, hiking, skeet shooting, airstrip, putting, tennis on grounds. Golf nearby. Dallas Gant, Jr., Innkeeper.*

*Directions: Rtes. 60, 89 and 93 bring you to Wickenburg. Ranch is 2 mi. west of town on Rte. 60 and 2 mi. south on Vulture Mine Road.*

# California

*Originally my contact with California came as a result of correspondence with Jane Way at the Sutter Creek Inn. On that first visit, I flew to San Francisco where I rode the cable cars at ten o'clock at night and then drove to the Monterey Peninsula and Carmel.*

*The next stop was the Mother Lode country where the main north-south road was called by an interesting coincidence, Route 49. Towns that I never knew existed like Volcano, Angel's Camp, Sonora, Murphys, Placerville and Amador City. History in this country is as recent as yesterday and I often have the feeling that Black Bart or Joachim Murrieta were trailing me down some of the old streets.*

*On a later visit to northern California I saw why for ninety years Californians attempted to secure federal protection for the magnificent Sequoia trees. The great event took place in 1968 when Congress authorized the establishment of Redwood National Park. Within its boundries are several sub-parks.*

*There are just no words to describe the awesome beauty and splendid serenity that surround the great trees. They are the world's tallest, and I understand the oldest living things on this earth. The Avenue of the Giants in Humbolt Redwood State Park is a 27-mile parkway winding among the huge columns of first-growth redwoods.*

## THE WINE COUNTRY INN
### St. Helena, California

The story of this inn is inspirational. It goes back a few years when Ned and Marge Smith visited me in Stockbridge, Massachusetts, and we talked about the ideals and objectives of innkeeping. They live in St. Helena, in the beautiful Napa Valley, where Ned is a prominent real estate broker. They were looking for the qualities that they most admired in country inns because they were interested in having an inn of their own. I was delighted that they stopped off to share some of their experiences with me.

After visiting about 15 New England inns they returned to California and began to give form to their ideas. A perfect site was found and the Smith family, all of them, began to work on building their inn.

In June of 1975 I called them to say that I was planning to come

to California in late August. "Wonderful," said Marge. "We'll be open by that time for certain." The day arrived and I drove down from Elk on the coast and approached St. Helena from the north on Rte. 128. At the outskirts of St. Helena, following directions, I turned down Lodi Lane and in about thirty seconds I saw a spanking new sign, "The Wine Country Inn."

After our reunion, we set off on a complete tour of every nook and cranny of the new inn. Ned explained that the building was carefully designed to fit the site which overlooks the upper part of the Napa valley in full view of Glass Mountain.

"We tried to arrange for every room to have a view. So some have intimate balconies and others have patios leading to the lawn. The natural wild mustard, lupin, poppies and live oak trees have been blended with plantings of oleanders, petunias and Chinese pistachios to accent the scenery."

Each room is individually decorated with country antique furnishings refinished and reconstructed by members of the family. Many of the rooms have fireplaces, canopied beds, tufted bedspreads and handmade quilts. There are no televisions or radios, but a generous supply of magazines and books and big, comfortable, fluffy pillows encourage the lost art of reading.

To top everything off there is a generous Continental breakfast served every day with fresh California fruit and muffins or delicious caramel pecan rolls served warm. When it comes to the evening meal the Smiths can make many helpful suggestions for they know every restaurant in the valley. In 1977, the Smiths plan on adding six more rooms in the Brandy House—a completely separate building with what Ned calls a "nifty" view and complete privacy.

The Wine Country Inn is a real thrill for me since I was in on it when it was just a gleam in the Smiths' eyes. The care and consideration that went into its designing and the result prove that a country inn doesn't necessarily have to be old or legendary.

It's the spirit that matters most.

*THE WINE COUNTRY INN, 1152 Lodi Lane, St. Helena, Ca. 94574; 707-963-7077. A newly built 15-room country inn in the Napa Wine Valley of California, about 70 mi. from San Francisco. Continental breakfast served to house guests, no other meals served. Open daily except December 22-27. No children, no pets. This inn is within driving distance of a great many wineries and also the Robert Louis Stevenson Museum. Golf and tennis nearby. Ned and Marge Smith, Innkeepers.*

*Directions: From San Francisco take the Oakland Bay Bridge to Hwy. 80. Travel north to the Napa cutoff. Stay on Hwy. 29 through the town of St. Helena, go 1¾ mi. north to Lodi Lane, then turn east ¼ mi. to inn.*

## SUTTER CREEK INN
### Sutter Creek, California

The gate in the white picket fence was unlatched so I stepped through, closed it, walked up the narrow path and started to knock on the double front door. A note caught my eye directing me to the back door. I circled the house past the flower beds and fir trees and knocked on the back door. Still no answer. Edging inside, I saw a beautiful big kitchen and large old fireplace with andirons in the shape of black owls. A long country Chippendale pine table was set with ten rabbit-eared chairs in place.

I heard a light step on the back porch and in came innkeeper Jane Way with an apron full of tomatoes. "Oh, hello Berkshire Traveller, would you like a nice ripe tomato? They're wonderful with salt on them."

And so back in 1967 began my first visit to the Sutter Creek Inn which is as neat a bit of old New Hampshire as you'll find west of New Hampshire. The house was built over 100 years ago by people who were homesick for the Granite State.

"I took a guess on the kind of a room that I thought you would like," she said. "We have many with fireplaces, some have canopied fussy and frilly beds, and others are tailored and simple. However, I decided that you would enjoy the Washroom, which is just off the

back porch and up the steps. The Oriental cook lived there for many years." (Since that time I have stayed at about every room in the inn.)

She finished washing the tomatoes and, laying them out on the table, suggested that we would both enjoy a glass of iced tea under the grape arbor.

"We serve breakfast here every mild morning at nine sharp. It's with the compliments of the inn." Jane explained the fact that other meals are not served at the inn this way:

"You see, there are so many fascinating things to do that our guests really prefer to spend the day roaming about. We have some unusual Serbian boarding houses nearby that serve simple food. We generally direct our guests to one of them."

Breakfasts are really great fun; the food is hearty and the talk is lively. Guests frequently decide to join forces for the day in exploring the Mother Lode countryside.

That's the way it has been for years now at the Sutter Creek Inn, deep in the Mother Lode country. Fireplaces blaze in cold weather and there are warm, lazy summer days to be spent in hammocks or out exploring this fascinating Gold Rush country. Sutter Creek, Jackson, Volcano, Murphy's, Angel's Camp and Sonora are all part of the great living legend of gold in California and they're all on or near Route 49 which runs along the foothills of the Sierras.

*SUTTER CREEK INN, 75 Main St., Sutter Creek, Ca. 95685; 209-267-5606. A 16-room New England village inn on the main street of a historic Mother Lode town, 35 mi. from Sacramento. Lodgings include breakfast. No meals served to travelers. Closed all of January. No children under 10. No pets. Water skiing, riding, fishing and boating nearby. Mrs. Jane Way, Innkeeper.*

*Directions: From Sacramento, travel on the Freeway (50) toward Placerville and exit at Power Inn Rd. Turn right and drive one block, note signs for Rte. 16 and Jackson. Turn left on Fulsom Rd., approximately ¼ mi., follow Rte. 16 signs to right for Jackson. Rte. 16 joins Rte. 49. Turn right to Sutter Creek. From San Francisco, follow Freeway (80) to Sacramento and take previous directions or drive via Stockton to Rte. 49.*

## HARBOR HOUSE
### Elk, California

The sound of sea birds awakened me rather gently. The first sight that came to my eyes was the tunnel formed over thousands of years by the Pacific Ocean in the huge rocks just a few yards offshore. The sun had risen over the hills to the east and the entire oceanside was golden in the light of morning.

I rose immediately, walked out on the sundeck and there was more ocean and sky than could be taken in at once. Small wonder that people come to Harbor House just to spend the day looking at the ocean, listening to the fabulous sounds created by waves rushing through the holes in the rocks, and watching the kites and sprays play tag.

In the summer of 1975, on my way south on the coastal route I stopped by at this tiny place, and there didn't seem to be anybody at home. I was just about to leave when a tall young man came around the corner and said, "Hi, I'm Rick Sutfin, the innkeeper. Can I help you with anything?"

We strolled around to the back of the inn and sat on a little terrace looking at the rocks and water. He explained that he and his wife, Pat, had come from a thriving California community where she was teaching and he was superintendent of schools. "We have always been interested in inns," he said. "When we heard this was for sale, we dropped everything and plunged in."

At that time I learned that the inn had been built in 1916 by the Goodyear Redwood Lumber Company as an executive residence. Construction is entirely of redwood taken from the nearby Albion forest. Lodging rooms located in the house have fireplaces. The little cottages with a sea view have Franklin stoves and picture windows. The winding path from the inn to a private sandy beach is unique on the rugged Mendocino Coast.

And how are things going with the Sutfins and their new way of life at the Harbor House? Here is an excerpt from a letter I received from Rick and Pat before we went to press:

"Our friends (guests) consistently return to visit us and record their evaluations in our guest book with comments such as 'fantastic,' 'a special spot,' 'unexpected.' " Our menus have broadened as our service has become more efficient. The view of the picturesque tunnel rocks widens as my chain saw opens various vantage points. Flowers abound outside. Most of our work is not readily seen as it is expected by the guests: hot water heaters, new wiring, plumbing, paint, wallpaper and clean, clean, clean—everything, all the time! Your inclusion of us in CIBR has been the primary reason why so many people all over the world have made it a point ot stay with us. (Thank you, Rick and Pat.)

There is much more to this inn by the sea than space will permit me to tell in this issue. For example, the effects of the fog, the beautiful flowers, the 30-foot high fuschia trees, and the barking of the seals. The Sutfins are having fun with their little inn, and I am sure that their guests are having fun as well.

*HARBOR HOUSE BY THE SEA, Hwy. #1, Elk, Ca. 95432; 707-877-3203. An 8-room seaside inn, 16 mi. south of Mendocino, overlooking the Pacific. Modified American plan omits lunch. Breakfast and dinner to house guests served daily. Open year-round. Ocean swimming, abalone and shell hunting, fishing and hiking on grounds. Biking, boating, deep sea fishing, golf, canoeing nearby. Rick and Pat Sutfin, Innkeepers.*

*Directions: Take Rte. 128 from I-101 to Coast. Turn south on Hwy.#1, 6 mi. to Harbor House.*

## HERITAGE HOUSE
**Little River, California**

Don Dennen was telling me and some of the other guests about the Heritage House:

"Many people have asked us about the history of this place. The original farmhouse is now our reception area, dining room and kitchen. It was built in 1877 by my grandfather, John Dennen, whose family settled here on the coast five generations ago. The first owners used the site as a shipping point for hand-split redwood ties. Back then it was known as Pullen's Landing.

"The house like many others in the Mendocino area reflects the Maine architecture of that period. The barn and outbuildings have long since vanished, but colorful stories are still told about the old days. At one time it was used as a base for smuggling goods and people into the country. A secret cave and traces of the old cables still exist. And during the frantic search for bandit Baby Face Nelson, authorities found out, too late, that the old, apparently abandoned house had sheltered him.

"While revisiting the coast in 1949, we spotted the familiar old house—by now quite abandoned—and conceived the idea of turning it into a quiet country inn. Within an hour, arrangements were made, and we set about restoring and rebuilding our 'Heritage House.'

"Although there are a few guest rooms in the main building, most of our accommodations are in the cottages tucked unobtrusively into the landscape. We've given them names inspired by early buildings of the area. For example, 'Scott's Opera House' was a center of entertainment on the coast offering traveling minstrel shows and later a hand-cranked moving picture operation (grandfather won the machine in a poker game!). Other cottages are named 'Country Store,' 'Bonnet Shop,' 'Ice Cream Parlor,' 'Barber Pole,' 'Stable,' and the like. Most of the furnishings have come from around here. Pieces like the tavern chairs date from a hotel of the 1860's. Knowing we wanted to preserve this era of history at Heritage House, many families have generously allowed us to have our choice when households are broken up. Many pieces were made by hand by local carpenters. We cherish them all."

Heritage House is different. It's a pleasant, intimate atmosphere without room telephones or televisions. There are no planned activities. The good food, peace and quiet, and the Pacific Ocean right outside the door are all that is needed.

*HERITAGE HOUSE, Little River, Ca. 95456; 707-937-5885. An elegant 45-room oceanside inn on Coast Highway #1, 144 mi. north of San Francisco, 6 mi. south of Mendocino. Modified American plan omits lunch. Breakfast and dinner served to travelers daily by reservation. Open from February through November. Don Dennen, Innkeeper.*

*Directions: From San Francisco, follow Rte. 101 to Cloverdale, then Rte. 128 to Coast Highway #1. Inn is 5 mi. north of this junction on Hwy. #1.*

**BENBOW INN**
**Garberville, California**

California is certainly a state of exciting contrasts. Earlier that morning I had left the almost semi-tropical climate in Carmel, and now, in the middle of the afternoon of the same day, I was traveling south from Eureka to Garberville on Route 101 amidst massive redwoods on a road running next to the wild Humbolt River in a green and brooding country.

Once again, I would be making a visit to the Benbow Inn to talk to Connie Corbett and Dennis Levett who by now are no longer called the "new" innkeepers since the inn has been in their capable hands for quite a few years.

I walked up the steps through the French doors and into a spacious living room which was dominated by a magnificent Persian rug. At one end there was a crackling fire, most welcome since this was mid-October.

Connie Corbett came toward me with his cheery words of welcome.

"Well," I said, "things look pretty much the same. Any significant changes since my last visit?"

"Yes," he replied enthusiastically. "You know we celebrated the Benbow's 50th birthday on July 9th, 1976, and our staff wore typical clothing from the 1920's through the entire weekend. Our guests thought it was delightful."

Perhaps I should explain here that the Benbow was actually designed and built by Albert Farr, a well-known San Francisco architect in the early 1920's. The design is Tudor, which was enjoying a very popular revival throughout the United States during those years. Today, the inn has furnishings that are reminiscent of those times, with much carved wood and stone work that would be virtually impossible to duplicate today. There are also many wrought iron lamps and massive tables which were characteristic of the period.

"We have just completed remodeling the last of twelve rooms on our fourth floor," he said. "You know, this has taken us about fifteen months. They were used by the staff and the guests' servants in the 1920's. I think we have maintained the same 1920's atmosphere in them as well.

"A little later on we can take a look at the beach area where we put a new patio."

Although the word "Tudor" may connote a feeling of formality, actually the Benbow is quite informal. Everyone is free to dress as they please, as long as it is in good taste. I found that a great many people travel a long way to get to the Benbow, and after a short rest they seem to be happy to come down and sit in the big living room and enjoy dinner without feeling it necessary to wear a coat and tie. There are frequent campers who like to get away from climbing and hiking long enough to come in and have a steak or abalone dinner.

The Benbow is both a resort-inn where people come and stay quite a few days and an overnight stop. They have a nine-hole, par 36 golf course, swimming, fishing and, of course, lots of walking in the redwood forests.

I did a little of this walking myself and in the evening enjoyed a beef Stroganoff dinner with Connie. Afterwards, I walked out on the terrace, where once again the peepers were peeping and the nightbirds were calling. The Eel River continued rippling by in front and the northern California blue velvet sky was turning to black.

Perhaps I would try once again for the morning job I missed on my last trip.

*BENBOW INN, Garberville, Calif. 95440; 707-923-2124. A 70-room inn in the heart of redwood country on Rte. 101, 2 mi. from Garberville, near Benbow State Park. European plan. Breakfast, lunch and dinner served to travelers daily. Open from April 1 through Dec. 1. Golf and swimming on grounds. Hiking and bicycles nearby. Cornelius Corbett and Dennis LeVett, Innkeepers.*

*Directions: From San Francisco, follow Rte. 101 200 mi. north and exit at Benbow.*

## NORMANDY INN
### Carmel, California

Mike Stanton, the innkeeper, had joined me for Continental breakfast in the French Provincial kitchen off the lobby of the Normandy Inn. We were talking about some recent changes.

"Well, we have been here 20 years and have now expanded to 44 lodging rooms," he said. "We have some cottages, some apartments with kitchens and woodburning fireplaces, and we've even added a few more luxurious suites for people who want to stay for a greater length of time."

The Normandy Inn is the epitome of gracious living conceived by the owners, architect Robert Stanton and decorator Virginia Stanton, who was one of the editors of *House Beautiful*. There are a great many unusual touches including king-size and extra-long beds

309

with down pillows, decorator linens, and large bath and dressing room combinations.

After breakfast, Mike and I walked outside along one of the galleries which give this inn an old-world atmosphere. We walked down the steps and over to the little swimming pool and patio which is hidden in the rear. It was a sunny day with bright yellow flowers lining the steps and porch. These flowers, which are generously distributed throughout the inn, are changed frequently. I commented on the beauty of the trees surrounding the inn. Mike explained to me that trees were such a vital part of the environment here that there are several town ordinances protecting them.

We gravitated to the front of the inn and Ocean Avenue and strolled up the street looking at the art galleries, restaurants, the many different shops and all the churches of different denominations. Mike pointed back down the hill and said that the beach was only two blocks away. "The blue water and white sand remind a lot of people of the Mediterranean."

I asked Mike what was the best time to visit this fascinating California community. "The best time is between October and April when all the golf courses are open. I must say that the town is more enjoyable when it is less crowded. There really is no specific season here," he continued. "People drive from San Francisco to spend three or four days every month, and more and more people are coming from the East Coast to visit the Monterey Peninsula. Quite a few of them," he added, "come in with copies of *Country Inns and Back Roads* in their hands."

The scenery, the nearby ocean beaches, the shops, and the

famous golf courses are the reasons to visit this beautiful part of the world. And whenever I go it is always a delight to return to the quiet elegance of the Normandy Inn.

*NORMANDY INN, Carmel, Ca. 93921; 408-624-3825. A 48-room French Provincial inn in the heart of Carmel, on Ocean Ave. between Monteverde and Casanova. Within walking distance of beach, shops and restaurants and near Point Lobos State Park. European plan includes Continental breakfast served to inn guests only. No other meals served. Open year-round. No pets. Tennis, golf, fishing, bicycles nearby. Mike Stanton, Innkeeper.*

*Directions: Follow Rte. 101 to Salinas, then Rte. 68 into Monterey Peninsula. Or, follow Coast Hwy. #1 which travels through Carmel.*

## VAGABOND HOUSE
### Carmel, California

The Vagabond House is at the corner of Fourth and Dolores Streets in Carmel. On my first visit I stood there for at least a full minute thinking that I had come to the wrong place. Then I walked up a few stone steps and entered an atmosphere that seemed almost magical. It was a secluded square surrounded by a great many trees including mock orange, magnolia and oak. There were bushes and birds and several resident squirrels. Camellias, primroses, tulips and daffodils were in bloom, and impatiens, rhododendrons, fuchias, and many other varieties of flowers reminded me of some of the gardens of the paradores I had visited in Spain.

This quiet, secluded guest house is the culmination of a dream for Chuck and Patsy Watts who, I am sure, were destined to become innkeepers.

The inn is made up of twelve rooms which border three sides of the square. Most of these have wood burning fireplaces and each room has a completely individual feeling about it.

Some of the rooms are done in knotty pine, others in brick and barn board. Entrances into each of them have a completely distinctive style. Some of them, incidentally, have their own kitchens.

Evidences of Chuck's enthusiasm about restoring and repairing clocks can be found everywhere.

On the other hand, Patsy's deftness at needlepoint can also be seen in every room with her many, many pillows. One thing I was glad to see were many books everywhere.

Continental breakfast is served each morning by Patsy and Chuck to their house guests, and they will be very happy to discuss the virtues of Carmel restaurants for luncheon and dinner.

Now that I think I have set the stage, I'd like to share a letter that I received from Patsy late in the fall of 1976 which has some very interesting news.

"We've done many new things to the inn since your visit. We have completely redecorated five rooms (paint, wallpaper, curtains, shutters, beds, brass headboards and new bedspreads). I have also been busy doing more needlepoint pillows for the rooms as well as calico collages of Victoria (British Columbia) houses. On our recent trip to San Francisco we picked up some lovely antique pieces for the rooms and, of course, some new (antique) clocks. The rooms are getting more homey all the time.

"The garden was exceptionally beautiful this summer, the guests raved about it and this makes all the work put into it so worthwhile.

"We returned yesterday from a two-week vacation in Victoria and Vancouver Island in British Columbia and visited many inns along the way, starting at the Benbow Inn where we met Connie Corbett and Dennis Levett, both charming gentlemen. They have completely redone the outside terrace in aggregate and wood, and it looks fantastic. I suppose you know that they have taken up the fourth floor and made 12 additional rooms. What a job well done.

"From there we headed north and finally arrived at delightful Whidbey Island . . . what a beautiful spot. We spent two nights at Captain Whidbey's and enjoyed every minute of it.

"Muffin (our blonde Afgan hound) is gorgeous. Just got back from the beauty parlor. You know how particular we are regarding pets. They must always be leashed and never left inside the rooms unattended. We love Muffin and we believe we know how to treat a dog."

I will be visiting Carmel in June 1977 to see Patsy, Chuck and Muffin, and also Mike Stanton at the Normandy Inn, who originally recommended the Vagabond to me. In the meantime, readers' letters and telephone calls as well as visits by other innkeepers including Helen Tobin of the Lincklaen House in Cazenovia, N.Y. and Barb Dove of the Springside Inn in Auburn, N.Y. make me very glad that I found my way into that hidden courtyard.

*VAGABOND HOUSE INN, Fourth & Dolores Streets, P.O. Box 2747, Carmel, Ca. 93921; 408-624-9988. A 12-room village inn serving Continental breakfasts to house guests only. No other meals served. Open every day of the year. Not ideal for children. Attended leashed pets allowed. Bike renting, golf, natural beauty nearby (see notes on Carmel-Monterey region). Chuck and Patsy Watts, Innkeepers.*

*Directions: Turn off Hwy. 1 on Ocean Ave. in Carmel. Turn right off Ocean to Dolores St. Go 2½ blocks to inn.*

## OJAI VALLEY INN
### Ojai, California

It was early March in Ojai, which is springtime in Southern California. The robins were nesting in the oak trees. The plantings on the patio of the Ojai Valley Inn were in bloom, and the golf course and tennis courts were in readiness. The putting green had already been swept free of the dew, and the air was so clear and dry I felt as though I could drive every green or ace every serve.

The native Indians named this sunny valley which is pronounced "o-hi." It means "the nest." It is most aptly named for it sits in the center of a vast amphitheatre of towering mountains. These mountains create an ideal climate year-round, and I understand that the average summer temperature is between 70 and 90 degrees. Winter daytime temperatures range from 60 to 85 degrees. There is no fog or smog or dampness because everything is 1,000 feet up in the dry, invigorating air. The days are warm and brilliant with sunshine and the nights are cool. I've slept under a blanket even after the warmest days.

This inn is a place where, throughout the year, guests can enjoy the four major outdoor playtime activities: golf, tennis, riding, and swimming.

The championship golf course, designed by Billy Bell, is 6,800

yards. "Tricky but fair" is one description. There's a heated swimming pool with cabanas and terraces for sun bathing, and luncheon and refreshments are served at poolside. There are hundreds of miles of riding trails in the mountains, valleys, and canyons surrounding Ojai. Horses are available at the inn stable. The tennis pro is always glad to arrange games, and I've already made quite a few tennis friends among the regular residents of this attractive town.

One other important feature that delights me at this inn is that there's plenty of fun for children. There's even a playground for them, and babysitters can be arranged.

At the Ojai Valley Inn gentlemen are requested to wear jackets and ties to dinner, and ladies usually wear dresses or pantsuits in the evening. When I commented on this to Innkeeper Bill Briggs, he said, "Our guests tell us that they prefer it this way."

The architecture of Ojai Valley Inn is Spanish Mission style. It is surrounded by beautiful oaks, evergreens, eucalyptus and an occasional palm tree. There are more varieties of birds than I could possibly count.

Golfers were already getting ready for the morning round. As two of them passed on their way to the first tee, I heard one say, "Do you realize that we're only an hour and a half from Los Angeles?"

*OJAI VALLEY INN & COUNTRY CLUB, Ojai, Ca. 93023; 805-646-5511. A 100-room resort-inn with its own championship golf course, 12 mi. northeast of Ventura on U.S. 33. American plan. Breakfast, lunch and dinner served to travelers daily. Open year-round. No pets. Tennis, riding, heated pool, golf and bicycles on the grounds. Bill Briggs, Innkeeper.*

*Directions: From the Ventura Freeway, exit at Hwy. 33.*

## THE INN
### Rancho Santa Fe, California

The two towering eucalyptus trees were benign sentinels on the path that led from the front entrance of The Inn straight down to the Village of Rancho Santa Fe. On either side of the broad front lawn, one side of which had a lawn bowling green, were two of the many rambling cottages which have been covertly placed among the spacious trees, lawns and gardens. The evening sky was the deepest blue, and stars were twinkling diamonds. No smog here. Discreet floodlighting accented the myriad shapes.

I was enchanted with the fragrances of Southern California. On this balmy, sub-tropical night, I couldn't possibly single out one from the dozens of varieties wafting from the vegetation.

It is impossible to consider The Inn without becoming involved in the concept of Rancho Santa Fe itself. It has been described as a *civilized planned community* where the homes and estates have been created in perfect harmony with nature's generous endowment of climate and scenery.

For one thing, the town fathers take an extremely hard line on the subject of anything which will in any way detract from the natural beauty of the area. As an example, a local ordinance states that no home garages may be built with an entrance facing the street! Steve Royce, the father of innkeeper Dan Royce, who was most courteous and patient about giving me a complete tour of Rancho Santa Fe, explained that everything is under strict zoning and architectural control.

In such a setting, nothing less than a model country inn would be appropriate. The Inn is a wonderful elegant little place with such unusual touches as triple sheets, turn-down service and real fireplaces blazing in the lobby and many of the rooms. At the same time, it is very warm and informal with great appeal to guests who enjoy outdoor living.

There are golf privileges available at one of the three nearby private country clubs, tennis and swimming on the inn's grounds and ocean swimming at nearby Del Mar beach where the inn has its own beach cottage. I was delighted also with the 4,000 book library.

In addition to the picturesque surroundings, the inn's location makes it a natural starting point for the unusual in sightseeing in California including Old Mexico, just an hour's drive away.

In May 1976 I joined a group of my innkeeping friends at a two-day conference at the inn. While most of them were from the West Coast, a surprising number came from the east as well. It was a most

enjoyable occasion and a perfect atmosphere for getting acquainted and exchanging ideas and solutions about innkeeping.

There was also time for play, too (which is part of the idea). I still remember tennis games with Steve and Barbara Apted and Mike Parker.

Our festive seminar ended with a super steak roast at the beach cottage.

As someone said the next morning at breakfast, "This is an innkeeper's inn."

*THE INN, Rancho Santa Fe, Ca. 92067; 714-756-1131. A 75-room resort-inn, 27 mi. north of San Diego Freeway #5, 5 mi. inland from Solana Beach, Del Mar. European plan. Breakfast, lunch and dinner served to travelers daily. Open year-round. Pool, tennis, putting green and bicycles on grounds. Golf and ocean nearby. Airport transportation provided. Daniel Royce, Innkeeper.*

*Directions: From I-5, take Exit S8 and drive inland about 6 mi.*

# Washington

*I have heard it said of Seattle that it is "like a handsome teen-age boy with an infectious grin who is still growing out of his clothes."*

*Seattle has so much! A continual view of great snowcapped mountains, an almost entirely water-oriented environment, art museums, science museums, the space needle, art, music, drama at the University of Washington, a marine aquarium, basketball, hockey, many parks and harbor tours.*

*One of the most fascinating features of Seattle is an interesting guided walking tour both above and below the ground in the Pioneer Square area. I understand that a fire destroyed most of Seattle in 1889. Instead of rebuilding the city they simply built over the top of that area and a restored section of the city can actually be found in the sub-basement.*

*The Puget Sound ferries which go everywhere can be favorably compared with the ferries in Scandinavia. In fact, it is surprising how similar the terrains are in certain places. In both places ferries are fast and, most important, very clean.*

## THE FARMHOUSE
### Port Townsend, Washington

I am most grateful to my dear friend, Joan White, for leading me from Seattle across the ferries to Port Townsend to meet Dorothy and John Ashby Conway at the Farmhouse. This all happened a number of years ago and I am the richer for not only frequent visits to this truly unusual gourmet restaurant but for my lasting friendship with the Conways themselves.

I believe the best way that I can explain this unusual dining experience is to describe it month by month. There is only one menu at a time which permits everything to be prepared from scratch. The patrons have a choice by choosing the day or month, and a telephone call can not only assure a reservation but also check the food specialty of that time. Incidentally, young children will find the food too sophisticated for them, and as John says, "An unhappy or unruly child can discommode an entire dining room." Minimal dress requirements are imposed—short shorts do not belong in the Farmhouse dining room. Dorothy says, "When campers inquire I tell them to wash their faces and wear their best camping clothes. Some diners come from the mountains, some from their boats and some come in evening dresses."

The inn is closed in January, and in 1976 the Conways visited Yucatan after an absence of 45 years. I suspect that there will be some Mayan and Aztec dishes on the menu in the future. February the menu features Mandarin food from North China. In March, there are delicious Lebanese specialties. April is the month for East Indian curries and sambals. They are not uncomfortably hot but there is plenty of hot oil for those who like to have their eyebrows singed!

May is the month of classic Greek food. The entree is leg of lamb broiled out-of-doors with charcoal with green peppers and

onions. John learned a great deal about Greek cooking in the Tavernas of Athens many years ago.

June, July and August moves into the summer schedule with dinners served on Thursday, Friday, Saturday and Sunday. Thursday is the Greek-style leg of lamb, Friday's entree is seafood, Saturday's is usually roast beef, and Sunday the entree is fowl. Be sure and check and see what the menu is on the night of your choice.

In September the weekend schedule resumes and Japanese food is featured. October is Italian month with regional cuisines from the Alps to Sicily, with a special emphasis on Tuscany. November brings back Hungarian food. John says that if you do not know this style of cooking you have missed a great treat. I suspect that it is one of his personal favorites. If the Farmhouse is open during December of 1977 it will feature a German menu including sauerbraten, red cabbage, spaetzle, and others.

A word about desserts. Two people from Munich declared that the Farmhouse strudel was better than Demel's in Vienna!

People from all over the world find their way to the Farmhouse including a professor of mathematics from the University of Moscow. Many of them are intrigued with the unusual gifts in the little shop in the inn.

Remember, one menu at a time and be certain that you call in advance. Please do not "drop in" on the Farmhouse. It is not an arduous trip from Seattle but it would be a disappointment not to be served. There are no rooms at the Farmhouse but the Conways can make recommendations for overnight lodgings nearby.

One more request: If you are traveling with CIBR, please be sure to give John my personal greetings.

*THE FARMHOUSE, North Beach, Port Townsend, Wash. 98368; 206-385-1411. A unique gourmet country restaurant, 50 mi. from Seattle. Meals by reservation only. Dinner served Thursdays through Sundays in June, July and August; dinner served Fridays, Saturdays and Sundays from September through May. Closed month of January, except New Year's Day. Dorothy and John Ashby Conway, Innkeepers.*

*Directions: From Seattle take Edmonds-Kingston Ferry and follow Rte. 104 over Hood Canal Floating Bridge to Rte. 101 N. Exit at Port Townsend and make inquiries for the Farmhouse before driving into town.*

## THE CAPTAIN WHIDBEY
### Coupeville, Washington

As I have mentioned in previous editions, the Captain Whidbey is a country inn that would be equally in place on the coast of New England as well as on the shores of an arm of the Puget Sound.

The fact is that innkeeper, Steve Stone, is from the Nantucket Island off the Massachusetts coast!

I've always wanted to spend part of the Christmas holiday at the Captain Whidbey but it is hard to be at 160 inns at the same time. With this in mind, I have asked Helen Chatfield who lives up the road from the Captain Whidbey and is a correspondant for the *Skagit Valley Herald*, to share her impressions of part of the holiday:

"The Christmas holiday mood at the Captain Whidbey Inn is heightened by the anticipation of the annual Charles Dickens dinner. Innkeepers Steve and Shirlie Stone and their son, John, take great pride in serving a traditional seven-course dinner by candlelight. The popularity of the dinner forced them to hold it for two nights this year. It's no wonder, when one examines the Olde English menu: A first course of oysters baked in a pastry, oxtail soup, apple salad, the main course of roast goose with dressing, game pie (beef, rabbit and lamb baked in a pastry), vegetables, potatoes, and a homemade chutney dressing. a steamed pudding flamed with brandy completes the feast, which is accompanied by a red wine.

" 'This is one dinner I manage from beginning to end,' Shirlie said. She joins the crowd during the last course, and enjoys the accolades from appreciative, completely content diners. Dickens never had it so good!

"Aside from the spicy smells and wonderful flavors of the Christmas dinner, guests are treated to a beautifully decorated tree, filled with handmade decorations, including a likeness of Captain Whidbey himself. A hobby horse at the base of the tree is surrounded by gaily decorated packages. Outside on the lawn stands a tall tree decorated with blinking lights, which is a cheery sight to the passing boats.

"The front door of the inn, covered with green pine boughs and marked 'welcome,' makes a visitor feel welcome even before opening the heavy oak door and stepping into the old-fashioned lobby centered with a mammoth rock fireplace. Christmas songs are sung by guests gathered in the Chart Room in the rear, and a memorable evening is had by one and all.

"The idea for seasonal dinners reflects the Stones' previous life-style. Steve served all over the world in the Army, giving Shirlie an opportunity to collect authentic recipes from each country. A Chinese dinner leads off the year in February, followed by a French meal in April and a German Octoberfest dinner."

Thank you Helen, that is a most expressive picture. It is almost as good as actually being on hand to sing carols and enjoy the roast goose!

Although this particular account happens to be about the Christmas holidays, the inn is open year-round and specializes in marvelous fish and other offerings from Puget Sound including crab claws, oysters, Dungeness crab, Pacific salmon and Pacific halibut steak.

The inn has grown most gratifingly in the years since I first visited it and now has 25 rooms. This is very fortunate because this particular section of Puget Sound has a great deal of natural beauty and is most attractive for vacationers and visitors.

*THE CAPTAIN WHIDBEY, Rte. 1, Box 32, Coupeville, Wash. 98239; 206-678-4097. A 25-room country inn, 50 mi. north of Seattle, 3 mi. north of Coupeville. European plan. 4 cottages with private bath; 12 rooms with private bath. Breakfast, lunch and dinner served daily to travelers. Open year-round. Pets allowed in cottages only. Boating and fishing on grounds. Golf nearby. Steve, Shirlie and John Stone, Innkeepers.*

*Directions: Whidbey Island is reached year-round from the south by the Columbia Beach-Mukilteo Ferry, and during the summer and on weekends by the Port Townsend-Keystone Ferry. From the north (Vancouver, B.C. and Bellingham), take the Deception Pass Bridge to Whidbey Island.*

## LAKE QUINAULT LODGE
### Quinault, Washington

It was ten o'clock on a summer evening and the big living room of the Lake Quinault Lodge was filled with a number of guests reading, talking, doing puzzles and playing bridge. In one corner some people were singing softly to the accompaniment of a guitar. The moon had risen over the lake and a light breeze was stirring the great trees on the mountains.

One of the guests who had been there about a week, dropped a couple of aromatic birch bark logs on the fire. Although it was a mild night, a small fire was quite welcome.

"Well," he asked me, "what did you do all afternoon?"

I replied that I spent most of the time just walking in the woods, getting the feel of the great trees. "Yes," he replied, "I think that's what almost every newcomer does. It takes time to get used to these two- and three-hundred foot giants that surround us."

This is indeed big tree country with cedars, redwoods, spruces, Douglas firs, hemlocks, and pines in profusion. My afternoon walk in the woods was an inspiring experience.

"It's interesting to watch people come into this relaxing atmosphere for the first time," my new friend continued. "They arrive tired and tight from city living and I can see them unwind. Finally they're sitting around like all of us without a worry in the world. I think that the saunas, jacuzzi and indoor swimming pool

321

help out a great deal, too," he added.

Most of the original lodge built in the 1920's remains today including some of the wicker chairs, and desks and tables in the lobby. The handsome floors have only gained in beauty from the years of use. There are beautifully stenciled designs on the beamed ceilings of the lobby.

The present innkeepers, Marge and Larry Lesley, have worked very hard to preserve the best of the old and, of course, to incorporate it with some of the improvements of today's conveniences. The result is a growing lodge in which the new rooms look out over the lake and command an excellent view of the mountains.

The Lake Quinault Lodge is a year-round resort-inn about three hours from Seattle and Tacoma. Frankly, I feel totally inadequate to describe the tremendous scope of the trees and the entire forest, mountain and lake experience.

Everything about the lodge is homelike and comfortable. There were a great many families sharing the experience and a dandy recreation room with various kinds of games for the irrepressible younger set to enjoy in the evening.

With so much time spent out-of-doors, it was easy to see why the dining room is an important part of the inn experience. I found homemade baked bread, Yankee pot roast of beef, and many other typical country inn items interspersed with things that are found only in the Northwest like Alder smoked Quinault salmon.

As the evening moved on I sauntered over to the corner where the people were singing to a guitar and joined the widening circle. About thirty minutes later the great old grandfather's clock in the corner tolled eleven. With this the group started to break up and say good night, all of them headed for another deep sleep here in the woods.

*LAKE QUINAULT LODGE, Southshore Rd., Quinault, Wash. 98575; 206-288-2571. A 52-room resort-inn in the Olympic National Forest of the State of Washington, about 40 mi. from Aberdeen. European plan. Breakfast, lunch and dinner served daily to travelers. Open every day of the year. $2 fee for pets; must be attended. Indoor swimming pool, chipping green on grounds. Hiking, mountain climbing, fishing, nature walks nearby. Marge and Larry Lesley, Innkeepers.*

*Directions: Use Quinault exit from Rte. 101. Proceed 2 mi. on south shore of Lake Quinault to inn.*

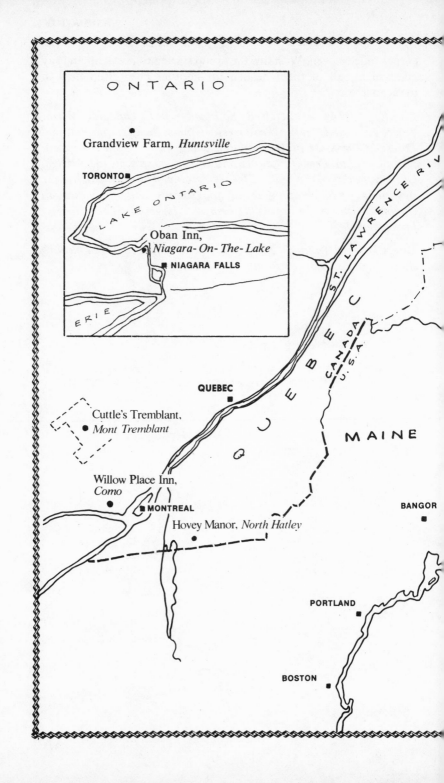

GULF OF
ST. LAWRENCE

NEW

BRUNSWICK

CAPE
BRETON

Kilmuir Place, *Northeast Margaree*

Shaw's Hotel, *Brackley Beach*

SYDNEY

P. E. I.

Inverary Inn, *Baddeck*

MONCTON

Marshlands, *Sackville*

NOVA SCOTIA

lm Lodge,
. *Stephen*

HALIFAX

AIS
Rossmount Inn, *St. Andrews*

Marathon Hotel, *Grand Manan Island*

ATLANTIC

ANNAPOLIS ROYAL
Milford House, *South Milford*

YARMOUTH

OCEAN

# Eastern and Maritime
# Canada

# Ontario

*Ontario is again represented in* Country Inns and Back Roads *by two inns. The first is the Oban Inn in Niagara-on-the-Lake which is just over the Canadian line north of Niagara Falls, New York. The other is about two hours north of Toronto in Ontario's lake and recreation area.*

**OBAN INN**
**Niagara-on-the-Lake, Ontario**

"The building," said Gary Burroughs, "has a great deal of very interesting history. It was once the home of Captain Duncan Malloy, a lake captain whose home was in Oban, Scotland, a beautiful seaport town. It was built about 1824 and later turned into an inn. In 1914 there were additions made, and the Oban Inn became an officers mess. It's been in my family for some years now, and I'm very pleased to make my home here in Niagara-on-the-Lake and make the inn a part of my way of life."

It was on the recommendation of Marthe Lane of the *Buffalo Courier-Express* that I visited the Oban Inn, and, infact, she was good enough to accompany me on this midday visit.

In many ways I was reminded of the Willow Place Inn in Como, Quebec, and its English innkeeper, Patrick Garbutt. The Oban is essentially a Canadian inn, however, because of its evident English heritage, I recalled other English inns I had visited such as the Crown in Chiddingfold which has the same cozy village air, and the Mermaid Tavern in Rye, where the atmosphere is also drenched in history.

The menu indicated that the Oban really has a mix of the Old World and the new. For example, among the appetizers was a homemade pate which is a tradition in England and the Continent. The main menu items have the ring of the English countryside: roast prime ribs of beef with Yorkshire pudding, and calves sweetbreads with bacon on toast. Desserts included Meringue Chantilly and strawberry mousse from France, but there is no doubt that pie a la mode is from the USA!

We were talking about the intermingling of cultures at the Oban when Gary said, "There is one thing that we have here that is undeniably British. Come with me and you will see what I mean." We walked from the main dining room down the corridor into a pub room that might well have been in Surrey or Sussex. It was decorated with many photographs of actors and actresses that have appeared at the Shaw Festival. At the center of a buffet bar was the star of the repast, a turkey pie with a big beautiful crust. There was also a large salad bowl, cold cauliflower, mixed peas and lima beans, cold sliced meats, sliced eggs and generous helpings of tomatoes, beets and pickles. It was quite British.

There was a mixture of patrons at that hour including business men from the town as well as a few Canadian and American visitors who were enjoying Niagara-on-the-Lake in the off-season. I noted a piano in one corner, and Gary said that in the evening there were informal, jolly sing-alongs as well as quiet entertainment. With the fire crackling away on a rather chilly day, it was all very heart-warming and hospitable. At the time I was there, the inn was decorated for Christmas with holly, wreaths and garlands of greens.

The hospitality at the Oban Inn extends to some very homelike lodging rooms. Some of them have a view of Lake Ontario and all are neat and quite typical of country inns with individual color schemes and furniture.

Gary and I talked extensively about local history, and as we were leaving, he said warmly, "I am sure that your readers will enjoy Niagara-on-the-Lake." I'm equally sure that they will also enjoy a visit at the Oban Inn.

Incidentally, in a subsequent column describing our visit to the Oban, Marthe Lane spoke of the inn in glowing terms.

*THE OBAN INN, 160 Front St., Box 94, Niagara-on-the-Lake, Ontario LOS IJO 416-468-2165. A 23-room village inn on a quiet street in one of Canada's historic villages approx. 12 mi. from Niagara Falls, N.Y., on the shores of Lake Ontario. Near Ft. George and Ft. Niagara, the Shaw Festival and Mime Theatre. All plans available. Breakfast, lunch, dinner served daily to travelers. Open every day of the year. Owner-controlled pets welcome. Golf, xc skiing, sailing, fishing, tennis nearby. Gary Burroughs, Innkeeper.*

*Directions: Exit Hwy. 55 at St. Catherines from the Queen Elizabeth Hwy. Follow signs to Niagara-on-the-Lake.*

## GRANDVIEW FARM
**Huntsville, Ontario**

"I wish you could see that tree during the Fall season. It turns the most gorgeous scarlet," said Bruce Craik. He and I were taking a leisurely walk around the grounds and buildings of Grandview Farm. "Yes, and during the summer, our dock has canoes, Lasers and inboards for touring the lakes or waterskiing. That's Fairy Lake, part of a chain of five lakes in this section of Ontario."

It was a strikingly beautiful day in early January. I had driven up from Toronto and then turned east on route 60 for a few miles through snow covered fields which were bathed in brilliant sunshine. The daisies and buttercups would carpet them in a few short months. I turned off at the little sign and drove to the top of the knoll with a series of friendly looking buildings and was promptly greeted by two equally friendly dogs. There was a young man out flooding the skating pond and we both agreed that it was a marvelous day. The snow was crunchy underfoot. As I approached the door to the main house which was flanked by trees, it was opened by Judy Craik who said, "Welcome to Grandview Farm. I saw you coming."

The first thing the Craik family did was to take me into a living room where a most welcome fire was crackling away on a raised hearth and a big picture window overlooked the lake. I was revived by some hot chocolate and we started visiting.

It is easy to visit with the Craiks because there are so many of them. In fact, a needlepoint design on one wall carried the message: The Craik Family: Bruce, Judy, Ian, Peter, Ginny, Sandy, Tim, and Heather—Grandview Farm 1975.

"Yes, everyone is involved here," said Bruce. "We are a resort-inn where most families have fun because we are a big family ourselves."

I found that in addition to being an inn with lots of different things to do during summer as well as winter, Grandview Farm Inn is also a restaurant serving three meals a day. "One of our specialties is roast beef with Yorkshire pudding which we serve on Wednesday and Saturday nights," explained Judy. "Other nights we offer three

different entrees, such as chicken done in many different ways, and we serve fish every night and there is stuffed roast pork, and veal. We pass the vegetables and offer seconds on everything."

Lodgings are in the main house and in six other attractive cottages set among some fine old trees on or near the lake shore, each with its own name. All the rooms are very comfortable, from the corner room in the inn with the four-poster to the fireplace rooms in the "Tree Tops" and those in the little waterside cottage called "Puffin Hill."

While I was browsing in the Rafters, the small gift shop at the inn, I picked up the Grandview Farm brochure. It was extremely handsome with full color photographs of all of the activities, the lake views, and the lodging rooms. I found it very helpful when writing this account.

Bruce and I had returned to the main house and he pointed out the patio which is on the west side overlooking the lake. "We serve lunch and dinner out here in the summertime." The scene reminded me of another most attractive Canadian inn, Hovey Manor south of Montreal in North Hatley, Quebec, overlooking Lake Massawippi.

*GRANDVIEW FARM, Huntsville, Ontario, Canada POA 1KO; 705-789-7462. A 25-room resort-inn on Fairy Lake, 142 mi. north of Toronto in a beautiful lake and mountain resort area. American and Mod. American Plans. Breakfast, lunch and dinner served to travelers daily. Open from mid- May to October 31; Dec. 26 to Mar. 31. Closed Christmas Eve and Christmas Day. No pets. Tennis, swimming, sailing, waterskiing, canoeing, xc skiing on grounds; Alpine skiing nearby. The Craik Family, Innkeepers.*

*Directions: From Toronto follow Route 400 North above Barrie, then Rte. 11 North, approx. 80 mi. near Huntsville. Turn right on Rte. 60 for 4 mi. Inn is on right.*

# Quebec

*I first visited Quebec a few years ago while touring inns in northern Vermont. From Stowe I went north on Route 100 and, after driving through the hamlets of Eaton Mills, Lowell and Troy, came to Newport, a surprisingly large community on Lake Memphremagog. At Derby Line I passed into Canada picking up the Stanstead Expressway. This led north to Lake Massawippi and North Hatley where I visited Hovey Manor.*

*From Montreal I drove 75 miles northwest via the Laurentian Auto Route 15 to St. Jovite and visited Cuttle's Tremblant Club and Mont Tremblant.*

*The Willow Place Inn in Hudson is just a few miles east of Montreal off the Trans-Canada Highway.*

## CUTTLE'S TREMBLANT CLUB
### Mont Tremblant, Quebec

I trained the telescope along the lakeshore and focused on a beautiful white Laser sailboat as it headed toward the middle of the lake. It seemed to almost fly over the water. I turned slightly to watch four people on the tennis court enjoying a final game of doubles before dinner. However, I kept returning to the slopes of Mont Tremblant immediately across the lake. It was easy to follow the many interesting ski trails and lifts that are so busy during the wintertime here in this Canadian Laurentians resort.

"It seems hard to realize that there will be six to eight feet of snow up here, doesn't it?" Jim Cuttle was at my elbow. "Incidentally we have a very active ski program here. We have our own instructors and even use video equipment to help our students improve their technique. In fact, it was skiing that originally brought Betty and me to the Laurentians. It doesn't seem possible that we have been here for 20 years."

Winter is a magic time here at Cuttle's. In addition to their downhill ski school and various ski weeks during the season, there is also emphasis on cross-country skiing weeks as well. Many trails begin right on the property and Mont Tremblant Park offers fifty miles of marked and groomed trails for Nordic skiers of all degrees of ability. A box lunch is available from the Club. A waxing room and repair bench are available. This is the time when there are ski movies, evening dancing and entertainment, and transportation back and forth to the ski area across the lake.

In the beautiful July twilight surrounded by poppies, marigolds and tulips, with swallows flitting among the maples and birches, winter seemed quite far away. Already dozens of tanned vacationers were gathering for the Thursday buffet, and Betty was taking care of the last minute details. She paused long enough to point out some water skiers on the lake.

I found the dinners a most interesting experience at this bilingual inn. There is an emphasis, of course, on French dishes including a cold seafood plate featuring fish from the Gaspe Peninsula, roast leg of veal, braised calf sweetbreads, stuffed rainbow trout done in the chef's own style and boned chicken Bayonnaise.

Although the word "club" is used in the name of this somewhat sophisticated resort-inn, it is nonetheless open to the public. Guests come in all seasons to stay for one night or three weeks! The interior has much paneling, and I found fireplaces in many of the beautifully designed rooms as well as in a few of the lodging rooms.

For many years I had hoped to find a warm personal resort-inn in the Laurentian Mountains north of Montreal. Cuttle's is the answer.

*CUTTLE'S TREMBLANT CLUB, Mont Tremblant, Quebec, Canada JOT IZO, 819-425-2731. A 32-room resort inn on Lac Tremblant facing Mont Tremblant, the highest peak in the Laurentians. Modified American plan omits lunch. Breakfast, lunch and dinner served daily to travelers. Open year-round. No pets. Tennis, swimming, sailing, boating, fishing and xc skiing on grounds. Golf, riding, trap shooting, Alpine skiing nearby. Jim and Betty Cuttle, Innkeepers.*

*Directions: From Montreal, 85 mi. northwest via Laurentian Auto Rte. 15 to St. Jovite. Turn right at church on Rte. 327N, 7 mi. to Lac Tremblant. Cuttle's is on the west shore facing the mountain.*

## HOVEY MANOR
### North Hatley, Quebec

"I know this is going to sound funny," I said, "but it seems to me that from out here on the lake the inn looks exactly like . . ."

"Like a replica of Mt. Vernon," said Bob Brown. "Excuse my interrupting you but I knew exactly what you were going to say, and many of our American guests notice the resemblance immediately. You see, Hovey Manor was built in 1900 by a man named Henry Atkinson who purposely made it as close to Mt. Vernon as possible. You know we even have a portrait of George Washington on the wall of our dining room that is painted on glass. It's over 150 years old.

"This part of Quebec has always had very strong American ties," he said. "A great many visitors from Georgia, Virginia, Maryland and Alabama built summer homes around Lake Massawippi at the same time Atkinson built Hovey Manor. There is a story that in 1900 some of these Southerners continued to feel such antipathy toward the Yankees that on the train trip north every summer they would draw the blinds while passing through New England."

Bob made another tack for the opposite shore of the lake and I asked him about the name. "Well, we renamed it Hovey Manor in honor of Captain Ebenezer Hovey who was an Empire loyalist from Vermont and one of the first settlers here in North Hatley. He came in 1804 and you can well imagine what the Eastern townships were like and how travel was pretty rough by ox team, sled and snowshoe.

"Betty and I have worked very hard and had a lot of fun making the manor house into an inn. We've been collecting authentic Quebec antiques and have put most of them into the sitting rooms and bedrooms."

I asked him about how many guests he had during the winter. "Well, there are five ski areas within easy driving distance from here. We have become a family ski resort as well as a family summer resort. There is outdoor activity here during most of the months of the year. Our boat dock and tennis courts are busy during the summer, and many people come to walk in the hills in the fall."

I happened to mention that I had a letter from one of my readers who told of enjoying the Saturday night steak party. "We are always glad to hear that," he said. "It's a very jolly time. We cook different kinds of steaks over the fire in our Carriage House and everybody gets acquainted very quickly when the fireplace is going. Have you ever noticed that?"

I said I had. "Well what about the haunted clock," I asked. He removed his pipe and knocked it against the side of the boat. "Well now that is an interesting thing," he said. "We have a Gothic-style 80-day clock in the reception lobby that never chimes on the hour. However, if I mention the name of one of the village's original inhabitants, who incidentally was something of a character and went around in a racoon coat in the summer, something strange happens. Within just a few minutes, the clock starts to chime vigorously. I don't do this very often because I am a man of moderation and certainly doubt the presence of ghosts. Nonetheless, I am beginning to have respect for something I don't understand." His eyes twinkled and I wasn't sure if he was kidding.

"Well, what is this person's name that seems to upset the clock so much?"

"That," he replied, putting a finger to his lips, "is a house secret."

*HOVEY MANOR, Box 60, Rtes. 10 and 55, North Hatley, Quebec, Canada JOB2CO; 819-842-2421. A 34-room resort-inn, 85 mi. from Montreal, 35 mi. from Newport, Vt. On Lake Massawippi and near major ski areas. European plan or Modified American plan which omits lunch. Breakfast, lunch and dinner served to travelers daily. Open year-round. Tennis on grounds. Golf, Alpine and xc skiing nearby. Bob and Betty Brown, Innkeepers.*

*Directions: From U.S., take I-91 across border to Rte. 55. From Rte. 55, take North Hatley-Kateville Exit 18 and follow Rte. 108 east. Turn right at blinker, approximately 5 mi.*

## WILLOW PLACE INN
**Como, Quebec, Canada**

Pat Garbutt is the very picture of an Englishman. He is well over six feet tall, a former footballer, and I could just imagine him among the English soldiery at the Battle of Agincourt or at the Red Fort in Agra. He is an Englishman who is now a Canadian by choice. "I love Canada," he said. "Both Zena, who is Scottish, and I are proud to say that this is our real home."

Pat and Zena are the innkeepers of not only one inn in Canada, but two. Besides the Willow Place Inn in Como, just about 35 miles from the heart of Montreal, they also keep the Elm Lodge in St. Stephen, New Brunswick.

"I wish you would find an inn about halfway between where we could stay overnight en route. It would make the trip much more enjoyable." I assured him that I would spend part of the summer of 1977 on the Gaspé in search of just such an inn.

The "Willow," which most everyone in the vicinity calls the inn, was built around 1820 as a private home and later became a store. It has undergone several different uses and managements but during the past few years it has been a wonderful experience for Pat and Zena.

The 14 rooms of the inn come in various sizes and are furnished in a comfortable country inn manner.

The menu includes steak and kidney pie, roast beef with Yorkshire pudding, Dover sole and cottage pie. There is also a generous sprinkling of French cuisine including coq au vin and escargots de Bourgogne. The menu is bilingual.

Here is an excerpt of a letter I received from Americans who have visited the Willow Place recently:

"We had made some reservations at various CIBR inns in Canada but oddly enough did not receive confirmation from the Willow Place. Nevertheless, while driving to Montreal I convinced my wife to take the side trip to Como to see what we were missing. When we got there we were 'eating our hearts out.' The narrow country road leading to the inn made us feel as if we were in Europe. We went inside hoping for one chance in a thousand that we would get a room on what was their Labor Day weekend. I couldn't believe it—the clerk told us that they were expecting us! She showed me a copy of a letter that they had sent to us which for some reason we had never received. Our room was waiting, a room with a private bath which we had requested two months before. To say the least, my wife and I were thrilled with Mr. Garbutt's faith in our 'informal reservation' and our chance to stay at their inn."

When I mentioned this to Pat at a recent innkeepers meeting, he said, "We try to keep our end of the bargain although some guests simply do not realize how inconvenient it is when they fail to make scheduled appearances. I remember these people very well and I am glad it all worked out."

The Willow is a meeting place for many kinds of people with varied interests. I found that the American-Canadian visitors mixed well with each other, and it was fun to practice my halting French in the "home pub" section of the inn.

Now I am off to the Gaspé to help make Pat's trips more pleasant.

*WILLOW PLACE INN, Box 573, Hudson, Quebec, Canada JOP IHO, 514-458-4656. A 14-room English inn, 25 mi. from Montreal on the shores of the "Lake of Two Mountains." European plan or Modified American plan which omits lunch. Some rooms with shared bath. Breakfast, lunch and dinner served to travelers daily. Closed Christmas Day, Boxing Day (St. Stephen's Day), New Year's Day and Good Friday. Swimming, sailing, bicycles and xc skiing on grounds. Tennis, golf and Alpine skiing nearby. Pat and Zena Garbutt, Innkeepers.*

*Directions: From Trans-Canada Hwy., take Exit 17 and follow Hwy. 342 north to Como Station Rd. and Bellevue Blvd. Turn left to inn. Near Oka Ferry.*

*It is possible to travel from upper Michigan, Missouri or southern Florida through the Northeast to New Brunswick, Prince Edward Island and Nova Scotia and stay at one of "our inns" every night. Once in New England, the traveler can use the land route through Maine and New Brunswick or take ferries from either Portland or Bar Harbor to Nova Scotia. The air flight to Halifax from Boston takes about an hour.*

# New Brunswick

*In 1975 I visited inns in St. Stephen (at the Calais, Maine, border crossing), St. Andrews and Grand Manan Island. It is a day's drive from these inns through the city of St. John to the Marshlands Inn in Sackville, New Brunswick. From here it is another day north to the inns in Cape Breton or south to the Milford House in South Milford, Nova Scotia.*

### ELM LODGE INN
### St. Stephen, New Brunswick

I have visited many country inns that have something unusual about them, and in fact, all of them are unique. However, the Elm Lodge Inn is my first inn where a college was started!

Pat Garbutt explained to me that St. Stephen's University is Canada's only four-year degree-granting interdenominational Christian university.

"It was started in 1971," he asserted, "to provide a place for a Christian center of higher learning reflecting a Biblical world-and-life view in all of its activities. In the first years the top floor of the Elm Lodge was used for student dormitories and lecture rooms."

I'm happy to report that this center of higher learning makes more progress each year and now it occupies a few of the nearby buildings in the residential area of St. Stephen. I was impressed with the academic opportunities at the college and would suggest that anyone wishing further information write St. Stephen's University, St. Stephen, New Brunswick, Canada.

The town of St. Stephen which is just over the St. Croix River from Calais, Maine, is a community that seems to belong to an earlier century. There are broad streets, huge elm trees, graceful homes, and a pleasant park.

The inn is a beautifully restored Victorian building with three huge elm trees on the lawn in front. Handsome coach lamps flank the main entrance and the building is considerably enhanced with large green shutters. There are flowerbeds on the lawn including a number of rosebushes. At the time of my visit the bluebells were in full array.

The interior of the inn tells a marvelous story. Pat and Zena Garbutt who also own the Willow Place Inn in Como, Quebec, have worked very hard over the past few years restoring this truly elegant house. The floors, walls and woodwork are all cleaned, polished and refurbished until everything shines. Victorian antiques and improvisation of different types of furniture make each of the three little dining rooms a separate experience. Zena and Pat have been aided in their efforts by young people, some of whom have come from the Willow Place.

Upstairs there are nine very handsome, comfortable rooms. Mine overlooked the lawn and broad street and had a canopied bed.

One couple who had stopped at both the Willow Place and at Elm Lodge wrote me a letter which said in part: "It was late when we arrived but there was still time to get some refreshment and, as was the case at the Willow Place, we enjoyed talking to the local people.

"We liked this inn very much. We were made to feel at home and invited to walk around anywhere we wished inside the inn. I took many pictures. One of my favorites is the one I took of my wife in the dining room that morning. We felt even more at home when one of the young men who works at the inn told us that he had been to our hometown in Minnesota just the summer before."

Naturally, the Garbutts' experience at the "Willow" has bene-fited the operation of Elm Lodge. The menu also reflects Pat and Zena's English and Scottish backgrounds with such things as steak and kidney pie, roast beef and Yorkshire pudding and much seafood from the waters of Passamaquoddy Bay.

The easiest route is to take the border crossing from Rte. 9 at Milltown, Maine, to St. Stephen, New Brunswick. The inn takes a bit of finding when coming from the Calais crossing.

A college that started in an inn! There is a great deal more to Pat and Zena Garbutt than meets the eye.

*ELM LODGE INN, 477 Milltown Blvd., St. Stephen, New Bruns-wick, Canada; 506-466-3771. A 9-room village inn on a quiet street near the Canadian-American border crossing at Calais, Maine. European plan and Modified American plan which omits lunch. Breakfast, lunch and dinner served daily. Open every day from Jan. 12 through Dec. 14. Dining room closed on Sundays from Jan. to May. Children welcome and pets who act like English gentlemen. Bicycles, sailing, swimming, nature trails, horseback riding, golf, canoeing, jogging nearby. Patrick and Zena Garbutt, Innkeepers.*

*Directions: From Bangor, Maine, follow Rte. 9. Cross at Milltown-St. Stephen border crossing. Inn is kitty-cornered to and within sight of Canadian customs.*

## ROSSMOUNT INN
### St. Andrews, New Brunswick, Canada

It was during the summer of 1975 when I saw the Rossmount through the eyes of a family from Virginia Beach, Virginia: Andrew Fine, his wife Barbara, their two sons, Matthew and Jeffrey and daughter, Katherine. They had been touring the Maritimes and using *Country Inns and Back Roads*. Almost as soon as we were introduced they told me that they loved the Rossmount and felt that it was the perfect combination of location, beautiful rooms, marvel-ous food and cordial, entertaining innkeepers.

"The children are having the time of their lives," exclaimed Barbara. "Today they are going to the big hockey arena downtown to watch the players from the summer hockey camp. The town also has some very nice shops and a fascinating waterfront. We all went to the Aquarium and Block House yesterday, and tomorrow we are planning to go deep sea fishing."

At this point the three young people in question came zooming up to ask if they could go fishing in the inn pool before lunch.

They were joined by the innkeepers' two children and, as soon as permission was given, they all scooted.

I ran into them later on at the hockey rink, and they said they were having the best time possible. "There's so much to do. Lots of time people forget we need our own kind of entertainment." This came from Jeffrey Fine, the elder of the two brothers.

Matthew, who has a lot of enthusiasm added, "We just love to run around in the woods. Do you know that the inn property goes clear to the top of Chamcock Mountain and you can see the whole harbor from the top? Besides that, the whole place is a wildlife refuge."

About two years ago, George Brewin, a successful English businessman, and his wife, Marion, acquired the Rossmount and contributed generous portions of hard work, dedication and good humor.

I saw ample evidence of their teamwork at dinner. Marion supervises all of the cooking and prepares each plate, and George serves each course personally, usually with generous dollops of humor. Every table soon rings with laughter as he offers a saucy comment with each serving.

George becomes serious however, when talking about Marion. "She's really the heart and soul of what we're doing here," he said. "She's very particular about everything. We serve only homecooked food and make our own breads, soups and chowders. We are especially proud of the creamed fiddlehead soup and our salmon and pollock dishes." Actually, Passamaquoddy is an Indian word which means "place of Pollock."

All of the public rooms and lodgings at the Rossmount are furnished with handsome antiques from around the world. These unusual furnishings are the most surprising and frequently the most memorable features of the inn. Guests wander up and down the hallways and around the second and third floors admiring all of the carved wood, handpainted chairs, tables, cabinets and other unusual pieces.

Since my last visit, the exterior of the inn has undergone what Marion Brewin described in a recent letter as a major face lifting. "We hope to see you in 1977," she added, "for it's going to be a beautiful year in St. Andrews-by-the-Sea."

It's already on my list.

*ROSSMOUNT INN, St. Andrews, New Brunswick, Canada EOG 2XO; 506-529-3351. A 20-room inn in one of Canada's most delightful towns. Located on the Passamaquoddy Bay in the Bay of Fundy. European plan. Breakfast and dinner served daily. Dining room closed Mondays out of season. No pets. Swimming, shuffleboard, pitch and putt golf, croquet on grounds. Golf, ocean fishing, cultural and scenic features nearby. George and Marion Brewin, Innkeepers.*

*Directions: To reach St. Andrews from Calais, Maine or St. John, New Brunswick, follow Rte. 1 and look for direction signs to St. Andrews via Rte. 127. Follow this road down the peninsula and look for direction sign to inn.*

## MARATHON HOTEL
### Grand Manan Island, New Brunswick

The ferry from Black's Harbour approached the wharf at North Head on Grand Manan Island. I could readily see that this was a place where men made their living from the sea. There were fishing boats, seining weirs, and rugged docks on tall stilts.

In the small crowd that was awaiting the arrival of the boat, I tried to pick out Jim Kennedy, the innkeeper of the Marathon Inn. As I came down the gangplank, he called, "Welcome to Grand Manan. We are going to have some great weather." This was the start of a most rewarding visit.

I learned that Grand Manan, Campobello, and Deer islands are known as New Brunswick's "Fundy Isles." Long before the coming of the French and English, Grand Manan was settled by United Empire Loyalists, but some think that the Vikings may have been here first.

It is a quiet, unspoiled island of great natural beauty 15 miles long and 4 miles wide—a paradise for naturalists, bird watchers,

photographers, artists, divers and rock hounds. In my explorations with Jim and by myself, I found many walking trails (not for sandals). Some went to the west where I found great cliffs and surf crashing against the rocks. There are little bays, inlets, beaches and sheltered rocks, rolling fields, and friendly people everywhere.

Jim told me that besides the beach combing, fishing, walking and exploring, golf and tennis facilities are available on the island. "Basically," he said, "this is a quiet, restful place. As I told one lady: If it is a swinging time you're after — go to the Bahamas."

Jim explained that during the summer months Grand Manan is literally covered with wild flowers. Wild berries are found all over the island. He said that John Audubon visited in 1833 and gave a glowing report: "It's birds that really own Grand Manan. There are over three hundred species that live at least a part of their lives here and that includes the Bald Eagle."

All of the outdoor activity here makes food of prime importance. Each night at dinner there is one main dish. A typical week might include: roast beef on Sunday served with the famous fiddlehead greens from New Brunswick; Monday night, baked fish; Tuesday night, baked chicken; Wednesday night, lobster; Thursday night, baked pork chops; Friday night, a scallop casserole; Saturday night, Rock Cornish hen. There are no fried foods served at the Marathon. Marjorie Kennedy, who does the cooking, added that, "We make all our own chowders, pies, rolls, breads, cakes and cookies."

The Marathon is exactly the kind of country hotel that I was hoping it would be. There were spotlessly clean rooms with white walls and furniture painted in gay colors. The open staircase reminded me of a flying bridge on board a boat. My room was on the top floor and, like most of them, had a spectacular view of the harbor.

I met some pleasant people from New Jersey who were having a marvelous time including a trip by charter boat to some of the nearby islands. One man especially recommended the museum at Grand Harbour where the Grand Manan birds have been so well preserved.

*MARATHON HOTEL, North Head at Grand Manan, New Brunswick, Canada EOG 2MO; 506-662-8144. A 38-room resort-inn on Grand Manan Island in the Bay of Fundy, 40 mi. from St. John in New Brunswick. Modified American and European plans. Open April 1-Oct. 15. Breakfast and dinner served to travelers daily. Pets allowed on ground floor annex. Beach combing, bird watching, swimming, fishing, hiking, diving, bicycles, golf and tennis nearby. James and Marjorie Kennedy, Innkeepers.*

*Directions: Grand Manan Island is reached by ferry from Black's Harbour which is just off Rte. 1, midway between Calais, Maine and St. John, New Brunswick. Be sure to check the ferry schedule when making car reservations. Arrangements may be made for cars to be left at Black Harbour, but if you're planning to take your car be sure to be in line no less than 60 minutes before sailing time. The late afternoon ferry sailing may not arrive in time for dinner at the Marathon, but the ferry snack bar has adequate food.*

## MARSHLANDS INN
### Sackville, New Brunswick

Every year I hear from a great many people who drive across Maine into New Brunswick to reach Nova Scotia, Prince Edward Island and Newfoundland the long way, by land.

Almost all of these letters make some reference to the Marshlands Inn, which is located just a few miles from the Nova Scotia Border and the P.E.I. ferry. This is what one couple reported: "Our first stop was the Marshlands Inn. We had planned a three week camping trip with an occasional overnight stop to get a bedroom and an adjoining bathroom, the pleasures you miss even in the best Provincial parks. Our itinerary brought us to the Marshlands Inn for a late lunch. We must admit the setting, decor and food exceeded our expectations." (I have many letters from people who stop at the Marshlands and mention the fact that they never expected to find such a sophisticated inn so far north.)

"While paying our bill we found a copy of *Country Inns and Back Roads*, perused the table of contents, and noticed your entry regarding the Marshlands. We found that we were in complete agreement with your comments and enjoyed your personal observations. Believe it or not we never expected that such a purchase would determine the roads that we would eventually take." Incidentally, that couple also visited the Inverary Inn and the Milford House, in Nova Scotia, both a single day's drive from Sackville.

My personal dilemma when visiting the Marshlands is to make a choice of entrees at dinner. The Atlantic and Miramichi salmon are very tempting but the curried lamb with Marshlands chutney is also very enjoyable. There are also lobsters, scallops, beefsteak and kidney pie, the famous fiddlehead greens, and many curry dishes. All the rolls, breads, ice cream and sherbets are homemade.

I am happy to say that Innkeeper Herb Read continues to pursue the Marshlands tradition of leaving a thermos pitcher of hot chocolate in the front parlor for guests who like a late snack.

Although the Marshlands seems like it is just a few miles from the North Pole to those of us who live below the Canadian border, it would be unusual in any setting. The dinnerware is sterling, the china is Spode and all the waitresses wear dark blue uniforms with white collars and aprons.

Many of the guests stay on for an extra night or two to see the famous "Tidal Bore" which is visible in the nearby Bay of Fundy, or to play golf and enjoy some hiking and swimming nearby. Curling is another popular sport in this part of Canada.

Incidentally, Marshlands is named after the Tantramar Marshes that surround the town of Sackville. Tantramar comes from the Indian word meaning "sound of bird wings." The marshes are home to millions of migrating waterfowl. This area, now largely controlled by Ducks Unlimited and the Marsh Reclamation Board, is one of the main flyways of North America. In the spring and fall huge flights of geese and ducks may be seen coming in to rest on the marshes.

The Marshlands is not only a place where East meets West, but also a place where North meets South.

*MARSHLANDS INN, Box 1440, Sackville, N.B., Canada EOA 3CO; 506-536-0170. A 10-room village inn near Tantramar Marshes and Fundy Tides. European plan. Six rooms with private baths. Breakfast, lunch and dinner served to travelers daily. Closed during the Christmas season. Golf, xc skiing, curling, hiking and swimming nearby. Herb and Alice Read, Innkeepers.*

*Directions: Follow Trans-Canada Highway to Sackville, then Rte.6, 1 mi. to center of town.*

# Nova Scotia

*The super back road in Nova Scotia is the Cabot Trail which winds around the top of the province next to the Gulf of St. Lawrence through the great forests and back down to Lake Bras d'Or. It includes the Cape Breton Highlands National Park and can be traversed it twice, once clockwise and the second time counterclockwise.*

### INVERARY INN
### Baddeck, Cape Breton, Nova Scotia

During the 11 years that I have been traveling throughout North America visiting inns and writing this book, there have been thousands of letters from readers who have been good enough to share their inn experiences with me. Here are some letters about the Inverary Inn:

"When we returned to Nova Scotia we stopped at the Inverary Inn as planned for two evenings. The first night we got there just in time for dinner, and in my rush to get to the dining room in time, I promptly locked the room key in our room! Mrs. MacAulay told me not to worry, so we enjoyed a delicious dinner of poached haddock.

"Our room was in the 'barn' and when I came back with a ring of

room keys to open our room another traveler mistook me for an employee and complimented me on the accommodations. He was a salesman, a native of Nova Scotia, who happened to come to the Inverary by chance. We sat in the lounge and talked for over two hours. A completely enjoyable experience. We introduced him to *Country Inns and Back Roads* and he was quite interested. He was really pleased to find a place like the Inverary Inn after a day of work. As is the case with most of us, he was used to staying in 'ho-hum' motels. While talking to him we discovered a lot about the people of Nova Scotia. It was very interesting. Never before have I had the opportunity to visit with other travelers like at the Inverary, but then the inn is arranged to induce such conversation among its guests."

Here is a portion of another letter:

"Thanks to your inviting description we spent two nights at the Inverary Inn which we thoroughly enjoyed. Our room was most pleasant and the food delicious, especially the Scottish breakfast. My husband thought it was the most enjoyable spot in Nova Scotia. The MacAulays were so warm and friendly that I felt that I had known them for quite awhile. I enjoyed standing and talking in Mrs. MacAulay's gift shop which is full of local crafts of high quality. I happened to mention that it was my older daughter's 12th birthday and Mrs. MacAulay presented her with a necklace from her shop and invited the family over to her parlor for ice cream and wedding cake (from her daughter's wedding three days before). My girls were delighted and I was truly impressed with the lovely lady who would take such an interest in her guests. Thanks so much for showing us the way to the Inverary Inn."

Here is an excerpt from still another letter:

"Your description of the Inverary Inn in Baddeck could not begin to characterize the warmth, graciousness and hospitality which we received. Mrs. MacAulay is among one of the most delightful people I have ever met, a person whose acquaintance I would feel fortunate to maintain. She made us feel as though we were her own daughters and gave us many ideas of how we might make the most of our stay. Let me say simply, 'Thank you, Berkshire Traveller' for helping my vacation to be more memorable."

Thank you all for sharing some of your Inverary experiences with me. The Inverary Inn, located on the shores of Lake Bras d'Or in the Scottish village of Baddeck, is already a Nova Scotia institution.

*INVERARY INN, Box 190, Baddeck, Cape Breton, N.S., Canada 902-295-2674. A 40-room village inn on the Cabot Trail, 52 mi. from Sydney, N.S. On the shores of Lake Bras d'Or. European plan. Some rooms with shared bath. Breakfast and dinner served to travelers daily. Open from May 15 to Nov. 1. Bicycles and children's playground on grounds. Boating and small golf course nearby. Isobel MacAulay, Innkeeper.*

*Directions: Follow Trans-Canada Hwy. to Canso Causeway to Baddeck.*

### KILMUIR PLACE
**Northeast Margaree, Cape Breton, Nova Scotia**

I love to get letters from Isabel Taylor. In some ways it is like hearing from people who are on a mountaintop in Tibet or in a valley in Terra del Fuego. Actually, she's in Cape Breton, Nova Scotia, but there are times when Cape Breton seems to be a long way off. Let me share one of her letters:

"Dear Mr. Norman (she always calls me Mr. Norman):

"I'm in my usual corner, the red chair by the window. I wish you could see the valley today. All of our trees and bushes are in full bloom, and I'm sure all of the birds are here for the summer. Ross is in the kitchen now making a couple of chocolate cakes so that he can take a few of our guests off to do some salmon fishing this afternoon. He sends his best.

"I thought of you the other day because I know how much you're affected by cooking aromas, and we had three freshly made apple pies and a mince pie that were cooling and filling the kitchen with the most marvelous aromas. Speaking of the kitchen, it has been a busy week for me because we've just finished laundering the red

calico curtains in the kitchen and have done over one corner of it. We're saving your comfortable chair and a few of the Canadian magazines that you liked, for you said you were coming up here soon again."

It seems like a short season at this little family-style inn in Cape Breton. On a recent visit I talked with some people who had been coming there for a number of years and then built their own houses in the vicinity. This is one of the great salmon fishing areas of the world, and there is a little salmon museum (which I found very informative) just up the road a short way from the Kilmuir Place. Naturally, everyone up here is concerned about preserving the salmon streams.

This is a very tiny American Plan inn with five or six lodging rooms, booked well in advance. Everybody eats at a big dining room table with silver and china that's been in the family for years. In addition to salmon and all of its variations, Isabel sets a table that includes roast beef, steak, lamb and lobster.

Guests sit in the family living room to talk and read some of the books and magazines, and they usually go to bed rather early.

Although the Taylors are most hospitable and kind, it is nearly impossible to drop in on the Kilmuir Place and be fortunate enough to find overnight accommodations available. Reservations, made well in advance, are a necessity. The dining room is not really public. It is for the convenience of the Taylors' house guests.

Ross and Isabel, I know you can't go on forever, but, please, at least for another fifty years!

*KILMUIR PLACE, Northeast Margaree, Cape Breton, N.S., Canada B0E 2H0; 902-248-2877. A 5-room country inn on Rte. 19, 28 mi. from Baddeck. American plan. Some rooms with shared baths. Breakfast, lunch and dinner served to house guests only. Open from June to mid-October. Salmon fishing in the Margaree River, touring the Cabot Trail and both fresh water and salt water swimming nearby. Mr. and Mrs. Ross Taylor, Innkeepers.*

*Directions: After crossing Canso Causeway to Cape Breton, follow either Rte. 19 (coast road to Inverness) and turn right on Cabot Trail at Margaree Forks, or follow Rte. 105 and turn left on Cabot Trail at Nyanza.*

## MILFORD HOUSE
### South Milford, Nova Scotia

I am very angry at one mosquito in South Milford, Nova Scotia. Last summer it was probably the only mosquito within a radius of several miles and yet it managed to bite the same Milford House guest twice within two hours after his arrival! Maybe this sounds funny, but in the 1976 edition I mentioned the fact that the mosquitoes in South Milford had disappeared.

So much for making specific statements about broad subjects. As Margaret Miller says, "While we like to describe our place as an unspoiled retreat, we have to admit that God also made mosquitoes and several other pests for what reason we cannot say. We would emphasize, however, that there are no poisonous insects, snakes, bugs or ticks. On the positive side I would point out that there is a complete absence of ragweed in our vicinity which is vitally important to some people."

The Milford House is a flashback to the early days of the 20th century when people from Canada and the United States came and stayed for months at a time. It is an old-fashioned place with turn-of-the-century furniture and decor. The parlors and living rooms have a "country elegance."

Lodgings are in the main house and also a group of extremely neat and well-furnished cabins that are spread out along the series of lakes within a short walk of the inn. Each has a dock, a fireplace, and all the conveniences including electricity and maid service. Meals are taken at the inn dining room.

In past years I've had a great deal of fun writing about my visits to the Milford House and also sharing letters with 16-year-old Wendy Miller, who is the daughter of Bud and Margaret, the innkeepers at the Milford House. Almost every letter I get about the Milford House mentions Wendy and how she is such a marvelous person with the guests of all ages. She was sort of unofficially nominated photographer for the honeymoon couples who find the Milford House very pleasant during the month of July.

Although I missed it myself, I understand that last summer Bud

Miller staged a "corn boil" for a group of families. A huge feast of chicken, corn and potato salad and sweets was put away in short order.

One of the funniest stories coming out of Milford House was about a college professor and his wife who complained that they were kept awake at night by a particularly large resident bullfrog. To the rescue came Curtis Orde, a resourceful Milford resident with a twinkle in his eye who works at Milford House during the summer. He caught this thoughtless disturber of the peace with a trout net and moved him into the next lake!

Because many of the same families have been returning to the Milford House for many years, there are quite a few very interesting guest traditions. One of the most touching is the custom of everyone standing on the front porch of the inn to wave handkerchiefs at departing guests. Tradition hath it that the guest who is leaving may wave in response only until he passes the big tree at the edge of the property. Then he looks straight ahead and never looks back. There is a similar tradition at Rockview Mountain Farm in upper New Hampshire where departing guests are sent off to the paen of many bells!

If anybody sees the errant mosquito, I hope they will pass along my feelings of ire, and instruct it to steer clear of the Milford House in the future.

*MILFORD HOUSE, South Milford, R.R. #4, Annapolis Royal, N.S., Canada, B0S 1OA; 902-532-2617. A rustic resort-inn with 24 cabins on 600 acres of woodlands and lakes, 90 mi. from Yarmouth, N.S., near Kejimkujik National Park. Modified American plan.* **Breakfast and dinner served daily with picnic lunches available.**

*Open from June 20 to Sept. 10. Tennis, fishing, croquet, canoeing, bird-watching and swimming on grounds. Deep-sea fishing and golf nearby. Warren and Margaret Miller, Innkeepers.*

*Directions: From Yarmouth follow Rte. 1 to traffic lights in Annapolis Royal. Turn right and continue on to Rte. 8, 15 mi. to inn.*

# Prince Edward Island

*Prince Edward Island is one of the great surprises in North America. I am sure that I, like most Americans, thought of P.E.I., as it is called, as being almost within sight of Greenland and much too cold for anything but birds and seals.*

*Nothing could be further from the truth.*

*For one thing, ocean water temperatures along the wide P.E.I. beaches average 68 to 70 degrees in summer. The sun is excellent for tanning.*

*One of Canada's finest national parks lies along the north shore of the island, stretching 25 miles along the Gulf of St. Lawrence and providing a public reserve for some of the finest beaches in North America. Wide seascapes, breathtaking views and an atmosphere of hospitality backed by more than a century of tradition, combine to bring visitors back year after year.*

*In the capital city of Charlottetown there is the Confederation Centre of the Arts. This was the site of the meeting that eventually resulted in the Dominion of Canada in 1864. The Confederation Centre is a memorial built by the people of Canada to the memory of the Fathers of the Confederation.*

*During the summer months there is an excellent theatre offering a choice of three musicals which play to capacity houses every night. The theatre was opened in 1964, and some of the shows have played in London, New York and the larger cities in Canada. The Tokyo show was Canada's contribution to the World's Fair. The play was "Anne of Green Gables."*

*"Anne of Green Gables," of course, is another facet of P.E.I. and Cavendish Beach is the locale of the Lucy Maude Montgomery stories of the famous fictional character. A small, gabled, green cottage has been built with some reminders of the "Anne" stories.*

*Prince Edward Island is very popular in July and August, so reserve well in advance, and be sure to obtain ferry information.*

## SHAW'S HOTEL
**Brackley Beach, Prince Edward Island**

"We open around June 15th and close around September 15th," said Gordon Shaw, "and I think that the first two weeks and the last two weeks are two of the best times of the season." We were sitting on the side porch of Shaw's Hotel watching all of the fun as a large group of children played with two big sheep dogs.

"It's very warm and pleasant here in June," he continued. "You know that because you were here yourself in June. September is always excellent and, since most of the young people have gone back to school, it becomes our 'quiet season.' We have 30 or 40 children at the height of the season."

Shaw's Hotel was a great discovery for me a few years ago. I went over to P.E.I. on the ferry from Caribou, Nova Scotia, to Wood Islands and shared the trip with a group of young French students who lived on one of the islands in St. Lawrence Bay. As I recall, they sang during the entire trip.

I found my way to the Brackley Beach area and visited several pleasant guest houses and resorts. However as soon as I walked through the front gates at Shaw's and saw old barns and the red-roofed Mansard house, I knew that this was something special.

"It all started in 1860," said Gordon Shaw, "and it has been in the family ever since. We have about 75 acres of the original Shaw pioneer farm, a property which was settled in the 18th century. We've added quite a few accommodations including cottages and some of these have two, three and four bedrooms because we have a lot of the families every summer. Five of the cottages have fireplaces.

"We still keep a lot of farm animals here because it's a wonderful opportunity for city people to become familiar with them. It's only a short distance through the forest to the beach. That's one of the principal attractions for all of our guests."

All of this summertime outdoor activity, including swimming, sailing on the bay which adjoins the hotel property, deep sea tuna fishing, golf, tennis, bicycling, walking and horseback riding contribute to very big appetites. Consequently the cooks at Shaw's are busy from morning to night preparing all kinds of dishes including salmon, lobster, mackerel, cod and halibut. Naturally the fish is fresh. Dinners are fun because everyone is eager for a hearty meal and the atmosphere is full of enthusiasm about the day's activities.

"I guess we are the oldest family-operated summer resort in Eastern Canada," exclaimed Gordon as he settled back into his chair. "I grew up here. It has been my home and always will be. What I enjoy most is sharing it with families like these every summer."

*SHAW'S HOTEL and Cottages, Brackley Point Road, Brackley Beach, Prince Edward Island, Canada COA 2HO; 902-672-2022. A 24-room country hotel within walking distance of Brackley Beach, 15 mi. from Charlottetown. American plan. Some rooms with shared baths. 10 guest cottages. Breakfast, lunch, dinner served to travelers daily. Open from June 15 to Sept. 15. Pets allowed in cottages only. Tennis, golf, bicycles, riding, sailing, beach and summer theatre nearby. Gordon Shaw, Innkeeper.*

*Directions: Prince Edward Island is reached either by ferry from Cape Tormentine, New Brunswick (near Moncton), or Caribou, Nova Scotia. In both cases, after arriving on P.E.I., follow Rte. 1 to Charlottetown, then Rte. 15 to Brackley Beach. P.E.I. is also reached by Eastern Provincial Airways, Canadian National Railways and Air Canada.*

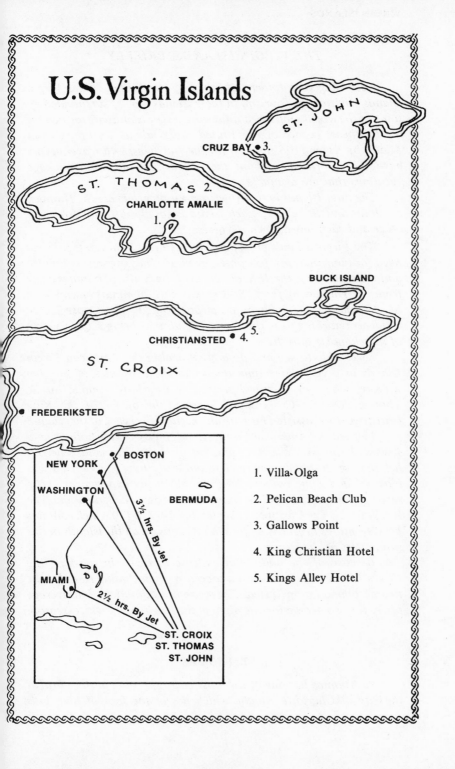

# U.S. Virgin Islands

ST. JOHN

CRUZ BAY ● 3.

ST. THOMAS 2.

CHARLOTTE AMALIE

1. ●

BUCK ISLAND

CHRISTIANSTED ● 4. 5.

ST. CROIX

● FREDERIKSTED

BOSTON

NEW YORK

WASHINGTON

BERMUDA

3½ hrs. By Jet

MIAMI

2½ hrs. By Jet

ST. CROIX
ST. THOMAS
ST. JOHN

1. Villa Olga

2. Pelican Beach Club

3. Gallows Point

4. King Christian Hotel

5. Kings Alley Hotel

## THE VIRGIN ISLANDS, BRIEFLY

*According to a folder published by the United States Virgin Islands Division of Tourism, in these islands one is "surrounded by some of the world's most beautiful water." The islands are located off the southeast corner of the United States about 2½ hours from Miami by jet and 3½ hours from the Northeast. All travel agents have full information about the airline schedules and package vacations that are available.*

*The three islands in the American Virgin group are St. Thomas, St. John and St. Croix. Each island is totally different from the other and each has its own devotees.*

*The Virgin Islands are a part of the United States so there is no need for innoculations, passports, or visas. The language is English and the currency is the U.S. dollar. St. John is just 20 minutes away from St. Thomas by ferry. St. Croix is only 20 minutes away from St. Thomas or St. John by an airboat called "The Goose." U.S. residents returning from the Virgin Islands may bring $200.00 worth of merchandise duty free.*

*I was able to see and do a great deal in the American Virgin Islands in a very short time thanks to the assistance of Marilyn McKay, who runs a travel service at Charlotte Amalie on St. Thomas. On St. Croix Betty Sperber, the owner of the King Christian Hotel assisted me with an excellent overview of that island.*

*I visited the American Virgin Islands on a working holiday, and I wanted sun, sea, a certain amount of tranquility, and generous helpings of outdoor activity. I found everything for which I was looking, and some country inns as well. If my experiences excite readers' curiosity, may I recommend Margaret Zellers' book,* The Inn Way . . . The Caribbean *(September 1977, BTP) which contains her adventures in searching for country inns on all the islands in this sunny part of the world.*

*Because of the additional expense involved in reaching the Virgin Islands, I have broken a precedent by including rates for the five accommodations listed. These are not quotations but average prices for two people for one night at the height of the winter season.*

### ST. THOMAS

*St. Thomas has one of the most beautiful ports in the world at the city of Charlotte Amalie which lies at the foot of high hills*

*with nearly perpetual blue sky and fluffy white clouds overhead. There is a continuous parade of visiting cruise ships and everything from Japanese cameras to Italian leather goods and English china are available at reduced prices. All of the Virgin Islands are duty-free ports.*

*I found the best way to explore St. Thomas was to rent a car and drive in and around the hills. With every turn there are spectacular views of the dozens of bays and inlets. St. Thomas has the most diversified terrain and is more heavily populated than the other two islands.*

## VILLA OLGA
### Frenchtown, Charlotte Amalie, St. Thomas, Virgin Islands

Marty Giovan and I were seated in the open dining room looking over the bay and watching the fascinating parade of water traffic. In addition to the pleasure craft and sailboats, there was also the excitment of frequent takeoffs and landings by the amphibious airplanes that serve the Virgin Islands.

"There is an unusual history at Villa Olga," she said. "It was the Russian consulate in the 1800's and has been the scene of more than 100 years of intrigue, romance and even violence. Over the years it was a gambling house as well as a fancy bordello. At one time it was the acknowledged center for many important island social events."

A few years ago Anthony and Marty Giovann decided to plunge into innkeeping and acquired the Villa Olga. "What you see now," she said, "represents a considerable amount of restoration. The place

355

was a shambles, the gardens were overgrown. We've been working on it continually."

Villa Olga has the feeling of the Virgin Islands the "way they used to be." There is a certain air of old-time elegance about it. It has a very informal atmosphere, and because the Giovanns have several children themselves, it is an excellent place for families where children have room to play and beaches to explore. Frenchtown is a section of Charlotte Amalie close to, but outside of, the hubbub of activity in the main part of the city.

*VILLA OLGA GUEST HOUSE, Box 4976, Charlotte Amalie, St. Thomas, Virgin Islands; 809-774-1376. A 12-room guest house in an unusual old waterside mansion. Luncheon and dinner served daily. Closed last two weeks in September and first two weeks in October. Snorkeling, swimming on grounds. All the Virgin Islands recreational activities are easily accessible. Rates: $35.00 E.P. Anthony and Marty Giovann, Innkeepers.*

## PELICAN BEACH CLUB
### St. Thomas, Virgin Islands

"Posh," is one of the best words to describe this resort-inn. It is located on the water with about 800 feet of beach reserved for the exclusive use of inn guests.

My first visit was in the early evening. I entered through a little pagoda. Soft, warm breezes carried a scent of night-blooming flowers. Overhead a full moon was shining through the swaying palm trees and a few wispy clouds raced by. On the beach were several Sunfishes, Sailfishes, and kayaks which would be back in the water with sunup tomorrow.

Lodgings are in either one-story villas or studio cabanas and both types are beautifully furnished.

Guests can either enjoy the restaurant for lunch or dinner or dine at one of the several other restaurants on the island.

Breakfast is carried to the individual lodging rooms as a leisurely prelude to the day's activities. Orders are left on the outside door before retiring and will be delivered at the time designated.

*PELICAN BEACH CLUB, P.O. Box 1371, St. Thomas, Virgin Islands 00801; 809-775-0855. A very chic 22-room resort-inn at the water's edge about 7 miles from downtown Charlotte Amalie. Complimentary tennis, boating, snorkeling exclusively for guests. Lunch and dinner served by reservation. Dec. 15-Apr. 15. Approximately $85.00 for two people (includes full breakfast).*

## ST. JOHN

*Two-thirds of the island of St. John is a U.S. National Park. Here the traveler can see what the world is like when nature is undisturbed. There are many, many beaches, some of them quite isolated with interesting tropical foliage which is almost jungle-like.*

*I was advised that the best way to see St. John was to take the ferry from St. Thomas to Cruz Bay and then hire a local car and driver. It was excellent advice. There are many people who go to the Virgin Islands and consider St. John ideal because it has comparatively few people and affords much opportunity for peace and quiet.*

*I drove out to Red Hook and while I was parking the car across the road from the ferry entrance I was delighted to run into Anthony Giovann, the owner of the Villa Olga. He manufactures all of the ice cream sold on the islands and was meeting the boat to take two cases of ice cream over to Cruz Bay.*

*The ferry turned out to be an oversized cruiser with a canvas awning for protection against the sun. Most of the passengers were daytrippers although there were some people planning to spend some time on the island.*

*The trip was choppy but fast. As we cruised along, I enjoyed the ever-widening view of St. Thomas. There were several sailboats on the bay and some of them sped toward us waiting for the last second to veer off as if playing a game. Cruz Bay Harbor was filled with sailboats and I thought of what fun it would be to spend a week or two sailing. We came rather close to one of these boats and the occupants seemed to be swathed in towels and suntan lotion. The boat docked at Cruz Bay and the first thing I noticed was the International Dive Club with its schedule of daily scuba and snorkeling trips. Snorkeling is super in the waters off St. John.*

*I came into the center of this small town with the strange feeling that I had seen it all in a South Seas movie. There was a string of taxicabs parked along the waterfront, but I was looking for one driver in particular — Lucy. I had been told that even without a description I would know her. Sure enough, there she was, a handsome lady with a flower behind her ear. "I am Lucy," she said, "and I know that you were looking for me." When I asked her how she knew, she said, "Oh, I have my ways."*

*After she helped me decide where to go, we proceeded on the winding roads next to the beaches climbing upward through the rich tropical foliage. The drive was a series of hairpin turns and changing views of bays and inlets. We finally arrived at Hawks Neck Beach which Lucy pronounced "as one of the best."*

*From there the road took us to the top of the mountain for a spectacular view. When I asked Lucy if she had ever considered leaving the island, she replied, "There is no reason for me to leave the island. I have everything that I would ever want right here." And I think that she was right.*

## GALLOWS POINT
**Cruz Bay, St. John, Virgin Islands**

In 1952 Richard Ellington and his wife came to St. John and decided they just couldn't leave. Gallows Point is a small cottage colony on a peninsula adjoining Cruz Bay Harbor about a five-minute walk from the village. Each cottage is completely equipped with modern housekeeping conveniences.

Life at Gallows Point is informal and friendly. Guests amuse themselves by swimming, snorkeling, hiking, sailing, fishing, shelling, and exploring the island by jeep.

*GALLOWS POINT, Cruz Bay, St. John, Virgin Islands 00830; 809-776-6434. A grouf of 8 cottages next to the waters of Cruz Bay. No meals are served, but each cottage has its own kitchen. Swimming, sailing, fishing. Ferry from St. Thomas to Cruz Bay leaves from Red Hook every hour from 7 a.m. to 7 p.m. Open year-round. Rates: $35.00. Richard Ellington, Innkeeper.*

## ST. CROIX

*St. Croix like the others, has mountains and gorgeous beaches as well as excellent swimming, snorkeling and scuba diving. It has two communities, Christiansted and Fredericksted. Each of these has picture book charm.*

*Fredericksted is the location of the Island Center, and under a roofed open-air theatre there is everything from art shows to ballet and rock.*

*St. Croix has a rain forest, an excellent Robert Trent Jones golf course, horse races, cricket, and baseball.*

*Buck Island, the only U.S. National Park that is under water, is located just off Christiansted.*

*Christiansted resembles many European towns. It has the same type and shapes of buildings that I saw in many towns in Scandinavia and Austria. The difference is that there are a great many colonnades — arches that support a gallery over the sidewalk. Shops are also located in very attractive arcades.*

\*     \*     \*

*My stay on St. Croix was quite brief, unfortunately. I had taken the "Goose" from St. Thomas late the previous afternoon and after skimming over the blue water and watching the outlines of St. Croix get closer and closer, we landed and I took the short walk through the shopping district to reach my hotel.*

*While I was looking for a restaurant that evening, I ran into Mr. and Mrs. Casper Meals of Camphill, Pa., who invited me to join them for dinner at the Top Hat Restaurant. There happened to be a fashion show in progress and the models were very pretty. There was lots of badinage each time they came to our table wearing a different dress. Incidentally, almost a year to the day I received a postcard from Casper which reported that they had once again had dinner at the Top Hat, the food was excellent and the fashion models just as pretty.*

*After dinner we wandered around the town for a bit, and then stopped at Frankie's Place where a retired naval commander plays the piano and sings great songs of the thirties and forties.*

### KING CHRISTIAN HOTEL
**Christiansted, St. Croix, Virgin Islands**

"I think we are very fortunate here on St. Croix," said Betty Sperber. "In addition to the King Christian, there are several excellent accommodations on many different parts of the island. More and more people are coming to St. Croix every year. I think it's because of the beaches, the tranquility, the golf course, and the fact that it is such an entirely different atmosphere."

Betty and I had been walking through the hotel and had stopped momentarily on a balcony overlooking the harbor. I remarked that the Kings Warf seemed to be the center of a great deal of activity.

"Yes, it's fun right here on the waterfront," she said. "You know this is a working harbor, and in addition to the pleasure craft and boats that are available for rent, there are also fishermen that go out every day. Our guests seem to like the feel of being near the water. We are in walking distance of museums, many art galleries and shops. The beach is just 300 yards away. Did you know that Alexander Hamilton spent his boyhood in Christiansted and worked within two blocks of where we are now?"

Since my last visit in March, 1976, I received a letter from Betty bringing me up to date. She writes in part: "We are doing many exciting things with the hotel. The swimming pool has been resurfaced and looks gorgeous. The entire building has been painted in a cream color and the shutters in deep blue. The restaurant outside patio area has been redecorated. The lounge is all done, with built-ins and super graphics using Marimeko prints on the cushions. It really does look lovely. If I should sound enthusiastic, it's because I'm watching my dreams come true one by one."

*KING CHRISTIAN HOTEL, Kings Warf, Christiansted, St. Croix, U.S. Virgin Islands 00820; 809-773-2285 (N.Y. reservations 212-661-7990). A 38-room waterfront hotel. Breakfast, lunch and dinner served daily. Open year-round. No pets. Swimming pool on grounds. Sailing, snorkeling, scuba diving, glass bottom boat rides, tennis and golf nearby. Rates: $44.00, E.P.; $70.00 MAP. Betty Sperber, Innkeeper.*

## KING'S ALLEY HOTEL
### Christiansted, Virgin Islands

I was floating on my back in the pool at King's Alley. Overhead, palms, banana and lime trees swayed in the breeze and the hibiscus, crotons, poinsettias and tramburgia enhanced the scene with their aromas and blossoms.

The blue skies stretched endlessly into the distance and an occasional pelican lazily flapped his wings heading out over the harbor. It was like swimming in a lush, private tropical garden.

One by one, guests who had been either swimming, walking about the town, or playing golf or tennis, came filing in and the chairs around the pool and the garden were rapidly filling. Everybody looked tanned and radiantly happy.

I climbed out of the pool, grabbed a towel, and struck up a conversation with a young couple.

"How did you happen to come to King's Alley," I asked. "Well, we wanted to come to St. Croix, and one of our friends had stayed here. They recommended it. Our room overlooks the garden and the harbor and we like it very much. There are lots of restaurants in town, and we have met a lot of other people who are also honeymooners."

King's Alley is just the right size to draw people together, and before long there were conversations flowing between tables as people were eager to share their experiences.

*KING'S ALLEY HOTEL, Kings Wharf, Christiansted, Virgin Islands 00820; 809-773-0103. A 22-room hotel overlooking Christiansted Harbor. European Plan. Open year-round. Swimming pool. Hotel has private marina. Sailing, scuba, snorkeling trips, tennis and golf nearby. Rates: $45.00 E.P. Victor Gilbert, Phyllis Simmons, Innkeepers.*

## BUCK ISLAND REEF

*A most informative four-color booklet published by the National Park Service provides enticing information about visiting this National Park. It says in part:*

*"Surpassing even the familiar beauty of the Virgin Islands is the world of the tropical reef. At its best this world is incredibly colorful and varied, intensely alive, the reef is nothing less than a joy to the senses. Swimming and snorkeling in the crystal clear lagoon just off Buck Island near St. Croix is an ideal way to see one of the best Caribbean reefs firsthand. Well suited to the beginner and expert snorkeler alike, Buck Island reef offers shallow-water snorkeling above the inner reef and deep-water exploring along the outer barrier.*

*"Getting to Buck Island reef requires only a visit to one of the skippers who operates small boats between St. Croix and the island All the boatmen furnish snorkeling equipment. The adventure begins in the morning with a trip directly to the reef with an hour and a half of swimming and snorkeling. Arrow markers and signs on the ocean floor guide the snorkelers along the Buck Island Reef nature*

*trail. By following the underwater signs the snorkeler can negotiate the trail in about thirty minutes.*

*"At lunchtime the boat stops at Buck Island and here you may eat, swim or take a walk on the primitive hiking trail through the tropical vegetation that covers the island. For a spectacular view of St. Croix and the reef areas, take the trail to the top of Buck Island. The National Park Service provides picnic tables, charcoal grills, a small house for changing clothes, sheltered pavilion and rest rooms."*

*I have talked to dozens of people who have never snorkeled before and who thought they would never be involved in this wonderful underwater sport. A trip to Buck Island on one of the boats in the harbor is all it really takes to make one a believer. It is probably the best way to be introduced to snorkeling because the instruction is so complete and professional. Snorkeling and scuba diving opened up a wonderful world and Buck Island is certainly one of the best places to start.*

# INDEX

ACCOMAC INN
Wrightsville, Pennsylvania, 169

ALEXANDER WITHROW HOUSE
Lexington, Virginia, 209

ALGONQUIN HOTEL
New York, New York, 138

ALMSHOUSE INN
Ghent, New York, 136

ANDOVER INN
Andover, Massachusetts, 47

ASA RANSOM HOUSE
Clarence, New York, 140

ASTICOU INN
Northeast Harbor, Maine, 111

BARROWS HOUSE
Dorset, Vermont, 68

BAY HILL CLUB
Orlando, Florida, 249

BAY SHORE YACHT CLUB
Fort Lauderdale, Florida, 255

BEEKMAN ARMS
Rhinebeck, New York, 142

BENBOW INN
Garberville, California, 307

BIRD AND BOTTLE
Garrison, New York, 143

BLACK POINT INN
Prouts Neck, Maine, 115

BLUEBERRY HILL
Goshen, Vermont, 70

BOONE TAVERN HOTEL
Berea, Kentucky, 237

BOTSFORD INN
Farmington Hills, Michigan, 278

BOULDERS INN
New Preston, Connecticut, 24

BRADFORD GARDENS INN
Provincetown, Massachusetts, 30

BRAMBLE INN
Brewster, Massachusetts, 35

BRAZILIAN COURT
Palm Beach, Florida, 253

BULL'S HEAD INN
Cobleskill, New York, 145

BUXTON INN
Granville, Ohio, 273

CANDLEWYCK INN
Green Lane, Pennsylvania, 171

CAPTAIN LORD MANSION
Kennebunkport, Maine, 117

CAPTAIN WHIDBEY INN
Coupeville, Washington, 319

CENTURY INN
Scenery Hill, Pennsylvania, 172

CHALET SUZANNE
Lake Wales, Florida, 251

CHESHIRE INN
St. Louis, Missouri, 282

CHESTER INN
Chester, Vermont, 72

THE CLAREMONT COTTAGES
Southwest Harbor, Maine, 113

CLARKSON HOUSE
Lewiston, New York, 147

COLBY HILL INN
Henniker, New Hampshire, 87

COUNTRY INN
Berkeley Springs,
West Virginia, 222

CURTIS HOUSE
Woodbury, Connecticut, 18

CUTTLE'S TREMBLANT CLUB
Mont Tremblant,
Quebec, Canada, 330

DANA PLACE INN
Jackson, New Hampshire, 109

DOCKSIDE GUEST QUARTERS
York, Maine, 119

DOE RUN INN
Brandenburg, Kentucky, 231

DROVERS INN
Wellsburg, West Virginia, 228

DURBIN HOTEL
Rushville, Indiana, 269

ELM LODGE
St. Stephen,
New Brunswick, Canada, 336

ELMWOOD INN
Perryville, Kentucky, 235

FAIRFIELD INN
Fairfield, Pennsylvania, 174

FARMHOUSE
Port Townsend, Washington, 317

GALLOWS POINT
Cruz Bay, St. John,
Virgin Islands, 358

GENERAL LEWIS INN
Lewisburg, West Virginia, 224

GLEN IRIS INN
Castile, New York, 148

GOLDEN LAMB
Lebanon, Ohio, 276

GRAVES MOUNTAIN LODGE
Syria, Virginia, 203

GRANDVIEW FARM
Huntsville,
Ontario, Canada, 328

GREEN MOUNTAIN INN
Stowe, Vermont, 74

GREENVILLE ARMS
Greenville, New York, 150

GREY ROCK INN
Northeast Harbor, Maine, 114

GRISTMILL SQUARE
Warm Springs, Virginia, 201

GRISWOLD INN
Essex, Connecticut, 20

HARBOR HOUSE
Elk, California, 304

HEMLOCK INN
Bryson City, North Carolina, 214

HERITAGE HOUSE
Little River, California, 306

HOLLOWAY HOUSE
East Bloomfield, New York, 152

HOLLYMEAD INN
Charlottesville, Virginia, 205

HOMEWOOD INN
Yarmouth, Maine, 121

HOUND EARS LODGE
Blowing Rock, North Carolina, 220

HOVEY MANOR
North Hatley,
Quebec, Canada, 332

INN AT CASTLE HILL
Newport, Rhode Island, 59

INN AT DUCK CREEKE
Wellfleet, Massachusetts, 33

INN AT PLEASANT HILL
Shakertown, Kentucky, 233

INN AT SAWMILL FARM
West Dover, Vermont, 76

INN AT STARLIGHT LAKE
Starlight, Pennsylvania, 176

INN FOR ALL SEASONS
Scituate Harbor, Massachusetts, 43

INN ON THE COMMON
Craftsbury Common, Vermont, 85

INVERARY INN
Baddeck,
Nova Scotia, Canada, 344

ISLAND HOUSE
Ogunquit, Maine, 123

JARED COFFIN HOUSE
Nantucket Island,
Massachusetts, 39

JOHN HANCOCK INN
Hancock, New Hampshire, 89

KEDRON VALLEY INN
South Woodstock, Vermont, 77

KILMUIR PLACE
Northeast Margaree,
Nova Scotia, Canada, 346

KING AND PRINCE
BEACH HOTEL
St. Simons Island, Georgia, 245

KING CHRISTIAN HOTEL
Christiansted, St. Croix,
Virgin Islands, 360

KING'S ALLEY HOTEL
Christiansted, St. Croix,
Virgin Islands, 361

LAKE QUINAULT LODGE
Quinault, Washington, 321

LAKESIDE INN
Mt. Dora, Florida, 247

LAMOTHE HOUSE
New Orleans, Louisiana, 257

LARCHWOOD INN
Wakefield, Rhode Island, 62
LINCKLAEN HOUSE
Cazenovia, New York, 154
LODGE ON THE DESERT
Tucson, Arizona, 296
LONGFELLOW'S WAYSIDE INN
South Sudbury, Massachusetts, 45
LOVETT'S
BY LAFAYETTE BROOK
Franconia, New Hampshire, 91
LOWELL INN
Stillwater, Minnesota, 288
LYME INN
Lyme, New Hampshire, 93
MAINSTAY INN
Cape May, New Jersey, 192
MARATHON HOTEL
Grand Manan Island,
New Brunswick, Canada, 340
MARSHLANDS INN
Sackville,
New Brunswick, Canada, 342
MARYLAND INN
Annapolis, Maryland, 198
MIDDLEBURY INN
Middlebury, Vermont, 79
MILFORD HOUSE
South Milford,
Nova Scotia, Canada, 348
MOSELEM SPRINGS INN
Moselem Springs, Pennsylvania, 177
MOUNTAIN VIEW INN
Norfolk, Connecticut, 26
NAUSET HOUSE
East Orleans, Massachusetts, 37
NEW HARMONY INN
New Harmony, Indiana, 266
NEW LONDON INN
New London, New Hampshire, 107
NORMANDY INN
Carmel, California, 309
NORTH HERO HOUSE
North Hero, Vermont, 81
NU-WRAY INN
Burnsville, North Carolina, 212
OBAN INN
Niagara-On-The-Lake,
Ontario, Canada, 326

OJAI VALLEY INN
Ojai, California, 313
OLD CLUB RESTAURANT
Alexandria, Virginia, 210
OLD DROVERS INN
Dover Plains, New York, 160
OLD FORT CLUB
Kennebunkport, Maine, 125
OLIVER HOUSE
Ancram, New York, 156
OVERLOOK INN
Canadensis, Pennsylvania, 179
PATCHWORK QUILT
Middlebury, Indiana, 271
PELICAN BEACH CLUB
St. Thomas, Virgin Islands, 356
PINE BARN INN
Danville, Pennsylvania, 181
PINE CREST INN
Tryon, North Carolina, 218
PUMP HOUSE
Canadensis, Pennsylvania, 184
RALPH WALDO EMERSON
Rockport, Massachusetts, 49
RANCHO DE LOS CABALLEROS
Wickenburg, Arizona, 298
RANCHO ENCANTADO
Santa Fe, New Mexico, 292
REDCOAT'S RETURN
Tannersville, New York, 166
RED GERANIUM and SHADBLOW
RESTAURANTS
New Harmony, Indiana, 268
RED INN
Provincetown, Massachusetts, 32
RED LION INN
Stockbridge, Massachusetts, 53
RIVERSIDE INN
Pence Springs, West Virginia, 226
ROBERT MORRIS INN
Oxford, Maryland, 196
ROBERT'S OF CHARLESTON
Charleston, South Carolina, 244
ROCKHOUSE MOUNTAIN FARM
Eaton Center, New Hampshire, 95
ROSSMOUNT INN
St. Andrews,
New Brunswick, Canada, 338

ST. GEMME BEAUVAIS INN
Ste. Genevieve, Missouri, 284

1740 HOUSE
Lumberville, Pennsylvania, 186

1661 INN
Block Island, Rhode Island, 63

SHAW'S HOTEL
Brackley Beach,
Prince Edward Island, Canada, 351

SILVERMINE TAVERN
Norwalk, Connecticut, 22

SNOWBIRD MOUNTAIN LODGE
Robbinsville, North Carolina, 216

SPALDING INN CLUB
Whitefield, New Hampshire, 97

SPRINGSIDE INN
Auburn, New York, 158

SQUAM LAKES INN
Holderness, New Hampshire, 99

SQUIRE TARBOX HOUSE
Westport Island, Maine, 128

STAFFORD'S BAY VIEW INN
Petoskey, Michigan, 280

STAFFORD'S-IN-THE-FIELD
Chocorua, New Hampshire, 101

STAGECOACH HILL INN
Sheffield, Massachusetts, 55

STERLING INN
South Sterling, Pennsylvania, 188

SUDBURY INN
Bethel, Maine, 126

SUTTER CREEK INN
Sutter Creek, California, 302

SWISS HUTTE
Hillsdale, New York, 162

SWORDGATE INN
Charleston, South Carolina, 242

TANQUE VERDE
Tucson, Arizona, 294

TAVERN
New Wilmington, Pennsylvania, 190

THE INN
Rancho Santa Fe, California, 315

THREE VILLAGE INN
Stony Brook, New York, 164

VAGABOND HOUSE
Carmel, California, 311

VICTORIAN INN
Whitinsville, Massachusetts, 41

VILLAGE INN
Landgrove, Vermont, 83

VILLAGE INN
Lenox, Massachusetts, 57

VILLA OLGA
St. Thomas, Virgin Islands, 355

WAYSIDE INN
Middletown, Virginia, 207

WELLS INN
Sistersville, West Virginia, 229

WELLS WOOD
Plainfield, New Hampshire, 103

WELSHFIELD INN
Burton, Ohio, 275

WHISTLING OYSTER
Ogunquit, Maine, 130

WHITEHALL INN
Camden, Maine, 132

WHITE HART INN
Salisbury, Connecticut, 28

WILDERNESS LODGE
Lesterville, Missouri, 286

WILLOW PLACE INN
Como, Quebec, Canada, 334

WINE COUNTRY INN
St. Helena, California, 300

WOODBOUND INN
Jaffrey, New Hampshire, 105

YANKEE CLIPPER
Rockport, Massachusetts, 49

YANKEE PEDLAR INN
Holyoke, Massachusetts, 52